THE IMPOSSIBLE CRAFT

THE IMPOSSIBLE CRAFT

LITERARY BIOGRAPHY

Scott Donaldson

THE PENNSYLVANIA STATE UNIVERSITY PRESS

UNIVERSITY PARK, PENNSYLVANIA

Library of Congress Cataloging-in-Publication Data

Donaldson, Scott, 1928– author.
The impossible craft : literary biography / Scott Donaldson.
pages   cm — (The Penn State series in the history of
the book)
Summary: "Explores the challenges and rewards faced by
literary biographers. Details the author's experiences
writing the lives of writers including Edwin Arlington
Robinson, Ernest Hemingway, F. Scott Fitzgerald, John
Cheever, and Archibald MacLeish"—Provided by
publisher.
Includes bibliographical references and index.
ISBN 978-0-271-06528-1 (cloth : alk. paper)
1. Biography as a literary form.
2. Authors—Biography—Authorship.
3. Authors, American—Biography—History and
criticism—Theory, etc.
4. Biographers.
5. Donaldson, Scott, 1928– .
I. Title.
II. Series: Penn State series in the history of the book.

CT21.D68   2014
920—dc23
2014035170

Yet again, and always,

for Vivie

CONTENTS

ABBREVIATIONS

Colby   Miller Library, Colby College: EAR papers

Columbia   Butler Library, Columbia University

Gardiner   Gardiner (Maine) Public Library: Yellow House papers
            (Richards family), Lawrance Thompson EAR Notes

Harvard   Houghton Library, Harvard University

JFK   Hemingway Collection, John F. Kennedy Library, Boston

LC   Library of Congress

Newberry   Newberry Library, Chicago: Malcolm Cowley papers

NYPL   New York Public Library: Lewis Isaacs papers, Macmillan Co.
            papers

Princeton   Firestone Library, Princeton University

Virginia   Alderman Library, University of Virginia

Yale   Beinecke Library, Yale University

JC   John Cheever

MC   Malcolm Cowley

SD   Scott Donaldson

FSF   F. Scott Fitzgerald

ZF   Zelda Fitzgerald

EH   Ernest Hemingway

EAR   Edwin Arlington Robinson

BEGINNINGS

Biography: A Background Sketch

The first biographies aimed to teach, on the assumption that the reader might learn by example from the lives of the great. Plutarch, as much a moralist as an historian, linked Greek and Roman figures in *Parallel Lives*, arranging them in tandem to illuminate their common virtues or, less often, failings. "Let us now praise famous men, and our fathers that begat us," the author of Ecclesiastes counseled, and for the most part early biographers adopted that policy. In medieval times writers celebrated lives of the saints—not the whole life but a few incidents testifying to sanctity—as the genre drifted toward hagiography, shrouded in what Samuel Johnson called "a mist of panegyrick" (Garraty, 43, 54–55; Fruman).

The magisterial Dr. Johnson (1709–84) was himself a biographer, writing a life of the poet Richard Savage in his youth and the six-volume *Lives of the Poets* in his final years. Johnson rebelled against the high-minded accounts of the hagiographers, recommending instead that biographers depict "the minute details of daily life" as well as "those performances and incidents which produce vulgar greatness" (quoted in Holroyd, "How I Fell," 98). That was exactly what his disciple James Boswell did in his masterly biography of Johnson. The much younger Boswell dogged the great man's footsteps for years, recording just about everything that happened. When Johnson declaimed brilliantly of an evening, Boswell wrote about it. When Johnson drank too much, he wrote about that as well.

This kind of account went by the boards during the blight of Victorianism, when close friends or family members assumed the role of official biographer. They presented subjects in the noblest possible light. Lives were tidied up to remove any humanizing hints of indecency—certain things were not to be spoken of—and to exemplify qualities schoolchildren might aspire to. Sometimes these long and excessively eulogistic effusions ran to two or three volumes of life and letters.

The effect on literary biography was disastrous. "Suppression, distortion, evasion, and outright falsehood" abounded in lives of the English Romantic poets. *De mortuis nil nisi bonum* became the standard. Charles Cowden Clarke, Keats's early mentor, maintained that no gentleman would ever knowingly publish anything that could give pain to a living person or reflect badly on the deceased. Wordsworth was furious when a biographer of Robert Burns revealed his drunkenness and sexual adventures, and enraged when Coleridge's biographers disclosed his opium addiction and abandonment of his family. It was considered far better to portray William Blake as an "enthusiast" than to raise the issue of mental illness (Fruman).

The most sensational case was that of Lord Byron, a bisexual who committed incest, a radical in politics, and a foe of conventional religion. While in exile from England, Byron wrote his memoirs for posthumous publication. These proved so incendiary that Byron's friends, gathered in the London offices of his publisher three days after the poet's death, duly consigned them to the flames (Fruman).

Family members set about shining up the image of Shelley, whose sexual exploits, revolutionary politics, and irreligious views rivaled those of Byron. The first generation of survivors delayed access to such sensational matters until potential biographers dwindled into respectable Victorians willing to forget or to conceal. In the second generation, Lady Jane Shelley took over the task of idealizing her ancestor, and a feminized bloodless figure of the poet emerged in the accounts of those apologists who gained her approval. It remained for Richard Holmes, in 1974, to present Shelley as agitator, atheist, and apostle of free love as well as brilliant poetic innovator: a gifted man who embraced rebellion whatever its cost (Lee, 12–15).

Toward the end of the nineteenth century, historians tended to subordinate personal character and accomplishment to great cultural movements of the past. The importance of individual human beings was similarly challenged by the economic determinism of Karl Marx and the rise of naturalism. Then the disillusionment of World War I made the touched-up portraits of the Victorian era seem foolish, even wrong. Lytton Strachey's influential *Eminent Victorians* (1918) introduced a new kind of debunking biography. In brief and incisive sketches of Cardinal Manning, Florence Nightingale, Thomas Arnold, and General Gordon, Strachey demonstrated the moral hypocrisy of the Victorians. "It is not the business of the biographer to be complimentary," Strachey declared. "It is his business to lay bare the facts of the case as he understands them" (quoted in Skidelsky, 6). But not *all* the facts, for such an exhaustive recital would militate against the selectivity that art demanded.

With Freud, everything changed. Biographers still wrote about people of achievement, but with a more or less uncomfortable awareness—Freud's ideas having pervaded the culture—that accomplishments derived from sublimated sex drives, that personalities were shaped in childhood, that everyone entertained fantasies. These concepts diminished the luster of the subject, as Freud felt they should. He had a lively interest in biography, and believed that his own case histories improved on the usual practice of the genre.

In his study of *Leonardo da Vinci* (1910), Freud argued that most biographers were "fixated on their heroes," for whom they felt a special, and very likely infantile, affection. As a consequence they smoothed over the rough patches and presented cold, strange figures with little resemblance to human beings. They sacrificed "truth to an illusion," abandoned "the opportunity of penetrating the most fascinating secrets of human nature," and failed to solve "the riddle" of character, a task Freud regarded as "the first step in biography" (Ellmann, "Freud," 261–62; Cassato, 1251). In later years, though, Freud began to doubt whether it was possible to decode the riddle, uncover the secret self, penetrate the hidden, locate what Leon Edel—author of the multivolume life of Henry James—called "the figure under the carpet."

Sigmund Freud's career overlapped with that of Lytton Strachey, and in 1928 the two men connected by correspondence. Strachey sent Freud a copy of his *Elizabeth and Essex*, a book which, unlike his previous work, manifestly owed a debt to psychoanalytic theory. It was far from Strachey's best, however, and Freud replied with cautious praise. He congratulated Strachey for tracing the character of Queen Elizabeth back to her childhood and for touching "upon her most hidden motives with equal boldness and discretion." At the same time, Freud acknowledged the tremendous barriers that all biography faced. "Our psychological analysis does not suffice [to divine men's motives and the essence of their minds] even with those who are nearest to us in space and time, unless we can make them the object of years of the closest investigation, and even then it breaks down before the incompleteness of our knowledge and the clumsiness of our synthesis" (Storr, 73–74).

Freud expanded on the point in rejecting Arnold Zweig's 1936 proposal to undertake a biography of himself. "To be a biographer," he wrote Zweig, "you must tie yourself up in lies, concealments, hypocrisies, false colourings, and even in hiding a lack of understanding." Freud may have been using overstatement as a way of evading Zweig. Instead he chose as *his* biographer the discreet Ernest Jones, who "skirted many of the issues that Freud would have dealt with in other men and, though a psychoanalyst, made no effort at psychoanalysis" (Ellmann, "Freud," 260).

After Strachey, after Freud, the pendulum swung further away from Victorian reticence toward intimate revelation. Strachey himself, who had initiated the antireverential movement, became the subject of a two-volume biography (1967–68) by Michael Holroyd, who declared that he was doing "something entirely new": giving prominent place to his subject's love life and treating the subject of homosexuality "without any artificial veils of decorum" (quoted in Glendinning, 56).

A half century later, what was new with Holroyd has become commonplace. The veils have been lifted, leaving no taboo subjects. Cruelty to family, disloyalty to friends, dishonesty in finances: every human failing has become fair game for the poaching biographer. Gays and lesbians are outed, along with bisexuals and serial adulterers. Racial and ethnic prejudices are routinely revealed. So too is the abuse of alcohol and drugs, particularly widespread among literary figures. Were we to follow Sir Edmund Gosse's early twentieth-century dictum against disclosing addiction to alcohol, Mark Schorer (biographer of Sinclair Lewis) pointed out, "what would the biographers of American writers have to write about?" (Schorer, 234). A valid point, yet in some recent cases the diligent debunker has seemed more interested in spreading disillusionment than in presenting a fair assessment of the subject.

Biography hence declined into what Joyce Carol Oates called "pathography," the word borrowed from Freud. Books of that sort, she wrote, "so mercilessly expose their subjects, so relentlessly catalog their most private, vulnerable and least illuminating moments, as to divest them of all mystery save the crucial and unexplained: How did a distinguished body of work emerge from so undistinguished a life?" (quoted in Schlesinger, 36). How did the subjects manage to get out of bed in the morning, much less create wonderful novels and poems? (Kaplan, "Culture," 6). Pathographers painted their pictures, warts and all, and sometimes added a few fake warts. Even when sticking to the facts, they often demeaned their subjects by attributing the worst possible motives to their behavior, as Lawrance Thompson consistently did in his embittered three-volume life of Robert Frost. Thompson had his reasons: he signed on early as Frost's biographer, and waited decades for his chosen subject to do the decent thing and die. During the long interim, Thompson became increasingly disillusioned with Frost, changing from devoted admirer to dedicated foe—and even sexual rival.

Thompson was not alone in committing what John Updike characterized as the Judas biography, in which disciples, friends, and lovers attack the person—or the corpse—of a former mentor. Such cases bring to mind Oscar Wilde's observation that every great man has disciples, but it is always

Judas who writes the biography (Pearce, xiv). Among others, Updike cited the example of Paul Theroux. After a falling out with V. S. Naipaul, Theroux attributed "a host of racist, misogynistic, cruel and vain remarks" to his longtime literary guide in *Sir Vidia's Shadow* (1998) (Updike, 28–29). Theroux argued in his defense that "the truest portrait of a writer can never be a study of virtue. . . . Any book that . . . invites the reader to see its subject as simple and lovable is a confidence trick" (Theroux, 39). But his suggestion— that by practicing their craft literary people necessarily leave the wounded in their wake—stretches credibility. Are there no admirable men and women among writers?

Contemporary literary biography has also been marked by its vast accumulation of detail. Not only did the writer in question shrink in stature as he or she was revealed to have been troubled by human failings at least as bad as the reader's own, but knowing the mundane quotidian facts— whether she liked eggs for breakfast, and if he could break one hundred on the golf course—inspired a spurious "mateyness" (Skidelsky, 11) between subject and reader. This heaping up of insignificant material led to bad books of sash-weight heft, yet, as James Atlas argued, it was not "girth" alone but "pedantry" that doomed them: "the insistence—prevalent especially among academics—upon entering every fact, however insignificant, into the biographical ledger merely because it has been found" (Atlas, "Subject," 25).

Despite such shortcomings, biographies have rarely been more popular than in recent times. People like to read about the failings of others, a somewhat distressing fact that has helped the present age become "a culture of biography," according to Justin Kaplan, biographer of Mark Twain and Walt Whitman. Ideas and issues fade in importance, he observed in 1994, as we pay attention instead to "celebrity, personality, and anecdote." At the low end of the scale lie supermarket scandal sheets and tell-all accounts of the disordered lives of the rich and famous. At the peak stands the occasional biography that, like Kaplan's own, "explores the intersection of history, society, and individual experience, renders character in the round, tells a generously contexted story that has a beginning, middle, and end, and may even suggest a degree of social continuity and personal responsibility" (Kaplan, "Culture," 1–3) and accomplishes these goals without moralizing.

The path toward production of such estimable books has hardly grown smoother. Malcolm Bradbury observed in a 1988 essay that we were living simultaneously in "the age of the Literary Life" and "the age of the Death of the Author"—"the age of the author studied, pursued, celebrated, and hyped, and the age of the author denied and eliminated, airbrushed from the world of writing" (Bradbury, 132–33). The "Death of the Author" had its origin in the recondite recesses of literary theory. At the middle of the twentieth century, the New Critics mandated "close reading" of fiction and poetry accompanied by a studied disregard for their creators and the times they lived in. They were succeeded by the Deconstructionists, who declared that the text was everything, and the author who produced it—in Michel Foucault's phrase—merely "the dead man in the game of writing" (quoted in Halperin, 149). In such a theoretical universe, "the reader" became more important than either author or text, for he or she alone could invest any given text with meaning.

Taken cumulatively, these theories called into question literary biography's central justification: that knowledge of the life throws light on the work and vice versa. Fortunately, neither the New Criticism nor postmodern Deconstructionism has spread its influence far beyond the halls of academe. Dedicated professional craftsmen continue to write biographies for an audience of interested readers. That will not stop until humans lose their curiosity about each other, and about the way they lived and loved and did their work.

Becoming a Biographer

I didn't start out to be a literary biographer. For a long time, I had no occupational plans at all, other than vaguely hoping to become a writer of some sort. In my first surviving postcard, when seven years of age, I asked my vacationing parents for a typewriter. In grade school my mother coached me to recite poems, very heavy on Kipling: "Gunga Din" and "If," which didn't make a man of me, not close, not yet. At Blake School, the country day school outside Minneapolis I attended alongside other children of privilege, I started writing pieces for the *Torch* ("Pass the torch to those who follow / With an undimmed light," the school song implored) and ended up being editor my senior year. That proved to be less than a distinction at Yale, where something like 10 percent of the freshman class also edited their school newspapers.

I went to Yale (1) because my older brother Frank, who'd been salutatorian at Blake, went to Harvard, (2) because my stepmother sent a son of hers to Yale, and (3) because it was the only college I applied to. That was 1946, when almost every Blake lad whose torch wasn't dim could count on being admitted everywhere, even the Ivies. But that was also the time when several years' worth of soldiers and sailors returned to swell the ranks of the class of 1950. Many of my veteran classmates knew exactly what career they wanted to pursue and what they planned to do about it during their bright college years. Having lost time to the war, they strode through Yale with purpose and a sense of urgency. The competition was tough. After a fine first semester—when I was by and large repeating courses I'd had at Blake—my grades drifted back to mediocrity. I was young for my class, and young for my years, and lazy to boot.

I majored in English in order "to read the best which has been thought and said," Matthew Arnold's Victorian remedy against galloping materialism, which, by the later twentieth century, guaranteed almost surefire protection against gainful employment. Arnold would have approved of the English curriculum at Blake, which was nothing if not high-minded. We read novels and plays that more or less openly provided moral instruction. *The Merchant of Venice* and *Julius Caesar. The Man Without a Country* and *The Cloister and the Hearth* and *A Tale of Two Cities*, climaxed by Sydney Carton's noble sacrifice. Somehow *The Return of the Native* and the racy Eustacia Vye slipped into the mix, and by that time—it must have been senior year—I'd discovered de Maupassant's salacious stories right there, uncensored, on the school's library shelves.

At Yale, the reading lists were more adventurous. In a freshman honors class taught by young instructor Douglas Knight (later president of Duke), I was introduced to T. S. Eliot and the challenging ten-minute quiz: "Prufrock's 'I should have been a pair of ragged claws / Scuttling across the floors of silent seas.' *Discuss.*" Matthew Arnold's dictates were not of much use. What most interested me were American writers only a generation ahead of mine. For a senior thesis I proposed a study of either Steinbeck or Hemingway, neither of whom was customarily taught in Yale's classrooms. Not Steinbeck, I was told, but maybe, possibly, Hemingway, if someone on the faculty could be found to direct my meanderings. That someone turned out to be the charismatic Charles A. Fenton, another young instructor who was about to embark on his dissertation/book *The Apprenticeship of Ernest Hemingway.* I learned a lot from Charlie Fenton, most crucially that it might be possible to make an occupation out of reading and writing about and teaching the work of authors who appealed to me. Through his example, and that of his Yale mentor Norman Holmes Pearson, I hazily envisioned such a future.

Barely too young for World War II, I was a prime candidate—fresh out of college, unmarried, in good health—to be drafted for the Korean War. To avoid that calamity, I enrolled in graduate school at the University of Minnesota and stalled around for nearly three years before taking a master's degree in English early in 1953. Then, knowing the draft was about to catch up with me, I enlisted in the Army Security Agency. That kept me from being shot at, but otherwise my experience in the army was about as screwed up as imaginable. I'd expected to go to the Monterey language school to study Mandarin Chinese—a sure thing, the recruiter assured me, since I had some facility with languages, and all I had to do was pass the test given to ASA enlistees during their first week. The week I joined, the quota was full and no test was administered. Then the army sent me to Camp Chaffee, Arkansas, for basic training as a preliminary step toward combat service in the artillery. I got pneumonia, recovered, and started basic again. The army noticed I was in the wrong place, and shipped me to Fort Riley, Kansas, to begin basic training for the third time. In the end I did eighteen weeks of what was supposed to be a rigorous eight weeks of basic training.

Only then did the Army Security Agency start training me as a Morse code intercept operator. I wasn't very good at the work, which consisted largely of copying five-letter code groups from barely audible radio signals. It did teach me for the first time how to use a typewriter, the one good thing that came out of my military experience. Otherwise it was one SNAFU after another. I got married over the Christmas holiday in 1953, and applied to stay at Fort Devens, Massachusetts, to teach other recruits the rudiments of code breaking. This proposal had the support of my C.O., and the papers were in preparation when contrary orders came in for further training at Fort Bragg, North Carolina. My wife was killed there in an automobile accident. We'd been married seven months. Not long thereafter I took a troop ship to Japan, again as the result of a mistake. We were asked to indicate our preferred overseas destinations. I chose EUCOM [Europe], Hawaii, and FECOM [Far East], in that order. The sergeant taking this down reversed the order, typing FECOM, Hawaii, and EUCOM. So it went.

Stationed near Kyoto for about fifteen months, I began to think about the future. I still wanted to be a writer, but had no idea what kind of a writer. I read Rudolf Flesch's *The Art of Plain Talk* and thereafter determined to communicate on paper as clearly as possible. I sent a fact piece to the *New Yorker* about the life of an enlisted man in the Orient—"Letter from Japan," I pretentiously called it—and am still waiting for acknowledgment of its receipt. I wangled an early discharge and went back to Minneapolis, where my luck changed. The *Minneapolis Star and Tribune* was expanding its coverage of the community's suburbs, which were burgeoning as a consequence of the postwar building boom. My guardian—both of my parents died while I was in high school—knew an executive at the papers, got me an interview, and I was hired at $61 a week to cover the growing pains of the south suburbs of Bloomington and Richfield.

It was an ideal assignment for a beginning reporter, for each of those communities had its own mayor and city council, its own school district, its own police force, and so on, and I was soon writing stories on a wide variety of topics, from government and politics to education to law enforcement. It made for learning on a much broader scale than if—like most reporters—I'd been covering only one beat. Most of my colleagues on the *Star* were veteran newsmen. Some had worked for larger papers elsewhere, in Chicago or New York. An unusual number of them were Irish by heritage—star rewrite man Frank Murray, for example, who could take down notes from another reporter on the telephone and magically convert them into a first-rate story, and the saintly (and therefore quite different from his colleagues, a fair number of them reformed drunks) Bernard Casserly, at the desk opposite mine, who transformed my First Amendment leanings into a vehement commitment to freedom of expression. I watched and listened to men like that, and every day cranked out two or three stories for the *Star*, the evening paper, in time for the late morning deadline.

I'd get to the newsroom by 7 A.M., assemble notes from the previous night's city council or school board meeting or personal interview, make a few follow-up phone calls, write my copy on a standup Royal in a crowded and noisy newsroom, and send it off to the copy desk in hopes of securing a byline. The assistant city editor didn't cotton to my material, which he marked up unmercifully: no bylines from him. Eventually, though, I had the thrill of seeing "by Scott Donaldson" above a story. That felt better than the obligatory $5 a week raise that came after six months. You couldn't make much of a living as a reporter, even on a metropolitan newspaper like the *Minneapolis Star*. Working there, though, taught me that it was possible through adequate preparation and concentration to produce a fair amount of copy every day, whether you felt like it or not. As Ernest Hemingway said about his early newspaper days, what he learned at the *Kansas City Star*— what carried over into his career as a writer—was discipline.

I left the *Star* sooner than I should have, for a public relations job at Pillsbury that immediately doubled my salary. The money was better and the work worse. I wrote articles for trade magazines in which I embedded mention of Pillsbury's bakery products. I coached executives on how to write an interesting letter. I was bored most of the time. When a proposal came along to start a weekly newspaper in suburban Bloomington, I was ready to jump.

The *Bloomington Suburbanite*, we called it, and we were in fierce competition with another weekly, the *Bloomington Sun*. Bloomington's population rocketed from about ten thousand in 1950 to one hundred thousand in 1960, and such rapid development resulted in a time of troubles and disputes that tested the limits of democracy and made for wonderful newspaper stories. Overbuilding to provide baby boomers with their first houses led to community-wide sewer problems. Wets and drys battled over whether to allow municipal liquor stores. Republicans and Democrats, split 50–50 in the populace, converted council elections into vigorously antagonistic struggles.

Those were lively days, and as editor and publisher of a fledgling weekly I was on a steep learning curve. The news side I understood pretty well, but I'd had no experience whatever in running a small business. It came as a shock to discover that some people—especially those who'd run ads in our paper—didn't pay their bills promptly, and that a few didn't pay at all. A printer in the shop disappeared with a small supply of company checks. The monthly balance sheet looked promising, until the bill for workmen's compensation came in—a cost I hadn't figured on. I had never worked so hard, and never would again. The opposition spread terrible rumors about us, while we attributed the worst possible motives to everything they did. Eventually we grew our circulation to match theirs, and after some difficult negotiations were able to buy them out. Probably we paid too much, but the surviving *Bloomington Sun-Suburbanite* prospered, becoming, in circulation at least, one of the nation's largest weeklies.

Then there was a merger with two dozen other weeklies serving the several suburbs around the Twin Cities. I became executive editor of that chain, which was much less rewarding than putting out one's own paper. Besides, I wasn't doing any serious writing of my own: no books, no articles in widely distributed magazines. In the fall of 1963, I went back to the University of Minnesota and enrolled in its outstanding American Studies program, emerging three years later with a Ph.D. and a dissertation on the contemporary American suburb viewed from the varying perspectives of novelists and architectural historians, sociologists and political scientists. That became my first book, called *The Suburban Myth*. I also placed an article on the gallery of characters in E. A. Robinson's poetry with *American Literature*, the leading journal in the field.

The university market was not yet overstocked with doctored candidates, and with these accomplishments I secured a post teaching American literature at the College of William and Mary in Virginia. There I could teach bright students—and myself—about great literature and take summers off to write material that would not be used, the following day, to wrap the fish in. It was an ideal way of working, and I stayed there thirty years, minus the odd semester off to teach overseas on Fulbright grants or to do research toward the next book-in-progress with awards from William and Mary and the National Endowment for the Humanities.

My newspaper background gave me an advantage over most academics. I was used to thinking in terms of what would be of general interest to readers, and of getting words down on paper as a daily regimen. I'd become a professional writer, but was a long way from knowing what kind of a writer. My principal interests lay in American literature and American intellectual history—the specialties of J. C. Levenson and David W. Noble, the two University of Minnesota professors who jointly directed my dissertation. It was only by accident that these interests morphed into biography.

I'd done well enough in Levenson's two-semester course in American poetry to serve as his assistant—and even, during a summer session, to teach the second half of the course myself (Dickinson to 1950) to fellow graduate students. Levenson liked my paper on Robinson and urged me to send if off to *American Literature*. He also acquainted me with a number of poets still practicing, and I took a particular liking to the work of Winfield Townley Scott (1910–1968). A New Englander who spent his last years in Santa Fe, Scott wrote powerful, plainspoken verse and had a consuming passion for the great writers who had preceded him. Once established at William and Mary, I decided to undertake a long article on Scott's work. To give the piece authority I spent a summer poring over his papers at Brown University's John Hay Library. During those sunny summer days in Rhode Island, sitting inside seven hours a day reading with fascination the letters and journals of a minor (but far from inconsequential) poet, my future was sealed. There was no clap of thunder, but I'd found something I could do, something I really wanted to do. I would tell the stories of American writers, the intersection of their lives and works with the times. I would be a literary biographer.

And Then I Wrote . . .

It did not occur to me that I could possibly make a living by writing literary biographies. Such books, if reasonably well done, usually found publishers, but few of them brought in substantial earnings. So my principal occupation remained that of a university professor, with biography relegated to the status of a passionately pursued avocation. I'd been lucky to land at William and Mary, which was undergoing a transformation from a sleepy southern college to one of the nation's best small universities. In the English department I taught bright and eager students about the very figures who would become my subjects. Most of these authors fell within the scope of the survey course in twentieth-century American literature. To go deeper into their work I initiated seminars in Fitzgerald and Hemingway, in what I called Gnomic American Poets (Dickinson, Robinson, Frost), and in writing nonfiction. In all of these I learned along with the students.

"What was that about?" I would ask my classes, and "how was it done?" Upon third or fourth reading of a novel and fifteenth or twentieth immersion in a poem, I (we) sometimes came upon answers to those questions. As a biographer I resisted the New Critics' obliteration of the author, yet at the same time embraced their insistence upon "close reading," a doctrine brilliantly advocated in I. A. Richards's *Practical Criticism* (1929). If you looked at a literary work often and carefully enough, one word at a time, a light might go on.

One such illuminating experience led to my second biographical work, *By Force of Will: The Life and Art of Ernest Hemingway* (1977). We'd been examining Hemingway's *The Sun Also Rises* in class, and I was struck, this time through the book, by the many detailed financial transactions Jake Barnes described and reflected upon. In an essay I argued that the morality of the novel was structured around a financial metaphor: in brief, that easy money was bad for people, and you had to earn your pleasure. I wrote an article on that theme, again for *American Literature*, called "The Morality of Compensation in *The Sun Also Rises.*" That got me thinking about Hemingway's attitudes on a number of issues. Why not do a book that took up a number of such topics? Hemingway and . . . Money, Love, Friendship, Sport, War, Death, Politics, Religion, Fame, and so on. From these fragments I might stitch together a collage depicting the kind of man and writer Hemingway was.

So much for the idea, but what of the process? I knew little about the making of biographies. It happened that Charles Norman, an accomplished veteran in the field who had written biographies of E. E. Cummings and Ezra Pound, came to William and Mary to present a talk on his work. He emphasized that as a preliminary step the biographer was obliged to read *everything*. I accepted that as gospel, and set out to read everything Hemingway wrote, from published fiction through journalistic essays to personal letters, and everything others had written about him as well. This took about four years, though it could have been accomplished in half the time were it not for teaching duties.

Most of the research was done at Princeton, where Carlos Baker had assembled vast stores of information for his *Ernest Hemingway: A Life* (1969), the first and still indispensable biography. There were also trips to New York, Boston, New Haven, Charlottesville, and Austin, Texas, where the Lone Star university placed a gatekeeper with a holstered .38 at the entrance to its manuscript collection. In the course of these research trips, I established a procedure that was to become routine. I assembled thousands of 8 1/2 by 11 sheets, labeled by category at the top, one sheet at a time and never anything on the reverse. At some stage during this accumulation of material the shape of the book began to clarify. Then it was time to shuffle the notes, put them in order, and confront the actual physical and mental labor of writing. Once I repaired to my typewriter, I worked more or less obsessively, seven days a week, half a dozen hours a day. On a good day when I was in my forties I could turn out about ten typed pages, with nearly half of the verbiage crossed out as I went along. Later, the daily output shrank.

To attract a publisher I prepared a chapter reflecting the overall scope and intention of the book. This chapter went out to several firms, either because they were interested in Hemingway or because I knew someone who worked there. Doubleday and Scribner's politely declined interest.

Then Malcolm Cowley, who took time off from his own writing to advise Viking Press, saw and liked the sample chapter and persuaded Viking to take an option on the book. The advance wasn't large, but it didn't have to be. Overcome with joy and anticipation, I plunged ahead.

One of the unacknowledged benefits of biography consists of the people you encounter along the way. In researching my book on Win Scott, I'd met Justin (Joe) Kaplan and Anne Bernays, the husband-and-wife literary team—he a biographer, she a novelist—who'd been friends of Scott's. They encouraged my efforts and offered extremely helpful advice. Upon reading a few early chapters, Joe wrote me a letter that might serve as a model for communications from the editor's desk. He began with praise, so commanding my attention. Win Scott was coming through very well, he said, and I'd done wonders for his poetry by way of explication. Next he pointed out a few apparent errors: "David Grayson was Ray Stannard Baker's penname, not vice versa, as you seem to imply." Then he got down to his principal criticism, which had to do with lack of variation in *pacing*. Specifically, he recommended that at crucial points I should do more to develop a particular scene or episode. By way of example he mentioned young Win Scott's pilgrimage to the MacDowell Colony to spend a few hours with Edwin Arlington Robinson. That was an important meeting, the aspiring twenty-year-old poet sharing conversation with the famous one of sixty, and the reticent Robinson gradually revealing more of himself as the interview wore on. It needed "some slowing down, building up, refocusing," Joe suggested (Kaplan to SD, 31 May 1970). I went back and tried to give that meeting the emphasis it deserved.

Editorial guidance of such sophistication was rare at that time (the early 1970s) and has almost entirely vanished in the twenty-first century. In that regard too, I was fortunate in working with editors at trade houses who helped me fashion biographies into finished form. "Who is your editor?" people frequently ask, on the assumption that writers and their editors at publishing houses are wedded together for the long term. That was not my experience at all. I had several editors at various firms, but—except for a brief period at the very beginning—only one agent, or rather two men at one agency: Sterling Lord and his successor, Peter Matson, of Sterling Lord Literistic. They knew that the marketplace was not exactly humming with demand for midlist literary biographies, yet managed to place almost everything I got down on paper. So I stuck to one agent while shuttling from one publisher to another, in that way profiting from the accumulated wisdom of some excellent editors. The best of these were Malcolm Cowley at Viking, Robert D. Loomis at Random House, and Peter Davison at Houghton Mifflin. Probably Cowley did more for my cause than anyone else.

I met Cowley at a British American Studies conference in 1972, when he was a distinguished visiting professor at the University of Warwick and I was teaching as the Bruern fellow at the University of Leeds. Cowley was an established literary eminence. Born in 1898, he belonged to the greatest literary generation of the twentieth century. I'd read *Exile's Return*, his wonderful memoir of Paris in the 1920s, and his long article for *Life* on Hemingway. I knew of his Viking *Portable Faulkner*, a volume instrumental in restoring William Faulkner's reputation. I'd used his anthology of F. Scott Fitzgerald's stories in my classes. Cowley brought a supple prose style and the authority of experience to his writing about these major figures, all of whom he knew and admired. It would have been daunting to approach him, had he erected any barriers against invasion. Instead he was among the most amiable men alive. With his round face, ubiquitous pipe, and deficient hearing—he was thirty years my senior—he drew me out on my ideas about Hemingway. He was a scout for Viking, he explained, and they might be interested.

This was tremendously exciting news, for as an American man of letters—poet, critic, freelancer, literary historian, editor—Cowley was rivaled only by the irascible Edmund Wilson. Yet his books and articles rarely brought in enough to support him and his family. He needed occasional academic assignments and the part-time job with Viking to make ends meet, just as, during the 1930s, he had relied on a salary from the *New Republic* to do so. In those peripheral roles, Cowley demonstrated his gift for locating and encouraging talent. As literary editor of the *New Republic* he rescued John Cheever's first publication from the trash pile, befriended the youth, and helped him shape his early pieces for the *New Yorker*. At Viking he found and promoted Jack Kerouac's *On the Road*.

The Editor's Hand: Hemingway

Not until I went back over our correspondence during 1974–76 did I realize how much I owed to Cowley at the beginning of my career. We were in it together, for he had recommended that Viking take a chance on my Hemingway book and wanted to make sure that the result met his standards. Therefore he played tutor to my tyro throughout the process of composition, alerting me to problems, suggesting revisions, challenging conclusions, and doing so with a combination of tough-minded criticism and uncommon tact. We communicated almost entirely by U.S. mail—I recall only two meetings, one at his home in Sherman, Connecticut, and the other in Viking's New York offices. As I finished chapters I sent them to Cowley for evaluation. In his responses, invariably dispatched within a few days, he mingled the occasional approving comment—how I listened for those!—with specific proposals for revision and lessons from the field.

In the first of the dozen letters from Cowley, usually running to a page and a half of single-spaced typewritten copy, he began with the good news that the two chapters I'd mailed him seemed to be "interesting, well researched and well written" and that therefore he'd asked executive editor Alan Williams at Viking to pick up their option. Then he launched into criticism. First of all, he detected a (quite unintended) bias against Hemingway in my prose, and that bothered him. As a contemporary of Hemingway—and of Faulkner and Fitzgerald and Dos Passos—he was disinclined to think badly of any of them. If I was writing "a tearing-down book," he warned, I had better show that it was a "considerable edifice" I was dismantling. Hemingway was for the early twentieth century what Byron had been for the early nineteenth, he pointed out. He was also possessed of "enormous charm," something I should take account of. Specifically, he warned against making too much of Hemingway's friendship with James Gamble, his Red Cross boss during World War I and his host during a 1918 holiday in Taormina. Theirs had not been a homosexual relationship, he felt sure, for Hemingway's puritan upbringing left him with "a horror of homosexuality."

Cowley corrected one error of fact in my sample chapters: Hemingway cut four thousand words from the beginning of *The Sun Also Rises*, not forty thousand as I'd written. More importantly, he questioned my interpretation of the politics in *For Whom the Bell Tolls*. I hadn't grasped how important the theme of "comradeship, brotherhood in the service of a cause" was in the novel, he thought. Something more than Jeffersonian individualism was involved, and Hemingway was more committed to the Loyalists in the Spanish Civil War than I seemed to believe. At the time we agreed to disagree, for I was then convinced of Hemingway's opposition to any and all sources of political authority. Thirty-five years later, after a more thorough study of Hemingway's involvement in that war, I concluded that Cowley was absolutely right in his assertion that "he [like his protagonist Robert Jordan] saw the weaknesses on the Loyalists' side and felt that, nevertheless, their cause was worth dying for."

Cowley took time to instruct me, as a newcomer, about copyright law. I'd better observe that law to avoid a costly court suit, he warned, for the courts generally ruled that biographers or historians could not quote from letters without permission of the estate. But I could avoid legal trouble, he counseled, by following the course of action he recommended. "You can't quote directly from letters, but you can always paraphrase what Hemingway said. Never put more than a single word in quotes," he advised, or simply omit the quotation marks. In one paragraph I'd quoted from Hemingway's letters to his wife Mary about financial affairs. "For that one Miss Mary would probably sue at the drop of a hat," he warned.

That passage was in the chapter on Hemingway and Money. In that chapter, Cowley observed, I hadn't made it sufficiently clear that Hemingway's attitude changed as he grew older. In his early years, he turned down some offers that were financially advantageous, and only after he became a famous author did he try to obtain the highest possible price for everything he wrote (MC to SD, 29 August 1974). Here he noted a shortcoming that was to affect almost every chapter. In assembling notes related to the topics under consideration, I occasionally failed to give chronology the importance it deserved, and to show how Hemingway's ideas about Love or War or Whatever developed and altered over time. Dividing a book into topical chapters automatically robbed it of the chronological order most readers expected. That was handicap enough. Within each individual chapter it was imperative to give chronology its due (MC to SD, 12 June 1975).

I wrote almost all of my book on Hemingway in the eighteen months between June 1974 and the end of 1975. It proved difficult to get the words down on paper while teaching a full load, so I managed to get a semester off in the spring of 1975 (the college president was a squash-playing companion). During that four-month leave I completed most of a first draft and shipped the new chapters off to Cowley. Almost all of these required rewriting, some more than others. Cowley was a diligent and sometimes stern editor. Even when he liked a chapter—like the one on Friendship, which traced Hemingway's repeated pattern of breaking off with friends—he proposed changes. "This chapter is so important, and good too, that I think it can be made still better" (MC to SD, 28 March 1975). With the beginning and ending chapters, he took a tougher line. He thought the opening chapter, on Fame, was too journalistic and breezy and advised me to put it back in the typewriter (Cowley to SD, 12 June 1975). And he was even more adamant about revising the concluding chapter on Hemingway's drive for Mastery in every kind of endeavor.

Last chapters were always a problem, he pointed out. "The writer wants to end with a bang; the reader expects him to do so, or at least to illuminate what has gone before by rolling it into one incandescent ball." But I hadn't done that, hadn't provided enough of a "sense of things ending" (MC to SD, 14 June 1975). Only after two rewrite jobs was he satisfied. "Last chapter arrived today. It *is* much better. . . . In fact the whole manuscript now begins to look like a book." So he wrote me on 2 January 1976, when he sent the script to Alan Williams with his endorsement.

"Scott Donaldson's Hemingway," Cowley commented, "is an interesting, thoughtful, and useful book, a character study of a great author rather than a critical study of his work. It contains a good deal of fresh material that became available after Carlos Baker wrote his biography and ends by presenting a rounded portrait of the man." He was less enthusiastic about the writing. "Donaldson writes pretty good prose, better now than in the first draft, clear, straightforward, and with not too many touches of the academic" (MC to Williams, 5 January 1976). One such "touch of the academic" he'd cautioned me about earlier—a tendency to start "too many sentences in succession with a participle or a prepositional phrase or an adverb." He also recommended avoiding clichés by deleting one of the two words so often coupled: "enemies" didn't have to be "mortal," innocent "lies" needn't always be "white" (MC to SD, 12 June 1975).

Again, I want to emphasize how unusual it was to be edited with such conscientious professional attention. Cowley went further than that, arranging for Carlos Baker to vet the semifinal draft. That process, too, considerably improved the book. I'd gotten to know Baker while doing research at Princeton. He was very much a gentleman-scholar, generous in helping others like Michael S. Reynolds and myself as we began our work on Hemingway. Baker guided me toward new information that had come to light after his official biography, *Ernest Hemingway: A Life Story*, appeared in 1969. He also allowed me to examine the papers in his office: the documents behind the "roughly 500–600 pages" he'd cut out of his book.

As the one person alive who had done the most research on Hemingway, Baker located many mistakes in my manuscript—more than I thought possible—in his report for Viking, and itemized them for correction. One egregious example: Hemingway's "arm, not collarbone, broken in car accident. It occurred west of Billings, Mont. while *returning* from the Yellowstone region, not driving west to Wyoming. In short, [Donaldson] has it all screwed up." In this case, as in several others, the problem derived from my trusting the proliferating literature about Hemingway, much of it incorrect. Specifically, Baker warned me against relying on the accuracy of A. E. Hotchner's *Papa Hemingway* (1966), and against using *any* quotations from an article in *Playboy* supposedly containing nuggets of Hemingway wisdom but "made up out of whole cloth." He took up each of the chapters in order, and recommended cuts in half of them. With his eight pages of "errors, queries, and disagreements" in front of me I undertook the final revision of *By Force of Will: The Life and Art of Ernest Hemingway* (Baker to MC, 7 August 1975). Baker did for that book what Cowley could not. I remain forever indebted to both of them.

Fitzgerald and the Craft

It made perfect sense, it seemed to me, to write a biography of F. Scott Fitzgerald once I'd had my say on Hemingway. But the market for another book on Fitzgerald was not promising in the late 1970s, when I started on my usual four-to-five-year gestation period. The unhappy saga of Scott and Zelda had been told several times over in biographies of uneven merit: Arthur Mizener's *The Far Side of Paradise*, Henry Dan Piper's *F. Scott Fitzgerald*, Andrew Turnbull's *Scott Fitzgerald,* Nancy Milford's *Zelda,* and Sheilah Graham and Gerold Frank's *Beloved Infidel.* Moreover, Matthew J. Bruccoli's *Some Sort of Epic Grandeur* (1981), easily the most thorough and fact-filled work, was in its final stages of preparation. Cowley, who knew the literary marketplace, advised me not to undertake yet another Fitzgerald book. But I was relatively young and foolish, and plunged ahead.

To justify itself, it was clear, any biographical portrait would have to look at Fitzgerald from an entirely new angle. After repeated rereadings of his novels and stories and several years of research (including a 1979 semester as a visiting scholar at Princeton, "reading Fitzgerald's mail" at the Firestone Library), I arrived at such an approach. The driving force in his life, it seemed to me, was a compulsion to please—a compulsion that could be traced to his boyhood in St. Paul. He had a tremendous drive to earn the approval and admiration of others, and since he wasn't much good at pleasing men, who thought he tried too hard and asked too many personal questions, he spent inordinate amounts of time and energy pleasing women, even women he did nor really care about. In his last years he was able to shake off this debilitating habit and stop the drinking that fueled it, realizing at last that it didn't really matter what others thought of him so long as he was doing the work that mattered. He died at only forty-four, yet by then had triumphed over his demons to become "a writer only."

My biography was constructed around this pattern, with a concentration on the women most involved: his mother, who invested her social ambitions in her handsome and talented son; the beautiful and wealthy Ginevra King, who jilted him in college; the daring southern belle Zelda Sayre, who caught him on the rebound and with whom he entered into a marriage that became a war for dominance; the ambitious Hollywood columnist Sheilah Graham, who stayed with him until the end. And of course this theme declared itself in Fitzgerald's finest fiction: *The Great Gatsby* and the early stories about the poor young boy in hapless pursuit of the unattainable and forever idealized rich girl, and *Tender Is the Night,* where Dick Diver's fatal charm actually captures just such a girl, a psychiatric patient of his who grows stronger under his care while he fades into obscurity.

In *Tender,* a great sprawling novel, Fitzgerald dramatized the war between the sexes that was becoming an obsession in his own life. In 1930 Zelda collapsed and underwent treatment for what her doctors diagnosed as schizophrenia. For the rest of her life—she outlived Scott—she was institutionalized most of the time. But there were occasions when she rallied while Scott grew increasingly dependent on liquor. It took him nine years to follow *Gatsby* (1925) with *Tender* (1934). Yet in 1932 alone Zelda produced a novel, *Save Me the Waltz*, during a burst of energy despite being confined at Phipps Clinic in Baltimore. He began to think of himself as the victim in a deadly competition with his wife. There was a bitter confrontation between them in May 1933, tape recorded by one of her doctors, in which Scott inveighed against Zelda's writing another novel or play based on their mutual experience. He was the professional writer, and she was poaching on *his* material, he insisted.

Shortly thereafter—as he was finally readying *Tender* for Scribner's— Scott set down some chilling comments that survive among his notes at Princeton: "As I got feeling worse Zelda got mentally better, but it seemed to me that as she did she was also coming to the conclusion that she had it on me, if I broke down it justified her whole life. . . . Finally four days ago told her frankly & furiously that had got & was getting rotten deal trading my health for her sanity." He proposed a diabolical plan to remedy the situation in a note I found at Princeton and included in *Fool for Love: F. Scott Fitzgerald*, my 1983 biography. Perhaps because it was my own discovery, noted by no one else, I thought this an extremely important document. Yet so far as I know, Fitzgerald's note has gone unmentioned in the articles and books devoted to him and his wife. Here it is again.

> *Plan—To attack on all grounds*
>   Play (suppress), novel (delay), pictures (suppress), character
> (showers??), child (detach), schedule (disorient to cause trouble),
> no typing
>   Probably result—new breakdown
>   Danger to Scotty (?)
>   "   " herself (?)
>
> *All this in secret.* (SD, *Fool*, 86)

There is no evidence that he actually carried out this plan, conceived as it must have been in desperation.

Fitzgerald's obsessive need to please gave my biography a guiding principle that removed it from a conventional cradle-to-grave account. That was all to the good, for there is almost always such a principle behind a life— what Leon Edel called the "life-myth" and Wallace Stevens "the presence of the determining personality." Or so I concluded, though with an awareness of the risk involved: the tendency to force evidence into supporting one's view. Though admirable in many ways, for example, Philip Young's book on

Hemingway rode its thesis—that almost everything about Hemingway could be accounted for by his wounding in World War I—pretty hard. As someone has remarked, once you adopt a thesis the whole world lies at your feet. I tried not to fall into that trap.

I worked on *Fool for Love* between semesters and during a sabbatical. The most productive period came during a visit to the MacDowell Colony in October 1980. As an admirer of Edwin Arlington Robinson, I knew of his many annual stays at the colony and his devotion to the place. I applied for a residency without much hope of success, but apparently my Hemingway book got me in. In preparation for a three-week stay at MacDowell I packed up the back seat of the Volvo with several boxes of notes and the upright Royal typewriter I'd been using since newspaper days in Minneapolis. (Not until the mid-1990s did I switch to word processing on the computer.)

The leaves turned red and gold as I drove from Williamsburg to Peterborough, New Hampshire. The routine at MacDowell was organized to make it almost impossible not to produce. Breakfast was served early, and colonists then walked to their studios in the woods. Each studio had a fireplace and a supply of wood to keep the place warm. Shortly before noon came a knock on the door. When you opened it, no one was there but a box lunch had arrived. There were no interruptions for the rest of the day, and no telephones in the studios. You were there with your materials—visual artists and musicians and composers as well as writers were in residence—and a tremendous amount of work got done. Dinner was plain New England fare with your fellow companions in residence, and you brought your own wine. Friendships and in some cases romantic attachments formed among colonists. Sometimes the professional bonding degenerated into competition.

Robinson recalled the evening a brash MacDowell fellow bragged about the several thousand words he'd got down on paper. "And what did you do today, Mr. Robinson?" he asked. "This morning," EAR answered, "I removed the hyphen from hell-hound. This afternoon I put it back" (SD, *Robinson*, 395–96). After dinner you might play cowboy pool, a blend of pocket pool and billiards that had become a MacDowell tradition, or someone might sing or play the piano. The entertainments did not run late, as the colonists repaired to their rooms to read and rest for the next day. Under this regimen I finished three chapters in three weeks—"Darling Heart," "Genius and Glass," and "The Glittering Things." To this day I think they were the best I ever wrote.

My agent at that time, Tim Seldes at Russell and Volkening, shopped the script far and wide before throwing up his hands. Luckily, at just that time I met Peter Weed through mutual friends Ann and Stephen Marlowe. Peter had recently established a small New York trade house, Congdon and Weed, and was on the lookout for books. Voila! *Fool for Love* found its publisher. This was not an entirely happy ending, for Congdon and Weed was sinking when the book surfaced in 1983 and could do little to promote it. At least the book did not vanish. It was my first book to be translated—into Spanish, as *Ansia de Amor*. Delta brought out a paperback in 1989, and much later—in 2012—the University of Minnesota Press issued another paperback edition with a new preface.

During these initial efforts at literary biography—books on Winfield Townley Scott, Hemingway, and Fitzgerald—I was learning as I went along. The most important lesson, probably, was that you had to begin with a strong enthusiasm for your subject. Merely being interested was not enough to keep you going through the several years of research and writing involved. Win Scott, for example, was an intensely American poet, conscious of his heritage in ways that had a tremendous appeal for me as a teacher of American literature. "It is so much easier to forget than to have been Mr. Whittier," his long poem on John Greenleaf Whittier begins, and that's both true and unfortunate. Scott's technique for keeping such memories green was to present them in moving vignettes—as of the ladies of Camden, New Jersey, for example, drawing "skirts and kids aside" to avoid contamination with Walt Whitman as the dirty old man hobbled past, "His basket on his arm / Filled with his book for sale."

Certain poems of Scott's, like "Mr. Whittier" and "Gert Swasey," made the back of my neck tingle. So did moments in Fitzgerald's and Hemingway's stories and novels that spoke to me the more powerfully because, like each of them a generation earlier, I was a middle-class youth who'd grown up in the Midwest. The excitement they generated made the long biographical process worthwhile. Within the academy, what I was doing remained highly suspect. At William and Mary, I resisted the developing tendency to reduce works of literature to studies in one of three categories: race, gender, and class. Actually the emphasis in most classrooms fell on race and gender almost exclusively. Students might major in Women's Studies or African American Studies, but there was not so much as a single course in Social Stratification. Yet the issue of class struck me as highly significant in our literature and culture. You could not adequately understand Fitzgerald or his fiction, for example, without an awareness of the precarious position he occupied, growing up, within the social hierarchy of St. Paul, Minnesota.

It's a curious thing, but almost all major American writers have had dominant mothers and ineffectual fathers. It's true of Fitzgerald and Hemingway, Faulkner and Frost, Melville and Hawthorne, Emerson and Thoreau. Emily Dickinson proved an exception, for in her case the tables were turned, with her father a powerful figure and her mother a virtual nonentity. There may be a sort of psychic kink that develops out of a strong mother-son or strong father-daughter relationship.

Mollie Fitzgerald, the dominant parent for Fitzgerald, pushed her son forward, sending him to St. Paul's best dancing school and prep school, where he was the only Irish-American Catholic boy with a newly rich mother and failed businessman father. Scott knew what his mother was doing, detested her for it, and at the same time felt compelled to struggle up the social ladder. It's an example of his ability, as with the double male-female side of his personality, to see matters from two different angles at the same time: a capacity he regarded as the mark of a mature and accomplished mind.

John Cheever, my next and most difficult biographical subject, faced a similar situation growing up in the Boston suburb of Quincy, Massachusetts, the son of a once-prospering shoe salesman fallen on hard times and an extremely competent mother who opened and ran a gift shop to support the family. The parallels between the two writers are striking. Late in Cheever's career, he wrote a biographical sketch of Fitzgerald for Louis Kronenberger's *Atlantic Brief Lives* (1971) that reads as if he were writing about himself.

Cheever's stories, many of them encountered in the pages of the *New Yorker*, tremendously appealed to me. Like no other writer of his time he commanded the physical and psychological territory of the upper middle-class suburb, and the American suburb had been the subject of my doctoral dissertation (and first book), *The Suburban Myth* (1969). In the late 1970s, I took time off from Fitzgerald research to write an extended essay on Cheever's work for Scribner's *American Writers* series. In that connection I visited Cheever briefly—it was our only meeting—at the Wauwinet Inn on Nantucket. We talked for a couple of hours about my project, about which he seemed amusedly tolerant. As he drove me back to the ferry, he remarked out of the blue that "most people have fathers and mothers. I had a brother": a startling comment that was to influence almost everything I was to write about him.

I was thus well started toward a Cheever biography before finishing my Fitzgerald book, and ready to go ahead when he died in 1982. Other than Susan Cheever's *Home Before Dark* (1984), the fine memoir of her father she was about to embark upon, there were no competing biographical studies. For the only time in my career, a number of publishers decided to bid on the book. Through that auction I was fortunate enough to land in the experienced hands of editor Bob Loomis at Random House. Loomis had a sharp ear for phrases that sounded not quite right, and an unerring eye for careless writing. He saw *John Cheever: A Biography* (1988) through its tortured passage toward publication, offering the support and encouragement I badly needed when the Cheever family tried to stop or at least cripple my biography. (That painful story is told at the end of this volume.) I regret that I never had another opportunity to do another book under his guidance.

The Amazing Archibald MacLeish

After my trials with the Cheever book, I was not exactly salivating to undertake another biography. Besides, I had no subject firmly in mind until, by happenstance, one presented itself. *American Playhouse*, under the direction of Miranda Barry, was interested in producing a several-part documentary for PBS on Gerald and Sara Murphy, the privileged yet star-crossed American couple who'd settled in Paris and on the Riviera in the mid-1920s and befriended many of the greatest artists of that time and place. Books had been and would be written about them, including Calvin Tomkins's *Living Well Is the Best Revenge* (1971) and Amanda Vaill's *Everybody Was So Young* (1998). In the public mind the Murphys came to represent the glamour of the Lost Generation, and their connections to Picasso and Hemingway and Fitzgerald and John Dos Passos and Archibald MacLeish gave their story a depth beyond Gerald's gift as a painter and Sara's as a great beauty.

The *American Playhouse* project, for whatever reasons, did not result in a televised documentary, although scripts for a four-part series were completed. But during the preliminary research stages a number of presumably well-informed people were brought in to serve as advisers. So it was that I landed in a conference room representing Hemingway, and there, across the table, sat William H. MacLeish as the authority on his parents, Archie and Ada MacLeish. I'd last seen Bill MacLeish in a senior Shakespeare seminar at Yale, where nine of us read almost all of the bard's work—the minor plays along with the major ones. We read *Henry VI, Parts 1, 2,* and *3,* along with *Richard III.* We read *Love's Labour's Lost* as well as *As You Like It.* We read *Titus Andronicus* and *King Lear.* There were stars in that seminar: the clever and brilliant William H. Buckley Jr. and the incipient Rhodes Scholar and eventual Pulitzer Prize winner Robert K. Massie. Then there were the rest of us.

Anyway, Bill MacLeish—an excellent writer himself—had a suggestion about what I might do next. R. H. Winnick had begun work on a biography of his father for Houghton Mifflin and then abandoned the effort to pursue other endeavors that would support his family. Before leaving the field, though, he'd tape recorded dozens of people who knew Archie and Ada MacLeish and had reminiscences to contribute. Several of those people were no longer above ground. There were more than a hundred hours of tapes. They could give me a head start, Bill suggested, if I wanted to embark on his father's life story.

The time period made sense. Archie MacLeish (1892–1982) was but a few years older than Ernest Hemingway and Scott Fitzgerald, and he and Hemingway had been close friends, off and on, through the years. But in fact I had not read much of the poetry and drama that won MacLeish three Pulitzer prizes. I'd seen a production of *J.B.*, his tremendously successful twentieth-century treatment of the book of Job. I knew the last lines of his widely anthologized "Ars poetica":

> A poem should be equal to:
> Not true
>
> For all the history of grief
> An empty doorway and a maple leaf
>
> For love
> The leaning grasses and two lights above the sea—
>
> A poem should not mean
> But be.
> (MacLeish, 106–7)

I didn't know much else about his writing, and even less about the wide arc of his life. *Very* wide arc. "Even in this heyday of second and third careers," as I pointed out in the preface to *Archibald MacLeish: An American Life* (1992), "it is daunting to consider that MacLeish undertook, and mastered, half a dozen: lawyer, journalist, librarian of Congress, assistant secretary of state and spokesman for the republic, teacher, playwright, and above all poet" (SD, *MacLeish*, ix).

To begin with, I went back to his *Collected Poems* and found them both interesting and uneven: at times stunning, as in, say, "The End of the World" and "You, Andrew Marvell" and "Epitaph," at other times less impressive. Still, it was clear that MacLeish deserved to be commemorated in a biography, and there was no one else on my immediate radar. So I went to see Richard McAdoo of Houghton Mifflin and signed on to write a MacLeish biography, with Peter Davison as editor, and got in touch with Winnick, who agreed to let me use his tapes.

Initially I hoped to produce an average-length book of perhaps three hundred pages, but I had not figured into my calculations either the ninety-year length of Archibald MacLeish's busy life or the complications attendant upon writing authoritatively on his separate careers. No other American writer had risen so high in the circles of government, for example. To do justice to the task, I had to acquaint myself with at least a rudimentary knowledge of such disparate matters as running a national library, directing wartime propaganda efforts, fighting off (as a dedicated liberal) the House Un-American Activities Committee and other attacks from the right, writing plays for Broadway and lesser markets, and teaching—at Harvard—some of the country's most promising young writers how to approach their craft. Archie MacLeish was manifestly a polymath, and I had to try to become one myself. And with MacLeish as with no other subject, it was mandatory to draw portraits in miniature of the many people who had helped to shape his personality and his work, beginning with his remarkable parents and exemplified in his mature years by his friendship with and devotion to the two men who, he said, could empty the air in a room simply by entering it: Franklin Delano Roosevelt and Ernest Hemingway. The finished book ran to 524 pages of text, with another hundred pages for acknowledgments, notes, and index. That's too long, and I don't know how it could have been shorter.

I wangled a semester grant from William and Mary to do initial research on the biography, and spent much of that time converting Winnick's tapes from conversation to usable quotations and, at their best, to scenes that could drive the narrative forward. Winnick had earned his spurs by serving as Lawrance Thompson's assistant at Princeton and after Thompson's death by finishing the third and last volume of his Robert Frost biography and then by doing an excellent job of editing the *Letters of Archibald MacLeish, 1907–1982* (1983). On tape, though, he did not always ask "the next question" of those he was interviewing. Sometimes he seemed to shy away from personal matters, as during his interview with Kay Bundy. Mrs. Bundy was patrician Boston, married to Archie's lawyer, Harvey Bundy, and mother of McGeorge and William Bundy. She knew both MacLeishes well, and remarked, on tape, about a welcome-home party when Ada and Archie returned from their 1924–28 years in Paris—years during which Ada was training her silver voice (she sang Mélisande with the Opéra Comique) while Archie was converting himself from successful Boston lawyer to established poet, and also years during which both of them may have had extramarital affairs. At the homecoming party, Kay Bundy said, Ada behaved scandalously. Next question on the tape: how long did your husband represent MacLeish as his attorney?

Then there was the mechanical problem of transcribing the tapes. (I've never tape recorded interviews myself, instead relying on rapid scribbling on yellow pads along with further notes made as soon as possible afterwards, often in motel rooms, sometimes in bathrooms.) Much of what was recorded proved to be of little use. I had to find a way of separating the gold of invaluable information and telling quotation from the more extensive dross. The solution came from Donald Hall, who had been MacLeish's student in

Harvard's English S class in 1949–50, along with such other talented young men as Robert Bly and George Plimpton. Participants in that year-long course were expected to complete a book-length manuscript. Hall came to know MacLeish well during that time, and on one of my interviewing trips I went to see him at his Eagle Rock farm in New Hampshire. Best known as a poet—he, like MacLeish himself, was eventually to serve as the nation's poet laureate—Hall was also a man of letters. In his fascinating *Life Work* (1993), he described in detail how he managed to earn his way in the financially unpromising vocation of freelance writer. When I went to see him, he was considering a biography about the actor Charles Laughton and had taped some interviews of sources. I asked him how he'd handled these recordings.

His method, Hall said, involved the use of not one but two tape recorders. First he listened to the interview on one recorder, stopping the tape whenever a significant quotation or revelation emerged, making notes, and talking the result into the second recorder. In that fashion he managed to boil the original down to a fraction of its original length and transplanted its important moments into accessible form, with comments added in his own voice. Then it was simply a matter of converting the shorter version on tape recorder number two into typewritten form. I did this chore myself, adding, subtracting, editing as I went along—doing these kinds of things in a way that no hired assistant or secretary could possibly do. I know that many biographers, some of the most prominent among them, have been able to shop out research chores to others, but it seemed to me that the result must inevitably reflect the researcher's ideas, opinions, prejudices— his or her decisions about what was and was not essential—and not those of the author who signed the book.

Then there were people to see and places to visit and large chunks of data to absorb. I spent a few days near Uphill Farm in Conway, Massachusetts, where Archie and Ada lived during their last decades, and visited the out-building where MacLeish would go to write without interruption. I talked with many of his students and colleagues at Harvard, among them William Alfred and Stephen Sandy and John Kenneth Galbraith and Edward Hoagland. I saw Alice Acheson, widow of Archie's classmate Dean Acheson both at Yale and at Harvard Law. Thursa Bakey, MacLeish's ever-reliable secretary when he was librarian of Congress, came down for an interview in Williamsburg. As much as possible, I tried to meet these sources face-to-face, but you can't be everywhere at once. Often I had to settle for telephone conversations, as with Elia Kazan, who'd directed J.B.

All of these endeavors supplemented heavy doses of reading, beginning with MacLeish's own extensive corpus, which included dozens of articles and speeches (and a couple of books) prepared in support of the war effort.

These were essentially propaganda, and like most propaganda did not age well. Yet there were high spots, too, among his governmental writings: the preamble to the United Nations constitution, for example, and the message of mourning that went out to the nation when FDR died. Every biographer has encountered readers who remark, by way of compliment, that "you must have done worlds of research." You say "Thank you very much" while thinking "Well, sure, it's part of the job." As David McCullough observed about his biography of Harry Truman, you have "to know what you write about, to get beneath the surface. You have to know what to leave out. . . . You have to know the territory" (McCullough, 29).

In broader terms, this meant immersing oneself in a particular period (in MacLeish's ninety-year life, several such periods) in order to understand the times and their distinctive climate of opinion. To detach one's subject from this web of conditions, Henry James thought, was to simplify the picture "fatal to the truth of history" (Nettels, 108). So in his own biography of Nathaniel Hawthorne, James tried to place him in connection with his contemporaries and circumstances, as well as in context with his antecedents and ancestors. What most interested James about Hawthorne was not what his heritage made of him but what he made of it (Nettels, 114). Almost always the great writer will rebel against the beliefs and assumptions of the culture he inhabits. Yet when we write about them, we must try to situate their accomplishments within the "intellectual present" (Skidelsky, 15) during which they thought and wrote and acted.

Peter Davison was highly qualified to edit the MacLeish biography. He was a distinguished poet himself, as his father had been before him. His mother had worked for MacLeish in the OWI (Office of War Information) during World War II. He'd been a devoted student of MacLeish's brother-in-law Alec Campbell, and a friend of MacLeish's son Bill for decades. He also was an editor and frequent contributor at the *Atlantic Monthly*. A long-time resident of Boston with connections to the intellectual and artistic community, Davison was well acquainted with most of the people whose paths crossed MacLeish's during his 1949–61 tenure as the Boylston professor of rhetoric and oratory at Harvard. And, most importantly, he'd known MacLeish himself and formed strong opinions about him. He respected Archibald MacLeish for his accomplishments but did not think highly of the man himself in his role as a famous literary personage. Besides serving as editor, then, Davison also acted as source.

An engaging and intelligent fellow who had done some acting and had dated Sylvia Plath when she was at Smith, Davison judiciously guided my steps through the long biographical process. He also recommended people for me to interview: it was at his suggestion that I went to see Donald Hall. The extent and importance of his editorial skill can best be judged in two letters from him six months apart, in January and June 1991. These letters were written in response to sections of the typescript I had sent him for comments and evaluation.

The first letter dealt with the opening twelve chapters—about half of a book that eventually ran to twenty-five chapters. Like Cowley before him, Davison opened with compliments before getting down to reservations. He had read the chapters "with pleasure and profit." Once the book got going, it moved "with great style." I had done "a splendid job on the poetry" and on MacLeish's years in Paris. Then, in a telling sentence, Davison summed up his attitude toward the man in question. "AM was an interesting man, not entirely attractive (but which of us is?), and the more he matured the more interesting he became."

As an editor, Davison had two critical points to make about the opening chapters on MacLeish's early family life and schooling, chapters before the book "got going." Davison thought that I had rendered "in bold perspective" the relationship between father and son but that "the relation between the son and his mother remain[ed] veiled and shrouded." His father, Andrew MacLeish, a Scotsman who immigrated to Chicago at eighteen, eventually became head of the Carson Pirie Scott department store. His mother, Martha Hillard, was descended from Puritan ancestors and believed in a life of service. She graduated from Vassar, taught there, and when she met Andrew MacLeish had just taken a position as principal of Rockford (Illinois) Seminary. She was half a generation younger than the man she married, and much closer to their three children.

Archie grew up in awe of his distant and demanding father, whom he thought of as "a foreign potentate," and gravitated toward his more youthful and less forbidding mother. He tried to satisfy both of them, and doing so—as Davison pointed out—began to shape his later life. "Old man MacLeish," he wrote me, "clearly gave him his model for the Person It Would Be Difficult to Please (Hemingway, Ezra Pound, Henry Luce, Roosevelt), but his mother gave him the model for responsibility, for social concern, for duty, arising from her educational bent. Isn't that plausible?" Indeed it was plausible, and in revision I kept those two models in mind—the competitive Scot driving the lad to excel at whatever he undertook, the public-minded Puritan directing him toward service to others.

The second point had to do with MacLeish's presentation of himself. Even in the early chapters, Davison felt, I needed to establish "Archie's narcissism, his acute sense of his own presence, his self-regard, which in later life grew inexorably, as his voice became more self-conscious, both in its lyrical croonings and its special hesitancies between the beautiful phrases." Davison supplied an anecdote by way of illustration. He remembered talking to MacLeish at a Harvard reception for the Argentine writer Jorge Luis

Borges, "with the blind old man standing side by side with the large-headed American, and noticing Borges' comparative lack of self-consciousness, his immediate response to questions, his outspokenness even when he was taking delight in puzzling his questioners, while MacLeish was as it were counting his syllables, adjusting his speech to take account of the effect of his brow, his profile, his pauses, before the Great Utterance came."

MacLeish's theatrical manner obviously troubled Davison, as it did others among the younger poets, including Robert Bly. And he was bothered, too, by what he called "an assumption of entitlement in AM's work and play" (Davison to SD, 10 January 1991). Still, these impressions were by no means universal among MacLeish's colleagues over the years, and out of admiration for his many and varied accomplishments and empathy for his complicated boyhood (for I too had grown up the son of a successful and somewhat distant father), I did not entirely accept Davison's views. I *liked* Archie more than he did, never mind that I had never met him, and it was going to be my biography of MacLeish, after all, not his.

I did labor mightily, though, to make the cuts that Davison called for after reading the second half of my draft. By that time the book had swollen to nearly eight hundred pages in typescript, and Davison confessed that he found it "disproportionately lengthy and even sometimes boring in its descending phase" (Davison to SD, 30 June 1991). That stung, all right, and I made the deletions he recommended, and looked for further ones elsewhere. The basic problem was that MacLeish's versatility and longevity required me to become at least modestly versed in such areas as *Fortune* magazine and the Spanish Civil War in the 1930s, the workings of government during World War II, the Broadway theater scene in the late 1950s, and the academic world during the next two decades. The more I learned, the more eager I was to display that learning on the page. Davison's good sense and tough language set me straight about that. As he was later to comment in an article, with specific reference to the MacLeish biography, "the editor's task is to know, and to persuade the author, when enough is enough" (Davison, 95–96). Besides, he ended his long letter with a note of praise. He pronounced the final chapter, which contained a number of MacLeish's poems about love and identity in old age, "quite wonderful."

Below I reproduce a passage from that last chapter as an example of what Davison liked. The setting is Conway, Massachusetts, where the MacLeishes lived out their eighties. In one of his last poems, Archie reflected on the person he had become.

Most poignantly and privately of all, he described that sense of otherness that had visited him in the tool shed at Craigie Lea at eleven and in his house in Cambridge at twenty-five when he looked in the mirror and saw a stranger's face. In "Epigraph," he suggests a reason for that alienation from himself, an overpowering feeling that in his inmost self he was not at all the Archibald MacLeish of vast accomplishment and international recognition, that in pursuing his goals he had shut himself off from companionship, that in adopting a public persona he had almost lost track of himself. (SD, *MacLeish*, 517)

Epigraph

This old man is no one I know
even if his look is mine—
or was when he first wore it in the jacket
photograph that advertised his book.

Everyone seems to know him: I don't know him.
People stop him at the post office to talk:
they don't stop me when I go walking.
I've lived here fifty years but they don't stop me.

It's him they want to see: the writer.
What I am they've never figured out—
only that I take to wood-lots evenings
crazing all the door-yard dogs.

Must be out for honey, way they see it—
lining up the late, last homeward flights
for bearings on a bee-tree somewhere.
Maybe I am but not their kind of honey.

I wonder, when they come to dig his grave
and find me lying in it, will they guess
whose death he died of, his or mine?—
Whose life I lived?—
                    Who wrote this line?
(MacLeish, *Collected*, 518–19)

Archibald MacLeish: An American Life won the 1993 Ambassador Book Award for biography.

A Dual Biography of Fitz and Hem

My next biographical enterprise was devoted to the story of the friendship of Ernest Hemingway and F. Scott Fitzgerald. In undertaking such a project, I was once more following the lead of Matthew J. Bruccoli (1931–2008), the gruff and energetic dean of Fitzgerald studies, who managed to write (or cowrite) and edit (or coedit) more than a hundred volumes on twentieth-century American writers during his incredibly productive career. Just as my *Fool for Love* had appeared in the wake of his *Some Sort of Epic Grandeur*, the book I decided to call *Hemingway vs. Fitzgerald: The Rise and Fall of a Literary Friendship* (1999) came out after not one but two books that Bruccoli produced on the same subject.

I first met Matt Bruccoli at the University of Alabama Symposium on Hemingway in the fall of 1976. I did a talk there on the role that "Frederic Henry, Selfish Lover" played in *A Farewell to Arms*, and in previous years I had contributed three short pieces to the *Fitzgerald-Hemingway Annual*, which Matt edited. We happened to leave the conference on the same early morning airplane and during the flight fell into conversation. He had already been up and at work for hours, Matt told me. He was about to launch a literary quarterly (it was one of very few endeavors he embarked upon that did not succeed) and asked for the right of first refusal on anything I might send him. I told him about my topical biography of Hemingway that was nearing publication. He asked what I planned to do next, and—more or less casually, thinking out loud—I mentioned that there hadn't been room in *By Force of Will* to do justice to the importance of the friendship between Hemingway and Fitzgerald. It deserved closer examination, I thought.

Matt Bruccoli thought so too. Two years later, his *Scott and Ernest: The Authority of Failure and the Authority of Success* (1978) appeared. Then in 1994, he returned to the subject with *Fitzgerald and Hemingway: A Dangerous Friendship*. These books provided "a documentary reconstruction of their friendship and estrangement." Matt, who was trained as a bibliographer and had a bulldog's determination when on the trail, uncovered just about everything that Fitzgerald and Hemingway wrote or said about or to each other. The documents he assembled—mostly unpublished letters and notes but also outtakes from the published writing—constituted an invaluable resource. Bruccoli did so much work on these two writers, manifestly accumulating more facts than anyone else, that he adopted a proprietary air toward them.

But I wanted to do a book building on that scholarship. In *Hemingway vs. Fitzgerald*, I set out to engage those documents, along with testimony from many others, in telling the *story* of the Fitzgerald-Hemingway relationship. So for example, in dealing with Fitzgerald's 1936 *Crack-Up* essays for *Esquire*, and Hemingway's dismissal of them as shameless whining in public, I brought in comments to and communications from a number of people, including Max Perkins, who edited both men for Scribner; Arnold Gingrich, the editor at *Esquire* who was printing articles from both of them; and John Dos Passos. Testimony from Gerald and Sara Murphy, Gertrude Stein, Morley Callaghan, Edmund Wilson, Budd Schulberg, and others enlightened other sections of the book. These included chapters comparing Fitzgerald and Hemingway's very different middle-class midwestern families, contrasting the jiltings they suffered in their youth (Scott by Ginevra King, Ernest by Agnes von Kurowsky), discussing the alcoholism that beset them both in differing ways, tracking the wildly uneven curves of their reputations.

The goal of *Hemingway vs. Fitzgerald* was to achieve an understanding of the initial friendship between these two great writers, its eventual collapse, and what that had to tell us about them and their work. I had been reading and writing and teaching about them for decades, with my interest stretching back retrospectively to the 1910s, when (or so I liked to think) my red-haired mother—just Fitzgerald's age and growing up in the same St. Paul neighborhood—may have danced with him. I became totally absorbed in the project.

When you are "living in the book," as Fitzgerald called it, the characters begin to occupy your life. They are in your mind as you work, and do not go away when you stop. Often they make a call during the night, waking you to make a note for the next day's writing. Sometimes they invade your dreams.

That happened with *Hemingway vs. Fitzgerald*. During the early morning hours of 31 March 1999, with a blue moon in the sky, I dreamed about Ernest Hemingway and F. Scott Fitzgerald. They were in the ring, boxing. This made no sense, for they never fought physically, and if they had, it would have been a dreadful mismatch between the small and slightly built Fitzgerald and the sturdy six-footer Hemingway. In any actual encounter Hem would surely have knocked Fitz out. (Fitzgerald was peripherally involved in one such bout, when he functioned as timekeeper for a 1929 boxing match between Hemingway and the writer Morley Callaghan, and let the round run late as Callaghan gained the upper hand).

There was no knockout in my dream. What happened was even worse. Traditionally boxers are taught to begin with blows to the body, and to deliver the knockout punch to the head when the opponent's arms come down. In the dream bout Hemingway went for Fitzgerald's upper arms instead. He jabbed at Scott's biceps until they grew numb, and he could do little to strike back or to defend himself. Then Ernest used Scott as a punching bag, hitting him with enough force to inflict pain but not enough to end the beating, which went on and on. It was terribly cruel (SD, *Hem vs. Fitz*, 9–10).

This was only a dream, and proved nothing, yet there was a logic to the dream fight. At the beginning—in 1925 and 1926, in France—the friendship between the two men was extraordinarily close. At that time, Fitzgerald was a well-established author who had just completed *The Great Gatsby* and had published two earlier novels and three books of stories. Hemingway was just beginning his career, his work having appeared only in literary quarterlies and limited editions. Scott went out of his way to help Ernest's career, notably by singing his praises to Max Perkins at Scribner's and by recommending important deletions at the beginning of *The Sun Also Rises*. The two men spent a lot of time together in the summer of 1925, and kept in close touch by mail through the end of 1926. Those letters back and forth make it clear that they deeply cared for each other. *If you don't mind, you're the best friend I've got*: that sort of thing. This feeling lasted longer for Fitzgerald than for Hemingway, who had a history of breaking off relationships. Fitzgerald had done him favors that proved hard to forgive. Time and again Ernest insulted Scott, and time and again Scott took the blows and came back for more. The dream suggested that Hemingway wanted or needed to strike out at his former friend much as Fitzgerald wanted or needed to be hurt. Ernest did the kicking, Scott wore the "kick me" sign on his backside.

In "Poor Butterfly," a section of the book documenting this pattern, I examined the way in which Hemingway committed a kind of murder by metaphor. This was not unusual for him—he often employed degrading comparisons in dismissing former friends and even relatives. Given his extraordinary competitiveness, Hemingway could not help seeing fellow writers as rivals, and did whatever he could to cut the ground from under them. Wolfe and O'Hara and Faulkner came in for this kind of treatment, but Fitzgerald bore the brunt of it, especially in *A Moveable Feast*, Hemingway's memoir written in the mid-1950s as Fitzgerald's reputation was on the rise. At various times in his correspondence, Hemingway demeaned Fitzgerald by comparing him to a fawning spaniel, a moldy slab of bacon, a washed-up ballplayer, a boxer who'd lost his nerve, a crooked mining prospector, and an unguided missile. In *A Moveable Feast*, he describes a reunion with Fitzgerald in 1931. He hadn't seen Scott for a year, and he looked older. "He showed his age, month by month, as perceptibly as cut flowers do each day and now, at thirty-five, if he had been in a vase at your house you would have thrown him out long ago" (SD, *Hem vs. Fitz*, 268–71).

The more subtly damning butterfly metaphor introduced the three chapters on Fitzgerald in the memoir: "His talent was as natural as the pattern that was made by the dust on a butterfly's wings. At one time he understood it no more than the butterfly did and he did not know when it was brushed or marred. Later he became conscious of his damaged wings and of their construction and he learned to think and could not fly any more because the love of flight was gone and he could only remember when it had been effortless" (Hemingway, *Feast*, 207–8). Here Hemingway likened Fitzgerald's talent not to a *butterfly* itself nor to the insect's *wings* nor to the *dust* on those wings but to the *pattern* the dust made. The pattern, which made the butterfly beautiful, was even more highly perishable than wilting flowers. Hemingway might have written that Fitzgerald's talent was fleeting or ephemeral or incredibly fragile. But he did not want to use adjectives. The metaphor said it better.

In this account of friendship and its rather bitter end, I tried to correct one of the best-known literary anecdotes of the twentieth century. This involved a famous exchange between the two authors. "The rich are different from you and me," Fitzgerald is supposed to have remarked, with Hemingway responding, "Yes, they have more money." So Edmund Wilson reported the conversation, and so it was cited in an essay by Lionel Trilling, the eminence of those two authorities lending credence to the tale. Wilson and Trilling were undoubtedly influenced by Hemingway's "The Snows of Kilimanjaro," as it appeared in the August 1936 *Esquire*. Midway through the story, the narrator reflects on the ways of the rich:

> [They] were dull and they drank too much, or they played too much backgammon. They were dull and they were repetitious. He remembered poor Scott Fitzgerald and his romantic awe of them and how he had started a story once that began, "The very rich are different from you and me." And how some one had said to Scott, Yes, they have more money. But that was not humorous to Scott. He thought they were a special glamorous race and when he found they weren't it wrecked him as much as any other thing that wrecked him.

Upon reading this attack (his own "Afternoon of an Author" appeared in the same issue of *Esquire*), Fitzgerald immediately sent Hemingway a note. Rather than simply reprinting his words, I used internal commentary (italicized in this case) to bring out what was unsaid: a device I'd never tried before.

Dear Ernest:

Please lay off me in print. (*Direct, and to the point.*) If I choose to write *de profundis* sometimes, it doesn't mean I want friends (*still friends, then?*) praying aloud over my corpse. No doubt you meant it kindly (*how could that have been?*) but it cost me a night's sleep. (*Only one night. I'm tougher than you think.*) And when you incorporate it (the story) in a book would you mind (*gently, gently*) cutting my name?

It's a fine story—one of your best—(*absolutely true, and under the circumstances insightful and generous*) even though the "Poor Scott Fitzgerald etc." rather (*putting it mildly*) spoiled it for me.

> Ever your friend (*despite all*)
> Scott

Hemingway's excuse for describing his erstwhile friend as "wrecked" was that Fitzgerald had in recent months published three essays in *Esquire* documenting his psychological Crack-Up: hence the *de profundis* comment in his letter. If Fitzgerald proclaimed he was washed up, Hemingway reasoned, it was "open season" on him. So it was only reluctantly—and after an interim attempt to alter "poor Scott Fitzgerald" to "poor Scott"—that Hemingway succumbed to Max Perkins's repeated requests and omitted Fitzgerald's name in the story as it appeared in book form, replacing it with "poor Julian." But the rest of the copy was unchanged, including the reference to the beginning of Fitzgerald's story "The Rich Boy," a story that powerfully illustrated—as did *The Great Gatsby* and *Tender Is the Night*—why and in what ways the very rich were indeed different from the rest of us.

In fact, according to Maxwell Perkins, it was Hemingway and not Fitzgerald who made the observation about the rich being different. During a lunch with Perkins and the quick-witted Irish writer Mary Colum, Hemingway was talking about his contacts with the wealthy sportsmen in Bimini who fished and partied off their yachts. He was getting to know the rich, he said. "The only difference between the rich and other people," Colum immediately responded, "is that the rich have more money" (Berg, 305). For Ernest to transfer this put-down of himself to Fitzgerald in "The Snows of Kilimanjaro" struck Perkins as "contemptible," he wrote his close friend Elizabeth Lemmon upon reading the August 1936 *Esquire* (SD, *Hem vs. Fitz*, 194–203).

I am not optimistic that this valid account of who said what to whom will supplant the false popular yarn about Ernest's making that "more money" wisecrack to Scott. In the construction of legends, truth has a hard time competing with fiction.

Hemingway vs. Fitzgerald is available in paperback, has been translated into half a dozen languages, and elicited more and better reviews than any other book of mine, along with the inevitable two or three dissenting ones. Writers are not supposed to be cast down by bad reviews of lifted up by favorable ones, for reviewers frequently demonstrate little understanding of the subject and less of the writing process. "You've done your job, people will respond in different ways, go back to your desk and get to work," you tell yourself, but still criticisms darken the day and compliments brighten it. So I fondly remember that several reviewers used the word "fascinating," and that the English edition (from publisher John Murray) had a number of excellent reviews. My favorite review came from Denise Gess in the *Raleigh News and Observer*. "*Hemingway vs. Fitzgerald* is fresh, risky, talky, bold, and ultimately brilliant. We close it deeply satisfied that we've read all there is to know about the men. Donaldson's stunning achievement is that he makes us want to return to Fitzgerald's and Hemingway's work, the one place their unique flames cannot be extinguished."

As *Hemingway vs. Fitzgerald* neared publication by Overlook—a first-rate small trade house where I had the good luck to work with Tracy Carns—Matt Bruccoli heard about it. On 28 June 1999 he sent me a one-sentence note characteristic of his aggressive nature. "Scott Donaldson: I strongly object to your use of my title *Fitzgerald and Hemingway*, and I intend to take appropriate action. Truly, Matthew J. Bruccoli" (Bruccoli to SD). I called to assure him that I was not, in fact, going to use that title, and did not want to confuse my volume with his. I did not say anything about my conviction that neither he nor anyone else actually *owned* the phrase "Fitzgerald and Hemingway," or the territory they occupied in American literature.

I knew that Matt Bruccoli felt most possessive of all of Fitzgerald. Through his amazing energy and fierce dedication and close bonding with Scottie Fitzgerald he managed to bring into print almost all of the writings that her father and mother produced. He staked out his territory and discouraged other settlers. When I was working on *Fool for Love*, my Fitzgerald biography, for example, I asked Scottie for permission to examine Zelda's medical records. She'd have to check, she said, and after consulting with Matt decided not to grant my request.

But Bruccoli's appropriation of all things Fitzgerald hardly rivaled the machinations of Leon Edel in establishing himself as the sole anointed authority on and biographer of Henry James. Edel managed to forbid access to James's papers to any and all rivals for decades: a process documented by

Michael Anesko in *Monopolizing the Master: Henry James and the Politics of Modern Literary Scholarship* (2012).

Recovering Robinson

I was first exposed to the poetry of Edwin Arlington Robinson (1869–1935) sixty-five years ago in Prescott C. Cleveland's senior English class at Blake School in Minneapolis.

> Miniver Cheevy, child of scorn,
>> Grew lean while he assailed the seasons;
> He wept that he was ever born,
>> And he had reasons.

I didn't know a feminine ending from a transit of Venus, but took delight in Robinson's own delight over the double rhymes in lines two and four of each stanza.

> Miniver loved the Medici,
>> Albeit he had never seen one;
> He would have sinned incessantly
>> Could he have been one.
> Miniver cursed the commonplace
>> And eyed a khaki suit with loathing.
> He missed the medieval grace
>> Of iron clothing.
> (Robinson, 347–48)

Miniver hooked me at seventeen, and further readings, both at Yale and in graduate school at Minnesota, expanded my interest in Robinson and his extraordinary gallery of characters. "Miniver Cheevy" was not at all a typical poem for him. Lazy, impecunious, and foolishly antiquarian, Miniver becomes a figure of fun and his poem an entertainment. It's a whimsical self-portrait of sorts, and even a down Maine New Englander was entitled to laugh at himself. Usually EAR—that was what he preferred to be called, for he disliked his name and was annoyed by the way people kept changing the "Edwin" to "Edward" (a mistake that still occurs in about half of everything written about him)—wrote about the derelict and downtrodden, the bereft and troubled, those who lost their way and led "scattered lives." He presented these men and women—more than two hundred of them—with deep compassion in a series of excellent short to medium-length poems. His portraits of the wronged wife in "Eros Turannos," of the too-proud mother in "The Gift of God," of the lonely old hermit proposing a toast to himself in "Mr. Flood's Party" stick in the mind and the heart.

From the first I was eager to write about Robinson and his work. My initial article for a literary quarterly, "The Alien Pity: A Study of Character in the Poetry of E. A. Robinson," appeared in *American Literature* in May 1966. Then the Robinson centenary in 1969 sparked a revival of interest in his work, with excellent critical studies by Louis O. Coxe and Wallace L. Anderson. As early as the mid-1970s, after finishing my book on Hemingway, I considered undertaking a biography of EAR. Two things stopped me at the time. First, Malcolm Cowley advised against it. A Robinson biography wouldn't sell, he assured me. Nonetheless I did some exploring in the EAR archive at Colby College in Waterville, Maine, and encountered another roadblock: EAR's nearly indecipherable handwriting. His letters would have to be a major source for any biography, and after spending an entire day at Colby's Miller Library failing to figure out the contents of a single Robinson letter, I abandoned the project, at least for the time being. Anderson, I knew, was working on what promised to become a several-volume edition of Robinson's correspondence. When it was published, perhaps I could come back to EAR. So I set Robinson aside, and instead committed books on Fitzgerald, Cheever, MacLeish, and the Hemingway-Fitzgerald relationship.

When I determined, at the turn of the twenty-first century, to tell EAR's life story, never mind that it wouldn't sell, his reputation had receded even further. There had been a flurry of attention in the 1990s, when three separate collections of Robinson poems were published. The two better ones swiftly went out of print. In one of them, poet-editor Robert Mezey characterized EAR's fall from public favor as "a national disgrace." In the other, poet-editor Donald Hall declared that "[w]e must bring Robinson back. We must restore him to the national pantheon" (SD, "Recovering," 148). I could not have agreed more enthusiastically, and set about on a biography with the mission of recovering Robinson. My book, I knew from the start, would have to present and unpack a number of EAR's best poems while telling the story of his long struggle toward recognition. I understood that was a risky procedure, for the narrative thread might unravel while I was busy explicating poems. But it was paramount to place some of the best of Robinson on the page, and fortunately, a number of those poems could be tied to his own experiences.

In order to undertake the task at all, I had first to locate the Robinson letters, for they had not been published after all. After making some phone calls, I discovered that Wallace Anderson's trove had been languishing in a Raynham, Massachusetts, warehouse for fourteen years. Before he died in 1986, Anderson found more than three thousand Robinson letters and acquired the Rosetta Stone that enabled him to decode their minuscule script. He had transcribed all of the letters and annotated most of them. Then it became a matter of persuading his heirs to liberate the letters from the warehouse and deliver them to a responsible university library where they could be catalogued and opened to researchers. Eventually—it took some time—the Anderson family agreed to transfer this invaluable resource to the EAR collection at Colby.

So I had this fresh material to work with, along with unpublished reminiscences—over a hundred pages each—by two of EAR's friends. And the support and encouragement of his grandnephews and grandniece, who believed as I did that Robinson was too little valued. Having them on my side proved absolutely essential, for the family had refused to cooperate with previous biographers. There were skeletons in the closet, including alcoholism, drug addiction, and suicide. Only the passage of time made it possible for Robinson's relations to let the unhappy story be told. Time, too, had outlasted the feuding between two contingents of EAR's friends—New Englanders vs. New Yorkers—that had crippled earlier attempts at writing his biography.

In the past the Robinson family and the townspeople of Gardiner, Maine, where EAR lived his first thirty years, erected barriers against invasive inquirers, but now I had the full cooperation and encouragement of both. David S. Nivison, EAR's grandnephew and a distinguished scholar of Chinese history and philosophy at Stanford, opened the doors to long-concealed family secrets and his own insights into Robinson's poetry. Danny D. Smith, the unofficial and extremely knowledgeable historian of Gardiner, went even further in support of my project. He guided me to the essential sources and documents about the small, once-thriving city on the Kennebec where EAR first encountered most of the people who in poetic disguise inhabit his early "Tilbury Town" poems. Whenever I visited Maine, Danny devoted his time to showing me around Gardiner and its sites most closely aligned to Robinson's upbringing, sharing his vast fund of information about the town and its social and political makeup as we strolled along Lincoln Avenue and across the Gardiner Common. He also introduced me to the splendors of the A-1 Diner downtown.

As with the MacLeish book, I ended up knowing too much to write the relatively short book I originally had in mind. And once again I was counseled to make deep cuts. Robert Mezey, who agreed to read the manuscript as it progressed, urged me to do delete substantial sections of the semifinal draft as well as to soften its treatment of the complicated relationship between EAR and Robert Frost, his rival for eminence in the 1920s and '30s. My writer's ego resisted Mezey's recommendation. It seemed to me that everything

I'd taken the trouble to put down on paper belonged in the book. But I recalled Robinson's dictum that "anything is improved by cutting" (SD, "Recovering," 150) and understood that Mezey, a sharp and sympathetic reader, wanted only the best for the biography. So I got out the scissors and slashed forty thousand words. Once I got started making deletions, it wasn't nearly as painful as I'd feared. And I have no doubt at all that the process helped tighten the biography and make it more readable.

The basic reason behind Robinson's decline in reputation was that he became unjustly stereotyped into a figure not modern enough to deserve attention. It was true that his earlier (and best) poems were written in rhyme and meter, that his late long poems relied on blank verse, and that he eschewed experimental free verse entirely: "I write badly enough as it is," he wryly remarked (SD, "Recovering," 151). His poetry *looked* old-fashioned on the page, alongside the verse of Eliot and Pound and Stevens. Matters of form aside, though, EAR was very much a revolutionary poet.

He started his career at the turn of the twentieth century, when the reigning taste preferred "gifted singers" who sang of tinkling water and redbellied robins in archaic, prettified verse. Robinson would have none of it, for he understood the power of ordinary language. Consider the opening of "The Clerks," a sonnet he slaved over for his first book, *The Children of the Night* (1896).

> I did not think that I should find them there
> When I came back again; but there they stood,
> As in the days they dreamed of when young blood
> Was in their cheeks and women called them fair.
> (Robinson, 90)

The diction could hardly be simpler or more elegant, and the subject matter—small-town dry-goods clerks in his native Gardiner, Maine—more quotidian. Robinson offered no florid rhetoric celebrating the natural world, none at all. He was far more interested in the people around him than in their surroundings. Editors didn't know what to make of his work. For eleven years, at the start of his career, he did not sell a single poem to a magazine: the market, at the time, that most poets depended upon for financial support. He was down and out in New York, surviving through odd jobs (as a timekeeper for the subway then abuilding, for instance) and an awareness of the location of every tavern or bar in lower Manhattan that offered "free lunch."

Teddy Roosevelt came to his rescue during 1905–9, violating his civil service convictions to manufacture a place for EAR in the New York Custom House. Robinson was to think poetry first and customs duties second, the president told him. Later a dozen benefactors banded together to contribute $100 each annually toward Robinson's support. Every summer for thirty years he lived and worked, free, at the MacDowell Colony in New Hampshire. His three Pulitzer Prizes descended when he was well past fifty. Only then did he begin to make enough money to pay his own way. When he had disposable income, much of it went to friends who were in greater need than himself. He did not marry (Emma Shepherd, the great love of his life, married his brother Herman instead). He drank too much for many years before finally overcoming that demon. He lived for poetry. It was his calling, and he pursued it as religiously as his Puritan ancestors had pursued theirs.

But Robinson would not advertise. He did not do public readings. He did not seek advancement through poetry societies or cultivate influential advocates. T. R. sought him out, not the other way around. What he did was to write poems, and in later years they grew longer and more convoluted, much as had the late novels of Henry James. Almost no one reads the long blank verse narratives of his last decade, which characteristically tell a tale of redemption. The basic plot: a hugely successful materialist tramples on others in achieving his fortune before repenting and trying to make up for the error of his ways. Unlike these long tales, Robinson's short to medium-length works of the years from 1897 to 1923 remain as fresh as the day they were written.

EAR did not believe that poetry had to be difficult to matter, yet he was often—and justly—charged with obscurity. He practiced a gnomic style that mandated extreme condensation of language. He would not say what he didn't know about the characters he depicted. He suggested and hinted and left clues about how it might have been, but refused to leap to conclusions. "Was ever an insect flying between two flowers / Told less than we are told of what we are?" he asked, and meant it (SD, "Recovering," 151).

For Robinson, those who categorized their fellow human beings were not only wrong: they were the enemy. In many of his poems they render their morally flawed judgments in a collective choral "we." In "Richard Cory," his best-known poem (thanks in part to Simon and Garfunkel), the townspeople envy the aristocratic Cory, not understanding that he is about to take his own life. In the last stanza they bitterly comment, "So on we worked and waited for the light / And went without the meat and cursed the bread," which sounds innocent enough until one takes account of the sacrilegious cursing of the bread. In "Eros Turannos," the chorus makes the town and harborside "Vibrate" with gossip at the expense of the wife who chooses to ignore her husband's infidelities. "Meanwhile we do no harm," the gossipers assure themselves. The obscurity in that great poem, as Donald Justice pointed out, is "expressive of the very understanding the poem is intended to convey" (SD, "Recovering," 151). We who can barely begin to understand ourselves are poorly equipped to stand in judgment on others.

Yet a biographer must arrive at a plausible comprehension of his subject. As with no other subject, the more I learned about EAR, the more I came to admire him. "This book derives from the conviction that Edwin Arlington Robinson was a great American poet and an exceptionally fine human being," the biography begins. And the very last words, following a list of forty-four "real poems" to remember him by, propose that due recognition of EAR's accomplishment "will come when enough of us open his book and—as he recommended—read one word after another" (SD, *Robinson*, 1, 481–82).

To advance that cause and make such a book more available to readers, I assembled a selection of the best of Robinson for the Everyman's Library of Pocket Poets, a slim volume that emerged within weeks of *Edwin Arlington Robinson: A Poet's Life*. The two books were reviewed together in several places during 2007, usually by practicing poets who welcomed the prospect of restoring Robinson to his place in American literature. I hope that will happen and that if it does, that my biography will have played a small role in the revival. It took seven years to complete the book, which was my seventh venture into the field. In none of the others did I invest so much time and energy and love.

Other Chores, On to Fenton

In addition to literary biographies, I continued over the years to crank out critical articles, edit books, serve on boards, make talks at conferences, and otherwise—more or less obsessively—perform chores to keep me in touch with the field. I did a four-year stint on the editorial board of *American Literature*, for example, reading about one hundred submissions each year and recommending a tenth of them for publication. For another four-year period I wrote the annual evaluation of books and articles published on Fitzgerald and Hemingway for *American Literary Scholarship*.

I made occasional forays into American literature at some distance from those two writers. These included a critical edition of Jack Kerouac's *On the Road*, a long introduction to Harold Frederic's *The Damnation of Theron Ware*, several articles on John Cheever's fiction, a collection of his interviews, and an introduction to Thornton Wilder's letters. But for the most part Fitz and Hem, Hem and Fitz constituted my academic-scholarly specialty. I edited three collections of work on them: *Critical Essays on F. Scott Fitzgerald's "The Great Gatsby"* (1984), *New Essays on "A Farewell to Arms"* (1990), and the *Cambridge Companion to Hemingway* (1996), and wrote forty-two articles of my own about their fiction and their lives. As the EAR biography was nearing completion, I decided to construct a book from the best of these. This involved a somewhat painful process of elimination. Some pieces were discarded entirely: the forty-two were reduced to half that number. The surviving essays were then subjected to extensive revision to bring them up to date and to fit into the pattern of the book. Much of this involved making cuts, for I was relearning yet again that less is more. One extensive essay was added, on Hemingway's involvement in and dedication to the Loyalist cause in the Spanish Civil War. The resulting book, *Fitzgerald and Hemingway: Works and Days*, came out in 2009, and by that time I was already immersed in two other projects.

One of these was a book—this book—on the difficulties of writing literary biography. For starters, I produced the case studies that constitute part 4 of *The Impossible Craft*. One of these, "Hemingway's Battle with Biographers, 1949–1954," explores his attempts to ward off biographical invaders of privacy and/or appropriators of material that he might put to use in his own fiction. Among them were Malcolm Cowley, Lillian Ross, and Philip Young, but the liveliest and most thoroughly documented of these battles pitted Hemingway against Charles A. Fenton, whose *The Apprenticeship of Ernest Hemingway* (1954) remains one of the best books ever written about him. Almost all of the letters between the two men survive, and they tell a fascinating story. Initially Hemingway welcomed the overtures of Fenton, at the time a graduate student / instructor at Yale. Before long, though, Hemingway became annoyed by Fenton's persistent inquiries. Eventually, he warned Fenton to "cease and desist" and threatened legal action. In one particularly incendiary letter, he invited Fenton to come down to the Finca Vigia in Cuba so that they might settle their differences. They could duel it out with fists or whatever weapons Fenton chose and use the Finca's fenced-in tennis court for the confrontation, Hemingway proposed. He'd like nothing better for his fifty-third birthday than an opportunity to face Fenton (twenty years his junior) in an enclosed space.

The Hemingway-Fenton relationship amply illustrated the almost unavoidable conflict between living writers and those interested in writing about their lives and work. But I had another reason for pursuing the matter, for during my undergraduate years at Yale (class of 1950) Fenton was one of my four instructors in Yale's famous Daily Themes class and was assigned to direct my senior honors' thesis on Hemingway's short stories. I knew him then, but not well. For the most part I admired him from a distance, as a charismatic handsome jaunty rebellious somewhat sardonic figure who'd flown deadly bombing missions with the RAF, written stories and a prize-winning novel, and served as a reporter on metropolitan dailies. Like many other students I looked up to him, and not only figuratively. It was as if he occupied a more elevated position than the rest of us.

> Whenever Richard Cory went downtown
> We people on the pavement looked at him.
> (Robinson, 82)

At the same time, though, Fenton provided me with an example of the kind of life I might eventually lead: teaching university students about American literature and writing books as I went along. I owed him for that.

When the news came that Charlie Fenton, like the princely Richard Cory, had done away with himself at forty-one—not with a bullet through the head but by a leap from the top of the Washington Duke Hotel in Durham, North Carolina, in July 1960—I wondered what could possibly have happened to drive this successful and attractive man to suicide. Forty-seven years later, after talking with his widow, Gwendy, about the combative Fenton-Hemingway correspondence, I set out in search of the answers. I knew that he'd gone to Duke from Yale with an unprecedented promotion from assistant professor to full professor with tenure, and there was a rumor that he'd fallen in love with one of his graduate students. The love affair was real enough, and when Gwendy heard about it she expressed her outrage publicly, then packed up and left for Connecticut with the children in tow. Charlie became a social pariah in Durham, and soon discovered that, despite his success in the classroom and as the department's leader in publishing—three books out, three more in press, Guggenheim and ACLS grants—he would be the only professor on campus not given a raise. He started looking for a position elsewhere and waited in vain for the clacking tongues to quiet down.

The separation was an important part of Fenton's story, then, but no more important than a traumatic boyhood beating, the stress of his World War II experiences, and his lifelong resistance to the dictates of authority. Fenton not only refused to accept the prevailing mores; he spoke out eloquently against them. At Duke, for instance, he deplored the university's policy against admitting African Americans, its overemphasis on football, and the privileges it extended to fraternities. He expressed these opinions openly and often, on the front page of the college newspaper. He was a rebel, all right, but for the best of causes. He was saying what needed to be said, and during a time—the notoriously conformist 1950s—when most of those who agreed with him prudently chose to remain silent. This was admirable, and dangerous, for it turned the powers-that-be against him.

It took several years of digging into family letters and reminiscences, academic and military archives, and hundreds of e-mails and telephone conversations with students and colleagues of Fenton's before I began to understand some of the reasons *why* he made that final fateful leap—began, in other words, to fathom the kind of man he was—and to write about it in *Death of a Rebel: The Charlie Fenton Story*. At first I maintained the authorial distance I'd learned in newsrooms and observed in other biographies. Midway through the actual writing, though, I dispensed with objectivity. This was going to be a book celebrating a teacher whose inspiring presence guided many students toward useful and even brilliant careers. Some of my best sources were men and women who felt an obligation to Fenton and were eager to have him remembered: among them Peter Matthiessen and James Stevenson and Matt Bruccoli at Yale, Merrill Skaggs and Frank Gado and Reynolds Price at Duke. They were part of the story, and so was I, a young, impressionable kid whose life had been shaped in no small part by the good luck of encountering Charlie Fenton.

The Edwin Arlington Robinson book had been shopped to a number of houses before landing at Columbia University Press, and that established a precedent for their publishing *Fitzgerald and Hemingway: Works and Days*. But they passed on the Fenton book, and so did almost everyone else. At the start my agent, Peter Matson, was confident that one of the better small trade houses would bring it out. The story was interesting: love and war and an appealing figure at odds with conventional values. The book captured a sense of the period (1940–60) and offered insights into the way that two famous universities conducted their affairs. Publishers' readers loved *Death of a Rebel*. It was beautifully written, they said; it was moving; they were enthralled. But no, the publishers would not take the book. It did not fit their current publishing model, they explained. And, besides, who the hell was Charlie Fenton, anyway (the very question, of course, that the biography-memoir set out to answer)? After two dozen or so discouraging rejections along these lines, Harry Keyishian at Fairleigh Dickinson University Press opted to take a chance on the book.

As a practical matter, Fairleigh Dickinson itself had little to do with editing or publishing *Death of a Rebel*. Once accepted, it went through the standard production procedures at Rowman and Littlefield Publishing Group (RLPG), a firm that annually processes up to fifteen hundred books for several small publishers. Almost all of these are scholarly monographs aimed at the academic marketplace, and although Charlie Fenton's dramatic life story did not fit into that category, it was treated as if it did. The book was priced well above prevailing standards, guaranteeing a small sale. The firm provided minimal promotional assistance, sending out but ten books to potential reviewers. As a consequence, I undertook a campaign on my own, alerting writers and journalists to the existence of the Fenton biography and shamelessly declaring its virtues. I also mailed copies to several dozen people who seemed likely to do reviews or otherwise spread the word. This was expensive, time-consuming, and demeaning. I'd never done this sort of self-promotion before, and will never do it again. Spending one's days trying to elicit praise was not what I signed up for when I went into literary biography.

An additional complication developed when some outrageous typographical errors found their way into the initial press run of the book, including three howlers on the very first page. When I immediately e-mailed a list of these to RLPG, publisher Julie Kirsch stopped sales of the defective copies and ordered a second print run with the corrections made. This was a sound and generous professional decision. I had my differences with Rowman and Littlefield, especially about their charging $65 for a two-hundred-page book (a year later, they issued a more reasonably priced paperback). Yet I remain grateful to Fairleigh Dickinson University Press for choosing to bring out *Death of a Rebel* after many other publishers chose not to.

TOPICS IN LITERARY BIOGRAPHY

Fact and Fiction

Leon Edel, author of a magisterial five-volume biography of Henry James, described his chosen field in highly favorable terms. "Biography is the art of human portrayal in words," he asserted, "and it is a noble and adventurous art." Like a painter working on canvas or a sculptor with clay or marble, "a biographer fashions a man or a woman out of the seemingly intractable materials of archives, diaries, documents, dreams, a glimpse, a series of memories" (Edel, "Figure," 20–21). Thornton Wilder, who took a lively interest in biography, also defined it as "human portraiture" and described the biographer's challenge as that of extracting "from the data of life the savor of personality, the shades of a soul, the image of a vital energy." The characters so portrayed had to be "built from the Inside Outward," he thought, a daunting task because "we cannot know others or ourselves" (Niven to SD). Unsurprisingly, Wilder's novels are full of epistemological uncertainties. Janet Malcolm, in her dual biography of Gertrude Stein and Alice B. Toklas, took a much less elevated view of the genre. "Biography and autobiography are the aggregate of what, in the former, the author happens to learn, and what, in the latter, he happens to tell," she wrote (quoted in Roiphe).

Edel and Wilder on the one hand and Malcolm on the other seem to be talking about two entirely different forms, and that may well be the case, for there are several distinct types of biographies. The subject can often dictate one's approach. Consider, for example, the irreverent faultfinding in celebrity biographies in contrast with the laudatory biographies of America's founding fathers. In his notes Wilder similarly subdivides the field, citing the "rhapsodic" biography vs. the "psychoanalytic" biography in which "the flaw is without remedy," the "prudish" biography vs. the "secret scandal and sin" biography (Niven to SD).

Then there is the question of what to include. In the "multiplicity of facts" book, the biographer sets down almost every scrap of information he has accumulated. These compendiums can run to prodigious length. John Updike, who was not "an especial devotee" of literary biography, nonetheless reviewed and read "a fair amount of it." He kept most of these books in his barn, including five-hundred-page ones on Edmund Wilson and Joyce Cary, six-hundred-page ones on Oscar Wilde and Ivy Compton-Burnett, Michael Holroyd's two volumes on Lytton Strachey and three on George Bernard Shaw, and Edel's five on James (Updike, 12–14). Sometimes the sheer length of such biographies is justified, sometimes not.

Edel quoted Thomas Sergeant Perry, an early twentieth-century man of letters, about the worst cases. "The biographer gets a dustcart into which he shovels diaries, reminiscences, old letters, until the cart is full. Then he dumps the load in front of your door. . . . Out of this rubbish the reader constructs a biography" (Edel, "Figure," 19). "Minutiae without Meaning," critic Stanley Fish called such works (quoted in Shipman, 85), and rightly so, for a biographer has done only part of his job by finding the facts and making them available. "Facts relating to the past, when they are collected without art, are compilations," Lytton Strachey pointed out. Such compilations might be useful, but "they are no more History than butter, eggs, salt and herbs are an omlette" (quoted in Nadel, x).

In its ideal embodiments—Justin Kaplan's books on Mark Twain and Walt Whitman, for example—biographies are selective in choosing what to include. They aim for the significant anecdote—or meeting or conversation—rather than a complete rendering of all such moments. It's a point more easily illustrated by failure than success, as in a biography of F. Scott Fitzgerald that time and again recounted the humiliations he brought on himself when drinking and another about Robert Lowell that repeatedly revisited his episodes of manic misbehavior. By choosing which facts to put in and which to leave out, the biographer attempts to give shape and definition to his account of another's life. "The aim of biography," according to the prolific biographer Sir Sidney Lee, "is the truthful transmission of personality." Yet as Virginia Woolf commented in an essay of the late 1920s, "on the one hand there is truth; on the other there is personality," and it would not be easy to weld together the "granite-like solidity" of truth and the "rainbow-like intangibility" of personality. In order to make the light of personality shine through, Woolf pointed out, one had to "manipulate" the assembled facts, with some brightened, others shaded (Woolf, *Collected*, 229).

The biographer, like the novelist, is first and foremost a storyteller, with the significant difference that he is expected to limit himself to the facts and not make things up. The novelist invents his characters and is free to do whatever he wants with them. But the biographer's hands are tied. Or, as Edel put it, "Novelists have omniscience. Biographers never do." They dig and dig to unearth a great deal of data and then hope and pray that a pattern emerges from that jumbled assemblage to give definition to their account of another's life. But they cannot alter the documents, for "to alter is to disfigure" (Edel, *Lives*, 15). In this sense, Woolf observed, "biography is the most restricted of all the arts" (Woolf, *Collected*, 221). She felt hemmed in, constricted by facts. "How can one cut loose from facts," she commented when writing her biography of Roger Fry, "when there they are, contradicting my theories?" (quoted in Nadel, 5). Similarly, the novelist Anne Bernays, when she embarked upon a memoir about her father, Edward L. Bernays, known as "the father of public relations," was struck by how *confined* she felt sticking to the facts, how *difficult* it was to bring another person to life without access to her inventive faculties.

In his 1984 book *Biography: Fiction, Fact, and Form*, the critical theorist and biographer Ira Bruce Nadel posed a series of questions about the requirement that the biographer maintain fidelity to the record. "To what extent," he asked, "is fact necessary to the biographer? To what extent does it hinder the artistic and literary impulse of the biographer? To what degree does the biographer alter fact to fit his theme and pattern?"

Nadel's apparent view, the British biographer Victoria Glendinning observed, was that the biographer "ha[d] every right to change facts in order to make a psychological or artistic point," an idea that made her "shiver." She cited in opposition Desmond MacCarthy's assertion that the biographer was "an artist under oath." Her unrealized ideal, Glendinning added, "would be to write a biography that had the tension and entertainment value of a novel, using any and all narrative techniques, but including nothing that could not be backed up by documents or other evidence, and suppressing nothing of significance, however inconvenient it might be structurally or artistically. This makes biography a challenge, a sort of game" (Glendinning, 54–55). That formulation strikes me as very nearly perfect. It's a game, one that's very hard to win, and you can't break the rules. What you can and must do, however, is to keep a sharp eye out for what Woolf called "the creative fact, the fertile fact" (quoted in Nadel, 7).

In recent decades the lines of demarcation between biography and novel have become blurred. In *Dutch* (1999), his biography of Ronald Reagan—he called it "a memoir"—Edmund Morris invented a fictional character named "Edmund Morris" who supposedly knew Reagan well in his youth, and even supplied footnotes to document nonexistent meetings and conversations, with no confession to the reader about these inventions. In *Wild Nights!* (2008), Joyce Carol Oates ingeniously imagined the last days of five American writers—Poe, Dickinson, Twain, James, and Hemingway—building on but going well beyond the facts. But by and large biographers continue to aim for realism and carry a banner—John Hersey's phrase—declaring This Was Not Made Up.

This emphatically does not mean that the biographer, any more than the historian, is or should be deprived of the use of his imagination, or intuition. In fact, such an imaginative grasp of materials is essential for the biographer as well as the historian. As R. G. Collingwood commented in his authoritative *The Idea of History* (1946), history will not be history if it does not tell the truth, and also if it lacks the faculty of imagination (quoted in McGrath, 116), and that is true of the biography as well. You pore over the documents. You absorb them into your psyche. You begin to perceive recurrent themes. You find a unifying attitude that provides a thematic line. You use the techniques of fiction in telling your story: the selection of significant events above all, but also scene and picture, suspense, foreshortening, echoes, contrast, shifts in point of view, high points emphasized, lower ones given less stress, and so on. And still you may fail to create a work of art. Back to Edel: "A properly assembled documentary biography is in effect a kind of miniarchive. It may possess the organizing imagination" and avoid descending into a shoveled-together clutter, but still "cannot lay claim to art" (Edel, *Lives*, 14).

The title of this book is *The Impossible Craft*, yet sometimes, rarely, immersion in another person's life can lead by mysterious paths to a lasting work of art. While still an undergraduate at Brown, Winfield Townley Scott (1910–1968) completed a biography of John Greenleaf Whittier (1807–1892), the American Quaker poet famous for "Snow-Bound" and his ardent abolitionism. Scott sent his book to Harper's and Knopf and Macmillan and Putnam's, and they all sent it back with the usual comments. It was well-written but not right for their list, they doubted it would sell, perhaps in better times they would have taken it. But the rejections were far from a dead loss, for Scott put the manuscript aside and then . . . but here is Scott himself on how he "got" his wonderful "Mr. Whittier" poem.

> It was my senior year and I had already begun to work on a biography of Whittier . . . and I even finished a whole book . . . it was rejected, thank God . . . [for] I was just twenty-one or so . . . and not equipped at that point to write such a book very well. . . . [This] was at the beginning of the 1930's; and somewhere in the very early 1940's, perhaps literally 1941, that poem . . . just poured out, everything. I didn't look up anything. I even

wrote some passages when there were visitors sitting in the room because I couldn't stop. I'd pick up my paper and write some more lines and just—swist—everything I wanted to say. I'd much rather have it around than that benighted biography. (SD, *Poet*, 118–19)

Here is the poem that just "poured out." No one who reads it will continue to think of Whittier as one of the genteel Fireside Poets of the nineteenth century, gazing from behind his beard in a deck of "Authors" cards along with Longfellow, Lowell, and Holmes. Whittier was no Boston Brahmin, far from it.

Mr. Whittier

It is so much easier to forget than to have been Mr. Whittier.
Though of course no one now remembers him when he was
     young.
A few old ladies who were little girls next door in Amesbury,
Or practically next door, have reminiscences of pears and apples
Given them by the famous, tamed, white-bearded saint with the
Still inextinguishable dark Hebraic eyes; and
Of course there is the old man—and I for one am grateful—who
Recalls the seedy coat, the occasionally not so clean high collar,
And that like many another he read his paper by the hour in
     the privy.
Carl Schurz, finding him rained in by the stove at the village
     store,
Thought "So superior to those about him, and yet so like
     them"; and
His official biographer decided that Mr. Whittier's poetry was
     the kind
"Written first of all for the neighbors." There are lesser and
     worse.

In any case, here is a city, founded in 1630, present population
     somewhere about
55,000—has been more in boom times, and has been a lot
     less;—say,
In three hundred years has birthed a couple of hundred
     thousand people
And one poet. Not bad. And as proof of the title I shall only
     remark

It is easier to leave *Snow-Bound* and a dozen other items in or
      out of
The school curriculum than it is to have written them. Try it
      and see.

Born where the east wind brought the smell of the ocean from
      Plum Island up-river,
At a brookside haunted in the foggy dark of autumn nights
By six little witches in sky-blue capes—Uncle Moses had seen
      them;—
Born on a farm to the *Bible*, *Pilgrim's Progress*, a weekly paper,
      the Quaker meeting-house,
To hard poverty, obscure, and a few winters of country school;
To die—though only after there were thirteen for dinner, and
      the clock
Suddenly stopped—ancient with fame, with honorary
      degrees, and
One hundred thousand dollars all made out of poems,—I say
Even this was not easy, though also it is not
What I am talking about, but is really incidental along with
Not liking Walt Whitman and never quite affording marriage.

Neither, under the circumstances, could it have been easy, and
      it was important,
To stand suddenly struck with wonder of old legends in a
      young land,
To look up at last and see poetry driving a buckboard around
      the bend,
And poetry all the time in the jays screeching at the cats in the
      dooryard,
Climbing with the thrush into the August noon out of the boy's
      sight
As he dawdled barefoot through poetry among the welts of the
      goldenrod;
But nothing is hardest which treads on nobody else's toes.

Let us not begrudge Mr. Whittier his white beard, his saintliness,
      his other foibles;
Let us remember him when he was young, not to begrudge
      his rise
As a goddam Abolitionist hated not only in the South,
Hated by manufacturers, politicians, the neighbors, our folk, all
Who hate the outspoken radical and know a safer way;

Denounced by the clergy—a serious matter in that time; by the
    good men who
Rotten-egged him in New Hampshire, burned him out in
    Pennsylvania,
Jailed those who read him, and twenty years later immortally
    froze
With Webster on whom he turned his scorn of compromise.
It is so much easier to forget than to have been Mr. Whittier.

He put the names of our places into his poems and he honored
    us with himself;
And is for us but not altogether, because larger than us.
When he was an old man, the Negroes came to him free to
    come and sang to him
"The Lord bless thee and keep thee;
The Lord make his face to shine upon thee and be gracious
    unto thee;
The Lord lift up his countenance upon thee, and give thee
    peace."
—No more begrudge their freedom than his tears. (Quoted in
    SD, *Poet*, 118–21)

The poem, in Scott's characteristic plain-spoken voice, presents a great deal of information in its fifty-four long lines. We have a physical image of Whittier as an old man, along with the judgment of statesman Carl Schurz that he resembled his fellow townspeople in Amesbury, Massachusetts— where, not incidentally, Winfield Townley Scott grew up. We learn something of Whittier's career as a poet and his idiosyncratic personal views. We witness the young man "struck with wonder" to find poetry springing up everywhere around him. Then, in its portrait of Whittier's political views, we discover why Scott has taken such pains throughout to differentiate what is easy from what is hard. Outspoken advocacy of abolitionism was *hard*. It *cost* Whittier to take up that cause, decades in advance of the Civil War. So of course we do not "begrudge" him his "foibles," much less his tears when the Negroes come to him "free to come" and sing their biblical blessing. We may even be moved to tears ourselves. The failed biography has been transformed into a brilliant and memorable poem.

Writers as Subjects

If biographers are artists under oath—committed to telling as much of the truth as may be ascertained—novelists and poets have no such obligation.

At their best they exist in the world of their imagination, not in the ordinary universe inhabited by the rest of us. Inventing is what they do. "Fiction-writing," Cynthia Ozick commented, "is make-believe, acting a part, assuming an identity not one's own. Novelists are, after all, professional impostors; they become the people they invent" (Ozick, 33). In other words—those of Victoria Glendinning—they are "licensed liars" (Glendinning, 57) at work, and quite often they lie about themselves under other circumstances as well.

Often the lies are designed to present those who utter them in a favorable light. Even birthdates may be altered for such purposes. When he first became a poet of public importance, Robert Frost changed his birth date from 26 March 1874 to 26 March 1875 (Hall, 17). His parents had married, he believed, in November 1873. In advancing his birth date by a year, Frost dissociated himself from that segment of the population conceived out of wedlock and made an honest woman out of his mother. Ernest Hemingway took the opposite tack as an almost embarrassingly young man, building his reputation among expatriate writers in Paris. He was born in 1898, he said, instead of 1899, thereby adding a year's worth of maturity. Hemingway was badly wounded while serving as a Red Cross ambulance driver in World War I, and was awarded a medal as well. Not good enough: he invented the yarn that he'd been fighting with the crack Italian Arditi. William Faulkner promoted himself to an RCAF pilot in the same war.

Writers sometimes become exasperated by the more extravagant liars in their tribe. Edward Newhouse, when I was interviewing him for my John Cheever biography, warned me not to trust *anything* that fellow fiction writer Katharine Anne Porter might say. On *The Dick Cavett Show* in 1979, Mary McCarthy commented that "every word [Lillian Hellman] writes is a lie, including *and* and *the*," leading to a lawsuit dropped after Hellman's death. Ben Hecht, an intermittent friend of Sherwood Anderson's for twenty years, believed virtually nothing Anderson said. An even closer friend acknowledged that Anderson, a man of boundless imagination and a wearer of masks, "was there to be seen but not always found" (Taylor, 4–5).

It may be too that writers are more likely than others to indulge in self-deception as a way of reconfiguring past misbehavior. "One lies more to one's self than to anyone else," Byron once observed (Edel, *Lives*, 17). According to Oscar Wilde, "man is least himself when he talks in his own person. Give him a mask, and he will tell you the truth" (quoted in Lang). Or tell you a story.

Perhaps the champion liar among twentieth-century writers was the poet James Dickey. In interviews and public statements, Dickey constructed an image of himself as an all-American hero. He had been a college football player with NFL potential, he claimed, a state champion high hurdler, a decorated World War II pilot who'd flown a hundred combat missions, an award-winning advertising executive on the Coca-Cola account, a Casa-nova who'd slept with two thousand women, a successful big-game bow-and-arrow hunter, a guitar player who'd composed the soundtrack for the movie *Deliverance*. None of it was true, and Dickey was not the least apolo-getic about it. He told his biographer Henry Hart, author of *James Dickey: The World as a Lie* (2000), that he enjoyed mixing fact and fiction until the two were indistinguishable. In a letter he pointed out that he made "no real distinction between fact, fiction, history, reminiscence, and fantasy, for the imagination inhabits them all." He regarded writing itself as a "creative lie" that "makes us see the truth" (Hart, "Enemies," 98, 115).

Reviewing the first volume of Lawrance Thompson's biography of Robert Frost, Dickey focused on the way Frost created "a complex mask, a *persona*, an invented personality that the world, following the man, was pleased, was overjoyed, finally, to take as an authentic identity": that of the genial New England farmer dispensing homely wisdom until the cows came home. Dickey complimented Thompson for going behind the mask to uncover a much less simple and less admirable human being. "Looking back on Frost through the lens of Dr. Thompson's book, one finds it obvious that the mode, the manner in which a man lies, and what he lies about-these things and the *form* of his lies—are the main things to investigate in a poet's life and work" (Hart, *Dickey*, xii). Dickey himself suggested "the world as a lie" as the subtitle for Hart's biography.

Hemingway reflected on the same issue—both lying to others and to oneself—in an item lodged among his papers at the John F. Kennedy Library in Boston. Like Dickey he thought it

> not unnatural that the best writers are liars. A major part of their trade is to lie or invent and they will lie when they are drunk, or to themselves, or to strangers. They often lie uncon-sciously and then remember their lies with deep remorse. If they knew all other writers were liars too it would cheer them. . . . Lying when drinking is a good exercise for their powers of invention and is very helpful in the making up of a story. It is no more wicked or reprehensible in a writer than it is to have strange and marvelous experiences in his dreams. Lying to themselves is harmful but this is cleansed away by the writing of a true book which in its invention is truer than any true thing that ever happened. (Hemingway, item 845, JFK)

Writers, then, frequently complicate the task of the biographer by invent-ing fictitious accounts of their past. It might be argued that the literature they create offers a compensating source of information—that, as Hemingway argued, their stories or novels or poems or plays present a kind of truth superior to that of mere factual data. But in that respect as well, the literary biographer must tread warily.

Paul Murray Kendall addressed the issue in his landmark 1965 *The Art of Biography*. Biographers were drawn to writers as subjects, he pointed out, partly because as "writers of a kind" themselves they felt a certain kinship with them. There were both advantages and disadvantages to pursuing literary biography. *Pro*: Men or women of letters were "schooled, by temperament and talent, to examine themselves rather more assiduously than other beings do," thus offering "eloquent source-materials" in the form of letters and journals and drafts. Furthermore, they tended "to project themselves by gesture as well as pen," thus providing "the biographer with provocative role-playings against which he can stage his own perception of character." *Con*: The literary biographer faced a significantly more difficult task than that of a colleague undertaking the life story of a historical or political figure, for "a novel-event or poem-event was much harder to translate into reliable and interesting information than an election campaign or a military battle" (Kendall, 6–7).

Danger lies in wait as the biographer begins to deal with works of literary merit. Summaries of novels or poems or plays temporarily interrupt the narrative flow of the life story. Longer explications or evaluations demonstrating how and why these works make the subject worth writing about—studies of the achievement—can bring the story to a full stop. Simply on artistic grounds, then, literary biographers try to connect the life and the work under examination. Sometimes, even often, they go too far in using a story, say, as parallel to and indicative of what was going on in a writer's private existence.

Earl Rovit discussed this dilemma in his 2011 essay on "Literary Lives." The biographer must not only be wary, he wrote, of identifying "the voice of the text with that of the author," for he or she may well be using an invented and unreliable voice to relate the tale. Then Rovit added a related problem. "Nothing comes from nothing," he observed, "and common wisdom insists that a writer's experience in the 'real world' must at least be ancillary to, and possibly generative of, the world inside the text. It would indeed be strange if writers did not exploit their own lives for the lyrical moments they inscribe, the stories they tell, the emotional predicaments and reactions their characters display. What then does the biographer do when he finds material that gives every indication of being authentically autobiographical even though fictionalized?" Can he trust such data as much as "documents from the author's nonwriting life?"

In answering those questions, Rovit commented that most authors "find ways of distancing themselves from naked exposure with elaborate masks, stylistic convolutions, displacements and condensations, invented diversions and detours." They may be concealing more than they reveal in their work, leaving it to aftercomers to assess the role of such evasions. As William Carlos Williams reminded us in *Paterson*, "Nothing is so unclear between man and his writing as to which is the man and which is the thing" (quoted in SD, "Definitive," 97). So the biographer must proceed with caution. He may be unable to resist finding lines of correlation between his subject's life and work, but he should resign himself to being wrong "a good percentage of the time" (Rovit, 232–33).

And yet there are instances when a biographer feels absolutely right about tracing an occurrence in a work of art to one in real life. That happened to me in connection with Hemingway's "Now I Lay Me," one of the twenty-four stories or story fragments in *The Nick Adams Stories* (1972). The first-person narrator—"Signor Tenente"—describes how he manages getting through the sleepless nights he is facing after a traumatic wartime wound. "I myself did not want to sleep because I had been living for a long time with the knowledge that if I ever shut my eyes in the dark and let myself go, my soul would go out of my body." It had been that way with him, the narrator says, ever since he'd been "blown up" at night. Well, we know that Hemingway himself was badly wounded at Fossalta di Piave shortly after midnight on 8 July 1918, and there is some evidence that for a long time thereafter he could not sleep without a night light. In any case, every biographer I know of has equated the voice of the narrator of this story—along with that of Hemingway's "In Another Country," also related by a soldier recovering from wartime trauma—with the voice of the author.

With "Now I Lay Me," though, there is another and better reason for regarding the story as autobiographical. "Signor Tenente" has devised several ways of occupying himself while he lies awake at night. He thinks back to trout streams he fished in his youth, for example. Sometimes he fishes four or five different streams by memory, starting at the source and going downstream and then, to make the time pass, reversing his course. Sometimes he "made up streams, and these were very exciting, and it was like being awake and dreaming." On other nights, he lay "cold-awake" and prayed for everyone he had ever known, a process that took up "a great amount of time." Or he tried to remember everything that had ever happened to him, and the two things that come to mind in the story present an indelible picture of his dysfunctional parents.

His mother, the *tenente* recalls, liked to "clean things out and make a good clearance." When the family moved to a new house—he was very young then—he could remember watching jars from the old attic being burned in the backyard and "how they popped in the heat and the fire flamed up from the alcohol." He could not even remember who burned those things at that time, but he has full recall of a later incident. This scene, described in detail, is central to the emotional impact of the story.

While his father was away on a hunting trip, his mother had "made a good thorough clearing out in the basement and burned everything that should not have been there," the *tenente* remembers, casting the account in the language his mother used at the time. The fire was still burning in the road behind the house when his father returned. But paraphrase won't do: here is the rest of the scene in the words Hemingway puts in the voice of his narrator, who in his boyhood was called Nick [Adams].

> I went out to meet him. He handed me his shotgun and looked at the fire. "What's this?" he asked.
>
> "I've been cleaning out the basement, dear," my mother said from the porch. She was standing there smiling, to meet him. My father looked at the fire and kicked at something. Then he leaned over and picked something out of the ashes. "Get a rake, Nick," he said to me. I went to the basement and brought a rake and my father raked very carefully in the ashes. He raked out stone axes and stone skinning knives and tools for making arrowheads and pieces of pottery and many arrowheads. They had all been blackened and chipped by the fire. My father raked them all out very carefully and spread them on the grass by the road. His shotgun in its leather case and his gamebags were on the grass where he had left them when he stepped down from the buggy.
>
> "Take the gun and the bags in the house, Nick, and bring me a paper," he said. My mother had gone inside the house. I took the shotgun, which was heavy to carry and banged against my legs, and the two gamebags and started toward the house.
>
> "Take them one at a time, Nick," my father said. "Don't try and carry too much at once." I put down the gamebags and took in the shotgun and brought out a newspaper from the pile in my father's office. My father spread all the blackened, chipped stone implements on the paper and then wrapped them up. "The best arrowheads went all to pieces," he said. He walked into the house with the paper package and I stayed outside on the grass with the two gamebags. After a while I took them in. In remembering that, there were only two people, so I would pray for them both. (EH, *Nick Adams*, 147–48)

The writing is as powerful here as in anything Hemingway ever wrote, because of his uncanny ability to convey emotion through things left out, or what he called the iceberg principle. "If a writer of prose knows enough about what he is writing about he may omit things that he knows and the reader, if the writer is writing truly enough, will have a feeling of those things as strongly as though the writer had stated them," Hemingway wrote in *Death in the Afternoon*. "The dignity of movement of the iceberg is due to only one-eighth of it being above water. The writer who omits things because he does not know them only makes hollow places in his writing" (EH, *Death*, 192).

This artistic idea is not much different from the frequently evoked one that stories should "show, not tell," thus allowing readers the pleasure of discovering, in a sort of collaboration with the writer, what is going on. In this scene Hemingway does not *tell* us that Nick's father was furious to find his treasured collection of arrowheads and other American Indian artifacts destroyed in his absence. He does not *present* a marital confrontation about this issue. And he says *nothing* about the way Nick is drawn into his parents' conflict or about his emotional distress. These things are not told, but surely shown. We feel them as strongly—more strongly—as if the writer had stated them. How does he manage to accomplish this?

Dr. Adams—we know his name from Hemingway's earlier story called "The Doctor and the Doctor's Wife"—comes home from his hunting trip, and his son Nick goes out to greet him. His wife remains on the porch, smiling. Husband and wife exchange very few words and nothing by way of physical contact. "What's this?" Nick's father asks upon seeing the burned artifacts. "I've been cleaning out the basement, dear," his mother answers. That ends their conversation.

Instead Nick's father issues a series of directives to his son. "Get a rake, Nick." "Take the gun and the bags in the house, Nick, and bring me a paper." (By this time Nick's mother has gone back inside the house.) And when the shotgun, heavy to carry, bangs against Nick's legs, "Take them one at a time. . . . Don't try and carry too much at once." These commands function as a painful attempt by Nick's exasperated father to express his authority, and as a way of involving his son in the silent struggle between husband and wife. The authority vanishes as his father rakes carefully among the ashes to recover whatever he can, and in the end he can only make an appeal for sympathy: "The best arrowheads went all to pieces." With this Dr. Adams takes his paper package of charred remains inside the house and Nick stays outside on the grass with the two gamebags for a while, reluctant to witness any confrontation between his parents and reflecting—and this is the crucial thing Hemingway left out—on how he has been made a party to *both sides* of their dispute.

When I initially commented on this story in *By Force of Will*, I assumed that in this case fiction was fact. Writing about "The Last Good Country," an autobiographical story Hemingway chose not to publish during his lifetime, I pointed out that Ernest/Nick had elaborated on his mother's techniques for controlling other members of the family, leading him and his sister "Littless" to fervently agree that they had "seen enough fights in families." From that I moved to bald statement: "In one memorable assertion of her superiority, Mrs. Hemingway gathered up her husband's treasured collection of Indian arrowheads and tools and tossed them all into a back-yard bonfire, an event which Ernest transplanted to his story 'Now I Lay Me' to illustrate the point that marriage was hardly likely to solve Nick Adams's problems" (SD, *Force*, 171).

That was a somewhat reckless leap from fiction to fact, but I found out later the leap was almost certainly justified. The evidence came from Paul Smith's invaluable *Reader's Guide to the Short Stories of Ernest Hemingway*. Smith spent countless hours working with the Hemingway collection at the John F. Kennedy Library in Boston, comparing the drafts each story went through on its way toward a finished work of art. The final typescript of "Now I Lay Me," he observed, implies that Nick was "at most an observer" of his mother's burning the artifacts. But in the manuscript draft there is this telling line and revision as the smiling wife meets her returning husband. " 'I've been cleaning out the basement, dear,' " my mother called from the porch, " '*and Ernie's /Nicky's/ helped me burn the things*' " (my emphasis). Smith knew of no other instance, anywhere in Hemingway's meticulously preserved manuscripts, "in which he inadvertently has Nick's mother call him Ernie" (Paul Smith, 173). When I first heard that passage—Smith was reading a paper at a Hemingway conference—the hair on the back of my neck stood up.

In this case, what is left out accomplishes two things. The slip from "Nick" to "Ernie" strongly suggests that the incident he is writing about actually occurred. And the fact that Nick's mother involves him in destroying his father's valued relics deepens the story immeasurably. The boy, still young enough that he needs both hands to carry his father's shotgun comfortably, has been drawn into the ongoing contest for dominance between his parents—a contest in which his mother has the upper hand. On the day his father is due back from a hunting trip, she decides to burn her husband's collection of arrowheads, just as in a previous year she had consigned his specimen jars to the flames. This time, though, she enlists Nick's assistance and makes him complicit in the ritual humiliation. Then his father arrives, and in his frustration orders the boy around. Nick can only watch as his father rakes through the ashes in a futile attempt to undo the damage. He has done what his mother told him to, and done what his father told him to. Something terrible has happened, he knows, but he has no words for it. No words at all, for he says absolutely nothing to either of his parents. He's caught, helpless, in the middle of his parents' marital dispute.

The story ends with an ironic discussion on the virtues of marriage between Signor Tenente Nick Adams, now grown and a lieutenant wounded while serving with the Italian army, and his orderly, an Italian who had spent some time in the United States and speaks English. The two of them lie awake, listening to the silkworms "eating very clearly in the night." The orderly, who is worried about his *tenente*'s sleeplessness, has recently married, and repeatedly tells his *tenente* that he too should marry. "A man ought to be married," he insists. "You'll never regret it. Every man ought to be married." "All right," Nick says. "Let's try and sleep a while." But as the last sentence reveals, the orderly feels quite sure about this matter. "He was going back to America and he was very certain about marriage and knew it would fix up everything" (EH, *Nick Adams*, 152–53). Even in this instance, though, one cannot conclude that the souvenir-burning episode took place precisely as Hemingway wrote about it in "Now I Lay Me." To do so would be to ignore what Olivia Laing in *The Trip to Echo Spring* (2014) calls the "shaping," "scissoring and moulding by which real life is converted into art." Even when writers draw deeply on events they've experienced or felt, she warns, "what they make of them is never straightforwardly factual" (79–80).

What does seem certain is that "Now I Lay Me" exemplifies Frank O'Connor's description of a story as showing a change in someone's life, a moment when "the iron was bent, and anything that happens to that person afterwards, they never feel the same about again" (quoted in Wilkinson, 44). It was one of the last stories Hemingway wrote about Nick Adams. Paul Smith dates its composition to 1932–33, a few years after Dr. Clarence Edmonds Hemingway killed himself in a suicide brought on, his son believed, by repeated knuckling under to his wife.

Most writers disparage such biographical explorations into their lives and work. I cite a few of their comments, arranged more or less chronologically. George Eliot: "Biographers are generally a disease of English literature." Gustave Flaubert: "The artist must make posterity believe that he never existed." Emily Dickinson: "Biography first convinces us of the fleeing of the Biographied." Oscar Wilde: Biography "adds to death a new terror, and makes one wish that all art were anonymous." Thomas Carlyle: "The biographies of men of letters are for the most part the saddest chapter in the history of the human race except the Newgate Calendar." Henry James: "The writer and would-be biographer [are] engaged in a contest in which the victim, the writer, like a hunted creature, struggle[s] to protect himself and frustrate his relentless pursuer." Willa Cather: Biographers are

"Tomb-breakers." W. H. Auden: "Biographies of writers are always super-fluous and usually in bad taste. . . . [The writer's] private life is, or should be, of no concern to anybody except himself, his family, and his friends." Gore Vidal: Biographers are "[b]irds of ill omen." Germaine Greer: Biography constitutes "rape . . . an unpardonable crime against selfhood." Vladimir Nabokov: Biography equals "psycho-plagiarism."

In efforts to advance their posthumous reputations, writers have often taken extraordinary steps to ward off future biographers. Bonfires, for example. Charles Dickens fed his papers into the fire and invited his children to roast potatoes and onions in the embers. "Would to God every letter I have ever written were on that pile," he said. Henry James, who in an exquisite ironic twist was to become the subject of Leon Edel's five volumes, burned thousands of letters accumulated over forty years in a great roaring fire in the garden of Lamb House in Sussex, and felt "easier in mind" afterwards (Edel, *Literary*, 38). He also urged his correspondents to burn letters he had written them, and told his literary executor of his "utter and absolute abhorrence of any attempted biography" and of his wish "to frustrate as utterly as possible the post mortem exploiters" (Nettels, 120).

Authors have also attempted to manage posterity by designating close relatives to write their biographies. In his will Sir Walter Scott directed that his son-in-law, the novelist and historian John Gibson Lockhart, undertake that task. The Victorian poets Browning and Tennyson shared an abhorrence against intrusions on their privacy. Each of them destroyed much of their correspondence and placed a son in charge beyond the grave. Hallam Tennyson's two-volume *Alfred, Lord Tennyson*, appearing within five years of his father's death, was specifically designed to "preclude the chance of future and unauthentic biographies" (Millgate, 1, 16, 23, 44–45).

Thomas Hardy went still further, in effect writing his own biography and concealing that fact from the public. Late in his long life (1840–1928), Hardy married his second wife, Florence Emily Dugdale, thirty-eight years his junior, who brought a modest record as a writer of children's books and excellent secretarial skills to their union. Together they concocted a scheme to control his reputation. Like others before him, Hardy was to dispose of most of his private papers. Before doing so, though, he used his notebooks and diaries, often altered to present himself in the best possible light, as source material for a biography: a biography of Thomas Hardy, by Thomas Hardy. His wife duly typed out the manuscript pages as they accumulated, all of this done secretly. Otherwise it was his work. Yet it was her name, Florence Emily Hardy, that appeared as the author of the two-volume biography published within two years of his death (Millgate, 122–27).

In *Keepers of the Flame* (1992), Ian Hamilton recounts a series of cases where widows or children or executors of a recently deceased author fought against biographers. "Relatives are the biographer's natural enemies," according to Janet Malcolm, like "the hostile tribes an explorer encounters and must ruthlessly subdue to claim his territory" (quoted in Hart, "Enemies," 106"). Even when they initially agree to cooperate with the exploiter-explorer-investigator, they may draw the line when it comes to revealing documents. For my biography of Archibald MacLeish, I had the invaluable support of his son Bill. He opened many doors for me, but would not allow access to the highly personal letters his parents exchanged. Justin Kaplan encountered a similar restriction when embarked upon a biography of Irving Berlin—one of "many unwritten books" in his career. (After writing biographies of Mark Twain, Lincoln Steffens, and Walt Whitman, he considered and abandoned several other subjects—Gertrude Stein, Willa Cather, Stephen Crane, and Edgar Allan Poe among them.) Two of Berlin's daughters, who had originally pledged a hands-off policy, reversed that position when Kaplan asked to see "an important cycle of letters and messages their parents had exchanged during their courtship": these were "too private, too sacred" to be examined, even for indirect background use. Kaplan understood that "even the most kindly disposed biographer enters an adversarial situation when family feelings about adored parents are involved," but could see further restrictions and concessions looming. "The venture had been irreparably compromised," he felt, and he bowed out (Kaplan, "Culture," 9–11).

One way writers have attempted to frustrate biographers is by writing their own memoirs or autobiographies. "Biographies are murder," Henry Adams observed. "They belittle the victim and the assassin equally." He conceived of his famous autobiography, *The Education of Henry Adams*, as a "shield of protection" against such assassins (quoted in Kaplan, "Culture," 6). Gore Vidal made a point of writing a memoir so as to have the first word on his own life, and so did Philip Roth and John Updike.

In a 1999 essay, "On Literary Biography," Updike expressed the reasons for his "decided reluctance" to be "the subject of extended biographical treatment." A fiction writer's life, he said, "is his treasure, his ore, his savings account, his jungle gym," and as long as he was alive, he didn't want anybody else playing on that jungle gym—disturbing his children, quizzing his ex-wife, bugging his present wife, seeking for Judases among his friends, rummaging through yellowing old clippings, and quoting at length bad reviews he would rather forget. To ward off such intruders, Updike published "an autobiography of sorts, *Self-Consciousness*" (1989), recounting "in sometimes embarrassing detail" significant or curious facts about his life. Some thought the book amounted to "a parading of wounds," but the wounds were his to parade "and no one else's." Others, he found, never managed to get things quite right. "The exact socioeconomic tone, the muddle and eddy of peculiar circumstances are almost invariably missed" (Updike, "Biography," 31–32).

Updike died in 2009, by which time his literary trust had erected substantial roadblocks to protect him and his works from exploitation. Following his wishes, the trust has not granted permission to publish any of his writing before 1953, except "in unique circumstances." In addition, Updike did not want his personal and professional correspondence to become public, and therefore the trust has not "entertain[ed] requests to publish, post, broadcast, or publicly read his correspondence." These provisions were relaxed after Updike's death and the sale of his papers to Harvard. According to Leslie A. Morris, curator of modern books and manuscripts at Harvard's Houghton Library, there are no restrictions on the use of this archive. So Adam Begley was allowed to make use of Updike's materials in *Updike*, his 2014 biography.

Several writers made preemptive strikes against biographers in their fiction. Offhand I think of Somerset Maugham in *Cakes and Ale*, William Golding in *The Paper Men*, Nabokov in *Pale Fire*, Roth in *Exit Ghost*. But the most famous and damning case is surely that of James's *The Aspern Papers*. As Kaplan characterized it, this "brimstone-and-hellfire" story is told from the point of view of the narrator or antihero or villain. He lies his way into the Venetian palazzo of an old woman in hopes of securing the private papers of Jeffrey Aspern, a famous deceased author who had once been her lover. This intruder will do almost anything to secure his prize. He takes advantage of the woman's poverty, and leads her "plain, dingy, elderly" niece to believe that he is prepared to marry her in exchange for the papers. In a climactic scene, he creeps into the room of Aspern's one-time lover, who lies abed and in ill health, in order to break into her desk. But she wakes and "hisse[s] out passionately, furiously: 'Ah, you publishing scoundrel!'" In the end the old woman dies and her niece burns the papers, leaving the frustrated intruder—"sly and manipulative, but rather thick all the same," in Kaplan's phrase—with an "almost intolerable" sense of loss (Kaplan, "Culture," 5).

One reason writers try to forestall biographical inquiry lies in the contrast between the great works of literature they have created and their otherwise insignificant or even reprehensible private lives. The most sympathetic biographers may try to focus on the stories or novels or poems or plays of their all-too-human subjects, but there is precious little drama in describing the *process* by which these accomplishments were achieved. By and large the biographer is confronted by what Henry James called "the turned-back of the writer" (quoted in Rovit, 229), who sits alone in a room scratching out words by hand or on a typewriter or computer screen or, worse, sits at a desk waiting for those words to come. Depicting what a writer does is boring, and so it is that films about authors are almost universally awful. To interest the reader—to interest himself—the biographer must turn to events and incidents drawn from the life, and seek parallels or contradictions between those and the works of art. Yet it may be regarded as "childish," as Nabokov commented in his afterword to *Lolita*, to expect a work of fiction to reveal significant information about an author. The critic Hugh Kenner maintained that he learned more about Samuel Beckett from watching a two-hour film of him playing billiards than from Deirdre Bair's long biography (Sisk, 455).

The task is made more difficult when the subject has adopted a public persona for the specific purpose of throwing off close inquiry into his personality and behavior. Robert Frost brilliantly fashioned his folksy image, for example, though he warned us in his first book of poems what he was about.

> We make ourselves a place apart
> > Behind light words that tease and flout,
> But oh, the agitated heart
> > Till someone find us really out.
> (Frost, 19)

Drawing analogies between the life with the work, and vice versa, is a risky enterprise, and often the biographer will fail. As Milan Kundera put it, "Overfamiliar metaphor: The novelist destroys the house of his life and uses its stones to build the house of his novel. A novelist's biographers thus undo what a novelist has done, and redo what he undid. All their labor cannot illuminate either the value or the meaning of a novel, can scarcely even identify a few of the bricks" (Kundera, 144–45).

Ethical Issues

In addition to his devastating portrait of the "publishing scoundrel" in *The Aspern Papers*, Henry James addressed the moral and artistic questions of biography in reviews, essays, letters, and other works of fiction. He was a biographer himself—author of full-length books on *Hawthorne* and *William Wetmore Story and His Friends* and of more than thirty sketches / portraits-in-prose on nineteenth-century English and American writers—and so was confronted with the basic ethical issues. These included, "What is the duty of the biographer to his subject and to the public? How much should the biographer tell? When, if ever, is it his duty to withhold facts? Should the artist be exempted from the standards by which other people are judged?"

In the confrontation between the writer/subject and his or her biographer, Elsa Nettels noted, James invariably took the side of the writer and opposed "detailed revelations" of scandalous or intimate behavior that pandered to public interest in the sensational (Nettels, 119–21).

Leon Edel, perhaps taking his cue from James, arrived at a similar position. Biographers needed to learn the lesson of relevance, and to ignore occasional dishonest or disloyal acts by subjects that had minimal impact on their life and work, he believed. There was a boundary that protected human dignity from unwarranted intrusion. The wise biographer would exercise tact and "a sense of certain lingering decencies" in order to avoid crossing that boundary (Sisk, 450). It's a problem that all serious practitioners of the craft must wrestle with. If they are capable and thorough researchers, they will discover things about their subjects that probably shouldn't be made public and other things that probably should. But which are which?

James Boswell himself worried the question in his *Life of Samuel Johnson, LL.D.* As Patricia Spacks pointed out in *Gossip*, Boswell's monumental work gained much of its power by avoiding the dullness of mere hagiography. Johnson is depicted as "at least briefly unkind, petty, fearful, or self-absorbed"—and hence more human and credible. But these revelations troubled Boswell. After a passage about Johnson's youthful sexual indulgences, he intruded with this remark: "I am conscious that this is the most difficult part of my biographical work, and I cannot but be anxious concerning it. I trust that I have got through it, preserving at once my regard to truth,—to my friend,—and to the interests of virtue and religion." This triple obligation sounded "high-minded" indeed, Spacks observed, but problems still remained.

> Maybe, despite [Boswell's] protestations, he wishes to reduce the stature of an uncomfortably gigantic figure. Perhaps people read biography not to confirm but to challenge the moral grandeur of larger-than-life public figures. If a life story uncovers weakness and folly, does it not serve leveling impulses, the desire to emphasize the limits of human possibilities so as to avoid the necessity of aspiration? The writer and the reader of biography may gratify malice and envy in the guise of serving truth, virtue, and religion. Where are truth's proper limits? Should everything known be told; should one seek knowledge no matter where the search leads? Need biography respect no privacies? (Spacks, 98–99)

Most people have fixed opinions on such questions. It's like arguing about abortion or capital punishment, biographer Ian Hamilton commented. On one side stand the concealers, on the other the revealers, and "the agents of reticence have no truck with the agents of disclosure" (Hamilton, vii). My early training as a newspaperman persuaded me that in most cases the public's right to know trumped privacy concerns, so I'm on the side of the revealers. At the beginning of *The Adventures of Augie March*, Saul Bellow's narrator says that if you hold back one piece of information, you tend to hold back the adjoining facts as well. I think that's true, and regrettable, and to be avoided. There are, of course, legal issues to consider, as your publisher's lawyers will remind you: libel laws and invasion of privacy ones as well. But *generally*, my position resembles that of Mark Schorer, who believed that "[o]ne should write in anything that is true and relevant to one's themes—anything, that is, that will not bring [you] into court" (Schorer, 235).

Generally, for a fuller understanding of the issue I have relied on Diane Middlebrook's 1991 "Telling Secrets: The Ethics of Disclosure in Writing Biography," an essay composed shortly after publication of her biography on the poet Anne Sexton. That book caused something of an uproar, for it was based in good part on hundreds of hours of audiotapes that Sexton's psychiatrist decided to share with Middlebrook. Sexton would have wanted it that way, they were both persuaded. Several commentators—in particular, members of the medical profession—criticized both biographer and psychiatrist for (as they saw it) violating the sanctity of the doctor-patient relationship. The controversy had particular interest for me. A few years earlier, armed with a letter of permission from his widow, I'd gained access to two psychiatrists John Cheever and his family consulted. In interviews, they spoke of their impressions of him, referring to notes they'd made during their talks. But neither of these doctors conducted long-term explorations of Cheever's psychological makeup, for he was a reluctant patient. Instead of releasing innermost thoughts and concerns, he entertained his psychiatrists by spinning yarns. He amused them for a while—only a few meetings—and then cut off therapy.

No one quarreled with my use of such interviews, and the psychiatrists I saw offered no more insight into Cheever's personality than friends and family members and lovers who knew him far longer. Nonetheless, I was eager to hear what Diane Middlebrook had to say about her experience and about the broader issue of disclosure when she presented her essay at the December 1995 meeting of the Modern Language Association.

Middlebrook based her view on the ethics of biography on Voltaire's saying: "We must respect the living, but only truth is good enough for the dead." The dead cannot have wishes, she commented, and we cannot know "what they would have wanted" in the absence of testamentary evidence. We owe the dead the truth, nothing less—and not judgment but insight, not criticism but understanding (Middlebrook, "Secrets"). From that standard she arrived at three ethical responsibilities of the biographer.

First, know as much as possible. That demanded a strenuous effort to obtain all available information, but there was a difference between information and the truth, and in seeking truth the biographer had an obligation to take into account the biases of one's sources and oneself. Telling truths about subjects' lives could not harm them, Middlebrook maintained. Biographers "honored the dead most effectively by trying to comprehend them as whole human beings whose faults are as significant as their virtues."

Second, do no harm. If the subject—in this case, Anne Sexton—was a writer, the work she left behind was cultural property, and belonged to the culture. But certain boundaries should be observed. The biographer should not speculate or purport to represent the thoughts of her subject without information. Nor should she violate the "penumbra of privacy" of the survivors. These relatives and friends had rights to privacy, and biographers' "ethical obligations to protect those interests [went] beyond our legal rights to publish truths." Every responsible biographer should not publish information—I can think of two such instances in my experience—that he knows will harm the living. Or at the very least, should not publish such information without securing permission to do so from those most affected.

Third, try to do good. A well-researched and reasoned biography represents a contribution to knowledge, Middlebrook pointed out, "and thus is a good in itself." In addition, confidential materials—and here she addressed her use of Anne Sexton's psychiatric tapes—offered insights "into the relationship between the individual human being and prevailing cultural values." We learn about ourselves and about our heritage by learning about others. Anne Sexton lived a deeply troubled life and wrote about it in her poems before committing suicide at forty-five. "[P]utting an undisguised account of [her] case on record," Middlebrook concluded, "seemed an important way to extend the legacy of one aspect of her work, which was, in her words, 'to help people like me feel less alone'" (Middlebrook, *Straw,* 47–50).

And besides, she was after the truth, for the biographer, like the historian and the journalist, justifies his quest by invoking the need for truth-telling. *But whose truth?* This is not a simple question. James thought that the truth should be "presented with kindness, urbanity, and discretion" (Nettels, 122). Dickey, albeit a consummate liar, advocated total candor in biography. In criticizing a book on Theodore Roethke, he declared that it was "no good to assert . . . that Roethke was a big lovable clumsy affectionate bear who just incidentally wrote wonderful poems." The "driving force" of Roethke "was agony, and to know him we must know all the forms it took" (Hart, "Enemies," 103). Agony inspired Roethke to lie in his poetry, Dickey believed, and for him that was not a misfortune. Dickey would have agreed with Picasso that art is a lie that tells the truth (Bram, 298).

How much of the truth? To begin with, any biographer understands, first, that absolute Truth about anyone cannot be known, and second, that depiction of the subject necessarily involves choosing what to include. You gather a vast amount of information, and use only a fraction of it in your work. You subtract, but must not add anything that cannot be verified. It's through the process of selection that you succeed or fail. "The governing principle of selection," historian Barbara W. Tuchman commented, "is that it must honestly illustrate but never distort. By the very fact of inclusion or omission the writer has tremendous power to leave an impression that may not in fact be justified. He must, therefore, resist the temptation to use an isolated incident, however colorful, to support a thesis, or by judicious omission to shade the evidence." It doesn't matter whether the biographer is a Marxist or a moralist, a psychologist or a revisionist, Tuchman went on. "What matters is that he has a conscience and keeps it on guard" (Tuchman, 145). Unlike the pathographers Joyce Carol Oates condemned, he must resist the temptation to emphasize "the sensational underside . . . to the detriment of . . . less dramatic periods of accomplishment and well-being" (Sisk, 449).

And the biographer had better bring a healthy skepticism to his work as well, for not all apparently valid evidence is to be trusted. Some people make up stories, for example, for notoriety or the charge of seeing their name and exploits in print. That's a lesson I was fortunate enough to learn from an early immersion in newspaper work. Every few weeks a plausible fraud would show up in the city room of the *Minneapolis Star* with a terrific story to tell—something absolutely untruthful that in print would make a first-rate feature, and maybe even earn a byline. The veteran reporters, who knew better, would send such dissemblers my way to see if the gullible young cub reporter would bite.

The dishonest among us sometimes invent fictitious documents for profit, like the eighteenth-century English biographer who had his ears cut off for fabricating and quoting from scurrilous letters about famous figures (Authors Guild, "Whose Life," 20). Or they lie out of sheer malice, like Iago using Desdemona's handkerchief to twist Othello into an unshakable conviction that she had been unfaithful. Or they concoct untruths for the best of military reasons, as in the elaborate ruse called Operation Mincemeat the British conjured up during World War II. They invented a complete identity for a corpse launched from a submarine in the Mediterranean. The corpse carried totally false documents about the Allied invasion plans "along with dog tags, love letters, family letters, overdraft notices, legal papers, tailor's bills, theater tickets, fiancée's photo, and the like": all wonderful "corroborative detail" designed to disarm enemy suspicion. A Spanish fisherman discovered the corpse washed up on shore and turned him over to the Germans, who swallowed the story whole. Justin Kaplan, writing about that deception, referred to it as a "fable of biography" (Kaplan, "Culture," 7). There are always many falsehoods in circulation.

Biographers inevitably face a moral dilemma as well. In 1978 I spent a semester at Princeton poring over the splendid F. Scott Fitzgerald papers in the Firestone Library. I did this chronologically, following Fitzgerald from childhood to youth and as much maturity as he was able to achieve in his forty-four years. It was deep research of the best kind, not aimed at any particular period or theme. Almost every day I came upon a note or a letter or a draft that revealed something new and important about Fitzgerald's life and career. Yet when friends or colleagues asked what I'd been doing, I'd chuckle somewhat uneasily and say, "reading Fitzgerald's mail." Manifestly, I was aware that my days in the Firestone made me something of a voyeur, or to put it more politely, an observer experiencing vicariously the trials and triumphs of the subject under examination.

Janet Malcolm addressed this issue in "The Silent Woman," her 1993 meditation on the craft. In that essay she compared the biographer to a "professional burglar, breaking into a house, rifling through certain drawers that he has good reason to think contain the jewelry and money, and triumphantly bearing his loot away." The loot, she suggested, amounts to nothing more than gossip, and that's what readers want. "The transgressive nature of biography is rarely acknowledged," she said, "but it is the only explanation for biography's status as a popular genre." I think Malcolm went too far, but as a biographer herself, she had every right to trash the profession. Another prominent biographer, Phyllis Rose, reluctantly came to agree with Malcolm's remarks. At the heart of the biographer's motivation, she wrote, was "some act of personal appropriation, some sort of psychic exploitation. . . . In some sense each biographer . . . exploits his or her subject." It amounted to an invasive "morally tenuous" procedure, and Rose paid the price in guilt.

At the same time, though, she acknowledged some of the joys of writing biography: "the voyeuristic thrill of reading someone else's papers, the aesthetic thrill when the narrative sucks up all the details and seems unstoppable, the simpler joy of burying yourself in a library and forgetting yourself for hours at a time, the satisfaction of getting people to tell you what you want to know, the pleasure of exercising your art on a story you've had only to discover, not invent" (Rose, "Confessions," 74). To which I would add: the wonderful sensation of finishing a book and believing that you had this once, miraculously, come close to capturing and conveying the personality of your subject.

Sources: Letters

Almost invariably, when I talk to others about writing biography, someone raises the issue of whether future biographers will have enough source material to do their job. "People don't write letters any more," they point out. They communicate by cell phone or Skype, or by e-mail, or by texting and tweets. Won't the paper trail slip away? The answer, I think, is that such a dire prospect is highly unlikely.

It was only a generation ago, after all, that writers like Leon Edel and Richard Ellmann, James Joyce's biographer, were bemoaning the vast collections of documents at major libraries. Gone were the days, Edel pointed out, when biographies were written "out of half a dozen shoe boxes, or pieced together out of little facts like the royal grant of wine to Chaucer, or Shakespeare's second-best bed." Now—it was 1979—the biographer was confronted by more information than he could reasonably absorb and digest. After spending a lifetime wading through "great masses of paper, Himalayas of photographs, microfilms, kinescopes," how could he possibly "emerge, if not suffocated, with any sense of a face or a personality?" Might he not succumb to merely collecting the facts in "books too heavy and too long"? (Edel, "Figure," 22–23).

The telephone was supposed to have done away with such masses of written communication, but in practice, as Robert Skidelsky noted in 1988, more scholarly material than ever was being generated. One good reason was that prominent people, aware that private papers constituted an important part of their estate, saw to it that they were carefully preserved. In the case of well-known authors, half a dozen university libraries were likely to bid for possession and archiving of these documents. Sometimes, Skidelsky suggests, famous persons manipulated this evidence to present themselves to posterity in a favorable light (Skidelsky, 8–9). More often, though, they simply preserved everything. Ralph Ellison, author of a single great novel, *Invisible Man* (1952), and his wife, Fanny, saved almost every scrap of paper, from tax returns to typescripts, for deposit at the Library of Congress. In reviewing Arnold Rampersad's excellent *Ralph Ellison: A Biography* (2007), Phyllis Rose suggests that the Ellisons might better have thrown some of those papers away, especially the ones that show Ellison as elitist, self-righteous, and possessed of a strong sense of entitlement (Rose, "Impulse," 125–26).

In the twenty-first century, the Internet has replaced the telephone as the supposed substitute for letters/diaries/journals/books. Our children and grandchildren grow up in a world very different from that of the 1920s or 1950s or the 1980s. They communicate by way of smart phones or iPads, and can reach anyone anywhere within seconds by texting and tweeting and e-mail. But they do still read, and are still interested in finding out about men and women of accomplishment. By going to search engines, they can Google almost anyone and scan through the information available online through Wikipedia and other sites—most of it accurate and reliable, and becoming more so all the time. Even a putative biographer might start that way, before proceeding, say, to the archival holdings listed in *American Literary Manuscripts*—a useful compendium last published in 1977 and badly in need of updating.

During the interim, of course, increasingly sophisticated techniques of information retrieval have been developed. Several projects are now underway, for example, to digitize thousands of American newspapers. In that way, researchers can run keyword searches to ascertain the whereabouts and activities of the object of their attention. A case in point. The legend was that Joseph Pulitzer bought the *New York World* on a lark in 1883. James McGrath Morris, working on a biography of Pulitzer, thought that story unlikely: it didn't fit the picture of the man forming in his mind. He figured that Pulitzer probably spent some time in New York considering his options before buying the *World*, but there was nothing in the newspaper's index to that effect. Then Morris consulted one of the digitized-newspaper sites, and in a few minutes discovered what would have cost him many musty library hours to find out. Pulitzer had been staying in New York hotels a year before his purchase, scouting out the territory (Mihm).

It seems likely, then, that the cybernetic revolution will provide biographers with more rather than less information in the future—that the Internet will develop fresh ways of digging out previously unmined strata. There are already so many ways of gathering data that it is possible to write a competent biography without any cooperation whatever from the family and friends of the subject. Consider the case of Edward Butscher, who managed to produce *Sylvia Plath: Method and Madness* in 1976. Plath was an extremely difficult subject for any biographer, because of the feuding between Plath's adherents and those of her husband and fellow poet Ted Hughes. But Butscher faced apparently insurmountable difficulties, for no one on *either* side of the Plath-Hughes feud—according to Janet Malcolm—was disposed to cooperate with him. Besides, an official biographer appointed by the Plath estate was already at work. Butcher nonetheless plunged ahead, and without support from any of the central figures and without access to the archival materials published a book that, again according to Malcolm, bore "a striking resemblance" to the work of later biographers allowed access to the published and unpublished letters and journals.

How, under such forbidding circumstances, did he amass his materials? In the introduction to an anthology of essays on Plath, Butscher set out to answer that question. "Facts as such are relatively easy to come by in a society where growing complexity has spawned a growing network of official institutions," he wrote. "Schools, libraries, newspaper files, governmental agencies, and the like are there for the plundering, as every credit house and FBI investigator well knows, and the laziest of biographers can still construct a reasonable collage from the bits and pieces resurrected from these bureaucratic mausoleums." In addition, he managed to uncover some of Plath's secrets by interviewing sources who decided to talk to him despite being discouraged from doing so. Malcolm cited one such instance, and from that example proposed "the Confidant's Law": a law of human nature that "no secret is ever told to any one person; there is always at least one other person to whom we feel compelled to spill the beans." So the secrets eventually emerge, and so, Malcolm ventured, does a great deal else. "Every cup of coffee we ever drank, every hamburger we ever ate, every boy we ever kissed has been inscribed on someone's memory and lies in impatient readiness for the biographer's retrieval" (Malcolm, "Silent," 143).

Novels and stories, poems and plays represent the first and most indispensable source for the literary biographer. So far as possible, he must read everything his subject/author wrote, both published and unpublished, do that close reading with sensitivity and perception, and then embark on the dangerous game of tracing lines of connection between those works of art and the life of their creator. Often manuscript drafts leading up to final copy will provide clues in that endeavor. This proved true of Hemingway's story "Now I Lay Me," and it's true as well of Cheever's novel *Bullet Park* (1969).

The critical consensus on Cheever's fiction holds that he is at his best in the short story and less successful as a novelist. The longer form demands a sort of coherence that he found it difficult to achieve. His first two attempts at novels—*The Wapshot Chronicle* (1957) and *The Wapshot Scandal* (1964)— are episodic works, consisting of a series of scenes and incidents. Cheever's brilliant command of prose makes these books joys to read, but they do not achieve the organic structure one expects of novels. His closest approach to mastery of the form came in *Falconer* (1977), a novel written after Cheever had stopped the drinking that ruined so many of his days. Unlike almost all of his previous work, *Falconer* takes place not in the superficially comfortable but actually dysfunctional upper-middle-class suburb that is the locale of most of Cheever's fiction, but in Falconer Prison (Cheever had spent some time teaching the inmates of Sing Sing, located near his home in Ossining, how to write). And, also unlike most of his writing, the book ends with a powerful affirmation. Ezekiel Farragut, incarcerated for fratricide, kicks his heroin habit, conquers his phobias, manages a miraculous escape, and directs himself and his readers to "Rejoice."

Bullet Park (1969) is a very different sort of novel. Here in Cheever's customary exurbia, Eliot Nailles—a chemist reduced to promoting the virtues of a mouthwash called Spang—goes through his days in a fog of tranquilizers. His much-loved son Tony lies abed for days at a time, succumbing to sadness. Then Nailles's alter ego appears in the form of Paul Hammer, a newcomer to Bullet Park who has taken a vow to murder a representative of the materialistic culture. Hammer and Nailles: this is not subtle, for Cheever here, as in much of his writing, wanted to draw attention to the dual and contrary nature of his protagonist. The two men are archetypal figures, representing different ways of responding to a malaise that has overtaken American life.

The book ends, like *Falconer*, with a nearly miraculous event. Hammer settles on Tony Nailles as the victim of the ritual murder he is bent upon committing. He plans to "awaken the world" by immolating the lad in the chancel of Christ's Church. But Nailles, alerted to the danger by a swami, manages to come to his son's rescue at the last minute. That should have amounted to a relatively happy ending, but such an interpretation is undermined by the novel's final words. In each of four possible endings (reconstructed from Cheever's notes and his correspondence) Nailles rides the commuter train to New York. The one Cheever decided upon is the darkest of the four: "Tony went back to school on Monday and Nailles—drugged—went off to work and everything was as wonderful, wonderful, wonderful, wonderful as it had been" (Cheever, 144). Nothing has changed. Nailles still needs tranquilizers to get through the day. The fourth "wonderful" brings out the bitter irony. In thrall to alcohol, his marriage in disarray, Cheever was close to suicidal when he finished the book. Its criticisms of contemporary culture projected his own despondency.

In this case, intelligent reading of a writer's novel and related journal entries, combined with painstakingly acquired knowledge of the course of his of her existence, functioned to cast light on both the work and the life. The literary biographer is entitled, even obliged, to pursue such intersections. But he must not expect to capture everything that way. "My own view," as Paul Valéry remarked, "is that we cannot really circumscribe a man's life, imprison him in his ideas and his actions, reduce him to what he appeared to be and, so to speak, lay siege to him in his works. We are much more (and sometimes much less) than we have done" (quoted in Epstein, 123).

"The soul lies naked" before us in personal letters, Dr. Johnson once observed (Johnson, *Letters*, 11). They can and often do convey emotions with power and immediacy. "Letters are the great fixative of experience," as Janet Malcolm commented. The passage of time "erodes feeling . . . creates indifference," but letters prove that we once cared. "Everything else the biographer touches is stale, hashed over, told and retold, dubious, unauthentic, suspect" (Malcolm, "Silent," 123). Well, perhaps, yet even the most sincere love letters are not always to be trusted. I think of young Nathaniel Hawthorne writing Sophia Peabody how devastatingly lonely and sorrowful he was to be separated from her—a posture adopted to emphasize his love for Sophia that led many people to think of him, quite wrongly, as afflicted with melancholy.

We write different sorts of letters to different people, donning the appropriate mask for each performance. The young Hemingway speaks in one voice to his parents, another to his fishing buddies, and a third to his fiancée. Leon Edel reported having to scour through the "mere twaddle of graciousness" in Henry James's correspondence to uncover the occasional kernel of importance (Schorer, 225). Sinclair Lewis told his nephew not to take his weekly letters to his aged father seriously: he was only telling his father what he wanted to hear. "People lie in letters all the time," Louis Menand observed, and even diaries—presumably still more private and believable—can become "sites for gossip, flattery, and self-deception" (Menand, 65). Nor can journals be accepted at face value. In his voluminous journals Cheever sketched out trial passages and scenes for his fiction, a valuable display of the artist at work. But he also used journal entries to castigate himself for his drinking and his wife for her "coldness," thereby purchasing immunity against his daily bout with the bottle. And, Reynolds Price observed, journal keepers sometimes seem to be living for their journals. "Maybe they are barely conscious of the motive, but I often detect an inward grin as they think 'Do *this*; It'll sound so fine in my journal'" (Price, 4).

Menand also issued a sound warning against "the Rosebud assumption": that the most telling information will crop up in a long-lost note, that a dozen letters in someone's attic in Davenport, Iowa, will reveal all. Donating one's letters to a library with the proviso that they may not be consulted by researchers for, say, fifty years automatically invests them with importance, on the presumption that what is being withheld must contain surprising disclosures. In my experience it has not worked out that way. Rosalind Richards, a young woman of considerable beauty and impeccable family, attracted the interest of Edwin Arlington Robinson, a young man growing up a few blocks away in Gardiner, Maine. After Robinson's death in 1935, she gave her correspondence with him to the Houghton Library at Harvard, stipulating that the documents be kept from inspection for an extended period. When I was working on my biography of Robinson in the mid-2000s, I managed to persuade a relative of Rosalind Richards to allow me access to their correspondence. In those letters, secreted from view for decades, I expected to discover a Robinson deeply in love. I did not. EAR, as he liked to be called, may have been in love with Richards, but you could not prove it from their correspondence. He was one of the most private persons who ever lived, carrying the New Englander's customary reticence to extraordinary lengths. In his letters, as in almost all of his actions, he remained buttoned up. Only in his poetry did he demonstrate the passionate empathy he felt for his fellow human beings.

The modern biographer, as James Joyce's biographer Richard Ellmann pointed out, is fully aware that the letter itself constitutes a literary form—one in which the writer and receiver "play a game of concealment and revealment. . . . For earlier biographers, letters were saints' relics; for biographers since Freud, they are likely to be duplicitous or at least incomplete" (Ellmann, "Freud," 265). As source material, what is set forth in a letter cannot be taken as invariably true. Yet reading through hundreds or even thousands of a writer's letters over a period of time, keeping all caveats in mind, can be of tremendous value, for beyond the wit and the pretensions, despite the slanted truths and outright falsehoods, beneath the flattery and the gossip, there will emerge a "profile of a personality." So Thornton Wilder believed, and the observation proved to be true as applied to Wilder himself. Assigned to compose a foreword to *The Selected Letters of Thornton Wilder* (2008), I read through his correspondence and arrived at a picture of him as a man "who fizzed like champagne," whose effervescence was like a force of nature (Wilder, *Letters*, xxv). No wonder that biographer Gilbert A. Harrison titled his book *The Enthusiast: A Life of Thornton Wilder* (1983).

Professionals in the field are divided on the issue of whether letters can legitimately be converted into dialogue. Probably most would agree with Stanley Weintraub that "the biographer must quote only the real thing" (Weintraub, 32), but a significant minority would disagree and sanction transforming the written words of a letter into conversation. Doing so has obvious artistic benefits: dialogue is easy to read, and offers the immediacy of a scene that presumably, if not actually, took place. And using correspondence to simulate talk can sometimes avoid copyright infringement. In his memoir *Papa Hemingway* (1966), A. E. Hotchner took language Hemingway wrote him in letters—words that Hemingway and/or his heirs could have copyrighted—and reproduced it in the form of dialogue between himself and the author. He also appropriated conversations about bullfighting Hemingway placed near the end of chapters in *Death in the Afternoon* (1932). In Hemingway's book, that dialogue takes place between himself and an inquisitive if not especially bright old woman. Hotchner switched her inquiries into the more commercially palatable mouth of Ava Gardner, Hemingway acting as instructor to a most attractive student. Mary Hemingway, Ernest's widow, attempted to halt publication of *Papa Hemingway* on grounds of invasion of privacy. She lost the case, but might have prevailed had she sued on grounds of copyright infringement.

The meticulous biographer should also seek out letters or journals or diaries by people who knew the subject, looking for comments written *about* him but not *to* him. Difficult to locate, these can be invaluable, for "here are the really candid opinions, . . . here is the many-sided nature of the man" as his friends and acquaintances saw him (Garraty, 211).

When I was nearly finished writing *Death of a Rebel: The Charlie Fenton Story* (2012), it occurred to me to ask the Beinecke Library at Yale if there were significant mentions of Fenton in the archived papers of his teacher and mentor Norman Holmes Pearson. Were there ever! Pearson, it turned out, had undertaken much the same task that I was embarked upon fifty years later: to try to understand what had driven the charismatic Fenton to jump to his death in July 1960. In the months after that suicide, Pearson corresponded at length with Gale Carrithers, a young English instructor who like Fenton had studied with Pearson at Yale before migrating south to Duke; with the psychologist Leonard W. Doob, who befriended Fenton during his decade at Yale; and—best of all—with Ginger Price, the Duke graduate student Fenton fell in love with, leading to the breakup of his marriage and making him a social pariah in the Durham academic community. The profound insights and indelible memories articulated in those letters sent me back to the memoir-biography with a firmer grasp of what went terminally wrong during Fenton's last days.

Sources: Interviews

I was a newspaperman long enough to acquire some useful experience interviewing sources. Assigned to a story about a visiting figure of importance first thing in the morning (when working for an evening paper), I'd arrange for a meeting by telephone, make a few other calls for background information, scan through the clips in the morgue (no Internet, no Wikipedia, no Google at the time), scrape together half a dozen questions, with one or two of them promising a local hook, armed with that minimal knowledge confront the celebrated visitor, furiously scribble down notes, and rush back to the city room full of clattering typewriters to make deadline. Once in a while the result was worth reading. I did a good piece on James Michener for the *Minneapolis Star*, for instance, but in that case I'd read his earliest work and during my Army Security Agency stay in Japan had gotten to know a few of the foreign correspondents who were his friends. That gave us things to talk about. More often, though, I was navigating unfamiliar territory on such assignments, and didn't know enough to produce a really interesting, much less authoritative, article.

In the longer form of a magazine feature story, as exemplified by the *New Yorker* profile, the procedure changed radically. Staffers or freelancers were expected to do a great deal of homework, and to reach out beyond the subject to others who knew him well. With the advent of the New Journalism of the 1960s and 1970s—Tom Wolfe, Gay Talese, Lillian Ross, *Harper's* under Willie Morris, and the two masters: John McPhee and Joan Didion—reporter-writers sought extended access, occupying the same space as subjects for several days or even weeks at a time, observing but not asking questions, ideally becoming no more intrusive than "a fly on the wall." That resulted in excellent writing, but required a substantial investment of time and money. Still more of both commodities were needed for book-length biographies, where an entire life came under investigation and, if possible, the circle of interviewees was widened.

"If possible": if, that is, the biography deals with someone only recently deceased, and in my books about twentieth-century American writers that has been almost universally the case. McPhee, who likes to diagram his technique, uses X to represent the person he's writing about and O's for "peripheral interviews with people who can shed light on the life and career of X." The more O's, the better: "her friends, or his mother, old teachers, teammates, colleagues, employers, enemies, anybody at all." One benefit of such thorough interviewing, he points out, is that cumulatively "the O's provide triangulation—a way of checking facts one against another, and of eliminating apocrypha" (McPhee, 39). Besides, even misrememberings may lead to enlightenment. Meryle Secrest, in *Shoot the Widow*, advises talking to *everyone*. "Most people will know the obvious facts about your character and that is all. They will give you a garbled version of a certain story. It doesn't matter. The point of the exercise is to hear the tale told over and over until the outlines are as familiar as your own hand and you are alert to the nuances and variations that will appear along the way" (Secrest, 28–29).

The discussion of interviewing that follows is based on my own observations, those of other biographers, and the transcript of an excellent 1982 Authors Guild symposium on "The Art of Interviewing," moderated by Irwin Karp with authors John Brooks, Merle Miller, Lee Hays, Gael Greene, and Martha Weinman Lear participating. How difficult is it to persuade people to sit for an interview? the panel was asked. The easiest thing in the world, according to oral historian Miller, best known for *Plain Speaking*, his book on Harry Truman. Along the same lines, Karp cited A. J. Liebling's comment that "there is almost no circumstance under which an American doesn't like to be interviewed. . . . We are an articulate people, pleased by attention, covetous of being singled out" (Authors Guild, "Interviewing," 13). There are of course exceptions: celebrities wary of the press and a few eccentrics in flight from public view—writers J. D. Salinger and Thomas

Pynchon, for example. But by and large Liebling's observation squared with my experience. Offhand I can think of only one person who simply refused to talk with me: the first wife of Winfield Townley Scott, who remained deeply angered by their divorce. Otherwise, once I'd established *bona fides*— that I was working on a book for such-and-such press, for example—the gates swung open.

As a newspaperman, with deadlines looming, I'd make initial contact by telephone. As a biographer, I wrote letters of inquiry, introducing myself and the project, asking for cooperation, and promising a follow-up telephone call in hopes of arranging a meeting. (That method of approach changed over the decades. Now I start with e-mail.) Almost always these meetings would take place on the interviewees' home ground, both as a convenience to them and as a way for me to understand the territory they inhabited. Sometimes it has been impossible to talk with people face-to-face, and I've had to resort to telephone interviews. But you lose a lot that way: body language and facial expression, for instance.

Once you've landed the interview, it becomes imperative to prepare for it. The reporter's conventional half a dozen questions won't do. You have to know a lot. As John Brooks pointed out, it is foolish "to go in cold. You won't ask the right questions, you won't understand the answers, they won't lead to subsequent questions." Martha Weinman Lear agreed. "I think you have a two-part project going and the first is to know as much as you can about the subject. The second, frequently, is not to show how much you know" (Authors Guild, "Interviewing," 15). Above all, when the interviewee repeats information or reprises a scene you have heard or read about, do not under any circumstances interrupt with "Oh, I know about that"—a remark that may well offend the person you're talking to. It's far better to let him go on, and later, tactfully, steer the conversation in a more productive direction.

The worst thing you can do, as Liebling warned, is to talk too much yourself. Often the best thing is to remain completely silent when there's a pause in the conversation. Most people don't like silence, Lee Hays observed. "Two people in a room are very uncomfortable with it. If you wait long enough, you will get things you never expected to hear." When someone is talking about himself and silence falls, Lear commented, "there is *always* something else that person has to say." Wait, keep quiet, and he or she will say it. Of course, you have to listen hard to what is being said, and—this is important—not let your mind wander ahead to the next question on the list you prepared in advance. "*Really listen*," Hays said, really care about what the person is saying, and you'll come up with a question you never would have thought of no matter how much research you'd done" (Authors Guild, "Interviewing," 19).

Unless it's unavoidable, it is unwise to interview two or more people at the same time. For the Cheever biography, my wife and I stopped to see Robert Penn Warren and Eleanor Clark at their summer home in West Wardsboro, Vermont. We spent a few pleasant hours in their company, but it was a social occasion, not an interview. Besides, husbands and wives have a way of inhibiting each other's comments. When Warren launched on a reminiscence of Cheever, Clark hushed him up with "Oh, never mind, Red. He doesn't want to hear about that." Later, when I went to see John and Jill Ker Conway for my MacLeish book, each of them had work to do, and so, while Jill was in her study, I interviewed John alone, and vice versa. This worked out well. The Conways had come to know the MacLeishes when Archie was teaching at Harvard, and the friendship grew still closer when MacLeish retired from teaching. Archie in his eighties and the much younger Jill used to take long walks together. "Archie fell in love with Jill," John told me, "but since he was thirty years older than me, there was no cause for anxiety" (SD, *MacLeish*, 506). He might not have said that had she been present. Carlos Baker, in the long slog toward his Hemingway biography, traveled to Chicago to see several people who had grown up with Hemingway in nearby Oak Park. But he made the mistake, he told me, of assembling them for a group interview. That would save time, and he hoped the old friends would draw each other out. Instead they backed away from any but the most mundane recollections.

Above all, avoid what Merle Miller called the "absolute disaster" of confrontation. Some beginners, brought up on Mike Wallace and *60 Minutes*, think of interviews as necessarily adversarial. But no, they shouldn't be. "You have to remember who the *star* is," Merle Miller observed. "You are not the star. The person you are interviewing is the star, and he is doing you, or she is doing you, a favor by talking to you" (Authors Guild, "Interviewing," 20). Meryle Secrest went out of her way to establish a friendly atmosphere for such conversations. Interviewing a number of people in or around Paris for her biography of Romaine Brooks, she "learned to arrive on time, wear my very best outfit, smile a lot, agree with everything, always take flowers and follow up with cascades of thanks" (Secrest, 129). This method required a lot of trouble, and a fair amount of insincerity, but it worked.

Secrest also cautioned that "certain questions should never be approached"—questions that ask interviewees to reveal something they would prefer to keep to themselves (Secrest, 205). I found that out the hard way. For my biography of poet Winfield Townley Scott, I naturally got in touch with his sister and sole sibling, Jeannette. She and her husband kindly asked me to dinner at their home, and there—perhaps under the influence of a second glass of wine—I broached a taboo topic. I'd been reading Scott's journal kept during his stay at the MacDowell Colony, and entries therein implied that he'd had a homosexual encounter. So I asked Jeannette if she'd observed any such inclinations in her brother, growing up. This resulted in total silence from host and hostess, a distinct chill in the air, and my early exit.

Unless you have somehow managed to poison the process, it is usually a good idea to follow up on an interview, either by phone call or another face-to-face meeting. Going over your notes, you will almost always realize that there remain important matters you didn't get around to discussing. So after an extended talk with William Maxwell, mostly devoted to his editing Cheever's stories for the *New Yorker*, I called to ask about the Cheevers in the late 1940s, when they were first married and living in New York. At that stage Maxwell volunteered a startling memory of an incident at a party when Cheever had fallen / been pushed from an apartment window—an occurrence that shed light on his difficult and complicated marriage. Such callbacks might be compared to Peter Falk in his "Columbo" trenchcoat, about to leave the suspect's place but turning at the door with the crucial "Oh, one more thing."

Normally you will be conducting interviews with many sources, and deciding which ones to interview first can be surprisingly important. In the early stages of her research for *Dorothy Parker: What Fresh Hell Is This?* (1988), Marion Meade interviewed Budd Schulberg in New York. Schulberg, author of *What Makes Sammy Run?* (1941) and of the screenplay for *On the Waterfront* (1954), had known Parker and her husband, Alan Campbell, in Hollywood when all of them were working as scriptwriters. He turned out to be a good source: "a perfectly pleasant guy with a bad stutter but acute observations and excellent recall." (I had a similar experience interviewing Schulberg for *Fool for Love*, my Fitzgerald biography.)

But Schulberg had made enemies in Hollywood when he "named names" of Communist party members and sympathizers before the House Un-American Activities Committee in 1951. When Meade attempted to interview veterans of the leftist movements in Hollywood who'd been blacklisted in the 1950s, they immediately asked, "Did you talk to Budd?" When she admitted that she had, doors were slammed in her face. Reflecting on that experience in 2012, Meade commented that it would have been wiser "to hold off on contact with Budd until after seeing his enemies. My other choice was to evade or lie, which is what I would do today" (Meade, "Schulberg," 3–4).

Most of the writers in the Authors Guild symposium taped their interviews. John Brooks, however, did not, Gael Greene resisted it, and so have I. Presumably, once you ask if it's all right and turn the recorder on, the subject will forget about it, but some people, Brooks believed, were put off by taping. More importantly, he wanted a conversation in which the subject was talking to him and not to the tape. You might give up word-for-word accuracy in that way, but as Brooks remarked, for "nine out of ten interview subjects, it would be an act of sadism to quote them directly off tape" (Authors Guild, "Interviewing," 17). Few people speak in sentences. Most sound better if you do them the favor of improving their syntax and grammar and of eliminating repetitions and parenthetical digressions. In any event, whether you use a tape or not, you should certainly make notes in addition to alerting yourself to the most significant comments—and as soon as possible thereafter transcribe those scribblings into coherent written form. Some people will try to impose conditions on the interviewer. At one stage or another they will stipulate that what they are about to say must be kept off the record. Or they will insist that they remain anonymous when you quote or paraphrase their remarks. Or they will demand the right to review the text before it goes to press. Whether you agree to such conditions will depend on the balance of power involved. Do you want the interview at any cost? Do they have something to gain by participating? But generally, the Authors Guild writers recommend refusing such conditions.

INTERVIEWEE: "Off the record?"
WRITER: "But surely we can talk with candor, and I will not put you in a bad light."
I: "Anonymity?"
W: "All right, just this once."
I: "Will you let me see what you've written?"
W: "No" whenever you can. (Authors Guild, "Interviewing," 14–15)

Under no circumstances, as Linda Wagner-Martin (who has written biographies of Sylvia Plath and Zelda Fitzgerald) warned, should you *offer* to send drafts or work-in-progress to sources for their approval. If you do that, "you'll be in for trouble" (Wagner-Martin). At most, allow review only for factual inaccuracy.

Which brings up the issue of whether sources can be trusted to tell the truth. The short answer is: not without checking. Oldsters are inclined to forget, younger ones may forget or get it wrong, those of any age may be lying. "The Survivors," Victoria Glendinning observed, "are at once the most valuable sources of information and the least reliable." She has had "spectacular help and gained valuable insights" from colleagues, friends, lovers, housekeepers, secretaries, and distant relatives of her biographical subjects. But survivors may also have "axes to grind, or opinions they want to impress," or feuds with the subject they want to revisit. Their memories may be bad, and often they will "overestimate their significance in someone else's life" (Glendinning, 57–58).

Some survivors won't see you, at least not at first. But keep after them, Deirdre Bair advises. "As time goes by and the book gets written, they'll see that the train is leaving the station, and nine times out of ten, they'll want to jump on." Some won't be forthcoming after consenting to an interview. In rare cases, they even may distort the truth. Carol Sklenicka, biographer of Raymond Carver, suggested a technique for establishing the reliability of sources. "Ask about what you do know, then see if they contradict you or not" (Munker).

As Mark Schorer put it, "the first problem with living witnesses is simply human vanity." Anyone who knows he is to appear in a book will want to appear "to the best advantage." When talking to the biographer he will either "be exasperatingly reticent or . . . dress up the circumstances. Then there are those who wish to be memorialized as having had a more important association with the subject than the facts will support" (Schorer, 224–25). Combine this tendency with the shortcomings of memory, and you enter the realm of the imagined. As Shakespeare wrote of a veteran of the battle of Agincourt,

> Old men forget; yet all shall be forgot,
> But he'll remember with advantages
> What feats he did that day . . .
> (*Henry V*, act 4, scene 3)

You don't have to be doddering to deceive yourself and others. I know of two instances in which my biographical subjects, both poets, led survivors to think of themselves as more closely connected to them emotionally than was the case. Winfield Townley Scott either told or allowed each of *three* different women to think that a love poem he wrote was meant for her alone. Edwin Arlington Robinson celebrated a young girl's charming wide-eyed curiosity in a sonnet. It was inspired by his niece Ruth, the Robinson family was certain. It was inspired by Arvia, the daughter of playwright Percy MacKaye, the MacKaye clan maintained. The poem appears under the title "For Arvia" in his collected poems, favoring the MacKayes' side. Yet it may have been written before Robinson met MacKaye, favoring the family view.

Sources are rarely pleased with the way they are presented in biography. They dislike the words (their words, shined up for company) that have been placed in their mouths, and resent being relegated to minor characters, mentioned only because of their acquaintance/friendship with the figure whose story is being told. E. M. Forster, in *Aspects of the Novel*, wrote about "flat characters" in fiction, invented by the author to enhance understanding of the more thoroughly portrayed major characters in a story or novel. Unlike them, as Janet Malcolm remarked, the flat characters of biography are "actual, three-dimensional people. But the biographer is writing a life not lives, and . . . must cultivate a kind of narcissism on behalf of his subject that blinds him to the full humanity of anyone else" (Malcolm, *Two Lives*, 205–6).

I've customarily consulted the resources of the Oral History Project at Columbia University for my literary biographies, with varying success. Usually, reading through those taped and transcribed interviews resulted in frustration, because of the questions that went unasked. On rare occasions, though, the person being interviewed will deliver a reminiscence of great value. Even then, however, one must keep in mind the fallibility of human memory and/or the interviewee's biases. John Hay and John G. Nicolay began work on their ten-volume biography of Abraham Lincoln immediately after his assassination in 1865, thinking that they would gain a huge advantage through personal conversations with his contemporaries. But, Hay reported, they soon discovered "that no confidence whatever could be placed in the memories of even the most intelligent and most honorable men when it came to narrating their relations with Lincoln" (Garraty, 211).

These problems and complications are exacerbated when the subject of a literary biography is still alive. In 1998 Greg Johnson published *Invisible Writer: A Biography of Joyce Carol Oates*. The book was "really well done," Oates thought, although Johnson's presentation did not entirely square with her own view of herself. "We tend to live our lives without any great sense of pattern or design," she remarked, but reading the biography she realized that Johnson had "invented [her life] to conform" to just such a pattern. He was extracting some things and dropping out others "in order to make up a story": that she was "a sort of Cinderella up from the ashes of upstate New York." The story was plausible enough, "and yet one could argue that it was a completely invented fairytale that my life could be used to exemplify" (McGrath et al., "Real Story," 125).

Much of what is incorrect will be contributed by sources the biographer has contacted, Oates believed. Even if people don't remember too much about you, she said, they will still deliver memories. They don't want to disappoint the interviewer, and "they also don't want not to be in a biography." So they'll "seem to remember some things and if it sounds good" they will go into the biography. But that's "confabulated. It's fiction." As Philip Roth said of a putative biographer, "I make up the stories . . . and now he's going to make up a story about me." Or the source may have an axe to grind. When biographer Bair approached the playwright Samuel Beckett, he said he would neither help nor hinder her efforts beyond introducing her to his friends. His enemies, he added, would find her soon enough. "And they did," she recalled. "I ended up in a psychodrama," James Atlas said of his biography of Saul Bellow. "One idolizes one's literary heroes only to have that idealism subverted by the reality" (Donadio).

The case of the poet Allen Tate (1899–1979) demonstrates the difficulty of presenting an honest account of a figure whose personal behavior was far from exemplary. Tate engaged in a number of extramarital liaisons, for example. In the mid-1960s he sold thirty cubic feet of his papers to Princeton, and almost immediately began to worry about what researchers lacking discretion might do with letters to and from his lovers. Four prospective biographers undertook to tell Tate's story during his lifetime, but all found Tate and each of his wives determined to shut the doors against unseemly revelations. Ned O'Gorman, one of the four, felt that there could be no biography without dealing with Tate's erotic life. "It was not a phase, a period, a flash of libidinous fever," O'Gorman pointed out. It was a persistent pattern that assumed "a fragmenting power" in his marriages and led to "a sundering loss of energy" in his creative life (Underwood, 214). In Thomas A. Underwood's 2003 *Allen Tate: Orphan of the South*, the only biography to appear so far, there is very little discussion of the issue.

Under such circumstances, it is not surprising that most authors discourage biographical treatment during their lifetime. "One *ought* to be left alone while one's alive," Elizabeth Barrett Browning objected after publication of an 1852 volume exposing her most intimate feelings. "The vultures SHOULD wait a little until the carrion is ready" (Millgate, 17). Biographers, too, may profit from dealing with figures safely departed and so unable to object to errors of fact or interpretation. It "is always better to wait until the subject of your biography is dead," Richard Ellmann advised, "since it reduces the possibility of authoritative refutation" (Ellmann, *Codgers*, 6).

Updike marveled at the willingness of his friends Joyce Carol Oates and William Styron to cooperate with biographers (Updike, 31). Styron's case, however, proved to be an exception to the rule: the relationship between biographer (James L. W. West III) and Styron did not turn sour, and resulted in West's first-rate *William Styron: A Life* (1998). He'd begun work on the book thirteen years earlier, after a meeting at Styron's summer home in Martha's Vineyard. "I seem to be working on a biography of you," West said. "If you want me to stop, I will. Otherwise, I'd like to keep going." Styron thought for a few moments before answering. "Why don't you just go ahead?" he said. "I'll be curious to know what you find." That was it: an oral understanding, with no legal documents to back it up. The very casualness of the agreement may have helped to solidify matters. So, surely, did West's repeated visits, two or three times a year. He would tell Styron about "the old girlfriends and schoolmates and fellow writers he'd been interviewing," and these sent Styron off on "flights of recollection."

When the biography was published, Styron seemed pleased with it without actually saying so, and he appeared with West a few times at book signings and on college campuses. The two men kept in touch for the remainder of Styron's life (he died in 2006). The relationship was amicable throughout. "I was lucky, I suppose," West acknowledged: lucky that his subject did not want to or decided not to control the process (West, "Boswell," 446, 448).

It remains to be seen how the biography of Philip Roth will turn out. In 2004 Roth reached a legal agreement granting his friend Ross Miller, the nephew of playwright Arthur Miller and professor of English at the University of Connecticut, full access to his papers as his biographer. Five years later, despite Miller's confidence that he was too far along on his work to face "the doomsday scenario" of Roth withdrawing his support, the arrangement between them was "abandoned by mutual consent." Miller continues to serve as editor of Roth's works for the Library of America, however. In September 2012 Roth signed "a collaborative agreement" along similar lines with Blake Bailey, who has written biographies of Richard Yates, John Cheever, and Charles Jackson (Donadio; McGrath, "Roth").

Roth's reputation has risen rapidly in the twenty-first century, as he has become the American writer most widely regarded as deserving of the Nobel Prize. Over the past three decades or so he has endeavored to shape that reputation through his own writing and that of others. Before announcing in 2013 that he was going to give up writing fiction, Roth was enormously productive as a "dazzling, funny, and audacious" novelist (Lee, *Roth*, foreword). In several of his novels he created as his protagonist a character named Nathan Zuckerman, whose background and capacity for literary gamesmanship closely resembled his own. In *Paternity* (1991) and *The Facts: A Novelist's Autobiography* (1997) he presented his own versions of segments of his life. Another book, to be called *Notes for My Biographer*, was announced in 2012 and has yet to appear (Berlinerblau). He granted cooperation, along with limited access to his papers, to Claudia Roth Pierpont (no relation) for her admiring *Roth Unbound: A Writer and His Books* (2013). The evidence suggests that Philip Roth, a brilliant novelist used to taking charge of the narrative, may well be joining the company of authors attempting in his latter years to shape what others write about him.

THE IMPOSSIBLE CRAFT

The Issue of Involvement

Any biographer who talks about his work in public is certain to be asked whether he liked his subject. So I was asked how *I* felt about Win Scott or Archie MacLeish or EAR, and about Cheever and Hemingway and Fitzgerald, after researching and writing biographies about them. Then, after I'd written about their troubled friendship in *Hemingway vs. Fitzgerald*, the query changed to "which of the two did you like better?"

My tendency has been to dodge such questions, retreating behind the barrier of objectivity. Or to respond with a this-and-then-again-that answer. I would celebrate Hemingway's extraordinary capacity for enjoying life, and deplore the way he cast aside his friends. Or admire Fitzgerald for his ability to put himself in the place of his characters, both male and female, while recognizing how impossible he could sometimes be in social situations. Or say that I was incapable of fantasizing a relationship with an author of great accomplishment. Who was I to imagine an afternoon at the bullfights with Hemingway, or an evening in Hollywood with Fitzgerald?

These naïve questions derive from a desire for instruction. As Victoria Glendinning noted, newspaper reviews of biographies often end "with a personal assessment of the subject, like a character reference," and readers want "to assess, to weigh, to get a picture of a significant person in the context of his times. We like and dislike the people we meet in books as we like and dislike the people we meet in life" (Glendinning, 55). Why not ask the biographer directly and escape the obligation of reading the book?

At the same time, though, they bring up a crucially important matter. "The relation of the biographer to the subject is the very core of the biographical enterprise," Leon Edel observed. "Idealization of the hero or the heroine blinds the writer of lives to the meaning of the materials. Hatred or animosity does the same" (Edel, "Writing," 14). And of course most biographies fall somewhere on the continuum between those poles.

Does it *matter* if the biographer likes the subject? The answer depends on who is asked. "Yes," according to Hermione Lee, author of *Virginia Woolf* (1996). "You have to have emotional [affinity] to do the work." When she completed her biography of Woolf, she felt a sense of bereavement at having to give her author back to the world. Nonsense, according to Peter Ackroyd, who's written about T. S. Eliot among others. "Biography is a job," and like or dislike doesn't really matter. Brenda Maddox, who has written books about D. H. and Frieda Lawrence and Nora Joyce, sides with Ackroyd by way of a telling metaphor. "Does the hunter like the fox?" she asks (Maddox). Maybe so, maybe not, but he or she wants the fox out of hiding.

It is mandatory, though, to begin with a strong interest in, even a fascination with, the person you have chosen to write about. Normally you will be spending several years with your subject—I've averaged about four years each with my biographies—inhabiting his surroundings, tracing the trajectory of his life and career, struggling to understand his way of thinking. It's a long-term commitment. "Above all," Justin Kaplan said, "there has to be an intimate link, not necessarily one of affection or sympathy—Adolf Hitler is an endlessly fascinating subject, as is Richard Nixon—but one of passionate, sustainable interest." Kaplan was lucky to discover such a subject his first time around. After a long literary lunch an editor suggested that he write a biography of Mark Twain. Kaplan said, "I'll do it," quit his "perfectly good editorial job" in New York, and spent the next seven years on *Mr. Clemens and Mark Twain* (1991), which won the Pulitzer Prize (Kaplan, "Culture," 8).

Digging into the particulars of anyone's life inevitably invites disillusionment. As Patricia Spacks put it, "the desire to worship and the desire for intimate knowledge oppose one another." When Boswell reveals Dr. Johnson in all his human imperfection—"scraping bits of orange peel, caressing his cat, losing his temper, fearing death and loneliness, appearing in public wearing shabby clothes and undersized wig, upholding untenable positions, abusing innocent bystanders and insulting Boswell himself"—he makes it impossible to regard Johnson as a saint: "intimate specificity modifies the myth of heroism." It is difficult for the biographer not to pass serial judgments on the subject, as one tracks him or her "across the decades and he or she evolves or changes and disappoints or ascends" (Spacks, 100–101).

As a literary biographer, I cannot conceive of writing the life story of an author without admiration for his or her work. Enthusiasm for the novels or poems or plays usually translates into admiration for their creator, but not always. Jonathan Yardley began (and ended) his biography of Frederick Exley—*Misfit: The Strange Life of Frederick Exley* (1997)—as an admirer of Exley's wonderful memoir/novel *A Fan's Notes* (1968). Yet in the course of learning about Exley's life, Yardley became impatient with the man himself, an alcoholic who died young after wasting much of his talent and who seemed to think that because of that talent the world and everyone in it was obliged to do him favors, financial and otherwise. Yardley finished his book wishing he could telephone Exley at three in the morning and tell him for Christ's sake to grow up. This would have been a singularly appropriate call, since Exley himself was in the habit of telephoning people from one bar or another well after midnight. Yardley had his share of those calls, and so did I, after I'd interviewed Exley for my Cheever biography.

Townsend Ludington suffered through a process of disenchantment when doing biographies of John Dos Passos and Marsden Hartley. After the books were done, he rather wished it had been possible to rearrange the facts to have his subjects meet with premature deaths. In his imagined scenarios, as he told them to Robert Richardson, Dos Passos would have been struck by a truck in New York City before his journey to the political far right, and Hartley would have fallen to his death from a ship before becoming a full-time practicing son-of-a-bitch (Richardson).

Peter Davison, editor and reader of many literary biographies, was struck by how often they revealed serious flaws of character. As a young man Thomas Hardy was sexually excited by the public hanging of criminals; later he "enthusiastically mourned" his first wife in a sequence of poems, although in fact they had not got along at all well. Despite his genuine sympathy for the disadvantaged, George Orwell emerged as "a surly and unpleasant friend." Katherine Anne Porter denounced her close friend Josephine Herbst to the FBI. Of the biographical subjects Davison encountered, only Anton Chekhov seemed to have been "without serious fault or flaw." Yet though easy enough to live with, Chekhov remained "one of the most difficult to understand" (Davison, 94).

Many writers live difficult, prickly lives. It may have something to do with the solitary nature of their work. It's not surprising, then, that their biographers often end as critics rather than supporters. John Updike observed that "Mark Schorer is supposed to have detested Sinclair Lewis by the time he finished his bulky biography of the man, and James Atlas could not have felt much more kindly toward Delmore Schwartz." Perhaps, Updike suggested, we read books that denigrate writers in order to feel superior to them (Updike, 25–26).

At the opposite end of the arena lie those biographies that refuse to acknowledge any failings whatever in their subjects. Such books are written,

Freud believed, by biographers "fixated" on heroes to whom they feel an emotional connection, a "special affection," from the beginning. "They then devote their energies to a task of idealization, aimed at enrolling the great man among the class of their infant models—at reviving in him, perhaps, the child's idea of his father." Biographers so smitten with their subjects smooth over their struggles and tolerate in them "no vestige of weakness or imperfection." Hence they "sacrifice truth to an illusion," and present cold, wooden, impossibly noble figures instead of human beings "to whom we might feel distantly related" (quoted in Ellmann, "Freud," 261–62).

Freud made these observations in 1910, and two generations later Richard Ellmann commented that the modern biographer who had read (or at least absorbed) Freud's ideas was unlikely to become so fixated upon and identified with his subject. In addressing the problem of immersion in one's subject, Douglas Day, author of *Malcolm Lowry: A Biography* (1973), posited a Hegelian three-stage dialectic the biographer should undergo.

Thesis: a strong sense of identification with the subject, sometimes with disastrous consequences. The first biographer of Lowry, Day pointed out, "fell into Lowry's personality" and followed his example by committing suicide. I took that as a cautionary tale, and so far have managed to write books about three suicides—Win Scott, Hemingway, and Charlie Fenton—without doing away with myself. Neither did Diane Middlebrook, although she found that as she delved deep into Anne Sexton's life, the demons that drove Sexton to suicide became the "focus of [her] life as well." One must sympathize but avoid total immersion.

Antithesis: withdrawal in order to see the subject from a distance, but without going so far as to lead to alienation or, even worse, boredom.

Synthesis: "the hard part"—recreating the subject as constructed by external events *and* by the unknowable things about his inner psyche one must seek for anyway. "One must be able to put oneself in the place of the subject," Day said, "both figuratively and literally" (Day; Middlebrook, "Straw," 48).

It has been my experience that if you devote enough time and energy to the task, you *do* eventually begin to inhabit the world your subject occupied. Ideally you should also occupy the *physical* territory for an extended stay: Cheever's Westchester County, Fitzgerald's St. Paul, Hemingway's several stopping places. As for the inner universe, after several years of accumulating information you get up and go to bed each day in the mindset of your subject. Consciously or subconsciously, you begin to identify with him or her. Thomas Underwood, researching his biography of Allen Tate at Princeton's Firestone Library, was startled one day when he looked at the register and saw that someone had signed in as "Allen Tate" and even more astounded to recognize that the signature was in Underwood's own hand-writing (Underwood, 219).

A very odd relationship develops between the writer of a biography and the subject, Millicent Dillon observed. "You find yourself pulled toward the subject, hating the subject, loving the subject, thinking you're the subject" (McGrath et al., "Real," 120–21). There is considerable disagreement about how close this relationship should become. Some commentators advocate as much intimacy as possible, believing with Voltaire that it's "a monstrous piece of charlatanry to pretend to paint a personage with whom you have never lived" (Garraty, 25).

By that standard, only memoir-biographies by family members or close friends would qualify for approval, and they are often both enlightening and moving: Alexandra Styron's and Susan Cheever's reminiscences about their fathers, for example. Yet such books are invariably tilted to concentrate on the particular relationship involved, and to that extent are basically "autobiographical rather than biographical"—two forms that are "intrinsically quite separate," autobiography coming from remembrance and biography from reconstruction (Garraty, 26).

In forging these reconstructions, most biographers write about accomplished figures they have never met. You can't time travel back to Hannibal, Missouri, to strike up an acquaintance with young Sam Clemens. Given this handicap, however, the biographer may either aim for judicious detachment from or emotional involvement with his subject. The British biographer Hugh Kingsmill proposed "the complete sympathy of complete detachment" as an ideal attitude. That sounds like an oxymoron. Yet, Simon Winchester said, he has been able to unite these seemingly contradictory goals in his own biographical writings, for as he disinterestedly gathered data in preparing to tell someone's story, enthusiasm and sympathy for his subject naturally developed (Winchester).

Most biographers would agree that emotional connections are inevitably formed as they investigate and write about their subjects. At the same time, however, they would also maintain that their goal was *objectivity*: assembling the facts and letting the facts speak for themselves. That goal is hard to reach. "You probably don't stay objective through the whole process," Jean Strouse commented. "You have enormous varieties in your relationships with these people, but you hope you ride that out . . . so you're not totally prosecuting or totally sanctifying that person" (Authors Guild, "Falling," 30). Then there are those, like Janet Malcolm, who believe that it's psychologically impossible not to take sides. "The pose of fair-mindedness, the striking of an attitude of detachment can never be more than rhetorical ruses," she declared. "If the writer *actually* didn't care one way or the other how things came out, he would not bestir himself to represent them"

(Malcolm, "Silent," 148). And besides, an entirely objective biography, a mere compendium of facts, would be almost unreadable.

"The matter of distance proves complicated in biography," Spacks observed. The biographical narrator "cannot risk too much coziness," cannot invade the consciousness of the subject with the confident recklessness of a novelistic narrator, cannot claim to know more than can be known, or the reader will rebel. Yet the biographer must know a great deal and get it down on the page. "The reader's trust will depend largely on the narrator's precise control of plausible distance," Spacks wrote, and that strikes me as absolutely right (Spacks, 93). The biographer earns authority by maintaining just such a *plausible distance*.

In an essay on "The Burdens of Biography," Mark Schorer retold an anecdote about James Boswell and Dr. Samuel Johnson. In his obsessive quest for more information, Boswell was blatantly interviewing a third party about Johnson in Johnson's presence. This was too much for Johnson, who "suddenly thundered" at Boswell, "You have but two subjects, yourself and me. I am sick of both." Schorer resurrected that remark following his "nine years' captivity" with Sinclair Lewis as applicable to the way his relationship with Lewis shaped "the substance" of his biography. Not the facts or the themes or the plot, but "the general attitude, the whole coloration, because that was I, or rather, the two of us together" (Schorer, 221, 238–39). The point is, in Paul Murray Kendall's words, that "on the trail of another man the biographer must put up with finding himself at every turn; any biography uneasily shelters an autobiography within it" (Kendall, x). To some degree, you end up writing about yourself in disguise.

The biographer may strive for objectivity with the best will in the world, but the process itself demands subjective decisions. It is necessary, for instance, to select the most significant of the many cold, hard facts he has assembled. As Stanley Weintraub put it in a complicated, complex sentence, the biographer "must regularly intervene among his materials to choose the compelling facts and the evocative details that converge at the angle of perception from which he wants the reader to view his subject." And in so doing, his own ideas and beliefs and emotions become "the subtle subtext of the book" (Weintraub, 42). Helene Moglen, looking back on her biography of Charlotte Brontë, found that while ostensibly searching for the "truth," she was actually pursuing her "own shadow through the beckoning recesses of another's mind" (Spacks, 118).

It is interesting in this connection to consider the role of gender. I have always written about male authors, feeling that it would be far more difficult to understand a female subject. Perhaps so, but sticking within one's own gender undoubtedly invites subjectivity. In an 1989 interview, Victoria Glendinning—who had by that time published biographies of Elizabeth

Bowen, Edith Sitwell, Vita Sackville-West, and Rebecca West—announced that she would "never write a book about a woman again." It was too internal, too navel-gazing. "You are exploring yourself all the time, *because* you can identify. You're comparing, saying 'I couldn't have done this, I could have done this.'" Then, she added, there was the danger of projecting herself into the picture. She'd write paragraphs late at night that seemed to be incredibly insightful, and in the light of day realize that she hadn't really been "writing about Edith or Vita or Rebecca," but about herself (Amanda Smith, 50). Glendinning stuck to her vow, choosing Anthony Trollope, Jonathan Swift, and Leonard Woolf as subjects for subsequent biographies.

Michael Holroyd took the somewhat contrary view that biography involved a two-step process of discovery leading to personal enlightenment. "As he pursues his research and finds out more about his subject, the biographer makes discoveries about himself. Features below the conscious level of his personality emerge, and what they are will depend upon the forces released by the meeting of two lives." This, Holroyd believed, was "a natural evolution in the making of a book," and by no means a bad thing (Holroyd, "How I Fell," 97). Those of us who write and read biographies should recognize that they are necessarily cooperative ventures. Biographers can't do their work, John Sisk observed, "without running the risk of revealing the patterns under their own carpets that help to determine both the subjects they choose and the figures they find" under the subjects' carpets. But that was a risk worth running, he thought. If biographers tried too hard to censor out the autobiographical component, their books would suffer from the strain (Sisk, 456).

Trying to Capture Hemingway

A remarkable number of people have entered the lists, gone on safari, fished the depths in attempts to catch the essence of Ernest Hemingway. He died one of the most famous persons on the planet, and within weeks a couple of slapped-together and highly inaccurate accounts of his life appeared. Books and articles followed from those who presumably knew him best: two wives, two sisters, two sons, his only brother, one long-term companion, and a handful of supposed friends, including one who met him once and once only on a train trip. Several serious biographers, most of them writing out of academic havens, dominated the field for twenty years. Then *The Garden of Eden*, posthumously published in abridged form in 1986, awakened interest in a Hemingway captivated by androgyny and the reversal of gender roles—an author quite unlike his public image as a macho sportsman-warrior. That led to several presentations of this new and different Hemingway, a corrective view largely ignored by the mass media, which in Woody Allen's *Midnight in Paris* (2011) and HBO's *Hemingway and Gellhorn* (2012) persist in depicting and making sport of the legendary masculine Papa.

For several reasons, the figure of Hemingway constitutes an almost irresistible subject for biography. The legend he himself was largely responsible for constructing offers an inviting target for attack, for as Carlos Baker pointed out nearly fifty years ago, he was a "complex and many-sided man," a walking bundle of contradictions. And, most importantly, there's a market for such material, for people remain interested in him and his work. So one after another have sat down at their word processors to have a crack at demythologizing the artist and taming his art. "No one else has understood him yet, but I have the keys, I have the answers, or at least I can come closer than anyone else." It's a form of arrogance, this explaining of greatness. It's also something of a competitive sport, with the more accurate and thoughtful biographers at the top of the standings and the less knowledgeable self-promoters at the bottom.

First of all, the Hemingway biographer must attempt to shunt aside the public persona as he seeks the man behind the mask. We all know about that "Ernest Hemingway." He liked to hunt and fish and fight, he loved the blood sports of boxing and bullfighting, he went to all the wars, he could drink everyone under the table, he loved many women and serially married four of them, he wanted to be champion at whatever he undertook, and incidentally, while he was living this well-publicized life, he wrote some of the twentieth century's greatest fiction. The stereotype is so firmly fixed that it gets in the way of understanding both the writer and his work. Tom Robbins said he "couldn't connect" with Norman Mailer's fiction "because the immense shadow of [Mailer's] public persona interposes itself between me and the page." It was the same with Hemingway, Robbins added, for he too "loom[ed] larger than his sentences" (Geeslin).

Like many another, Leon Edel was acutely aware of the inaccuracy of this public Hemingway, and felt it should be supplanted by his "hidden personal myth," "the reverse of the tapestry," "the figure under the carpet." What was Hemingway saying to us in all his books and all his actions? "A great deal," Edel believed, and "much that is exactly the opposite of what he seems to be saying. A manly man doesn't need to prove his masculinity every moment of the day. Only someone who is troubled with himself and with his role puts up his fists" as often and as belligerently as Hemingway (Edel, "Figure," 26). And why was it, as in one cartoon, that there was a rose in that hairy fist? Had Hemingway shaped his public personality as a shield against his own sensitivity? Various biographers have undertaken to answer questions like these. So far he has eluded his pursuers, guaranteeing that the search will continue.

A. E. Hotchner's *Papa Hemingway: A Personal Memoir* (1966) was the first biographical treatment of Hemingway to command a wide readership. A professional writer himself, Hotchner befriended Hemingway and over time became his traveling and drinking companion. His book is based on those encounters, and does not resemble the conventional cradle-to-grave life story. Hotchner was inclined to magnify his own role and to circulate as fact some of Hemingway's most outrageous yarns—the time, for example, when Ernest supposedly captured pigeons in the Luxembourg Gardens to alleviate starvation. In this respect, Hotchner belonged in the company of those that Martha Gellhorn, Hemingway's third wife, characterized as "apocryphiars" (Junkins, 144–45). He also earned the enmity of Mary Hemingway, Ernest's fourth and final wife, by revealing the great man's descent into depression and paranoia. His readable if not entirely reliable account may have influenced the public's perception of Hemingway more than the work of any other chronicler, with the possible exception of Philip Young.

Young's *Ernest Hemingway* (1952), amended in *Ernest Hemingway: A Reconsideration* (1966), presented a psychological portrait of a man compelled to repeatedly confront danger—a reaction, Young believed, to the severe wounding Hemingway suffered at Fossalta di Piave in the summer of 1918. This interpretation has considerable merit; it helps to account for the extraordinary series of fractures and concussions Hemingway underwent as time and again he demonstrated his bravery in combat and in confrontation with fierce animals. But the argument is less persuasive when applied to Hemingway's writing.

Carlos Baker spent seven years preparing *Ernest Hemingway: A Life Story* (1969), the first and only authorized biography. This groundbreaking book collected a multitude of facts and corrected dozens of errors that had accumulated around the bearded image of Papa Hemingway. Baker had no thesis to advance, hoping to convey his subject's personality through the cataloguing of incident. "If Ernest Hemingway is to be made to live again," he wrote in his foreword, "it must be by virtue of a thousand pictures, both still and moving, a thousand actions in which he was involved, a thousand instances when he wrote or spoke both publicly and privately of those matters that most concerned him" (vii). Baker assembled those thousands of pictures, instances, and comments without overtly directing the reader as to how they should be interpreted. He aimed for objectivity, and largely achieved it. Perhaps too much so—one yearns for guidance, for hints of approbation or blame. Both Mary Hemingway and Malcolm Cowley felt that Baker also failed to communicate Hemingway's tremendous capacity for enjoying life and for conveying that enjoyment to everyone around him. But no one has successfully captured that quality on paper, and Baker's thorough and evenhanded biography remains an essential resource for anyone interested in Hemingway.

My *By Force of Will: The Life and Art of Ernest Hemingway* (1977) had a brief run without becoming a canonical work of Hemingway scholarship. To a certain degree, it was hampered by the approach I took, with each chapter devoted to a single topic: Hemingway and Love, Death, Sport, and so on. This resulted, almost unavoidably, in good chapters, those in which I felt on firm ground with the evidence, and not so good ones, in which my command of the material was shakier.

Another decade would pass until, between 1985 and 1992, five biographers took their turns at understanding Hemingway: Jeffrey Meyers, Peter Griffin, Michael Reynolds, Kenneth S. Lynn, and James R. Mellow. Meyers, who may be the quickest study among all extant biographers, produced *Hemingway: A Biography* in only eighteen months. It's a well-written book, somewhat handicapped by the author's apparent stance of superiority to his subject. When close to completion, Meyers asked fellow biographer Michael Reynolds if he could see the FBI file on Hemingway that Reynolds secured after months of badgering bureaucrats to release it on freedom of information grounds. In a spirit of collegiality, Reynolds copied off several hundred pages (many of them with material blacked out) and sent them along. Soon thereafter the *New York Times* ran a front-page story on the revelations about Hemingway in the FBI records—most of them tracing back to his strong antifascism during the Spanish Civil War—as discovered by biographer Jeffrey Meyers.

Both Reynolds and Griffin embarked on several-volume approaches to a life full of vivid and remarkable events. Griffin finished two of his projected three volumes before his untimely early death. Both *Along with Youth: Hemingway, The Early Years* (1985) and *Less than a Treason: Hemingway in Paris* (1990) earned critical acclaim, particularly from writers. The first book contained five previously unpublished stories from Hemingway's apprentice years and benefited from access to a large number of letters between Hadley and Ernest Hemingway. On occasion Griffin took scenes from the fiction and treated them as fact, an unfortunate habit. On the other hand, he did not let discovery of Hemingway's shortcomings dampen his admiration. He tried to identify with his subject, to recreate his life from the inside—and at his best, he succeeded.

I first met Mike Reynolds at a University of Alabama symposium on Hemingway in the fall of 1976. He and I were the upstarts on a program that featured heavy hitters Alfred Kazin, Philip Young, and Mary Hemingway, and we immediately became friends. Probably it helped that there was no sense of rivalry between us. I'd completed *By Force of Will* before that gathering in Tuscaloosa, and had been advised by Carlos Baker, always generous to aftercomers, to be on the lookout for Reynolds's *Hemingway's First War: The Making of "A Farewell to Arms"* (1976). This young fellow down at North Carolina State, Baker said, has turned up some interesting new material.

Another decade would pass before Reynolds brought out the first of the five-volume Hemingway biography that became his life's work. During that time we corresponded fitfully, occasionally vacationed together, and on two occasions I arranged for him to teach a semester at William and Mary when I was on leave. I also did some editorial vetting of his *The Young Hemingway*. As it happened, that book, Meyers's *Hemingway*, and Griffin's *Along with Youth* all appeared within six months of each other. At the MLA convention in 1986, three of us took turns arguing the merits of these books. Jackson Bryer, as advocate for Meyers, pointed to the *range* of his book, based as it was on Meyers's command of English as well as American literature. George Monteiro, who had known Griffin during his student years, praised his book for its narrative power. But I had the strongest case to make on behalf of Reynolds, for he had dug deeper and harder than the others, unearthing valuable new data, and it showed.

Reynolds loved doing research, and like the distinguished British biographer Richard Holmes (in *Footsteps*, his 1985 book, Holmes describes his travels on the trail of subjects), he made it a priority to see for himself the many places where Hemingway had lived. He found a copy of Hemingway's high school yearbook, misfiled, in the Oak Park school's attic. He uncovered a hotel register for March 1926 in a remote Austrian village, revealing when and for how long Gerald and Sara Murphy and John Dos Passos had come for the winter skiing in the Vorarlberg with Ernest and Hadley. Small matters, perhaps, but highly significant when multiplied.

Reynolds confessed the pleasures of his detective work in the front matter for his first book. He had begun with a question: how closely did Hemingway's account of the Italian retreat from Caporetto in *A Farewell to Arms* square with the historical records of World War I? "As with all good questions," he found, "every answer produced more questions. . . . Friends who knew of my research finally stopped asking me how it was going for fear I would tell them in endless detail. My questions had become an obsession; pursuit was happiness. . . . There have been many electric moments that would seem sentimental or curious in the retelling. Finally, I have had to admit that I can pursue it no further. There are still questions unanswered: it will always be so. Perhaps no good book is ever finished" (Reynolds, *First War*, vii). He was right about that. Sooner or later, you have to quit collecting information and write the damn book.

Reynolds was to spend the time left to him in happy pursuit of the endless questions and writing his five-volume literary biography, which stands as the best and most complete record of a remarkable life: *The Young Hemingway*

(1986), *Hemingway: The Paris Years* (1989), *Hemingway: The American Home-coming* (1992), *Hemingway: The 1930s* (1997), and *Hemingway: The Final Years* (1999). Reynolds finished the last volume in time for the centenary of Hemingway's birth, and died of cancer a year later.

Valuable as they are, Reynolds's volumes differ from each other consider-ably in approach and style. In all of the books, he communicated a sense of the times, using quotations from newspapers and magazines to convey, for example, exactly what was going on in Paris when Hemingway's marriage to Hadley was falling apart. But he became a more accomplished and pro-fessional writer as he went along. The last volume does a brilliant job of tracing the disintegration of Hemingway's marriage to Mary Welsh and the mental and physical illnesses that drove him to suicide. Reynolds profited throughout from the support of his wife, Ann, who despite her painful rheu-matoid arthritis traveled everywhere with him. She functioned as an auxil-iary memory and as an acute observer of personal relationships. If he couldn't summon a name, there she was with it. If he wasn't sure how to interpret something, she'd bring her own sensitivity to bear.

Reynolds was especially worried, early on, by the advance publicity for Kenneth S. Lynn's *Hemingway* (1987). He was afraid that Lynn's long and widely praised book would leave him with nothing left to say, and relieved to find, as it seemed to him, that Lynn was not much interested in EH as a writer (always Reynolds's focus) and instead used the writings to prove his thesis about EH's psychological problems. These problems, Lynn believed, derived largely from Mrs. Hemingway's twinning of Marcelline and Ernest, her first two children, born but a year apart. She dressed both children alike until they were six years old, Ernest in dresses most of the time, and held Marcelline back so that they entered school together.

James R. Mellow's *Hemingway: A Life Without Consequences* (1992), like all of Mellow's work, was handsomely written and presented. The book did not read as persuasively as his earlier biographies of Nathaniel Hawthorne and Gertrude Stein, or his later one of Walker Evans, possibly because Mel-low could not summon a sense of identification with Hemingway and his style of life.

Hemingway was a hard man to feel neutral about, and easy to find fault with. He was often cruel to his friends. He married serially, and did not devote much time and attention to the children of the discarded marriages. In a 1991 essay, Donald Junkins criticized several of his biographers—Philip Young, Carlos Baker, me, Jeffrey Meyers, Kenneth Lynn, and Mike Reyn-olds—as "moralists" projecting "their own shadows onto their subject, cre-ating Hemingway the Bad Guy." As Junkins saw it, we had all failed "to perceive that the dark side of Hemingway's psyche was the vital and neces-sary root house of his creativity, his personality, and his genius" (142). I resisted Junkins's conclusions at first, for I'd tried to eliminate personal disapproval of Hemingway's behavior from *By Force of Will*. But Junkins convincingly documented the various and sometimes "subtly shaped put-downs" (146) of Hemingway in each of the biographies, including mine. Quite unintentionally, without meaning to do so, we all passed judgment on him.

There were plenty of clues to Hemingway's conflicted sexuality in the fiction published during his lifetime, most notably in the male-female role exchanges of Frederic Henry and Catherine Barkley in *A Farewell to Arms* (1929). Not until the gender-bending revelations in *The Garden of Eden* (1986), though, did commentators begin to explore these at length. Four books of the 1990s presented this "new" Hemingway, sharply at odds with the machismo of his public image: Mark Spilka's *Hemingway's Quarrel with Androgyny* (1990), Nancy R. Comley and Robert Scholes's *Hemingway's Genders: Rereading the Hemingway Text* (1994), Carl Eby's *Hemingway's Fetishism: Psychoanalysis and the Mirror of Manhood* (1998), and Debra A. Moddlemog's *Reading Desire: In Pursuit of Ernest Hemingway* (1999). Then in the 2000s two other volumes testified to the long-term effects of sexual inversions stretching across the generations: Valerie Hemingway's *Running with the Bulls: My Years with the Hemingways* (2004) and John Hemingway's *Strange Tribe: A Family Memoir* (2007). Valerie was at one time married to Hemingway's youngest son, Gregory, a transvestite who as "Gloria" died in the Miami women's jail; John was Gregory's son from an earlier marriage. Both books offered sympathetic portraits of Gregory, and *Strange Tribe* used poignant father-son letters to document Gregory's troubled relationship with Ernest.

Two thousand eleven saw the publication of Paula McLain's best-selling *The Paris Wife* and Paul Hendrickson's splendid *Hemingway's Boat*. Each of these books focused on segments of the author's life rather than trying to tell the whole story. McLain's book offered a well-written fictionalized account of the beginning and end of Hemingway's first marriage to Hadley Richardson. Hendrickson's used the author's love for boats and deep-sea fishing as a background against which to explore previously unexamined relationships with figures such as Arnold Samuelson and Walter Houk, and to arrive at a persuasive understanding of Hemingway himself.

Whoever writes the next full-scale Hemingway biography is going to have to take into account his posthumously published work, which in addition to *The Garden of Eden* includes two versions of "the African book," *True at First Light* (1999) and *Under Kilimanjaro* (2005), and two of "the Paris book," *A Moveable Feast* (1964 and 2009), as well as *Islands in the Stream* (1970) and *The Dangerous Summer* (1985). Then there are Hemingway's invaluable letters. Carlos Baker edited a selected edition of these in

1981, a useful resource but representing only a small fraction of the six thousand letters Hemingway wrote. To remedy this situation, the Hemingway Society and Foundation and the Hemingway family have undertaken to print all of the surviving letters. The first two of a projected sixteen volumes of *The Letters of Ernest Hemingway* were published in 2011 and 2013, under the excellent general editorship of Sandra Spanier at Penn State.

These documents mandate future biographers to present a far more complicated Ernest Hemingway than the macho figure in the public eye. Even without such discoveries, though, a biographer launching on a book about Hemingway two generations after Baker's initial venture will necessarily arrive at a different understanding of the writer. As Emerson told us, each age must write its own books. Or, in Stanley Weintraub's formulation, "in biography, there is no last word even if there is no new information. As our fashions in people change, we grind fresh lenses to see them anew" (31).

What this means is that there is not and will not be a *definitive* (a critical catchphrase, often used by reviewers) biography of Hemingway or of anyone else. Attitudes and impressions alter over time. And besides, as Freud warned us, the truth about another human being "is not accessible" (quoted in SD, "Definitive," 93). Forbidding words those, for it is precisely truth and understanding that the biographer sets out to achieve.

Victoria Glendinning confessed her own shortcomings in this regard, finding herself guilty of producing "lies and silences" in her work: silences because of gaps and mysteries that no amount of investigation can clear up (what *happened* to Whitman on his trip to New Orleans?), and lies because of the passion to make sense of what is irreducible to sense. How was she to reconcile Edith Sitwell's view that her mother was cruel, spoiled, scornful, and unloving with her brother Sacheverell's conviction that the same woman was "a vision of loveliness and security, indulgent and comforting" (quoted in SD, "Definitive," 93). Or, closer to home, should we regard Grace Hall Hemingway as an all-American bitch with handles, in her son Ernest's view, or as a wonderfully supportive mother, in his sister Marcelline's? Some puzzles defy solution.

The Mythical Ideal Biographer

Just as there can be no work of biography so splendid and comprehensive, so valid and insightful, so attuned to the past, in harmony with the present, and anticipatory of the future as to merit the term "definitive," neither can we conjure into existence any single *ideal* practitioner of the craft. In his notebooks F. Scott Fitzgerald observed that "there never was a good biography of a good novelist. There couldn't be. He is too many people if he's any good" (quoted in SD, "Definitive," 99). I don't mean to equate biographers with novelists, for they are often very different creatures indeed. Yet Fitzgerald's remark makes sense when applied to the mythical perfect biographer, who—if she were to exist—must manage to be several different people bound up within a single human form.

To begin with, as Mark Schorer discovered during his long confinement with Sinclair Lewis, the literary biographer must begin and end as a *drudge*, a tireless accumulator and organizer of information. In Schorer's case, that meant reading Lewis's "twenty-one novels, all but five of them of small literary worth and some of them almost unbelievably poor," along with his hundred-odd stories, "almost all of them worse than poor." And then reading most of this execrable fiction a second or a third time, in order to arrive at a pattern of the mind that created it. For even if the novels and stories were not autobiographical in the usual sense—and Lewis's were not—they nonetheless coalesced into "an autobiography of the spirit." A single theme emerged in almost all of Lewis's fiction—that of a character trying to escape from some form of confinement. This motif corresponded to Lewis's "frenetic and endless and impossible attempt to escape" from the restrictions of custom and convention and from those he imposed on himself. In arriving at that conclusion, and hence giving his massive biography a coherent form, Schorer segued from the drudge toiling away at his task to the *critic* who arrives at an interpretation of "what is basically there" in the work under examination (Schorer, 232–33).

If you are fortunate or clever enough to commit yourself to "someone in the early stages of rigor mortis" (Kaplan, "Culture," 8), with private papers and any number of friends and family members still on the scene, you have the opportunity and obligation to collect as much intelligence as possible from these sources. But this is not a simple matter, for there will be contrasting and contradictory accounts to resolve. Simply getting the facts right and weighing the reliability of various witnesses can be arduous tasks. Important documents sometimes turn up in improbable locations: Hemingway letters at Knox College and Central Michigan, for instance; reminiscences of Fitzgerald at St. Paul Academy; and even, occasionally, long-forgotten letters in someone's attic we read about in newspaper feature stories. You have to be persistent, to keep mining when the vein seems to have run out and you're only collecting dross. It can be an enervating process.

When Charles A. Fenton completed his study of Hemingway's apprenticeship as a writer, during which he engaged in a highly combative correspondence with the great man, he wrote to Schorer (then still at work on Lewis) in humorous frustration. Were he ever to undertake another biography, Fenton said, the subject would have to meet certain requirements. "He must have been thoroughly anti-social, and absolutely without either friends or enemies; he must have lived his entire life in a single community, preferably in one dwelling place from birth to death; he shall have been a bachelor and childless; and he shall have kept a scrupulous list of all correspondents and all contributions to magazines, books, anthologies, symposiums, and lecture circuits" (SD, *Death*, 71).

Having assembled the data and beginning to make sense of it, the *drudge* and *critic* must undergo another transformation to emerge as an *artist* who can bestir an inert mass of materials into life. In other words, the ideal biographer will know how tell a story. She will have command of all the techniques of fiction short of outright invention, including suspense, foreshadowing, symbolic clustering, alternating peaks and valleys, and above all mixing narrative and description. "ACTION IS CHARACTER," Fitzgerald noted, and he meant the capital letters. The biographer as artist must animate her subject by way of scenes: scene and picture, as Henry James advised, scene and picture. And the action dramatized in those scenes must be both significant and characteristic, in concert with the events and ideas of the subject's own time (SD, "Definitive," 101).

At this stage the *artist* takes on the role of *historian*. Ideally, she will be able to time travel comfortably into the same universe her subject occupied, a journey made possible only by near-total immersion in the past. In extraordinary cases, it can be done. As for instance by Hershel Parker, who invested decades of concentrated study in his two-volume *Herman Melville: A Biography* (1996, 2002). I once heard Parker deliver a paper on Melville and Thomas Powell, a British con man and would-be litterateur, and it was immediately obvious that he was intimately acquainted with these people and with the world they inhabited. Parker knew them as well as if they had been his contemporaries. It was as if they lived down the block (SD, "Definitive," 98).

In addition this model biographer must acquire the persistence of the *investigative reporter*. When Stephen B. Oates, researching his book on Martin Luther King, found that sources were reluctant to talk to him and important documents closed, he had to undergo a personality transformation. "The trouble was, my parents had raised me to be a gentleman. I took 'no' to mean 'no.' Now . . . I had to be aggressive, devoid of shame, and rude if necessary, and I had never to take no for an answer. I was terrible at it. I hated to intrude on other people's privacy, to ask them to remember things that could be painful. Who gave me the right to do that?" (quoted in Weinberg, B16). Who indeed, and yet that sort of imposition on others is part of the job, as every reporter finds out when he must telephone the widow of a suddenly dead spouse to ask how she is feeling and by the way does she have a recent photo of the departed.

A certain callousness is part of the equipment, along with a related determination not to quit when confronted with difficulties. In my own case, it would have been easy to abandon my John Cheever biography when—after I'd done three years of research—his family decided to shut whatever doors they could and threaten legal action. I was tempted to give up (there were other things to do, and I hated making enemies), but with the encouragement of my wife decided to plug ahead. It was the right decision; it would have been wrong, even cowardly, to do otherwise. As Justin Kaplan observed, to write biography "you need oxlike endurance, resignation to the swift passing of time without much to show for it, and the capacity to feed on your own blood when sources run dry." You're committing "a serious act of literature," after all (Kaplan, "Culture," 8). To do the job right, "you must know everything about everything—history, sociology, politics, economics, psychology, religion, popular culture, etc." (Weinberg, B17).

And the most important of these several disciplines is that of psychology. For our hypothetical *drudge-critic-artist-historian-investigative reporter-polymath* must have the empathy and imagination to create a life story about which the subject's ghost might say, "that's as close to me as anybody else could be expected to get" (Davison, 99). That is to say, she must be an amateur *psychologist* capable of putting herself in the neighborhood of someone else's mind. The "real problem" with Lawrance Thompson's uncharitable biography of Robert Frost, according to James M. Cox, was traceable to Thompson's inability to get inside other people's minds (Cox). Discovering Frost to be sometimes cruel, Thompson leaped to the assumption that he was always cruel.

That *psychologist* must also explore the daunting territory of family dynamics. Perhaps, as Jane Austen observed, "nobody who has not been in the interior of a family can say what the difficulties of any individual of that family can be" (quoted in SD, "Definitive," 98). Nonetheless, it is crucially important for the biographer of Ernest Hemingway to try to envision what it was like, say, to grow up the son of a moderately successful suburban physician who loved the outdoors and his musically gifted and domineering wife. Nature as well as nurture combine in this enterprise. "How shall a man escape from his ancestors, or draw off from his veins the black drop which he drew from his father's or his mother's life?" as Emerson rhetorically asked (SD, "Definitive," 98–99).

Jeffrey Meyers, who wrote his Hemingway biography in less than two years, felt that by the end he knew not only Hemingway's tastes and habits but also how he would think and act in any situation. One may doubt the accuracy of Meyers's claim without disparaging the goal he aimed for: an intellectual and psychological empathy so complete as to enable him to occupy the mind and heart of his subject. Leon Edel acknowledged the necessity for undertaking such a quest. "We go beyond the necessary routine [rooting through archives, etc.] into the search for an individual's hidden dreams of himself," he observed. "The biographer who writes the life of his subject's self-concept passes through a façade into the inner house of life." The facade, Edel felt certain, concealed the "secret myth" that lay hidden within every creative life (Edel, "Figure," 32). Phyllis Rose arrived at a similar conclusion in her study of Virginia Woolf. The inner life of a writer "is as much a work of fiction . . . as novels and poems," and it was the task of the literary biographer "to explore this fiction," reveal this "personal mythology" (quoted in Kaplan, "Naked," 46).

In his essay "The Wound and the Bow," Edmund Wilson explored one such explanatory notion: that the creative drive of the writer was related by way of compensation to human weaknesses deriving from a wound or wounds suffered in childhood. In considering this theory, John Updike brought up the case of Franz Kafka.

Any biographer of Kafka, he pointed out, would have to deal "with his insomnia, his unnatural awe of his father, his ambivalence toward his own Jewishness, his inability, until fatally weakened by tuberculosis, to achieve a liaison with a woman—the entire psychological paralysis, in short, dramatized in his superb comedies of modern bafflement." Updike went on to acknowledge the strangeness and mysteries in the lives and works of Melville and Hawthorne. "The vocabularies of psychoanalysis and of literary analysis become increasingly entwined," he concluded, "though we must not forget that these invalids receive our attention because of the truth and poetry and entertainment to be found in their creations. A wound existed, but also a strong bow, and a target was struck" (Updike, 24–25).

As Hermione Lee reminded us, Freud disliked biography in good part because of its tendency to "explain" everything on the basis of a single hidden principle, like Edel's figure under the carpet. Human lives did not lend themselves to "straightforward intelligibility" (Lee, 118). In *Life Histories and Psychobiography* (1984), William McKinley Runyan used the example of Van Gogh to demonstrate the complications behind any one action. We all know about what he did: "Late Sunday evening December 23, 1888, Vincent Van Gogh, then thirty-five years old, cut off the lower half of his left ear and took it to a brothel, where he asked for a prostitute named Rachel and handed the ear to her, requesting that she 'keep this object carefully'" (Runyon, 38). Over the years, Runyon found, various commentators advanced fourteen alternative explanations for this extraordinary act. There's the bullfight analogy, and jealousy of his brother Theo, and homosexual impulses involving Paul Gauguin, and a Christian interpretation in which Van Gogh symbolically repeats the scene at Calvary by "giving the mother surrogate, Rachel, a dead segment of his body" (Runyon, 41). Then, too, he might have acted as a consequence of temporal lobe epilepsy. The explanations vary widely in plausibility, and it may well be, according to the principle of "over-determination," that several of them were motivating Van Gogh when he mutilated himself.

In tackling such conundrums, it is essential to have a lay person's command of psychology. "A biographer, like any other civilized man, should know about the developments of modern psychology," Mark Schorer observed, "but I do not think he should write as if he were a psychoanalyst." Paul Murray Kendall cited some of the differences. Psychoanalysis, he wrote, was about *analysis*: classification, providing names for concepts, the clinical record. "But a biography is not *about* a man's life; it is the simulation of that life in words" (Kendall, 121).

And yet there are striking similarities between the two fields, according to Victoria Glendinning, who was a psychiatric social worker before turning to biography. "Casework, which is a lot of listening and enduring silences and reading between the lines metaphorically and waiting, is exactly what you do in biography—reading a person's work and their letters, trying to listen to them, though they can't talk to you, listening to the witnesses, the survivors, the people who knew them, that same technique of enabling somebody to say the unsayable" (Amanda Smith, 49).

Jay Martin, a biographer as well as a practicing analyst, outlined some of the parallels. Both fields assume that chronology is important, and both are interested in *development* over time, in their separate narratives looking "for the unfolding of meaning through representation and interpretation of development." Both also believe that *all* the material collected, whether through biographical research or extended consultations, is meaningful, and that no single piece of information should be interpreted in isolation. The entire body of research formed "a dynamic web of meaning," in which "any part touched by investigation will cause vibrations of meaning elsewhere." In addition, biographer and psychoanalyst alike realize that their reconstructions of another person, no matter how elaborately detailed, were "not to be thought of as *being*" that person. Instead, they "correspond" to his history, "represent" the structure of his past, "imitate" the story of his development. Both operate "in the realm of interpretation, where 'fictions'— probable truths—predominate" (Martin, 328–29, 337).

And of course there are differences as well. The psychoanalyst has the advantage of regular meetings with a patient, often over a considerable period of time, and of the opportunity to form a collaborative relationship in the search for data and its interpretation. The literary biographer, on the other hand, has several advantages of his own: an entire life to examine, a wealth of outside sources to consult, and the creative work to draw upon. As psychiatrist John Cody, author of *After Great Pain: The Inner Life of Emily*

Dickinson (1971), observed, "Emily Dickinson, surely, possessed a greater capacity for the perception and discrimination of psychological processes and a greater ability to find appropriate words to express her inner experiences than any patient who has ever been psychoanalyzed" (quoted in Runyon, 205).

Perhaps the worst mistake the biographer-as-amateur-psychologist can make is to fix upon a particular theory and let it take over the process of interpreting a subject's life. A friend of Mark Schorer alerted him to what she called "the Pollyanna Paranoid": someone who conceives of an impossibly wonderful future and feels betrayed when it does not develop. That concept, Schorer thought, would have explained a lot about Sinclair Lewis, but probably it was just as well that he became aware of it after he'd finished his biography (Schorer, 237). As Richard Ellmann, biographer of James Joyce, commented, relying on "certain patterns made available by psychoanalysis may have a blurring effect." He took Freud's idea of the anal erotic as an example. That particular character trait, Ellmann said, could easily be attributed to Ernest Hemingway, who "unlike his prodigal friend Fitzgerald was always gathering, absorbing, hoarding, withholding." In his writing Hemingway used language sparingly, and took pride in what he left out. In life he coveted his secrets, saved almost every scrap of paper, and discoursed on the benefits of deprivation. "Though he wanted to be known as swashbuckling," Ellmann concluded, "his strength came from self-concealment."

This interpretation makes a certain degree of sense, and an unwary biographer might be inclined to let it dominate—and so, in effect, replace—his thinking. But Ellmann added a warning. Wasn't it odd that anal eroticism applied both to Hemingway and, as Edmund Wilson asserted, to Ben Jonson as well, a very different kind of writer? Could it be that this particular character trait was "pretty general" among writers? And simply advancing the concept was liable to do damage, for *one thing was sure*: "the daring innovation in style of Hemingway, its fanatical economy, like the humor and lyricism of Ben Jonson, may be disparaged by offering it in the context of anal eroticism" (Ellmann, "Freud and Literary Biography," 267).

I should not leave this topic without confessing my own susceptibility to psychoanalytic concepts applicable to Hemingway. In preparing to write *By Force of Will* I had arrived at a more or less comprehensive view of his personality, without reference to any of the psychological studies about him. That view was reflected in my working title for the book: "Hemingway: The Man Who Would Be Master." It struck me that Hemingway set out to master, to become expert at, every enterprise that interested him. Moreover, he felt compelled to discourse on this knowledge to others, instructing Dorothy Parker, for instance, in the intricacies of six-day bike racing. This was as true of fishing and drinking, boxing and bullfighting, love and war, as it was of writing itself. And of course this drive had to end in defeat and depression, for no one could achieve that kind of universal mastery.

Then, nearing the end of my labors on the Hemingway biography, I happened to read a psychological interpretation that comported with this pattern. The argument, by Irvin D. and Marilyn Yalom, held that Hemingway created for himself an idealized self-image impossible of achievement: that of master of all he surveyed. Such grandiose self-images were characteristic in children who met lack of acceptance from their parents, the Yaloms pointed out. The theory agreed so well with my own conclusions that I used it in the chapter on Mastery.

> Ernest sought to transfer to his idealized self those same . . . attributes which, in a May 1950 letter, he assigned to his "God." That marvelous personage, he wrote, had painted many wonderful pictures and written some excellent books and fought Napoleon's most effective rearguard actions and cured yellow fever and sired Citation. He was the best god-damned God anyone had ever known. Above all, he was incredibly independent, sufficient unto himself. He was, in short, such a creature as never . . . lived, and therein lay Hemingway's downfall. The godhead he aimed for eluded him forever. (SD, *Force*, 260–61)

Perhaps I was unwise to adopt the Yaloms' concept so eagerly. It was true that they spoke from positions of authority, their 1971 article having appeared in the *Archives of General Psychiatry*. And they went on to fashion distinguished careers, Irvin as an existential psychiatrist, his wife Marilyn as a professor of comparative literature, and both of them as writers. Yet I knew—they made it clear—that they were basing their interpretation of Hemingway's personality not on firsthand evidence but largely on the testimony of General C. T. (Buck) Lanham and on letters he exchanged with Hemingway. Lanham commanded the regiment Hemingway attached himself to as a war correspondent during some of the fiercest fighting of World War II, and the two men became friends. Lanham thought of Hemingway as the bravest man he'd ever seen under fire, yet was disturbed by his habit of blatantly elaborating on the truth when he described his wartime exploits. The Hemingway he'd come to know during the battle of the Hürtgenwald in the summer of 1944, a courageous man with a sound military mind, was beyond reproach. Why, Lanham wondered, had Hemingway felt the need to inflate himself?

That seemed to me a splendid example of acting out to meet the impossibly high standards of the idealized self-image the Yaloms posited. No heights Hemingway reached satisfied him; he constantly set the bar higher.

And his actual admirable bravery in combat fit into a related psychological pattern: what Otto Fenichel called the "counter-phobic attitude." The counter-phobic person, instead of fleeing the sources of fear, actively seeks them out instead in the hope of overcoming the fear. In boyhood Hemingway loudly announced himself "'fraid of nothing," a declaration that his mother noted in her scrapbook. Yet in "Three Shots," the opening section deleted from "Indian Camp," the first story in his first book (*In Our Time*), Hemingway depicted the boy Nick Adams—the character who most resembles his creator—as succumbing to fear of the dark and the unknown. It followed that he had to obliterate that weakness, to prove himself under duress. After the trauma of his wounding in World War I, Hemingway repeatedly placed himself in dangerously confrontational situations: in the Spanish Civil War as well as World War II, in hunting wild animals in the African bush, in fistfights and other compulsive competitions for dominance. He paid the price in an astounding series of concussions and broken limbs. He could not entirely do away with the fears attendant on every human being, of course. The goal—the idealized self he sought—was beyond achieving.

I didn't become aware of the concept of counter-phobia until I was working on my memoir-biography of Charlie Fenton, thirty-five years after *By Force of Will*. But if I had known about it, it would have found its way into that earlier book as a plausible way of understanding a lot—by no means all—about Hemingway. Psychological concepts like the idealized self-image and the counter-phobic personality do not, by themselves, prove anything. (I make no case at all for anal eroticism.) Moreover, anyone in the grip of such apparently authoritative ideas must be wary of distorting or ignoring evidence that contradicts them. Yet such concepts can help biographers organize mountains of information as they try to assemble what groups together into an approximation of the truth.

What Biography Can't Do

"On Friday noon, July the twentieth, 1714, the finest bridge in all Peru broke and precipitated five travelers into the gulf below" (Wilder, *Bridge*, 15). So begins Thornton Wilder's Pulitzer Prize–winning *The Bridge of San Luis Rey* (1927), a novel that has a great deal to say to all of us, and more to would-be practitioners of the craft of biography. Brother Juniper, a Franciscan friar only recently arrived in Peru, happens to observe this terrible incident—he was waiting his turn to cross the bridge—and seizes upon it as a test case by which to justify the ways of God to man. He knows in advance the conclusions he will reach, seeing "in the same accident the wicked visited by destruction and the good called early to Heaven." He devotes six years to collecting every scrap of information he can about the five who lost their lives. He knocks on all the doors in Lima, asks thousands of questions, fills scores of notebooks. "Everyone knew that he was working on some sort of memorial . . . and everyone was very helpful and misleading" (Wilder, *Bridge*, 20–22).

The longer he works, the more confused and confounded Brother Juniper becomes, feeling as if he were "stumbling about among great dim intimations." People keep supplying him with contrary comments.

> The Marquesa de Montemayor's cook told him that she lived almost entirely on rice, fish and a little fruit and Brother Juniper put it down on the chance that it would some day reveal a spiritual trait. Don Rubío said of her that she used to appear at his receptions without invitation in order to steal the spoons. A midwife on the edge of the town declared that Doña María called upon her with morbid questions until she had been obliged to order her away from the door like a beggar. The bookseller of the town reported that she was one of the three most cultivated persons in Lima. Her farmer's wife declared that she was absent-minded, but compact of goodness.

"The art of biography," the narrator drily remarks, "is more difficult than is generally supposed" (Wilder, *Bridge*, 217–18).

Hampered by his assumption that the disastrous deaths must have fit into God's plan, Brother Juniper never discovers "the secret passions" driving Doña María's life and those of the other victims. Then, lest we rely too much on the manifestly perceptive narrator, Wilder has him issue his own caveat. "And I, who claim to know so much more [than Brother Juniper], isn't it possible that even I have missed the very spring within the spring?" (Wilder, *Bridge*, 23).

This theme of epistemological uncertainty, a conviction that we cannot fully understand other people, runs through all of Wilder's writing. But as a sensitive and acute guide he steered us toward understanding in his fiction, and he believed that biographers too had an obligation to grasp for the ineffable, " to extract from the data of life the savor of personality, the shades of a soul, the image of a vital energy." In quest of such intangibles, we do the research, accumulate the facts, look for patterns, and impose a kind of order on "the loose threads, the chaotic lurching, the random choices, and the unwanted compulsions" that make up most lives (e-mail, Niven to SD, 4 February 2011). What we're searching for—what the reader may demand— is coherence, structure: a life that makes sense on the page, never mind if it did so in actuality.

"There is no life that can be recaptured wholly," the protagonist observes in *Dubin's Lives* (1979), Bernard Malamud's novel about a biographer. "Which is to say that all biography is ultimately fiction. What does that tell you about the nature of life, and does one really want to know?" (quoted in Kaplan, "Pursuit," 24). Well, yes, "one" does, if a biographer, and of course it matters tremendously what one's own personal propensities may be. If, as Wilder thought, "we cannot know others or ourselves," we had better begin with ourselves, in concert with the sensible prerequisite of psychoanalysis that the professional undergo analysis before treating anyone else.

At its core, writing a biography is necessarily a subjective process. "If you put two biographers down in front of exactly the same archive and they spent five years reading through it, they would write very different books," Jean Strouse said. "Biography is an imaginative interaction between the writer and the subject" (Authors Guild, "Falling," 29). The course of that interaction will vary widely according to the writer's personality, for in relating someone else's life he is always, to some extent, writing about his own as well.

So, in my case, it mattered to the books I wrote about them that I identified with Fitzgerald's need for approval and insecurity about social status, and did not share Hemingway's passion for blood sports and compulsion to prove himself in dangerous situations. And surely it was far easier to imagine how it might have been for Fitzgerald as a spoiled, cocky, and not particularly popular adolescent at St. Paul Academy when a generation later (and sharing some of Fitzgerald's boyhood traits) I attended Blake School, SPA's rival college preparatory boys' school across the Mississippi in Minneapolis. I even fantasized that my mother, who was Fitzgerald's age and went to St. Paul Central High School, like several of his youthful friends, might have met and danced with him in her youth. But neither these real or imagined connections in Fitzgerald's case nor the lack of them in Hemingway's (though he too grew up in a midwestern middle-class environment) mattered nearly as much as the admiration I began and ended with for the literary accomplishments of both men. It was the legacy of the remarkable work they did that drove me to undertake their life stories, as well as those of such disparate authors as Winfield Townley Scott, John Cheever, Archibald MacLeish, and Edwin Arlington Robinson.

How accurately did I recount their lives? The best—the only—answer is: as well as I could. Like John Garraty, I know that "the average man is so contradictory and complicated that by selecting evidence carefully, a biographer can 'prove' that his subject is almost anything" (Garraty, 12). And yet there are those in the field who believe that by long perseverance and judicious exercise of their powers they can bring their subjects to life.

Leon Edel acknowledged the difficulties of the task but was persuaded that the biographer as artist might still succeed. Edel quoted Robert Louis

Stevenson on the differences between life and art: "Life is monstrous, infinite, illogical, abrupt and poignant; a work of art, in comparison, is neat, finite, self-contained, rational, flowing and emasculate. Life imposes by brute energy, like inarticulate thunder; art catches the ear, among the far louder noises of experience, like an air artificially made by a discreet musician." As applied to biography, Edel observed, this meant that "a writer of lives must extract individuals from their chaos yet create an illusion that they are in the midst of life—in the way [switching the metaphor from music to visual art] that a painter arrives at an approximation of a familiar visage on canvas" (Edel, *Writing*, 15).

In her *Virginia Woolf's Nose* (2007), Hermione Lee celebrated such pictorial moments. "What makes biography so endlessly absorbing," she wrote,

> is that through all the documents and letters and witnesses, the conflicting opinions and partial memories and fictionalized versions, we keep catching sight of a real body, a physical life: young Dickens coming quickly into a room, sprightly, long-haired, bright-eyed, dandyish, in a crimson velvet waistcoat or tartan trousers; . . . Joyce with a black felt hat, thick glasses and a cigar, sitting in Sylvia Beach's bookshop; Edith Wharton and Henry James, veiled and hatted, tucked up comfortably in the back of the Panhard behind the chauffeur, exchanging impressions as they zoom along the empty French roads. (Lee, 2–3)

Through the raw material of words, then, the biographer must become a creator, "the dustman reassembling the dust, the God of Genesis breathing life into a few handfuls of earth." Over several years, he shapes and selects and reorders the evidence of "tapes and letters, discarded drafts and manuscripts, directives and memos, testaments and check stubs, the feel of names and places revisited, people known perhaps still among the living, words transcribed, written, uttered" until a figure "begins to live again in our imagination" (Mariani, 133–34). And we can *see* him as he was, or might have been. The quotations are from Paul Mariani, who felt he'd come close to this goal in his biography of William Carlos Williams.

Most successful biographers, Mariani thought, experience a "moment of light," a sort of epiphany when the inner life of their subject is suddenly revealed and they apprehend clearly what had previously been blurred and shadowy. He had had such a moment of revelation when he saw "how central the myth of success through repeated failures" had been for Dr. Williams, Mariani wrote. The most rewarding of confirmations of that insight came from Williams's younger son. "Reading your biography," he wrote Mariani, "I can remember Dad's conversations over the dinner table. You brought them back to me. Apparently you were there too" (Mariani, 139, 142). That was heady praise indeed, considering the source.

As against such optimistic views on the potential of biography to summon up an accurate picture of its subject, there stands an impressive assembly of critics—and biographers—who doubt the veracity of such portraits. We say that after fifty, or forty, or sixty, people get the face they deserve. The assumption is that the saintly person's visage will shine with beauty and health while the sinner's turns dark and ugly. But we know from experience that the scoundrel may keep his youthful appearance, as the ravages of age are visited upon the virtuous. Consider the case of Dorian Gray. In the drive to impose order on chaos, organize the clutter, make sense of evidence that resists apprehension, are we not susceptible to imagined epiphanies of the kind that came to Mariani? Would the same "moment of light" shine for another equally intelligent and devoted biographer? Shouldn't we agree with Roland Barthes, who called biography "a novel that dare not speak its name"? (quoted in Davison, 92).

Virginia Woolf posed a frustrated query when embarking on her biography of Roger Fry. "How can one make a life out of six cardboard boxes full of tailors' bills, love letters and old picture postcards?" (quoted in Edel, *Figure*, 19). Also from Woolf: "there are three rules for writing biography, but unfortunately no one knows what they are." And: "yes, writing lives is the devil!" (quoted in Edel, *Writing*, 17).

In her 1939 essay "A Sketch of the Past," Woolf focused on a particular problem. It was extremely difficult to give any account of a "person to whom things happen," she observed, because that person—any person—was "immensely complicated." As an example, she cited her own childhood feelings about looking at herself in a mirror. She only did it when she was alone. She was ashamed of it. "A strong feeling of guilt seemed naturally attached to it." Why was this so? she asked herself half a century later.

The answers were various and inconclusive. She and her sister Vanessa were tomboys who scrambled over rocks, climbed trees, and didn't care about clothes. It may be, she speculated, that looking in the glass violated their tomboy code. But her problem went deeper, she thought. The women in her family were famous for their beauty, she took pride and pleasure in that, and still she could not gaze upon an image of herself without shame. What gave her that feeling unless it were that she'd inherited "some opposite instinct" from her father, who was "spartan, ascetic, puritanical," or her grandfather, "who once smoked a cigar, liked it, and so threw his cigar away and never smoked another." Also, very likely, she "must have been ashamed or afraid" of her own body. Once when she was "very small" a male visitor stood her up on a slab and began to explore her body. She hoped he would stop, squirmed and wriggled, and resented it when he touched her private parts. That must have been "instinctive," she concluded, deriving from instincts "acquired by thousands of ancestresses in the past."

This was a relatively simple matter, Woolf pointed out. She'd tried to explain why she was ashamed of looking at her own face and offered some possible reasons. But there may have been others, she knew. And she was working from the misleading source of memory, while "the things one does not remember" might be even more important. Woolf did not suppose, in other words, that she'd got at the truth. What was the likelihood of arriving at that goal when dealing not with oneself but with another person entirely? Any one human being, she believed, could have "as many as a thousand selves" (Woolf, "Sketch," 64–65, 68–69).

Victoria Glendinning proposed a nursery tale as a comedic example of the conundrums confronting the biographer.

> Little Miss Muffet sat on a tuffet
> Eating her curds and whey.
> Along came a spider
> Who sat down beside her
> And frightened Miss Muffet away.

This incident, which surely would interest a biographer of Miss Muffet, seems to be related from her point of view, hence raising "the problem of perspective." In other words, Glendinning asks, "are you going to write someone's life as it appeared to that person" or take into account the perceptions of others? And if the latter, what about the Spider: "what was his record, what were his real intentions, and did it all happen just as Miss Muffet said?"

You could so go on from there to puzzle out some of the archaic language. Curds and whey mean cottage cheese, but is a tuffet a three-legged stool, as some say, or "a little grassy bump big enough to sit on," according to others? Surely it is important to know what *kind* of a spider made so bold as to sit down next to the little girl. A more or less harmless specimen, or a black widow, a tarantula, a brown recluse? If possible, we should try to find out whether our spider was gratified or disturbed by Miss Muffet's rejection of his company. Digging into the past, what can we make of the interesting fact that Miss Muffet's apparent father was a British entomologist who died in 1604? What credence should be given to the idea, generally dismissed by Mother Goose scholars, that the rhyme is really about Mary Queen of Scots' fear of the Scottish religious reformer John Knox?

This is "a silly example," but it illustrates how some of the biographer's difficulties "are readily observable in the transactions of everyday life." If a group of friends attend the same party, and all agree to write down afterwards what happened at the party, Glendinning points out, "the accounts will all be quite different. Each person will have had his own encounters and experiences, besides which each person has different attitudes, perceptions and prejudices. Also, most importantly, not everyone will tell the truth about what happened or did not happen to them that evening." Alternatively, consider what happens when a married couple breaks up. Listening to each in turn "pouring out his or her dissatisfaction and resentment, the listener often just cannot put the two stories together," and may even arrive at an interpretation that both interested parties would reject. "Is the story of your life what happens to you, or what you feel happens to you, or what observers see happening to you?" she asks, leaving the question open for us to chew upon (Glendinning, "Lies," 50–52).

Craig Brown's *Hello Goodbye Hello* (2012), a book that recreates 101 actual "remarkable meetings" of famous people, testifies to the unreliability of witnesses. Often Brown ran across varying accounts of such encounters and was reduced to siding "with the most likely" among the alternatives. Meetings at parties were especially likely to be remembered differently, he found, for they were "subject to the vagaries of memory and further obscured by layers of gossip and hearsay and inaudibility, the whole mix invariably transformed even more by alcohol." James Joyce and Marcel Proust, for example, met at a Paris dinner party that lasted well past midnight. (Picasso and Stravinsky were also in attendance.) Brown came across seven versions of that encounter between literary lions. Among these, Joyce's recollection—he'd been drunk on arrival, according to Brown—is perhaps the most entertaining. "Our talk consisted entirely of the word 'No.' Proust asked me if I knew the Duc de so-and-so. I said "No." Our hostess asked Proust if he had read such and such a piece of 'Ulysses.' Proust said, 'No.' And so on" (Kakutani).

In *Flaubert's Parrot* (1984), the novelist Julian Barnes addresses such issues directly, even brilliantly. Barnes is no friend of biographies, especially those of creative writers. They tend to tidy things up, he thinks, and cannot be trusted to convey the way their subjects lived. "There's never a chapter called 'The Boring Bit,'" he observed in a BBC interview: never an account of the subject rising late one day, having toast and a soft-boiled egg for breakfast, watching a soccer match in the afternoon. Instead of recording everyday life, the biographer concentrates on the exceptional times-those are the ones that people remember, after all. Barnes's remark struck home with me, for one reviewer of my Cheever biography roundly—and rightly—criticized me for recording in detail one such banal day.

Flaubert's Parrot demonstrates the futility of the craft of biography in several ways. The novel was apparently inspired by Barnes's reading of Jean-Paul Sartre's massive *The Family Idiot: Gustave Flaubert, 1821–1857*, the first volume of which was published in English translation in 1982. Barnes wrote a review of that book, calling it "admirable but mad. . . . A work of elucidation couched in a lazily dense style; a biography seemingly concerned with externals but in fact spun from inside the biographer like a spider's thread; a critical study which exceeds in wordage all the major works of its subject put together." On the very first page, Sartre asked, "What, at this point in time, can we know about a man?" His answer: quite a lot, once we abandon the traditional academic approach—"the search for documentation, the sifting of evidence, the balancing of contradictory opinions, the cautious hypothesis, the modestly tentative conclusion"—in favor of Marxist analysis of the social background, Freudian analysis of the personality, and "free-wheeling imaginative hypotheses" to fill in the gaps (Barnes, "Double," 22).

On the surface, Flaubert seems an unlikely subject for biographical examination. The author of *Madame Bovary* maintained that the writer's text was everything and his personality of no importance whatever. "The artist," he declared, "must manage to make posterity believe that he never existed." Flaubert's ultimate goal was to write a book about nothing (making him, by the way, predictive of the 1990s' *Seinfeld*, which Jerry Seinfeld and Jason Alexander pitch as a television show "about nothing"). Despite or perhaps because of such statements, however, posterity continues to search for clues and divert itself with fantasies and surmises about the author and his characters (Barnes, *Parrot*, 86).

No one searches with more diligence and dedication than Geoffrey Braithwaite, the protagonist of *Flaubert's Parrot*. Braithwaite is a retired doctor who travels around France accumulating facts, facts, and more facts to give body to Flaubert's ethereal spirit. In his obsessive quest for minutiae, no detail is too trivial to escape his attention. He attempts, for example, to establish the exact dimensions of the closed cab in which Léon Dupuis seduced Emma Bovary, concluding that theirs must have been a crowded and awkward copulation.

The book begins and ends with Braithwaite's account of his search for the actual stuffed parrot that sat on Flaubert's desk while he was writing "A Simple Heart." That novella tells the story of Félicité, a Norman peasant woman who serves her mistress and her family for fifty years, selflessly giving of herself and receiving nothing in return. Finally the servant has only her parrot, Loulou, to love. When Loulou dies, Félicité has her stuffed. As her own death approaches, she confuses the parrot with the dove that symbolizes the Holy Ghost. "[A]s she breathed her final breath she thought she saw, as the heavens opened for her, a gigantic parrot hovering over her head" (Barnes, *Parrot*, 17).

Braithwaite, on the trail, discovers that two museums—one in Rouen, where Flaubert grew up, and the other in Croisset, where he spent his last years—have each placed on exhibit a stuffed parrot identified as the one that once occupied a place on Flaubert's desk. Braithwaite, determined to find the truth, spends two years trying "to solve The Case of the Stuffed Parrot." The letters he writes to Flaubert experts yield no useful information. Some of them are not even answered. "Anyone would have thought I was a crank," Braithwaite by way of Barnes reflects, "a senile amateur scholar hooked on trivia and pathetically trying to make a name for himself. . . . One of the academics to whom I wrote even suggested that the matter wasn't really of any interest at all" (Barnes, *Parrot*, 180, 182). Imagine that!

Alas, after his two-year quest, Braithwaite finds that neither the parrot on exhibit in Rouen nor the one in Croisset can be authenticated as Flaubert's. Both of them had been borrowed by the provincial museums from the Museum of Natural History, and that museum had fifty stuffed parrots in its reserve collection. "Une cinquantaine de perroquets!" The one that found its way to and from Flaubert's desk might have been any one of them. Such are the trials confronting the dedicated researcher.

Obsessed though Braithwaite may have been with Gustave Flaubert, Barnes nonetheless makes him spokesman for his own reservations about biography. "Why does the writing make us chase the writer? Why can't we leave well enough alone?" Braithwaite asks. And he makes a sorry example of Sartre's *The Family Idiot*—the title a reference to the attack of epilepsy that struck Flaubert at twenty-three and led to his being thereafter invalided, the "hermit of Croisset," free to write his fiction and escape obligations. "Look what happened to Flaubert," Braithwaite comments. "A century after his death Sartre, like some brawny, desperate lifeguard, spent ten years beating on his chest and blowing into his mouth; ten years trying to yank him back to consciousness, just so that he could sit him up on the sands and tell him exactly what he thought of him" (Barnes, *Parrot*, 12, 86).

In other passages, too, Braithwaite holds forth on the shortcomings of the biographical enterprise. He elaborates on this argument by way of metaphor.

> You can define a net in one of two ways, depending on your point of view. Normally, you would say that it is a meshed instrument designed to catch fish. But you could, with no great injury to logic, reverse the image and define a net as a jocular lexicographer once did: he called it a collection of holes tied together by string.
>
> You can do the same with a biography. The trawling net fills, then the biographer hauls it in, sorts, throws back, stores, fillets and sells. Yet consider what he doesn't catch: there is always far more of that. The biography stands, fat and worthy-burgherish on the shelf, boastful and sedate: a shilling life will give you all

the facts, a ten-pound one all the hypotheses as well. But think of everything that got away, that fled with the last deathbed exhalation of the biographee.

Attempting to seize the past, Braithwaite concludes, was like trying to grasp a piglet smeared with grease (Barnes, *Parrot*, 38, 14).

Flaubert's Parrot is by no means solely a disquisition on biography. Written with wit and brio, it qualifies as "high literary entertainment." As Peter Brooks observed in his review, Barnes presents "a kind of collage, pasted up from a multitude of quotations from Flaubert, 'facts' from his life (often at odds with one another), literary-critical excursuses, an examination paper for Flaubert students, [and] an imagined version of [his] famous love affair told from the point of view of Louise Colet, a Romantic poet of too many words and too familiar sentiments" (Brooks).

Among the more interesting departures from straightforward narrative is the list of animals Flaubert compared himself to during the forty years from 1841 to 1880. The bear predominates. Flaubert kept a bearskin rug in his study. He spoke of himself as a stubborn bear, a mangy bear, even a stuffed bear, and—in the last year of his life—he wrote that he was still "roaring as loudly as any bear in a cave." But there are many other creatures in "The Flaubert Bestiary" as painstakingly compiled by Braithwaite. Flaubert resembles a lion, a tiger, a boa constrictor, an ox, a bittern, an elephant, a whale, an oyster or a snail in his shell, a hedgehog, a lizard, a warbler, a cow, a donkey, a porpoise, a mule, a rhino, a gorilla (Barnes, *Parrot*, 50–51).

In this chapter, too, there is a section on dogs and their place in Flaubert's life: *The Dog Romantic, The Dog Practical, The Dog Figurative, The Dog Drowned and the Dog Fantastical.* "What happened to the dog is not recorded," the narrator observes after each anecdote. And at the end, set off in a paragraph all its own: "What happened to the truth is not recorded" (Barnes, *Parrot*, 60–65).

Barnes has said that he does not think he could write a biography. In his skeptical fashion, he would presumably distrust himself at every turn. A number of professional biographers are inclined to the same view of their enterprise. In her early (and to my mind her best) book, *Psychoanalysis: The Impossible Profession* (1981), Janet Malcolm reached the disturbing conviction that all personal relations were "tragic" because "we cannot know each other," cannot see each other plain. "'Only connect,' E. M. Forster proposed. 'Only we can't,' the psychoanalyst knows." She'd learned as much from her own analysis (Malcolm, *Psychoanalysis*, 6).

Later, in her exploration of the lives of Gertrude Stein and Alice B. Toklas, Malcolm extended the point to take in the instability of all human knowledge. "Almost everything we know we know incompletely at best. And almost nothing we are told remains the same when retold" (Malcolm, *Two Lives*, 186). After ten years of working on his biography of Saul Bellow, James Atlas drove up to Bellow's house in Vermont. "So tell me," Bellow said, "what have you learned?" Atlas said, "What I've learned is that you can't know anyone" (quoted in McGrath et al., "Real," 126). Citing Einstein, Heisenberg, and Whitehead, Hemingway biographer Michael Reynolds pointed out that reality itself was "variable, multiple, and ultimately unknowable" (Reynolds, 171). As Louis Menand put it, "All any biographer can hope, and all any reasonably skeptical reader can expect, is that the necessarily somewhat fictional character in the book bears some resemblance to the actual person who lived and died, and whose achievements (and disgraces) we care to learn more about. A biography is a tool for imagining another person, to be used along with other tools. It is not a window or a mirror" (Menand, 66).

It follows that we should be suspicious of enthusiastic reviewers who tell us that a biography has managed to capture its subject as a living and breathing person. And of books that sound too knowing, glide past gaps in the life, smooth over the rough spots, and fail to acknowledge "the swarm of possibilities" (Henry James) and "the baffle of being" (W. H. Auden) that complicate any life (Lee, 1; Epstein, 189). By way of contrast, one might cite the modesty of N. John Hall's *Max Beerbohm: A Kind of a Life* (2002). The subtitle could hardly sound less authoritative, and in the text Hall occasionally attaches an "I may be wrong" or "this may be mere biographical fancy" to his assertions—an approach that Joseph Epstein, one of those skeptics "who do not quite believe in biographical truth," thought "rather refreshing and even admirable" (Epstein, 188–89).

In Justin Kaplan's 1986 essay "What Biographies Can't Do," he concludes that at best biography amounts to "only a plausible, inevitably idiosyncratic surmise and reconstruction, severely limited by historical materials that are loaded with duplicities and evasions." Presumably he included his own excellent biographies of Mark Twain and Walt Whitman in that summary. For confirmation, in fact, he turned to the prefatory note Twain wrote for his autobiography: "What a wee little part of a person's life are his acts and his words! His real life is led in his head, and is known to none but himself. All day long, and every day, the mill of his brain is grinding, and his *thoughts*, not those other things, are his history. . . . These are his life, and they are not written, and cannot be written. Every day would make a whole book of eighty thousand words—three hundred and sixty-five books a year." "Biographies," Twain warned, "are but the clothes and buttons of the man" (Kaplan, "Can't Do," 9).

When next he came to write a biography of Walt Whitman, Kaplan well understood the limitations of his craft. In *Leaves of Grass* the poet himself issued a warning to all would-be chroniclers of other people's lives.

> When I read the book, the biography famous,
> And is this then (said I) what the author calls a man's life?
> And so will some one when I am dead and gone write my life?
> (As if any man really knew aught of my life,
> Why even I myself I often think know little or nothing of my
>   real life,
> Only a few hints, a few diffused faint clews and indirections
> I seek for my own use to trace out here.)
> (Whitman, 8)

And Yet . . .

"Why not admit," the poet and philosopher Paul Valéry asked, "that man is the source and origin of enigmas, where there is no object, or being, or moment, that is not impenetrable, when our existence, our movements, our sensations absolutely cannot be explained, and when everything we see becomes indecipherable from the moment our minds come to rest on it?" (quoted in Epstein, 121).

Why not indeed? And as Valéry's rhetorical question is reconfigured for biographers, whose minds come to rest over several years on the existence, the movements, the sensations of another person: why go to all that trouble? There must be more productive ways of occupying one's time. If the quest is doomed from the start, why bother?

Here is Edel in reply. "Some write biographies because they have fallen in love with their subjects (as Boswell fell in love with Johnson)." *More on this later.* "Some make biography into their trade: they seek lively and lucrative subjects, celebrities and popular lives—actresses, murderers, tycoons, gangsters, presidents." *Not the path of the literary biographer.* "All biographers understandably seek a measure of fame for themselves." *Well, yes, and thanks for sharing.* "A few—a very few—write biographies because they like the energy and economy, the order and form of a work of art." *Among that very few, surely, Edel himself.* (Edel, *Writing*, 13.)

Meryle Secrest chose her subjects—among them Bernard Berenson, Stephen Sondheim, and Frank Lloyd Wright—because she wanted to see worlds and meet minds that otherwise would have been closed to her. She saw herself as the learner, lucky enough to be attending school under the great. Biography was a "completely selfish enterprise," she thought. Ambition had something to do with it, and "the joy of discovery for its own sake." In addition, and not least, she "fell in love with almost all of [her] subjects." *Again, more on this later.* (Secrest, 229–30.)

An interviewer asked Stacy Schiff, author of books on Antoine de Saint-Exupéry, Vera Nabokov, Benjamin Franklin in France, and Cleopatra, why she'd become a biographer. "Some people will do anything to get out of writing about themselves," she answered (quoted in Solomon). *Or at least out of writing directly about themselves.*

Let's say that you accept the conclusions of Mark Twain and Paul Valéry, Thornton Wilder and Julian Barnes, Sigmund Freud and a host of others that you cannot take up residence in anyone else's mind. Then the writing of biography assumes the status of any undoable task, and appeals to the human desire to challenge boundaries. "A man's reach should exceed his grasp," as Robert Browning observed in "Andrea del Sarto." People climb a mountain because it's there, and try to climb the highest and most treacherous because it can't be done. What motivated the leopard whose carcass was found, according to Hemingway, near the top of Kilimanjaro?

But back to biography and away from analogies. You cannot go inside another human being's heart and head: agreed. You cannot reconstruct his bone and blood in a word portrait: also agreed. But it may be that if you are diligent and devoted, persistent and perceptive enough, you may come close.

And, of course, the *writer* of biographies is driven by that "universal hunger to penetrate other lives" (Spacks, 93) that makes so many eager to *read* biographies. For both reader and writer, satisfying that natural curiosity can be a good and constructive process. "We learn about ourselves by reading about the lives of other people," Menand remarks (66). "What we really want to know is, 'How do I live?'" biographer Nancy Milford comments (quoted in Stephen Oates, 3). "Reading about the lives of others," novelist James Salter observes, "is one of the things that gives us the courage to change our own, the courage to struggle against our own, I suppose" (Salter, *Letters*, 89).

Where literary biography is concerned, we come back to the subject of love. It is possible, as most of us know, to fall in love with a work of art—and like all lovers, to want to know as much as possible about the genius who created it. "If we love the poem, it is natural to be curious about the poet" (Hall, xii). Or, in John Updike's formulation, the first and most worthy reason to read literary biography "is the desire to prolong and extend our intimacy with the author—to partake again, from another angle, of the joys we have experienced within the author's oeuvre, in the presence of a voice and mind we have come to love." Updike mentioned two books that, he believed, succeeded brilliantly in accomplishing this result. George Painter's splendid two-volume biography of Marcel Proust, he observed, "allows us to enter the vast mansion of [*Remembrance of Things Past*] by the kitchen door." And Richard Ellmann's "superb biography" of James Joyce enables us "not only to revisit Joyce's Dublin but to understand how Joyce, modernism's wonderworker," managed to produce "rare and comprehensive art" from the drab environment of that provincial capital. What Updike remembered best from Ellmann's eight hundred pages was the way that Joyce, exiled in Trieste and Paris, pestered his friends in Dublin for details about the models for characters in *Ulysses*. "Get an ordinary sheet of foolscap and scribble any God damn drivel you may remember about these people," Joyce commanded his aunt (Updike, 15, 18–19).

In summary, Updike conceded that literary biography may prove useful in enhancing "our access to literature," but lamented its tendency to deflect attention from the work of art itself "in its necessary aloofness and mystery" to the "more or less meager and ignoble and practical facts" of the author's life (Updike, 36–37). That seems a reasonable judgment on the craft coming from one great creative writer on behalf of his fellow artists. And yes, there are biographers who seem bent upon diminishing the accomplishments of the authors they are depicting: biographers who fall out of love with their subjects and end by disparaging them.

For the most part, though, biographers remain supporters and friends of the author they are writing about, no matter what odious discoveries emerge during the long period of research. The very digging process—wanting to know everything—is a sign of love, Barnes's Geoffrey Braithwaite maintains in *Flaubert's Parrot*. "With a writer you love, the instinct is to defend." He conjures up a hypothetical case to demonstrate the point. "They say [the subject author] strangled an entire pack of Wolf Cubs and fed their bodies to a school of carp?" Surely not, he initially reacts, but pursue the truth he must, and if it turns out to be true . . .

"A pack of Wolf Cubs, eh? Was that twenty-seven or twenty-eight? And did he have their little scarves sewn up into a patchwork quilt? And is it true that as he ascended the scaffold he quoted from the Book of Jonah? And that he bequeathed the carp pond to the local Boy Scouts?" And later, "Take the long view: did we need so many Wolf Cubs? They would only have grown up and become Boy Scouts" (Barnes, 127–28). This is comedy, but comedy with a point. We so revere the work that we can forgive its creator almost anything. "An intense involvement with absent people from the past is what moves biographers to write," as Michael Holroyd put it (Holroyd, *Secrets*, 230).

Then, too, there are the pleasures of the process itself. If you begin from an academic base, what you are doing differs sharply from that of most of your colleagues. They are writing exegesis or theory, discoursing on literary texts, and they can do this in their office or their back porch, while you must travel, interview, and consult archives. But biography has considerable compensations as well. As James L. W. West III puts it, it is "a human activity, pleasurably engaging and messy." You are telling a story, writing narrative instead of argumentation. People like to read biographies, so that you are almost certain of commanding an audience for your work. You ordinarily get reviews in publications beyond the usual scholarly journals, and earn something in the way of royalties as well. And ideally you are doing a service on behalf of your subject author, interesting others in reading his work as you chronicle the life it came from (West, e-mail, 22 November 2013).

In my own case, I ended by regarding each of the seven figures I have written about over five decades with deep affection despite their varying personalities and sometimes undesirable behavior. It could hardly have been otherwise, after spending four or five years going to bed at night and waking up in the morning thinking about each of them in turn. The more I learned, the more I understood. The more I understood, the greater the fellow feeling.

John Cheever used to think of his readers as camping out in the woods behind his house. Let us suppose we are a company of two—a biographer and a reader taking a walk in those woods together, and talking about an author we both admire. It is one of those rare times when we can speak honestly and openly, and I do most the talking, for I have delved deep into the author's life and have much to communicate. This, it seems to me, is how the biographer might ideally approach his work, in communion with readers who share admiration for and curiosity about the subject author.

The poets first.

Winfield Townley Scott. Win Scott was a fine minor poet, a role that has no standing in American life. He wrote several well-received books of poetry and had his collected poems gathered into one volume. His best work took him into the lives of real and imagined characters: "Gert Swazey" and "Mr. Whittier" in poems, for example, and Emily Dickinson and Mark Twain in wonderful essays. But he did not and could not think of himself as having earned his way to success. It did not help that he married the boss's daughter and gave up his job on the *Providence Journal* to escape into relative idleness in Santa Fe. What does a poet do during the twenty-three and a half hours a day when he is not actually writing lines of poetry? Scott drank, and became riddled by self-doubt, and took an overdose of sleeping pills that in toxic combination with alcohol killed him. He was a gentle and likable man, short on ego strength. I slept in his bed in Santa Fe, a semiterrifying experience. Probably because Scott was less famous than the other authors I was to write books about, his survivors—particularly his widow Eleanor—were eager to see his life and accomplishments memorialized and facilitated my every endeavor. It was as if they were "cupping their hands" around the flickering flame of a literary reputation, as Norman Holmes Pearson, who knew everyone among the modernist poets of the twentieth century, once told me.

It was appropriate that, having started in literary biography with the little-known Winfield Townley Scott, forty years later I should write a life of Edwin—*not Edward, please*—Arlington Robinson, the poet who most inspired him. When he was an undergraduate at Brown, Scott drove up to see Robinson at the MacDowell Colony in Peterborough, New Hampshire—a meeting that helped shape the course of his career. EAR was notoriously reticent in social situations, but he unbuttoned his reserve for the visiting youngster. At the peak of his reputation, Robinson told Scott that if he was determined to live a life in poetry he might possibly manage to make as much money as a good carpenter. Alternatively, he might starve.

Robinson knew whereof he spoke. He skated for twenty years on the edge of the abyss, broke and lonely and unappreciated, before recognition began to come his way. He regarded poetry as his calling, and never married. Because of that lifelong bachelorhood and because of his New England reserve, some think of him as a distant and unapproachable figure. One of the first persons I talked to, once I'd committed to writing a Robinson biography, was a charming and intelligent woman living in the Head Tide, Maine, house where EAR had been born. He seemed such a "cold" man, she said, so withdrawn and uninvolved in life. In writing his biography, I wanted above all to correct that view.

Robinson did love, and deeply, but the great love of his life was married to his brother. He also had multitudes of friends. The closest of these were the companions of his youth in Gardiner, Maine, of his two years at Harvard as a special student, and of his early poverty-stricken days in New York. He would do almost anything to assist them.

More significantly, I can think of no other poet who invested so much empathy in his word-portraits of the downtrodden and bereft. Eben Flood in "Mr. Flood's Party," wending his way to his upland hermitage with the jug he has bought in the town below, proposing solitary toasts to himself as he goes. "The Poor Relation" in a New York apartment, determined not to impose her lonely distress on visitors. The maiden "Aunt Imogen" coming to visit her sister's family for a few weeks, making the occasion a delight for the children, and carrying their laughter with her to last for the rest of the year. The butcher "Reuben Bright" unable to cope with his wife's death, in his rage tearing down the slaughterhouse. The wronged wife in "Eros Turannos" shutting her ears to the townspeople's gossip about her unfaithful husband. The misguided mother in "Gift of God" idealizing her quite ordinary son to the heavens. The hilarious Miniver Cheevy yearning for days of yore.

With the Robinson biography as with no other I hoped to send readers back to poems like these. I also wanted to absolve Robinson of the wrong-headed judgment that because he used conventional rhyme and metrics he could safely be pigeonholed as old-fashioned. So I saw to it that a generous sampling of his poetry, briefly explicated, accompanied the narrative of *Edwin Arlington Robinson: A Poet's Life*. The poems could speak for themselves.

Telling Archibald MacLeish's life story presented a very different problem. Unlike my experience with Win Scott and Win (as he was called in his Maine boyhood) Robinson, I did not begin my half decade with MacLeish with a devotion to his work. I knew something of his honors, and of his having mastered the arts of statecraft as well as those of literature. But I was no better acquainted with his poetry than most academics specializing in twentieth-century American literature. I'd read the standard anthology pieces. My wife, Vivie, alerted me to "The End of the World." But that was all. If this biography was to be a labor of love, the feeling would have to develop over the course of time. And so it did.

MacLeish could hardly have been more differently constructed as a man than Robinson or Scott. He was brought up in a world of privilege and of obligatory service to others. At Hotchkiss and Yale and Harvard Law, he excelled both in and out of in the classroom. He captained Yale's water polo team, scored a touchdown against Notre Dame, was tapped for Skull and Bones, and graduated at the head of his class. He relished competition and carried himself with an air of confidence that struck some as a sense of entitlement. He was not shy, not withdrawn, not disadvantaged. He conquered one field after another: the law, journalism, the government: head of the Library of Congress and the wartime Office of Facts and Figures—propaganda, mostly—and assistant secretary of state, the theater: with his Pulitzer Prize–winning play *J.B.* (1958), the academy: as a mentor to brilliant young writers at Harvard. It seemed almost wrong that so much success should attend any one person's endeavors.

It was only in old age—he lived ninety years—that MacLeish captured me. Living out his semiretired days (he never really stopped working) at Uphill Farm in Conway, Massachusetts, he wrote a series of quite wonderful and very little-read poems about growing old and about married love as it mellowed but did not die. What moved me most, though, were his reflections on the cost of his success. In his several roles MacLeish had courted and gained the kind of recognition others could only dream of. To his neighbors in the Berkshires, he was "Archibald MacLeish," a public figure they felt proud to claim as one of their own. But they did not know Archie MacLeish, and he could not know them. At the end he wondered whether, along the path that carried him to one triumph after another, he had somehow lost command of who he really was and dwindled into his public persona. That old man, suddenly vulnerable and beset by doubts, was someone worth knowing and caring about.

MacLeish's two closest friends, he used to say, were Dean Acheson, his classmate at Yale and Harvard Law who was to become secretary of state for Harry Truman, and Ernest Hemingway, whom he met in Paris in the mid-1920s. The friendship with Hemingway was periodically rocky. It could hardly have been otherwise, inasmuch as they were two of the most competitive human beings who ever lived. They became close friends in late 1926 after Ernest and Hadley Hemingway separated. Hemingway kept his bicycle in the front hallway of the MacLeishes' Paris apartment, and he and Archie took bicycle trips together to Chartres and other destinations. These were not leisurely excursions. Both men pushed themselves to the limits of physical endurance as they raced in friendly but intense competition.

Years later, they quarreled bitterly during the Spanish Civil War. Both were ardent supporters of the antifascist cause. Hemingway spent months on the ground in Spain during the war, and accused the dedicated liberal MacLeish, who was doing his bit by way of propaganda and films back in the States, of not going far enough in his support of the Spanish Republic. That led to a break that took years of getting over.

Hemingway was notorious for his mistreatment of friends and family. He went through three divorces, and tried for four. He broke off friendships with almost all of his literary friends, often nastily. He was wounded in his youth by a father he could not respect and a mother he could not forgive for dominating his father. He was wounded in war, and by the nurse he fell in love with who jilted him. He wanted no one close, no one to care so much about as to risk the pain of rejection. He ended with a coterie of fishing and hunting buddies and boxers and bullfighters, a fourth wife he could not shake free of, and paranoid delusions that others—the CIA, the IRS, the pilot of the plane flying him across the Atlantic—were out to destroy him.

Hemingway was, I believe, the greatest of all the authors I did time with, as well as the most tortured. He set himself unreachable goals, and was devastated when he failed to reach them. The illusory enemies of his paranoia, projections of his own self-loathing, closed in on him, as did the physical consequences of a reckless and alcoholic life. He knew he could not write any more. So he stole downstairs early one morning and killed himself.

I felt a closer kinship with Fitzgerald than with any other subject. I grew up in Minneapolis, across the Mississippi River from Fitzgerald's St. Paul. I went to Blake school, the country day school for boys that rivaled his St. Paul Academy. My mother, a contemporary of Fitzgerald's, attended St. Paul Central High, as did several of his boyhood friends. He and I came from much the same background thirty years apart, well-off midwestern kids, yet not among the socially dominant. He was sensitive about the divide that separated him from the elite, and it's a major theme in his writing, not only in *The Great Gatsby* and *Tender Is the Night* but also in many stories, perhaps most powerfully in the great "Winter Dreams." I could understand why that mattered so much to Fitzgerald and his young protagonists, who were forever in quest of the uncapturable golden girl. I even thought, at times, that I could imagine my way into his head.

Along with the similarity in background, I shared with Fitzgerald a sometimes humiliating desire to make others like me. He understood this proclivity of his very well, as is evident in two major works of his during the 1930s. In *Tender Is the Night* (1934), he created in Dick Diver a protagonist weakened and finally undone by his compulsive exercise of charm. That novel demonstrated in fictional form the disastrous effects of Fitzgerald's own persistent drive to earn the approval both of women (he was usually successful in that) and of men (much less so). In boyhood his doting mother trotted him out to entertain visitors with recitations of famous poems. As an adult he looked back on those incidents with disgust, but it was not easy for him to overcome the habit of pleasing others. Sometimes he acted out in retaliation.

There was almost no one he knew whose friendship he coveted more than that of Gerald and Sara Murphy, a couple of social standing superior to his own. Fitzgerald earned his way into their notice by way of his writing. Yet at their parties he behaved abominably by getting drunk, insulting guests, picking fights, breaking expensive crystal. On the morning after such performances—and they occurred with others as well as with the Murphys—he would be desperately contrite, and try to repurchase favor with elaborate apologies. These usually worked, but not always. Sara Murphy ordered him off the reservation for an extended period of time. Another hostess refused to be moved by his contrition. "I'm terribly sorry about last night," he told her. "Are you?" she replied, and turned her back.

At the end of "Handle with Care," the last of the three essays in *The Crack-Up* (1936), Fitzgerald used a debilitating metaphor to excoriate himself. For too long he had concentrated on pleasing others, but in the future, he wrote, he would become a different kind of dog entirely, one who no longer likes "the postman, nor the grocer, nor the editor, nor the cousin's husband." He would only lick your hand now, Fitzgerald said, if you threw him a bone.

The confessional *Crack-Up* essays were written at the bottom of his long slide into depression and alcoholism. Probably they had a therapeutic effect. During the four years that he had left, Fitzgerald went to Hollywood, worked hard at crafting film scripts, and met his obligations to Zelda, institutionalized, and Scottie, at prep school and then Vassar. He gave up drinking, finally. He also gave up worrying what others thought of him. He would be no one's fawning lap dog. He would become at last what he was meant to be: a writer only; and he was well along on what promised to be a wonderful novel about Hollywood when the heart attack struck (SD, Fitzgerald and Hemingway, 186).

John Cheever's life and career closely resembled that of Fitzgerald. Both writers had strong mothers and unsuccessful fathers. Both were acutely sensitive to the workings of social class. Both could evoke epiphanies in flowing, seemingly effortless prose. Both were subject to appalling lapses in discipline brought about or exacerbated by drinking. Both managed to kick the habit near the end, and Cheever also came to terms with his long-concealed bisexuality. Both remained astonishingly hopeful in their last works of fiction (SD, *Cheever*, 352–53).

The subject matter was similar too. Fitzgerald often situated his stories of relatively poor young men courting rich young women in the fashionable outskirts of cities—"Black Bear Lake" for Dexter Green and Judy Jones, "East and West Egg" for Jimmy Gatz and Daisy Buchanan. Cheever went even further in his concentration on the suburbs and exurbs, where his protagonists clung to their positions as marital discord and financial ruin threatened to overtake them. Like no other writer, he captured the trials and troubles and occasional triumphs of the midcentury upper-middle-class suburbanite.

Cheever was different from Fitzgerald—and from any other American author of his time—in his extraordinary gift for invention. Time and again, miracles invade the otherwise mundane surroundings of his fiction. This was true of his early stories about New York City, "The Enormous Radio" for example, and the terrifying "Torch Song." It was also true of such later work as "The Swimmer," *Bullet Park*, and *Falconer*. Cheever was exploring the territory of magic realism before it became critically recognized and admired. And, like all great writers, he wrote in a distinctive voice of his own. If we cull out the first and last paragraphs of any work of his—and the same would be true for Fitzgerald and Hemingway—we know immediately who is doing the storytelling.

By the time it occurred to me that I had an obligation to write about Charlie Fenton, he'd been dead for almost half a century. An adventurer, a rule breaker, a rebel, Fenton was a talented writer who turned to the academy to support himself. I first saw him in the fall of 1949, when the lean and youthful Fenton was talking to the ninety or so Yale students who'd decided to take Daily Themes. At the time Fenton was only midway through the academic mill: an instructor doing course work for his doctorate, with the dissertation that became *The Apprenticeship of Ernest Hemingway* (1954) still five years in the future. But he was already a legend around Yale for his good looks, his irreverence for received wisdom, and his sardonic wit. Most of the rumors that circulated about him turned out to be true. He'd done more than his share of drinking and womanizing in a misspent youth. He was kicked out of Yale, once, and left a second time to enlist in the Royal Canadian Air Force prior to Pearl Harbor. He'd flown two dozen dangerous bombing missions over the Ruhr during the worst of the air war, and survived to write stories and a prize-winning novel about it. He'd worked as a newspaper reporter afterwards, and briefly for Time-Life. But he refused to become an organization man at a time when most others were doing so. He did not fit into any collective environment. In prep school and the war, he conceived a deep distrust of authority. He was opposed to "brass" in any form, whether military, corporate, or academic.

"Charismatic" is an over-used adjective, but Fenton was charismatic, all right—a glittering figure like Robinson's "Richard Cory" and, like Cory, destined to take his own life. He had the misfortune of being assigned to direct my senior thesis on Hemingway's short stories, and in the course of that duty I learned something from him that was to have a tremendous effect on my future.

Death of a Rebel: The Charlie Fenton Story is 95 percent about him, and heaven knows his story was a fascinating one, but I felt compelled to introduce myself into the narrative, for there was an obligation to acknowledge. One summer day I drove up to see Fenton at his modest home near the shore in Madison, Connecticut. He made a few suggestions about my Hemingway thesis, told me about the courses he was taking for his doctorate, and gave me a paper he'd done on the mostly unremembered first novels of twentieth-century American authors to read. Quick now, what were the first novels of Faulkner, Dos Passos, Steinbeck?

Then he left me to go back to work in his cluttered home office. Two young children scampered by. His wife poked her head in to ask what he wanted for dinner. And suddenly it occurred to me that this was the kind of life I might lead: reading and writing and teaching about authors and books that interested me, with a supportive wife and family. (I did not, in 1950, think of the possibility of marrying a woman with a career of her own.) I drove back along Long Island Sound with that idea in the back of my mind. As it turned out, I followed a career path that mirrored Charlie Fenton's, first as a newspaper reporter and editor, then as a college professor and writer of biographies. That might not have happened but for that June day in 1950.

Later, too, memories of Fenton vividly returned. He killed himself in July 1960, jumping from the top of the Washington Duke Hotel in Durham, North Carolina. He was a full professor at Duke by then, and had written three books with several others in the works. He'd won a Guggenheim, a Morse fellowship, and only recently an ACLS award for a book on "The Last Great Cause": the Spanish Civil War. He was a great success in the classroom, and students clamored to work with him on their master's theses and doctoral dissertations. At forty-one he was in every sense a star in the academic firmament. But he was also deeply depressed that summer, living alone in an un-air-conditioned apartment and nearly broke. Like most suicides, his could be traced to many causes, but prominent among them was that Fenton had fallen in love with a graduate student and his marriage had broken up. As a consequence it was clear that he'd have to leave Duke.

In the fall of 1977, teaching at William and Mary, I also fell in love with a graduate student. Three years later, she and I decided to end our marriages and commit to each other. We did so openly, leaving our respectable domiciles and moving in together. I don't think we could have done it otherwise. This created a local scandal, and as at Duke twenty years earlier, clacking tongues around Williamsburg, Virginia, accused us of the worst. So that, too, represented a parallel between Charlie Fenton and myself.

But I was luckier than him. I was less subject to depression, for one thing, and luckily times had changed. Divorce carried less of a stigma in the late 1970s than it had twenty years earlier. No one suggested that I should leave William and Mary. Over time the children, seeing that we were happy together, forgave us. We've been married more than thirty years now. It looks as if it will last.

The craft may be impossible, but I feel fortunate to have pursued it these past fifty years. As Richard Ellmann summarized the issue, "we cannot know completely the intricacies with which any mind negotiates with its surroundings to produce literature. The controlled seething out of which great works come is not likely to yield all its secrets. Yet at moments, in glimpses, biographers seem to be close to it, and the effort to come close . . . , to know another person who has lived as well as we know a character in fiction, and better than we know ourselves, is not frivolous. It may even be, for reader as for writer, an essential part of experience" (Ellmann, *Codgers*, 16).

You begin writing a biography with love or at least a strong admiration for your subject, and with a complementary curiosity about what sort of person was able to accomplish such wonders. You do your dutiful yet often exhilarating research, discovering illuminating remarks and unexpected actions along the way. You read and reread and assemble boxes full of notes. Eventually the notes begin to fall into a pattern. You shape your book along the lines of that pattern. You hope to end with understanding. Invariably you end with a profound sense of loss when it is time to let Scott or Ernest or EAR go back to his resting place. If that feeling communicates itself, so that the reader feels the same way at parting, you will have done what is next to impossible.

CASE STUDIES

Telling Robinson's Story: The Fight over a Poet's Bones

How strange it is that a gentle, reasonable spirit like E. A. should have his afterglow
clouded by a mist of hates, envies, selfish ambitions and blindnesses and that these
should have been released around Hermann [Hagedorn], a soul as true and friendly as
his own. Yes, it is strange, but stranger still is the fact that I have, three times before, seen
a measure of the same conditions following the death of gentle poets.

It is as though the poet, by the power of his harmony, gathers under his rule many dis-
cords which are released when he lays down his wand.

—RIDGELY TORRENCE TO LAURA RICHARDS, 4 DECEMBER 1938 (GARDINER)

Competing Candidates

After his death at 2:30 A.M., Saturday, 6 April 1935, editorials in the major
metropolitan dailies hailed Edwin Arlington Robinson (or EAR, as he liked
to be called) as the nation's foremost and most illustrious poet. Robinson
was also the very opposite of the performance poets who sought public
approval. Three times a Pulitzer Prize winner, he would not recite his poems
before audiences and avoided publicity, devoting himself to his work and
refusing every opportunity to capitalize on his reputation. EAR never married, but he had many friends, and a way of making each of them feel that
only he or she really understood him—this despite consistently withholding the most intimate information about himself, his family, his loves. In a
series of brilliant poems Robinson encapsulated or at least hinted at the
defining characteristics of such arresting figures as Isaac and Archibald,

Reuben Bright, Miniver Cheevy, Richard Cory, the husband and wife in "Eros Turannos," Mr. Flood, and Aunt Imogen. His inmost self he did not reveal, living and dying something of a mystery. Attracted by his eminence and eager to unlock the doors, would-be biographers lined up to tell his story.

Two candidates were keeping the death watch at New York Hospital on East Sixty-Eighth Street: Carty Ranck and Chard Powers Smith. Ranck, a small, irascible, mentally unstable playwright from Kentucky, met EAR at the MacDowell Colony in Peterborough, New Hampshire, in 1912, soon became his adoring disciple and promoter, and began collecting information toward a biography. Robinson liked Ranck, and—though fully cognizant of the man's condition—did not discourage his Boswellizing. Over time, Ranck formed an alliance with George Burnham, probably EAR's closest friend of all, tracing back to their years at Harvard in the 1890s.

Chard Powers Smith occupies a curious niche in literary history. Poet, novelist, historian of Puritanism, and eventually—in 1965—author of *Where the Light Falls: A Portrait of Edwin Arlington Robinson*, Smith also met Robinson at the MacDowell Colony, in the summer of 1924. Smith had recently returned to the United States from a sojourn in Paris. There, his fellow expatriate Ernest Hemingway depicted Smith and his wife in unflattering terms in "Mr. and Mrs. Elliot." Hemingway's story strongly suggested that Mrs. Elliot/Smith was a closeted lesbian, and in correspondence the outraged Smith accused Hemingway of character assassination. Hemingway responded that he would welcome a confrontation with Smith any time, anywhere, and that he was looking forward to knocking him down as often as necessary to keep him from getting up. No such confrontation took place.

Robinson felt sorry for Smith, whose maligned wife had died a few months earlier, and valued him as a skilled partner in the after-dinner games of cowboy pool that constituted part of his MacDowell Colony routine. The two men occasionally met in New York thereafter, and Smith, twenty-five years Robinson's junior, fancied himself well qualified to write his biography. But first he had in mind a long poem about the death of a great poet. In quest of material, Smith repeatedly presented himself at EAR's hospital bedside, demanding access even when it was obvious that Robinson did not want visitors. It fell to Lewis M. Isaacs, a composer by preference and lawyer by profession who served as Robinson's advocate during his final months in the hospital, to see to it that Smith's visits were restricted.

Isaacs, too, first encountered EAR at Peterborough (Robinson spent every summer at the MacDowell Colony from 1911 through 1934), and the two men formed a lifelong attachment, based on a shared love of music and Isaacs's patent admiration for the poet's work. For several years when Robinson was down and out, Isaacs and another New Yorker, Louis V. Ledoux, spearheaded a group of a dozen friends who each contributed $100 annually to the poet's support. By way of recompense, EAR gave both Isaacs and Ledoux original manuscripts of his work. Despite his general reclusiveness, Robinson felt comfortable in these benefactors' households—he got along best of all with Jean Ledoux—and when it came time to appoint executors to oversee his affairs, he chose Isaacs and Ledoux as joint caretakers. He expected Isaacs to look after the legal aspects of his legacy and Ledoux to concentrate on literary issues, but this division was not spelled out.

Ledoux, like Isaacs, was a well-to-do New Yorker, whose inheritance of a successful metallurgical business enabled him to pursue his artistic interests. A crack tennis player growing up, Ledoux turned to poetry as a young man and got to know Robinson through their mutual friendship with the poet and playwright Ridgely Torrence. Ledoux dedicated one of his five books, *The Soul's Progress and Other Poems* (1906), to Robinson and Torrence, a gesture EAR reciprocated by dedicating his 1915 play *The Porcupine* to Ledoux.

Both Isaacs and Ledoux took their duties as executors conscientiously, though they were not always in agreement about how to proceed. The first order of business, it seemed to Ledoux, was to protect Robinson and his reputation from the wrong sort of biographer. EAR died early Saturday morning, a memorial service was held on Sunday, and early on Monday Ledoux called George P. Brett Jr., president of Macmillan (Robinson's publishers). Ledoux was very much concerned that several unqualified people were liable to start writing biographies. To head them off, he wanted Macmillan to announce the appointment of an official biographer as soon as possible. Ledoux had an ideal candidate in mind, one who also came recommended by the eminent Harvard professor Bliss Perry: Ridgely Torrence himself.

Torrence was one of Robinson's oldest literary friends. The two young poets, both scratching out meager existences in New York, met in the spring of 1900 and saw a good deal of each other during the years immediately after. From 1906 to 1909 they both had rooms at the Judson Hotel at the south end of Washington Square. Also in residence there was freelance writer Olivia Howard Dunbar, whom Torrence married in 1914. Both men were tall and thin, but differed widely in personality. Torrence was sprightly and mischievous, a gifted mimic and a natural entertainer. When drinking—as he often was in those days—Robinson might join in conversation and even lift his voice in song. For the most part, though, he withdrew into himself in social situations. At the Judson, Dunbar watched with amusement as one woman after another tried and failed to penetrate his reserve.

Torrence was a poet with an established reputation, and could be depended upon to depict EAR with sensitivity and tact—qualities that recommended him as biographer to Robinson's executors and publishers. Even the bumptious Chard Smith, at a May 15 luncheon meeting with Macmillan's George Brett, acknowledged that Torrence would be the best one to write EAR's biography—unless he himself was. Torrence knew Robinson far better than he did, Smith admitted. He and EAR had only been close during three years or so before Robinson quit drinking. But Torrence would not be able to address the question of EAR's love life openly, he warned. Robinson never married, but, Smith told Brett, he believed that at least three women entered his life "in a big way." His "greatest amour," Smith believed, was Olivia Dunbar, who married Torrence, and Robinson and Torrence had become estranged for a time because of their rivalry as her suitors. If Torrence were to write the biography, Smith warned, that episode—a turning point in Robinson's life—could not be forthrightly told. According to Brett's memo, he did not "particularly like Smith's attitude with reference to Robinson's connection with women. He paints it as pretty lurid and especially the affair with Mrs. Ridgely Torrence" (Brett memo, 15 May 1935, NYPL). The approach smacked of sensationalism, not at all what EAR's executors were looking for. Besides, Smith was wrong about Olivia Dunbar, for as became clear with the passage of time, the great lasting love of Robinson's life was his brother Herman's wife, Emma Shepherd Robinson.

Chard Smith, in effect, talked himself out of the running as biographer in what he intended as a sales pitch to George Brett. And although Carty Ranck did not know it, he too had no real chance to meet the standards of the executors—especially Isaacs, with whom EAR had corresponded about Ranck as early as 1921. In that year, Ranck's marriage to Reita Lambert was about to collapse, in good part as a consequence of his mental breakdown. Robinson was much distressed about the breakup, and wrote to Isaacs asking for his advice. "I can only hope that R[anck] will find himself again before long," EAR commented (Edith Isaacs memo, 6 August 1921, NYPL). In fact, though, subsequent breakdowns continued to darken Ranck's days. His plays never took off, and to make ends meet he was reduced to cranking out freelance articles for newspapers.

Fond of Ranck and not averse to his adoration, Robinson did what he could to advance his career. In 1930, when approached by Boston and New York newspapers for a feature article on his life and work, he recommended Ranck for the job. In 1934 he wrote an introduction to Ranck's play *The Mountain*, whose hero—a Kentucky moonshiner who made and sold corn liquor in violation of federal statutes—was modeled on Ranck's father. This gesture was unusual for Robinson, for at about the same time he turned down requests from both Chard Smith and Hermann Hagedorn to write introductions to books of their poems. Yet he may well have had doubts as to whether Ranck was fully competent to tell his story of his life. He never put into writing any endorsement of Ranck as his biographer.

In addition to Smith and Ranck, several others aspired to the role of biographer. Among them was Howard G. Schmitt, a young collector of EAR's work from Buffalo. In a letter of 22 May 1934, Robinson asked Isaacs to show Schmitt his private collection of Robinson books and manuscripts. But, EAR added, "please discourage [Schmitt] in regard to any projected biography, for he is one of half a dozen enthusiastic youngsters who seem to be possessed with that particular demon" (Colby).

Within hours after Edwin Arlington Robinson's death the well-known playwright Percy MacKaye wrote a letter to Isaacs proposing himself as biographer. MacKaye came to know Robinson during the years (1905–13, approximately) when the impoverished poet, bitten by dramatic fever, attempted in vain to write commercially successful prose plays. Born to a theatrical family, MacKaye turned out a series of such plays himself, and encouraged EAR in his efforts. MacKaye was every inch a showman, with flashing dark eyes and an excess of energy. Robinson thought him a genius, and visited MacKaye and his family at their home in Cornish, New Hampshire.

In 1919 MacKaye was instrumental in orchestrating a fiftieth birthday tribute to EAR. Working behind the scenes with Macmillan, he asked seventeen other poets to write brief appreciations of Robinson's work. Some of these were themselves more or less famous: Robert Frost, Vachel Lindsay, Amy Lowell, Edwin Markham, Edgar Lee Masters, and Sara Teasdale. Others had close acquaintance with EAR, including Hagedorn, Ledoux, MacKaye himself, and Torrence.

These tributes—or sixteen of them, for one poet, Frost, declined to participate—appeared in the *New York Times Book Review* for Sunday, December 21, accompanied by an introduction from Bliss Perry comparing Robinson to Donne, Whitman, and Browning. All of this was managed surreptitiously, so that Robinson awoke that morning—the day before his birthday—to the surprise of finding his career celebrated in the morning newspaper. "Hagedorn and Ledoux hold you entirely responsible for some recent doings in the *Times*," EAR wrote MacKaye in gratitude. It was good to know that there were "men alive" like him (SD, *Robinson*, 353–54).

In his querying letter to Isaacs, MacKaye mentioned both Torrence (not really interested, he thought) and Hagedorn ("wonderfully well qualified") as possible biographers, but asked the executors to hold off on a decision until MacKaye, then at the Cosmos Club in Washington, D.C., had a chance to present his case (MacKaye to Isaacs, 6 May 1935, NYPL). At that stage, it was not clear in MacKaye's own mind exactly what he wanted to do to commemorate Robinson. He wrote Laura Richards in Gardiner, Maine—

Robinson's hometown—asking for information about the thirty years EAR lived there. He was about to undertake a biography, MacKaye said, or possibly a memoir. Then, in correspondence with Ledoux, he suggested himself as chairman of a committee of three (including Ledoux and Torrence) charged with selecting letters for a volume of EAR's correspondence. He had a letter from Robinson more or less endorsing such a volume.

Probably MacKaye retired from the field as a candidate for official biographer when Ledoux made it clear that Torrence was his choice for the task. As Ledoux wrote him on 27 April 1935, he hoped and expected that Torrence would be asked to write the biography—and the sooner this could be settled, the better. Since EAR's death, Ledoux explained, "Ridgely and I and the Macmillan Company have been besieged by a strange collection of people who wished to write his biography or threatened to write it, and some of these seem to be seekers after notoriety who would handle the book in a most undignified and tactless manner. Some even wish to make something sensational" (Ledoux to MacKaye, 27 April 1935, Harvard Theatre Collection). As he wrote in a separate letter to EAR's beloved niece Ruth Nivison, "[t]he life of a man like your uncle should be handled with the dignity and reserve, and the high mental and moral plane that would be appropriate to him" (Ledoux to Nivison, 26 April 1935, Colby). A public announcement of an official biographer by Macmillan, Ledoux felt confident, would have the salutary effect of discouraging other publishers from taking some of these unfortunate books.

With that end in mind and without a specific biographer on board—Torrence was still considering the matter—Ledoux and Isaacs worked with Brett on a broadside that went out to major newspapers throughout the country late in April: "The Macmillan Company, acting with the consent of the executors of the Estate of Edwin Arlington Robinson, request that anyone possessing letters from him send them as soon as possible to George P. Brett, Jr., in care of The Macmillan Company, 80 Fifth Avenue, New York City, for use in connection with a forthcoming critical biography of the poet and a possible volume of selected letters. The letters that are sent will be acknowledged, carefully preserved, and returned to the senders, as soon as they have accomplished their purpose" (Ledoux to Brett, 22 April 1935, NYPL).

The letters, presumably, would provide basic material for the biography. In due course this notice elicited many letters from EAR's correspondents, but by no means all of them. On June 12 the publishers sent a follow-up appeal to several people who were likely to have letters and who had not yet come forward with them. Please send any such correspondence by registered mail, the firm suggested, and the letters would be copied promptly and returned by registered mail. "We appreciate the splendid way in which

Mr. Robinson's friends are cooperating with us through the lending of these letters for the benefit of the official biographer," the appeal from Brett added. Only in that way, he declared, would it be possible to bring out a book worthy of its subject (Brett to Louis Untermeyer, 12 June 1935, NYPL).

These notices rather alarmed EAR's relatives in Gardiner, the most involved among them being Emma Robinson, Herman's widow, and Ruth Nivison, the oldest of Emma's three daughters and the one closest to the poet. Mrs. Nivison objected to the prospect of "a possible volume of selected letters," and Louis Ledoux went to some pains to reassure her. "I agree with you entirely about the delicacy of publishing a man's correspondence," he wrote her. Any such action would only be taken "with the greatest discretion," eliminating anything "too personal for publication." Ledoux himself would have been reluctant to authorize any such volume, he added, had Percy MacKaye not shown him a communication from EAR making it clear that the poet contemplated "the possible publication of some of his letters" (Ledoux to Nivison, 7 May 1935, Colby).

The issue of whether or not to publish a book of Robinson's letters struck the first note of discord between the executors in New York and his family in Gardiner. These notes were to be sounded time and again, swelling into a cacophony, as the biography—preceding the book of letters—moved toward completion. The trouble owed a good deal to the difference in outlook between EAR's friends among the sophisticated New Yorkers, who were confidently trying to do their best for his reputation, and his sister-in-law and nieces in Maine, who were motivated by New England reticence and family pride to avoid public disclosure of the skeletons in the Robinson closet: his brother Dean's drug addiction and suicide; his brother Herman's alcoholism, which led to separation from his wife Emma and an early death; and EAR's own, eventually victorious, battle with the bottle, as well as his emotional involvement with Emma. It was unfortunate, too, that neither Emma nor Ruth had any real acquaintance with Isaacs or Ledoux, or vice versa. At EAR's funeral, Ledoux had been surprised to learn of the nieces' existence.

This New York–New England division between Robinson's various supporters was reflected in—and to some degree resulted from—his annual perambulations between the two regions. For the last two dozen years of his life, he followed a regular schedule. From late fall to late spring, approximately December through May, EAR lived in New York City. He was drawn there by a love of the city's musical offerings, especially opera, by its importance as a center for artists and writers and publishers, and by the many friends who lived there. He occupied single rooms in boardinghouses or hotels or apartment buildings during much of that time, before moving into quarters designed specially for him in the East 48th Street home of the sculptors James Earle and Laura Gardin Fraser in 1925.

As spring moved into summer, Robinson headed north to New England, sometimes stopping to stay with Lewis and Edith Isaacs or Louis and Jean Ledoux at their summer retreats in Pelham and Cornwall, New York. After a regular stop in Boston to visit his close friend George Burnham, he proceeded to his summer headquarters at the MacDowell Colony. Robinson became a fixture there, a distinguished figure who spent the months from June through September in its rustic surroundings. He wrote almost all of his poetry at the colony. Then, worn down by the demands he'd made on himself over the summer, he decompressed for a month or more in Boston, living in a rented bedroom in the same building as Burnham, before returning to New York for the winter.

There was some overlap among the people who knew EAR in New England and in New York, but for the most part he kept these two groups separate, rarely speaking of Burnham, for example, while in communication with Ledoux, or vice versa. Gardiner, of course, occupied another space entirely, a small city with virtually no ties to New York. Boston, easily accessible by water and rail and in its genteel way the very model of New England reticence, was the city that mattered to Gardiner residents. In the competition for control of the way Robinson's life should be presented to the public, EAR's family in Gardiner formed an alliance with his friends in Boston against the executors and others in New York.

Two memoirs and a collection of tributes appeared in advance of the "official" biography. Rollo Walter Brown's *Next Door to a Poet* (1937) set down memories of Robinson at the MacDowell Colony. James Earle Fraser assembled encomiums to EAR from the nation's newspapers and magazines in a booklet. And—the most noteworthy of these early publications—Laura E. Richards in *E. A. R.* (1936) presented a sympathetic portrait of the poet during his formative years in Gardiner. Mrs. Richards occupied a prominent place in the world of letters. The daughter of Samuel Gridley Howe and Julia Ward Howe, who wrote "The Battle Hymn of the Republic," she grew up in Boston society and married Henry Richards, a cousin of the Gardiners who gave the Maine town its name. In her long lifetime Laura Richards produced more than eighty volumes of light verse and children's fiction (including the classic *Captain January*), as well as more serious work, including a two-volume biography of her mother that won the Pulitzer Prize.

In Gardiner the Richardses were regarded—and regarded themselves— as aristocrats. They devoted their energies to building and improving the small city where they lived: the library, the hospital, the high school all owed much to their initiatives. Mrs. Richards even invited the most promising local boys to come to tea in order to acquaint them with good manners and polite conversation. But the family remained Boston patricians, and did not make close friends in the small Maine city where fate had plunked them down. The attitude was one of *de haut en bas*.

Thus Laura Richards, the community's leading literary professional, chose not to participate in the meetings of the Gardiner Poetry Society, the collection of ambitious local amateurs who encouraged EAR in his boyhood attempts at verse. Still, she recognized talent when she saw it, and when the neighbor youth—twenty years her junior—brought out *The Torrent and the Night Before* in 1896, she summoned him to call: "Prithee, good Hermit Thrush, come out of thy thicket!" Robinson complied: "I shall be glad to come to see you on Monday. I am not a Hermit Thrush." So began an abiding friendship between the two of them, one that continued by correspondence after EAR left Gardiner for New York a few years later (SD, *Robinson*, 127–29).

The letters reflected their personalities. The laconic EAR, struggling to establish himself as a poet, often verged on the edge of despair. The relentlessly optimistic Mrs. Richards advised him to cheer up and, working behind the scenes, used her connections in the literary world to advance his career. Because of her friendship with the poet, Mrs. Richards later took an interest in Emma Robinson and her daughter Ruth Nivison, who continued to live nearby in Gardiner. It was only to be expected that, after EAR died, she should have decided to do a brief volume based on his early years in his home town. Nor was she the only one eager to have her say.

"As to memoirs, etc!" she wrote Lewis Isaacs on April 23. "We smile sadly, do we not? Everybody who knew him is rushing into print; everybody wants to tell the story, to paint the picture, to show the Man as he saw him. We can see E. A.'s smile too, can we not? No sadness in that; only the slow, wise, comprehending smile that we would give so much to see again. . . . He would be infinitely amused, somewhat touched, on the whole pleased" (NYPL).

Memoirs were one thing, and a thoroughgoing biography something else. Carty Ranck wrote a friendly note to Mrs. Richards, whom he had never met, and telephoned Isaacs in New York by way of advancing his cause. It was rumored that he had accumulated notes two feet deep, on 8 1/2 by 11 inch sheets of paper, toward his prospective book. As Isaacs dryly observed, "Mr. Ranck . . . is planning a biography, as, no doubt, are many others." Ledoux, he added, was "much exercised" at the prospect of these "more or less authentic" attempts, as the process of anointing a biographer dragged on (Isaacs to Richards, 16 April 1935, Colby). Not until late summer did Torrence, Ledoux's friend and first choice, definitely remove himself from consideration. He would work on EAR's letters, Torrence decided, but not on his life story.

From the point of view of EAR's family, all of these prospective biographers were outsiders. None of them showed up for the May 12 memorial service in Gardiner. Among his friends from elsewhere, only George Burnham came down from Boston for the ceremony and stayed with the Nivisons. Burnham had run away from his prosperous Hartford home at seventeen, traveling west and supporting himself in various temporary jobs. On a freezing January night in Montana, he was caught in a blizzard and kicked the trunk of a tree through the night to keep from falling into deadly sleep. The next morning he dragged himself to a town, where both feet were amputated. He met Robinson in 1891 when both enrolled as "special students" at Harvard. The two men bonded as fellow members of the Corn Cob Club, made up of a number of "specials": students generally older than the ordinary run of undergraduates and admitted on different grounds. (Later in the 1890s, Robert Frost and Wallace Stevens also studied at Harvard under the auspices of that program.)

At Harvard Burnham was notable for his choleric temper. He once charged the umpire at a Harvard-Yale baseball game (on his wooden legs) to protest a call, and in the heated discussions of the Corn Cob Club inveighed against any show of sham or pretense. He took his law degree at Harvard, but gave up the practice of law when he determined that in good conscience he could not represent the materialistic interests of his clients. By 1901, when he and Robinson were living in neighboring rented cubbyholes in New York, Burnham had become a disciple of Hindu Vedanta philosophy, believing that spiritual growth could only come through personal impoverishment. Thereafter he took a lowly clerk's job with the New York, New Haven and Hartford Railroad in Boston, practicing celibacy and allowing himself only the skimpiest of indulgences. Robinson was at ease with Burnham as with no one else. They talked when the spirit moved them, and lapsed into long silences without any tension whatever. EAR thought Burnham very nearly a saint, tried to take care of him in any way he could, and left him $3,000—more than for anyone outside the family—in his will.

EAR also brought Burnham together with Margaret Perry, the daughter of Thomas Sergeant and Lilla Cabot Perry. Robinson met the Perrys for the first time in August 1913 at their summer home in Hancock, New Hampshire, near the MacDowell Colony, and forged a lasting friendship with both of them. The Perrys came from socially prominent Boston families, she a Cabot and he the grandson of naval hero Oliver Hazard Perry. Tom Perry was an accomplished man of letters with a wide acquaintance among books and those who wrote them. Oliver Wendell Holmes thought him "the best read man [he had] ever known." For a number of years Perry taught at Harvard—French and German as well as English literature. He and his wife traveled widely, living for three years in Paris and three years in Japan. Perry maintained an active correspondence with Henry James, William Dean

Howells, and other literary lights. After he died in 1928, the Perry family asked Robinson to edit a volume of those letters, the only such task he ever undertook. In the introduction he characterized Perry as "a great reader, a great friend, and a great gentlemen" (SD, *Robinson*, 283–84, 440).

A talented painter, Lilla Cabot Perry shaped her work after the French Impressionists. In 1889 she and her husband rented a house in Giverny to be close to the great Claude Monet. Later she turned to poetry, producing three volumes of verse. Robinson encouraged her in these efforts, but did not stint in criticism of her work. Personally she was lively where her husband was inclined to be shy, and in company she was one of the few whose cheerfulness could release EAR from his customary taciturnity. The Perrys were old enough to be Robinson's parents, and they came to regard him as more or less an adoptive son. Their daughter Margaret, the oldest of three siblings, also became EAR's friend. They called him Rob, or Robbie, although no one else did, and the name signified what the Perrys considered to be true: that they understood and loved him as no one else could.

After EAR died, Margaret Perry struck up a friendship with Ruth Nivison, with whom she shared a November birthday and a determination to protect the poet and his family's reputation. She could not be in Gardiner for the 12 May 1935 observances, but received a full report on the proceedings from George Burnham, or "M. F. B." (my friend Burnham), as she referred to him. Her letter of May 23 ridiculed Kenneth C. M. Sills, president of Bowdoin, who had delivered a singularly generalized and dull eulogy at the memorial service. What most bothered Margaret Perry, who continued to live in Hancock and to support the MacDowell Colony, was that Sills had not so much as mentioned the colony in his remarks. As she put it in characteristically vivid language—Miss Perry was a woman of opinions, and eager to express them—"the poor ignorant man [Sills] in his rude, untutored way left out the only important fact of yr. uncle's life [his time at MacDowell]. He sh'd be taken out behind the barn & shot at dawn, or otherwise disposed of. He is a worm and no man" (Perry to Nivison, Colby).

This established the tone Margaret Perry would follow in succeeding months, as she repeatedly advised Ruth Nivison to have as little to do as possible with "those people who try so hard to feather their nests at old Rob's expense." During the three years before the biography appeared, Miss Perry became a close family friend of the Nivisons, visiting them so often that young David—only twelve in 1935—came to think of her as almost a member of the family. She was unlike anyone he'd ever met, and he liked her a lot. He remembered her as "of moderate height, late middle-aged, perhaps a bit heavy, brown hair not quite graying, a large face, loose fleshed, often jolly"—the first of a succession of brainy people that EAR's death brought to Gardiner. She was unmistakably female, but mannish in appearance. One evening David embarrassed his mother by announcing at dinner, "Miss Perry, you look just like Joe E. Brown," a movie comedian whose comically wide-visaged face the boy had become acquainted with at the local cinema. Miss Perry at once smoothed matters over.

On another occasion the Nivisons, who were moderately religious Episcopalians, took Margaret Perry to church with them. After the service a number of people gathered around the church entrance to chat, and Miss Perry was introduced to some of them. She was not impressed by the company. "What that parish needs," she later commented, "is some well-selected funerals." She was the sort of person, David Nivison realized in retrospect, who could say something like that and not only get away with it, but have it preserved in memory. In token of friendship, Miss Perry gave the Nivisons one of the Shetland sheep dogs (Jock) that she raised (David Nivison to SD, e-mails 8 May and 12 May 2009).

More importantly, where EAR was concerned, she became a leading figure in the group of New Englanders who set themselves up in opposition to the New York contingent. No one did more to undermine the New Yorkers and what she regarded as their self-seeking machinations—including the biography and the book of letters they were bent upon producing—in the mind and heart of Ruth Nivison than Margaret Perry.

In the afterword of *Where the Light Falls*, the memoir of EAR that he published in 1965, Chard Powers Smith summed up the difficulty posed by separate groups of EAR's friends/advocates. Each of these compartmentalized groups, he observed, believed that "it alone represented the utmost discipleship, and was alone accredited to protect him against the uncomprehending, insensitive and obviously predatory rest." The "dominant New York group" centered around "two moderately wealthy and cultivated families"—the Isaacses and Ledoux. Both of these, Smith wrote, were "highly respectable in the later Victorian sense which E. A. admired," and both "were extraordinarily protective, which is to say possessive, of him." Smith did not, however, discuss the New England group in any detail, probably because he did not know much about it. His own involvement had been solely with the New Yorkers, against whom he may have felt a certain animus. Smith had, after all, hoped that if Torrence turned down the assignment, Isaacs and Ledoux would ask him "to do the official biography" (C. P. Smith, 356–57).

Smith was still harboring expectations along this line when he wrote Mrs. Richards in August 1935 about the section of her memoir that had appeared in the *New York Herald Tribune Books*. He also felt compelled to write something about E. A., Smith said, for only in that way could "the unique flavor of the man survive. Scholarship may dig up facts and dates a century hence, but the personality must be inscribed by those who knew him intimately, or it will be lost" (Smith to Richards, 21 August 1935, Colby).

Perhaps so, but by that time George Brett at Macmillan had taken matters into his own hands and pretty much settled on Hermann Hagedorn as EAR's official biographer.

With Torrence out of the picture, Brett approached Hagedorn and received an encouraging response. "I have felt for years that I should love to have the opportunity to do E. A.'s life," Hagedorn wrote Brett on August 15. He was not interested in a critical biography, Hagedorn made clear. "I am seeing the book primarily . . . as the story of a man who happened to be a great poet, . . . not as a study of the works of a poet who had incidentally a noble and attractive personality." Biography interested him primarily "as portraiture," he added. Over the years Hagedorn had converted himself from poet to professional biographer, producing a popular book for young adults on Theodore Roosevelt, as well as life stories of General Leonard Wood and businessman William Boyce Thompson. He sent Brett a copy of *The Magnate,* his just-published book about Thompson, adding that he was at the moment writing a biography of Robert S. Brookings, founder of the Brookings Institution, but that he expected to complete his work by the spring of 1936 (Hagedorn to Brett, NYPL).

Ledoux was not initially enthusiastic about Hagedorn as biographer. On the positive side, as he wrote Brett, he liked Hagedorn and admired his early verse. Furthermore, Hagedorn had known Robinson quite well and was "a gentleman . . . whose tact and judgment could be relied on." But Ledoux had not seen Hagedorn or read any of his books for at least fifteen years, and there were questions that troubled him, some of them deriving from the anti-Teutonic bias of his French heritage. "Has [Hagedorn], for example, any sense of humor? E. A. R. had a great deal. Would the German background of his bringing up detract from his ability to estimate properly a man who, both in his personality and his work, was thoroughly a product of New England?"

Before agreeing on Hagedorn for the job, Ledoux asked publisher Brett to sound out Bliss Perry at Harvard (no relation to Thomas Sergeant Perry) as a candidate. Hagedorn needn't know about this overture (Ledoux to Brett, 22 August 1935, NYPL).

Brett did as executor Ledoux advised. "You knew E. A. R. as few knew him," he wrote Bliss Perry early in September, and he felt sure that the distinguished Harvard professor would "do just the biography that we would want to publish." Perry promised to consider the matter, but set down a series of daunting difficulties. First, he was nearly seventy-five and wrote slowly, while Brett seemed to want a rapid turnaround. He also wondered how much "letter material" had been gathered for the use of a biographer. Above all, though, he saw EAR's "extraordinary reticence" as a giant stumbling block. Robinson spoke freely about his books and the process of writing them, but kept silence "about his boyhood, his Harvard days, the N.Y. Custom House days, and all those personal matters contemporary biographers dote upon." Perry knew Robinson had been a drinker, for the poet admitted as much himself. But he didn't even know if EAR had ever been in love, and felt reluctant to invade any territory Robinson preferred to keep to himself (Brett to Bliss Perry, 5 September 1935; Bliss Perry to Brett, 10 September 1935, NYPL).

On these grounds, Perry withdrew, and despite Ledoux's reservations Hagedorn became the anointed biographer. A contract was duly signed, in which Hagedorn was apparently guaranteed a certain sum—the amount is unknown—to do the job as quickly as possible.

Hagedorn on the Trail

Ten years EAR's junior, Hagedorn had been a brilliant student at Harvard, and was chosen class poet in his senior year. When he met Robinson in the summer of 1910, Hagedorn was only three years out of Harvard and determined to devote his energies toward a literary career. Tall, handsome, somewhat authoritarian in manner, he was also well-to-do, his father—an immigrant from Germany—having made a fortune in the New York Cotton Exchange. On their first meeting, Hagedorn urged Robinson to apply for a summer residency at the MacDowell Colony. Later, he sent EAR occasional loans to help him survive the poverty-stricken years of 1911 to 1913. Robinson vowed to pay these back, and may even have done so after the financial success of *Tristram*, his long Arthurian poem of 1927. The very idea of writing blank verse about Arthurian figures derived in good part from the example of Hagedorn's "The Great Maze," a 1916 work which refashioned the material of Greek tragedy—the story of the house of Atreus—in modern dress. Shortly after reading that "altogether stunning" poem, EAR wrote his first two long Arthurian poems, *Merlin* (1917) and *Lancelot* (1920).

Perhaps as a consequence of obligations owed, perhaps because of a twinge of envy Hagedorn felt about the extraordinary success of *Tristram*, perhaps because EAR refused Hagedorn's 1930 request to write an introduction to a volume of his poetry, the friendship between the two men cooled during Robinson's last years (SD, *Robinson*, 264, 273–74, 329, 419, 443). Ledoux and Isaacs and Brett probably knew little about this drifting apart. It may be that no one except the two men themselves knew that Hagedorn sent EAR funds during his darkest days. And it would be unjust to conclude that the eventual failure of Hagedorn's biography resulted from any personal resentments. There were plenty of other obstacles confronting him as he set about the task of commemorating the life of Edwin Arlington Robinson. Most of these derived from animosity between the poet's executors and friends in New York and his family and friends in New England.

Trouble developed soon after the selection of Hagedorn when Lewis Isaacs sent Ruth Nivison, her sisters, and her mother, Emma Robinson, a document to sign that would have granted Isaacs and Ledoux sweeping powers over EAR's biography and a volume of his letters. This document, composed in the insensitivity of legalese, was to be signed by the family members Robinson designated as his heirs:

> We, the undersigned, residuary legatees named in the Will of Edwin Arlington Robinson, do hereby authorize and empower you, the Executors named in said Will, and, in the event of the death of either of you, the survivor, to take such action and to make such decisions with respect to the publication of a proposed biography of Edwin Arlington Robinson, and of a collection of his letters, as you may in your uncontrolled discretion from time to time determine upon, whether or not you shall have therefore rendered your account of proceedings as Executors and shall have been discharged from your duties and obligations as such; it being our intention to vest in you, and your survivor, continuing power and authority to determine all questions which may arise with respect to such biography and letters.
>
> We understand that it is your intention now to approve a contract about to be entered into between the Macmillan Company as publishers, and Hermann Hagedorn, as author, for the writing of the biography, in connection with which you propose to agree that the biographer shall be given access to all available letters and other documents, and the privilege to use and quote from same, without payment of any compensation therefor to the Estate; and we specifically ratify and confirm such action on your part. We further understand that in connection with the publication of any collection of letters, you may or may not be in a position to arrange that royalties or other compensation be paid to the Estate; and we specifically authorize you to make such arrangement in connection with such publication as to you seems most desirable, even though such arrangement shall not call for the payment of any compensation to the Estate or to us as residuary legatees.

By the time this letter reached her in Maine, Ruth Nivison had emerged as contact person and spokesman for the Robinson family. She was well qualified for the role. She graduated at the head of her class at Bradford Academy, took a nursing degree, and practiced that profession for a number of years before marrying William Nivison, foreman (and later superintendent) in the

Gardiner mill of the Hollingsworth and Whitney Paper Company. The Nivisons had two sons, both of whom were to achieve unusual success in life: Bill as an admiral in the United States Navy, David as an eminent scholar of Chinese history and philosophy at Stanford. Ledoux and Isaacs sent her a series of amiable communications during the months after EAR's death, but she was put off by the document printed above, and understandably so.

Considered objectively, this missive seemed designed to eliminate any need for the executors to secure approval—or seek cooperation—from the family during the process of producing a biography of EAR and a book of his letters, even if the time involved extended beyond completion of their legal duties as executors. Ruth Nivison thought these provisos "very terrifying" and refused to sign.

Her position was not based on financial grounds, nor (at that time) on any objection to Hermann Hagedorn as designated biographer. Speaking for her mother and siblings, Nivison replied that "[w]e agree most gladly and willingly (a) to waive all potential and possible profit from the publication and sale of the proposed biography, and (b) to aid in every way within reason in providing material for the biography and in securing letters of E. A. R. for whomsoever may publish a volume of the same in the future whether the present executors be dead or living." It was unfortunate that Carty Ranck had not been given proper consideration as a biographer, she commented. Nonetheless, the family was "very much pleased" with the choice of Hagedorn, "as we feel that his skill in presenting the subject is very great." Her objection to the document granting absolute authority to the executors stemmed from the family's desire to maintain its privacy as much as possible, to be consulted on "suitable information" to be disseminated in any biography, and to delay publication of any book of letters well into the future (Isaacs to Nivison, October 1935, 6 November 1935, 19 November 1935, 14 November 1937, Colby).

Ruth Nivison sent a copy of her response to Margaret Perry, who applauded her for taking a stand. "Of course this whole question proves . . . what everybody knows, viz. that it is impossible to write a definitive life within 50 years of a man's death," Miss Perry said, and she was even more adamant about the prospective volume of letters. When approached by a collector who offered to purchase Robinson's letters to her husband and herself, her mother, Lilla Cabot Perry, had indignantly observed that she was not in the habit of making money from her correspondence with friends. In much the same spirit, when George Brett at Macmillan asked Margaret Perry to send her parents' letters from EAR for the biography, she first pointed out that at least one of them contained information that should not be circulated, and that if it could not be withheld she could "settle the matter satisfactorily by burning the letter" (Perry to Nivison, 13 November 1935, Colby). Eventually she refused to send Brett any letters at all.

As Isaacs pointed out, the Robinson family's decision not to sign the document meant that he and Ledoux would have to confine their efforts to the exact limits of their legal authority. Isaacs concluded formal administration of the estate by the middle of June 1936, sending four checks for $498.51 to each of the heirs (Isaacs to Nivison, Colby). By that time, he and Ledoux had contracted with Macmillan both for Hagedorn's biography and a volume of EAR letters. Despite the disagreement between them, Isaacs maintained a friendly tone in letters to Mrs. Nivison, urging her and her husband to come to New York, or to the Isaacses' summer home in Pelham, so they might better get to know each other. Ledoux made similar comments in writing Ruth Nivison, but it was not until October 1936 that he actually came to Gardiner to meet the Robinson family members. Had the executors and the family foregathered earlier, some of the bitterness about the biography and the letters might have been averted.

Hagedorn at least was careful—and professional—enough to present himself in Gardiner ("Gardner," he unfortunately spelled it) in mid-December 1935. "I know that you must be a little anxious wondering what this stranger may do with a life—indeed with various lives—which were close and dear to you," he wrote Mrs. Nivison. On this visit he simply wanted to introduce himself to the Robinson family and to Laura Richards. He would stay only a weekend, and would not expect to gather material. Then he would return for a month or so in the summer (Hagedorn to Nivison, 2 December 1935, Colby).

This procedure inspired a few rare favorable words from Margaret Perry, whom Ruth immediately informed about Hagedorn's forthcoming visit. "I think you will find H. H. [Hagedorn] a pleasant appreciative and sympathetic human being," Miss Perry commented. He was hardly to be blamed for Ledoux and Isaacs "snatching after power" and Macmillan "snatching, deviously, after pelf." She advised Mrs. Nivison to be "perfectly frank and perfectly friendly" with Hagedorn. It would be "unfair to him and unfair to old Rob" to antagonize the biographer. She further cautioned Nivison, though, to make it clear to Hagedorn that she was anxious to do what her uncle would have wanted. EAR wanted "certain things" to go unmentioned, she knew. For example, he'd warned that whoever wrote his biography should leave his unfortunate brothers out of it.

In his introduction to the letters of Thomas Sergeant Perry, EAR demonstrated the kind of restraint that was called for. Perry's later years, Robinson observed parenthetically, "were clouded by a long bereavement to which he seldom referred, and for which nothing more could be done"

(Perry, *Selections*, 11). No one who did not know the circumstances could possibly have guessed that EAR was referring to the mental illness of the Perrys' daughter Edith. That, both Robinson and Margaret Perry thought, was the way it should be. According to the New England code of reticence, some things were not to be spoken of or written about—at least not before the passage of time alleviated the pain.

Miss Perry discussed the matter with Burnham ("M. F. B."), she added, and she offered to dispatch him to Gardiner in advance of Hagedorn should Ruth want his counsel. Under no circumstances was Ruth to mention her name to the biographer, Margaret cautioned. She did not want Hagedorn descending on her in Hancock. "Darling, I am just thinking with my pen in hand," she concluded her letter of advice. "[D]on't think I have the incredible conceit to try to tell you what to say or do" (Perry to Nivison, 8 December 1935, Colby).

Following his get-acquainted weekend in Gardiner, Hagedorn went directly to Boston in an attempt to make peace with George Burnham and Carty Ranck. Ranck was out of town, but after a pleasant dinner with Hagedorn, Burnham wrote Ruth Nivison that he thought the biographer would "write a most satisfactory book about your uncle" (Burnham to Nivison, 17 December 1935, Colby). After talking with Burnham, Hagedorn wrote Ruth Nivison, he was beginning "to see the framework of a great story appear" (Hagedorn to Nivison, 18 December 1935, Colby).

Hagedorn got off to a good start, then, arousing in Nivison only a slight sense of unease that he seemed rather too sure of himself. It was understood that he would be back in Gardiner for three or four weeks in the summer of 1936, "really to get to know the town and the country roundabout, and the people," and he expected to make still another pilgrimage to EAR's hometown on a later occasion.

At just this time Hartford insurance executive H. Bacon (Bac) Collamore was emerging as a major figure in the ongoing dispute over how best to preserve Robinson's reputation. A devoted collector or EAR's books and manuscripts, Collamore aligned himself with Miss Perry, Mrs. Nivison, George Burnham, and to a lesser degree Carty Ranck in opposition to the New York contingent, which now included Hagedorn, Percy MacKaye, and Ridgely Torrence as well as executors Ledoux and Isaacs, all five of whom were to serve as coeditors of the book of Robinson's letters.

Collamore had called on Isaacs when he first began collecting Robinson's works, and the two men—rivals through their common pursuit of Robinsoniana—remained on superficially good terms. Soon after EAR's death, an important cache of letters that he wrote to Edith Brower during his early struggles to establish himself came up for sale. It was obvious that these would be "a treasure for a biographer," as Edith Isaacs, Lewis's wife, commented, but the price was too high for Isaacs, and Collamore bought them instead. Initially Collamore was inclined to let Hagedorn consult these letters to Brower, but then he changed his mind and withheld them from the biographer and from the contingent of coeditors for the letters book. In so doing he earned the gratitude of the Robinson family, who strongly opposed publication of a book of letters. Also, by spurning Hagedorn, Collamore hoped to advance the cause of Lawrance (Larry) Thompson, a young scholar then eager to write a biography of EAR. (Later, Thompson switched subjects to Robert Frost.)

The lines were thus drawn between two cadres of Robinson admirers. Each felt sure that it was proceeding exactly as the poet would have wished, and attributed the worst possible motives to the opposing group. As Margaret Perry expressed it in a letter to Ruth Nivison, the two of them belonged to a secret society called the "Friends of Robinson," while the New York group was made up of "Exploiters of Robinson" seeking personal gain or power (Perry to Nivison, 6 August 1936). Edith Isaacs in New York, on the other hand, spoke of a "genuine cabal" of the New Englanders (note to letter of 19 May 1934, NYPL).

Where EAR's letters were concerned, both Ruth Nivison and her mother believed that any volume of correspondence should be postponed for many years, in order not to call public attention to the dysfunctional family and cause acute discomfort among its survivors. Once again, as she had six months previously, Mrs. Nivison expressed herself on this matter to Ledoux, who was the driving force behind the letters volume. Writing her on 10 January 1936, Ledoux said that in many ways he agreed with her about publication of letters. "Sometimes," he said, the prospect of doing so made him "squirm." But EAR seemed to want such a volume to appear, and so "the whole question" boiled down to the choice of people to do the editing "and the preservation of perfect dignity in the volume itself."

Ledoux also expressed the opinion that he and Isaacs had the right as executors to allow or prevent publication of EAR's letters. He thought that Ranck, for example, could not print his letters from Robinson without obtaining their permission. But Ledoux went on to add that "after the closing of the estate the heirs would have a similar right of restraint" (Ledoux to Nivison, 10 January 1936, Colby). They exercised that right. When the estate officially closed several months later, the Robinson family and its allies saw to it that EAR's extensive correspondence with Edith Brower and that with his friend Harry de Forest Smith did not fall into the hands of Hagedorn or anyone else in the New York editorial group.

These were the two most important holdings of Robinson letters extant. The correspondence with Harry de Forest Smith, EAR's closest friend in high school, covered the period when Smith was studying at Bowdoin while

Robinson languished at home, EAR's two years at Harvard, and his return to Gardiner determined to fashion himself into a writer: crucial formative years in the poet's development. Like Robinson, Smith was a literary lad—the two of them embarked on a collaborative translation of Sophocles' *Antigone* into blank verse—and the youthful EAR openly unburdened himself to Smith about his aspirations and family difficulties.

Still more vital were the letters to Edith Brower for their insights into the next half dozen years when EAR lived in abject poverty while struggling for recognition—and his next meal—in New York City. Brower was visiting manuscript doctor Titus Coan's office in New York when she happened upon a copy of Robinson's *The Children of the Night*, immediately decided he was a genius, and wrote him to say so. Perhaps because he knew Brower at a distance—they met only once, when EAR made a pilgrimage to her home in Wilkes-Barre, Pennsylvania—he abandoned his usual reserve and wrote to her of his inmost hopes and fears. Hagedorn, however, was unable to examine either of these invaluable sources, and as a consequence his biography only skimmed the surface of EAR's career beginnings. Robinson's letters to Smith were eventually published in 1947, and those to Brower in 1968, in separate volumes from Harvard University Press.

In its continuing quest for Robinson letters, Macmillan issued two separate appeals in June 1936, a year after the firm's first public requests. "Friends of the late Edwin Arlington Robinson are planning to collect and edit a volume of his letters which Macmillan will publish," the *New York Herald Tribune* "Book Notes" for June 18 observed (Box 87, NYPL). Anyone having such letters was urged to send them by registered mail to Hagedorn at 28 East 20th Street, New York, with a promise that they would be returned. In that way, they would be useful first for the biography and later for the book of letters. Personal requests were also mailed to Robinson's friends and acquaintances asking to see their communications from EAR. Ledoux wrote directly to Ruth Nivison, for instance, asking that she "get for [him] from the family any letters" she would be willing for the five coeditors of the letters volume to see. All "tactful discretion" would be exercised, he assured her, and none of the letters would be printed without the family's approval (Ledoux to Nivison, 2 June 1936, Colby). There were a number of EAR letters in the possession of Ruth Nivison and Emma Robinson. They forwarded none of them to Ledoux, or to Hagedorn.

In midsummer 1936 Laura Richards published *E. A. R.*, her memoir of the poet's youth in Gardiner. This slim and engaging book left the family secrets in the closet, and did not unduly displease Ruth or Emma. Nonetheless, a division was springing up between the Richardses and Robinsons. As a professional, Mrs. Richards threw her support behind the New York executors and their chosen biographer. She sent *her* letters from EAR to Ridgely Torrence, and her daughter Rosalind, who struck up an animated correspondence with Torrence, did the same. This placed them at odds with Ruth Nivison, who was becoming increasingly dubious about both Hagedorn's biography and the proposed volume of letters.

At the beginning of August, Hagedorn and his wife came to Gardiner on a research trip. He interviewed a number of people, including Emma Robinson and Rosalind Richards—the two women the young poet had fallen in love with. Hagedorn made his headquarters at Ruth Nivison's home during this visit, where the relations between the two turned chilly. She was put off by his overconfident manner, and by the fact that Macmillan was paying him a fee to write the biography: "the very idea reeked of being inauthentic," she told her son David (David S. Nivison to SD, e-mail, 8 May 2009). So she followed the advice of Margaret Perry, going to bed early so as to avoid confidential evening conversations and doing as little as possible to assist Hagedorn's research. She shouldn't feel remorseful about this, Miss Perry counseled her, for Hagedorn and "the whole gang [were] perfectly selfish and self-seeking" (Perry to Nivison, 9 August 1936, Colby). The atmosphere became so bleak that the Hagedorns spent only one week of the projected three or four in Gardiner.

Collamore also commiserated with Ruth Nivison about Hagedorn's visit. "I am sorry you are having so much difficulty with searchers after knowledge," Collamore wrote. He hoped she could keep the family in line, and promised her that he and Miss Perry, both "pretty good scrappers," were prepared to back her up (Collamore to Nivison, 15 August 1936, Colby). By way of advancing that cause, Collamore sought out Harry de Forest Smith at Amherst and encouraged him to withhold his EAR letters from Hagedorn. "I know you will be pleased to hear that [those letters] are not going to be turned over to Hagedorn et al.," he reported to Ruth Nivison on September 28 (Colby). The only thing Smith agreed to do when Hagedorn called on him was to answer specific questions, if he felt they were appropriate.

Despite the disastrous August visit, Hagedorn still hoped to win over Mrs. Nivison (and so gain access to the letters) by his address at a memorial ceremony for Robinson in Gardiner on Sunday, October 18. That event, organized by Laura Richards, culminated in the unveiling of a ten-foot granite tablet on the town common, only a few blocks from EAR's boyhood home. Hagedorn, the principal speaker, characterized Robinson as an "anchorite" who existed "outside space and time, conscious of an eternal Eye upon him and upon the work of his hands." By all accounts it was an excellent talk, eloquently delivered. As Emma Robinson wrote Mrs. Richards, thanking her for organizing the memorial, "Mr. Hagedorn's address was a masterpiece . . . and I was *thrilled*. . . . Now if the biography will only be all right . . . and Ruth get some rest and peace of mind, we can all be happy once more" (Emma Robinson to Laura Richards, 27 October 1936, Gardiner). Ridgely Torrence was similarly impressed. The address bolstered his increasing confidence that Hagedorn would produce "something very much worth while" in his biography (Torrence to Richards, 22 November 1936, Gardiner).

Inclined to agree, Ruth Nivison was tempted to abandon her stand against Hagedorn. The occasion of the memorial had brought almost all of the leading adversaries together in one place: Ledoux as well as Hagedorn and Torrence from New York, Collamore and his wife (who stayed with the Nivisons), Lawrance Thompson, and Margaret Perry of the New England cadre. Both camps were aware that Mrs. Nivison was more or less under siege by opposing forces. Ledoux, for example, described her as "a rare person with a good deal of her Uncle's quality" who was unfortunately required to wear "the chain mail that sometimes is necessary when a number of curiously divergent types of people come down on one like a flock of buzzards" (Ledoux to Rosalind Richards, 21 March 1937, Gardiner). Margaret Perry vehemently expressed herself on the New York–based flock—"what dreadful pests all those people were"—in an incendiary letter written immediately following the memorial celebration.

Miss Perry said she was "slightly alarmed" by something Ruth said after hearing "H. H. orate": that she felt "she must now collaborate" with him. That was "sheer piffle," she declared, and she brought in a voice of authority—that of Mrs. Edward MacDowell, widow of the composer and longtime head of the Peterborough colony—to instruct Mrs. Nivison how to proceed. Mrs. MacDowell "adjures you not on any account to assume any responsibility towards the biography. Don't read one page of it, don't take any part in its arrangement." Otherwise Macmillan might advertise the book as written with the family's cooperation. "Keep out of the whole mess," Miss Perry advised Nivison. She expressed herself with such urgency because she was "terrified lest those crooks should wear you down." If Ruth stuck to her guns, Hagedorn might even give up. He'd looked worried at Gardiner, Margaret Perry pointed out. Ruth "had all the cards in [her] hand and he knows it" (Perry to Nivison, 21 October 1936, Colby).

Hagedorn did not give up. During the two full years that elapsed between the EAR memorial in Gardiner and publication of his *Edwin Arlington Robinson* in October 1938, he—and Ledoux, and Torrence, and Isaacs—tried repeatedly to pry the Brower and other letters out of confinement. But Ruth Nivison stuck to the course of action—or more accurately, inaction—that Margaret Perry laid out for her. Early in 1937, Emma Robinson did cooperate with Hagedorn to the extent of supplying a family genealogy and some letters written by EAR's mother and his brother Herman, her husband. In that way, as from other sources, Hagedorn became apprised of Herman's addiction to drink. This was a subject that could hardly have escaped any serious biographer's notice, but Emma apparently hoped that a "sweet and gentle" fellow such as Hagedorn appeared to be when extolling EAR's virtues might ignore the matter in the book he was writing.

Hagedorn planned one more visit to Gardiner for two weeks in July and August 1937. Mrs. Richards offered him the use of her house and also dictated ten pages of notes to her daughter Rosalind for Hagedorn's use. "Hermann, dear," she added, it might seem absurd to gather all these threads together, but she and Rosalind felt they "must not fail in any smallest item that might conceivably help" (Gardiner). Ruth Nivison, on the other hand, was resolved not to help at all. Hagedorn canceled his projected visit to Gardiner after learning from Rosalind Richards that Ruth would have nothing to do with the biography, would not "go through the ordeal" of discussing the matter with him, and was prepared to leave town should he turn up. Under the circumstances it seemed better to stay away. Collamore's keeping the Brower letters from him, Hagedorn concluded, was part of "a general boycott" of the biography by Mrs. Nivison, Miss Perry, Mr. Collamore, and Ranck. He was inclined to think that Collamore was "behind it all" (Hagedorn to George Burnham, 22 July 1937, Colby).

Only Louis Ledoux of the New York group managed to establish friendly relations with Ruth Nivison. They got along well when Louis and his wife Jean came up for the October 1936 memorial, and the Ledoux invited Ruth and her family to visit them at their summer home in Cornwall. That did not happen, but Ledoux and his son Pierre came to see the Nivisons in the spring of 1938.

In two letters of the previous August, Ledoux proposed strategies to get around the impasse with Hagedorn. He commiserated with Ruth Nivison about the "tactlessness" the biographer had exhibited during his week at her house in Gardiner, attributing it to "the thoroughness inherited from his German ancestors." Then he trotted out a plan to provide this clumsy Teuton with at least partial access to the letters Collamore was withholding. Couldn't Collamore show her all the letters, and then she could pass on any she didn't object to for consideration by the group doing the collected letters and "for the help of a much distressed Mr. Hagedorn?" The second suggestion had to do with a rough draft of twelve chapters Hagedorn was circulating to interested parties for comments and suggested emendations. Ledoux was to see the manuscript soon, and next Hagedorn planned to send it to Mrs. Richards. Then, Ledoux proposed, Mrs. Richards could pass it along to Ruth Nivison before returning it to Hagedorn with suggested revisions of both of them. This seemed "a providentially simple way to get the manuscript before you for your criticism," Ledoux commented, and had the advantage of bypassing any need for direct communication between

Mrs. Nivison and Hagedorn (Ledoux to Nivison, 3 August 1937, 26 August 1937, Colby).

Neither of these proposals worked out. As to the Brower letters, Ruth Nivison took the position that she had no control over them at all. As to reading a draft of the biography-in-process, she preferred not to do so "unless asked to by the author with some assurance of power to make corrections." He could not guarantee any such ceding of power by Hagedorn, Ledoux responded, for "what you might consider a correction might seem to him a misinterpretation of fact or something that would throw an entirely wrong light on the subject" (Ledoux to Nivison, 1 September 1937, Colby).

Soon thereafter Emma Robinson sent Hagedorn a heartfelt communication, designed to appeal to his better nature. Without alluding directly to the problems of the three Robinson brothers—Dean's drug addiction and death by overdose, the alcoholism that ruined Herman's marriage and career, and EAR's own long (and finally successful) battle with the bottle— she pointed out that what represented Hagedorn's "bread and butter" was "to us . . . having to publish a grief we thought buried forever." Robinson wrote to leave poems behind him, "*not* for notoriety or to have his family life exposed" to a pitiless public. She realized she had no power to change anything, Emma said, but she hoped that in writing the biography Hagedorn would "be merciful." That way, some time in the future they might "again be friends" (Lawrance Thompson, EAR Notes, Gardiner).

This letter provoked replies from both Hermann and Dorothy Hagedorn. Mrs. Hagedorn's assured Emma that the life of EAR was safe in "my Hermann's" hands. He was honest and sympathetic, he loved Robinson, he was acutely sensitive in regard to Emma and to Ruth and her boys, and no one else would write a better biography. She mentioned the unfortunate visit the Hagedorns had made to Gardiner a year earlier—"a rather ghastly experience for us"—and thanked Emma for making it possible for them "to stay even as long as they did" (Dorothy Hagedorn to Emma Robinson, 5 September 1937, Colby).

In his businesslike response, Hagedorn came right to the point. "I wish I could do as you wish, and leave out of the book all reference to alcohol," he wrote Emma, "but it would be the worst possible tribute to EA. His triumphant struggle against the Demon is one of the essential and glorious facts of his life." In the book, he also told her, he'd pointed out that her husband Herman "had pulled himself together and was trying to make a fresh start" during the year before he died. "Honesty is the best friend of any man's reputation, living or dead," Hagedorn asserted. However, there was more than one way of telling the truth, and he intended to present the facts in such a way that they offended no one (Hagedorn to Emma Robinson, 9 September 1937, Colby). Emma Robinson was not reassured by these observations, nor was her daughter Ruth.

With Hagedorn's biography nearing publication, the New York contingent made two additional attempts to liberate the Brower letters. In December 1937, after running into Collamore at a book sale, Lewis Isaacs issued an appeal to Mrs. Nivison. The reason he would not allow access to the Brower letters, Collamore had told Isaacs, was that Ruth had asked him not to. If that was the case, wouldn't she release Collamore from this obligation? Were she to do so, it would help Hagedorn produce the best biography possible of her uncle. Moreover (here Isaacs was making a new concession), the letters would be seen only by Hagedorn, and not passed on for use in the later volume of EAR correspondence. Collamore, who was sent a copy of Isaacs's letter, suggested to Mrs. Nivison that she tell Isaacs the letters had not yet been fully transcribed (which was true, for Robinson's handwriting was extremely difficult to construe), and so she had no way of knowing whether it was appropriate to divulge their contents. Ruth Nivison chose to reply to Isaacs more directly. She had not exacted any promise about her uncle's letters to Brower, she said, but was delighted to find that Collamore agreed with her about the sanctity of personal letters (Isaacs to Nivison, 14 December 1937; Collamore to Nivison, 15 December 1937, Colby).

Five months later Hagedorn brought up the issue again in a final entreaty. "I have reason to believe that Mr. Collamore and Miss Perry have refused to let me see their letters because they felt that you didn't want me to have them," he wrote Mrs. Nivison. He wasn't sure how important the Perry letters might be, but was convinced that the ones to Brower contained material of vital importance regarding Robinson's early years in New York. Time was running short, Hagedorn pointed out; he was about to ship his manuscript to the publishers. But if he had the chance to see the letters within the next fortnight, he could still make revisions and produce a book that would do greater justice to EAR's memory. "Won't you, before it's too late, speak a persuasive word?"

Ruth Nivison drafted two different replies to Hagedorn. The one she sent followed the same lines as her response to Isaacs. She had not asked either Miss Perry or Collamore to withhold their letters, but they were all agreed against any use of them at present. The reply she did not send betrayed more than a trace of exasperation. Hagedorn's letter painted her "in lurid colors," Ruth said, for she had already told both him and Isaacs that she "did not consciously exact any promise." It also addressed the strongest reason behind her unwillingness to cooperate. "When the biography was first under discussion, I protested that such an undertaking was utterly futile without going quite thoroughly into family affairs which at the present time is unsuitable, and I still believe this to be true. Equally unsuitable, I think, is the use of letters concerning contemporary persons" (Hagedorn to Nivison, 16 May 1938; Nivison to Hagedorn (2), 18 May 1938, Colby).

Apprised of this final plea from Hagedorn, Collamore actually offered to unbend, and to let the biographer see approximately the one half of the Brower letters which had been transcribed, if Mrs. Nivison and Miss Perry thought that appropriate. "I should hate to feel that I was being unkind or unjust," he observed—a remark Miss Perry would surely have characterized as "sheer piffle" (Collamore to Nivison, 20 May 1938, Colby). On a trip to Colby College that same week, she vigorously expressed her opposition to Macmillan and all those involved in the forthcoming biography and book of letters. "[EAR's] publishers have acted most ungenerously toward his estate," Miss Perry told Colby's Carl Weber. "Hagedorn is not the one to do the biography, and that jackanapes MacKaye is certainly not the one to edit the letters." Even worse, she thought, was the way people "camp[ed] down" on poor Mrs. Nivison, worrying her for this or for that (Perry, "Reminiscences of Edwin Arlington Robinson," 21 May 1938, Colby). "Confound H. H.," she wrote Ruth directly. "I wish to Heaven he'd stop pestering you" (Perry to Nivison, 20 May 1938, Colby).

Collamore's offer may well have been a hollow one, in any event. Torrence, who more or less took over as the principal editor of the letters (MacKaye, Ledoux remarked, was often out of the country "being tragic"), inveighed against "the person named Collamore" in a letter to Mrs. Richards of 18 September 1938. "In buying the (Brower) letters he evidently felt that he paid for a hold on E. A.'s coat tails," Torrence wrote. By refusing access to them and gaining a sensation of power, "he probably feels that he is getting his money's worth." Having given up on Collamore's trove, Torrence asked Mrs. Richards's assistance in securing the letters EAR wrote to Harry de Forest Smith. She would know how "to work the spell," he observed (Torrence to Richards, Gardiner).

There was no spell, however, potent enough to change Harry Smith's mind, or Ruth Nivison's, or Margaret Perry's, or Bac Collamore's. The New Englanders awaited the publication of a biography they'd had as little as possible to do with, half in dread and confident they would find in it much to dislike. They were not disappointed.

The Revolt in Gardiner

Feeling that he had achieved his goal of writing "such a good book that it [would] never have to be done again," Hagedorn sent an advance copy of *Edwin Arlington Robinson: A Biography* to Ruth Nivison. "Under the circumstances," she said in her devastating reply, he should not have done so. "I am sorry I cannot offer praise but, with a full appreciation of the work you have put into it, to strip a dead friend of all his reticence for public display, in order to extol others, is not consistent with my code of friendship." In addition to baring the family secrets, the biography was full of inaccuracies, she added. These could have been avoided had he shown "a little cooperation" with her mother Emma, who was in considerable distress over the book (Nivison to Hagedorn, 5 October 1938, Colby).

Three days later Hagedorn's daughter Mary wrote Ruth Nivison in defense of her father. She argued that the biography would be inspirational for readers young and old through its depiction of EAR's victory over the obstacles confronting him. She knew that her father—like Mrs. Nivison herself—"loved Mr. Robinson and would never tolerate anything which might . . . reflect anything but tribute to his memory." Besides, Mary Hagedorn added, consider the alternatives. "If Dad hadn't written a sincere, complete picture (as complete as he could with the material at his disposal) critics knowing more of the facts would have laughed at the book's incompleteness [apparently a reference to EAR's battle with the bottle] and few would have known the deeply moving story of Mr. Robinson's life and great achievement. Then, perhaps, some opportunist would have come along saying, 'Ah, but I have the real inside stuff!' And thus might have come into being what he would call the 'True Story of E. A. R.'—liberally seasoned with falsehood and false innuendo—sensational and disturbing" (Mary Hagedorn to Nivison, 8 October 1938, Colby).

Ruth Nivison may have felt uncomfortable about Hagedorn's daughter acting as his paladin. In her letter to Lewis Isaacs of October 10, she attempted to address the merits of the book as dispassionately as possible. Isaacs asked what she thought of Hagedorn's book. "[I]t seems to me," she answered, "like a eulogy to a group of Uncle Win's friends at the expense of himself and his family—distressing at the present to us, but possibly not important to anyone a generation hence" (Nivison to Isaacs, 10 October 1938, Colby).

In that summary, she accurately described the approach of Hagedorn's book. Hampered by the notorious reserve of EAR himself and the unavailability of invaluable source material, almost by default he presented the poet's life as refracted through a series of laudatory portraits of his friends and benefactors. Notably these included the New Yorkers, close friends of EAR's mature years, who chose Hagedorn as official biographer: Louis and Jean Ledoux, Lewis Isaacs, and Ridgely Torrence. In Gardiner, his admiring gaze fell on Mrs. Richards and her family (he'd been a classmate of her son John at Harvard), who were depicted as offering EAR badly needed solace and support. A favorable review of Hagedorn's book for the *Kennebec Journal* in Maine maintained that these portraits of men and women who knew Robinson well formed "a constellation of brilliant lights" with the poet shining "as the sun of the system" (Lord). But he was a pale sun indeed, for Hagedorn's EAR does not glow with anything like the brightness of, say, the effervescent Torrence. In addition, "the sun" is consistently portrayed as indebted, financially and otherwise, to the members of the constellation. (Circumspectly, Hagedorn did not mention his own loans to a down-and-out EAR.)

The eighty-eight-year-old Laura Richards, who with her daughter Rosalind emerged as Hagedorn's staunchest supporters, noted only two passages she would have deleted in the book's opening sections: an account of EAR's tobacco chewing in boyhood and Hagedorn's "kindly but excessive mention of [the Richards] family." Otherwise she thought the biographer's treatment of Gardiner was "good, very good" (Richards to Torrence, 5 October 1938, Gardiner). For confirmation of her judgment, Mrs. Richards asked both Torrence and Ledoux what they thought of the book, and received less than enthusiastic responses.

Torrence, whose attention was concentrated on the volume of EAR letters, said merely that he thought "E. A. would pass [Hagedorn's book], be willing with one or two elisions to approve of it" (Torrence to Richards, 11 October 1938, Gardiner). Ledoux's response was more complicated. In his role as literary executor, he had consented to Hagedorn as official biographer, but he had done so reluctantly. Then too, he had grown fond of Ruth Nivison and her family. So after learning from Mrs. Richards that Ruth was filled with "wrath and anguish," he adopted a somewhat defensive attitude about the book. Hagedorn had done his best "in a thoroughly conscientious manner," Ledoux observed, and produced an entirely "competent but not inspired piece of work." He hadn't been his first choice for the job, or his second, Ledoux pointed out, yet he felt certain that making a public announcement of his appointment as official biographer had "kept certain people from rushing into print with very much worse, and in some cases psychopathic accounts." He felt "really profound sorrow over Mrs. Nivison's reaction," Ledoux said in closing. "She has no idea of what she missed" (Ledoux to Richards, 31 October 1938, Gardiner).

The reviews of Hagedorn's *Edwin Arlington Robinson* ranged from excellent to terrible. The most favorable were Howard Mumford Jones's in the *Boston Transcript* and Percy Hutchison's in the *New York Times Book Review*. Jones praised the biographer's thoroughness in hunting up sources and consulting "every bit of documentary evidence available to him (and certain collectors unfortunately refused him the courtesy of reading manuscripts in their possession)." As a result, Jones concluded, "the man [EAR] is now revealed, and the personality, shy and reticent and troubled, shines convincingly through Mr Hagedorn's careful and sober pages." His book promised to be "the standard life, which future biographers must always use" (Jones).

Hutchison was equally complimentary. "Edwin Arlington Robinson was the foremost of American poets in our time, and the story of his life could not have fallen into happier hands than those of Hermann Hagedorn, himself a poet and for many years an intimate friend of Robinson." His biography was "witty and tender by turns, and deeply understanding throughout." Hutchison particularly admired Hagedorn's "skillful" and "delicate" passages delineating minor figures in the background of the story, as for instance his description of the poet Josephine Preston Peabody: "[a] slight, incandescent being, with black, unmanageable hair . . . curiously vibrant, almost as a humming-bird is vibrant" (Hutchison).

Horace Gregory in the *New York Herald Tribune Books* provided a more balanced assessment. He noted especially Hagedorn's oblique approach to his subject. "[H]is book has the character of a novel in which the central figure is made visible through the lives of those around him." Hagedorn knew those people, as he knew the New York of the early years of the century where EAR came to seek recognition. As a source book, then, the biography was successful, and would "remain invaluable to other and future biographers of more sharply defined critical insight, of greater social and psychological penetration" (Gregory).

In a devastating attack, Louis Untermeyer in the *Saturday Review* expanded on Hagedorn's lack of understanding. Poet and anthologist, Untermeyer knew EAR from various meetings and as a fellow MacDowell colonist. In a closing paragraph, he summed up his impressions of Robinson—impressions largely shared by Robert Frost, whom Untermeyer served as a disciple. "Some day a biographer will explore the depths beneath Robinson's deceptive surfaces," Untermeyer wrote. The resulting book "will explain the reasons back of [EAR's] distrust of most men and his fear of almost all women, the causes of his limitations, and the desperate sublimation of the laconic, lonely man, a man obsessed by failure and in love with death." Untermeyer also objected to the "prevailing pedestrian style" of the book, and to Hagedorn's attempts to compensate "by fashioning sporadic bits of 'pretty prose,' sticky paragraphs which [Robinson] himself would have found not only incongruous but insufferable." For example, he cited a description of EAR in Gardiner, playing Uncle Win to his nieces: "The next hour was the children's, when he would romp with them, take them pickaback, toss them, and feel the fierce possessiveness of little arms. With a light in his eyes like a star in a well, he would play the fiddle for them." In this passage, as in the one Hutchison liked about Josephine Peabody and many others, Hagedorn revealed himself as a showy writer calling attention to his cleverness. His style was neither Robinsonian nor particularly winning (Untermeyer).

A truly awful review came from Robert Hillyer in the *Atlantic*. Hagedorn's book read like "an extended obituary," Hillyer asserted. Although Hagedorn intended to fashion "a portrait of a man and a poet he greatly admired," his book instead built up "a figure who, whatever the merits of his verse, was despicable as a man. This creature was spineless and whining. He looked forward to inheriting an income because 'jobs and he could not live together.' He sneered at his benefactor, Theodore Roosevelt. . . . He had a gnawing feeling of inferiority" and was constantly trying to prove to the citizens of Gardiner, Maine, that he was just as good as they were. And so on. Surely Hagedorn did not mean to create such a character, Hillyer said, but he was too close to his subject and "counted the pores while the general features eluded him" (Hillyer).

These notices led Mrs. Richards to feel anxious for the "good Hermann who has tried so hard and done so well" and who was suffering, she feared, "from scarification of soul." And in fact, Hillyer's review in the December *Atlantic*, appearing well after publication of his biography, saddened and depressed the biographer. He had, after all, issued a caveat in his foreword to the book, warning readers not to expect too much of a book written so soon after the demise of its subject. "The Robinson who emerges from these pages is not the whole Robinson; he is only the Robinson whom the author, with the evidence at his disposal, has been able to discern, or, with his personal limitations, to comprehend. Others, no doubt, will see deeper and farther" (Hagedorn, x).

In his reaction to the biography, Bac Collamore took his cue not from reviews but from Ruth Nivison. Had she read the book? Collamore asked her in a letter of October 11. He was halfway through it himself, and thought the job was "a good one" but a bit sketchy, leaving "many gaps" to be filled. A week later, after hearing from Mrs. Nivison, Collamore no longer had anything good to say about Hagedorn's book. Instead he proposed a plan to supplant it. "Carty Ranck says that now he must write his book, and I hope he will follow through. Mr. Burnham and I think it would be an excellent idea for him to do this and then let someone, probably Larry Thompson, edit it."

To advance this plan, Collamore organized a dinner in New York for various friends of Robinson who "felt very badly about Hagedorn's effusion." There wouldn't be any controversy, he assured Mrs. Nivison. He and Burnham were agreed that it would be unwise to air their objections in public. Collamore's plan was to find a publisher for the proposed Ranck-Thompson volume (which never materialized, Ranck being unable to produce more than a hundred and fifty pages, mostly consisting of transcriptions of newspaper and magazine articles on Robinson), and add "a discreet introduction which might, without even mentioning Hagedorn's book, take care of it nonetheless" (Collamore to Nivison, 11 October 1938, 18 October 1938, 26 October 1938, Colby).

Apparently Collamore liked to work behind the scenes, making arrangements, scheduling meetings, and consistently aligning himself with Mrs. Nivison. Soon after EAR's death, for example, he joined with Margaret Perry and the Robinson family to purchase the house in Head Tide, Maine, where the poet was born, in order to convert it into a memorial museum of sorts, with George Burnham as curator in residence. This scheme foundered in short order, but it established the Hartford insurance executive as a principal figure in the New England group. In the years that followed, the opposition in New York—unwilling to condemn Mrs. Nivison, who was admired for her intelligence and resemblance to her uncle, and largely unaware of Miss Perry's role—concentrated on Bac Collamore as the villain of the piece. It was only after Collamore "began cultivating" Miss Perry that she decided not to provide her parents' letters from EAR, they believed (Ledoux to Rosalind Richards, 24 November 1938, Gardiner). And they regarded Collamore's withholding the letters to Brower as an unseemly show of authority: he'd bought the letters, and they only gained in value the more others wanted to see them. As late as 1961 Hagedorn still felt bitter about it. "If ever there was a dog in the manger," he remarked (Hagedorn to C. P. Smith, 31 October 1961, Yale).

In late October, while Collamore was organizing his dinner in New York, an unlikely leader emerged in Gardiner to stir up the very sort of controversy the Hartford insurance man had warned against. This was Eben R. Haley, a bona fide Yankee eccentric. A native of Gardiner, Haley graduated from Bowdoin, taught at the Kent School in Connecticut for a decade, and retired at thirty-five to come home and pursue his interests in interior decorating and needlepoint. Ten years EAR's junior, Haley did not know Robinson well, but he did call on him one afternoon at the MacDowell Colony and thereafter made the poet's cause his own. After his death, Haley concentrated his admiration on Emma Robinson, Herman's widow. He sent her notes on Thanksgiving, on one occasion setting down Robert Browning's famous lines from *Pippa Passes*:

The lark's on the wing;
The snail's on the thorn;
God's in His Heaven—
All's right with the world!

On another Thanksgiving day, the message was more personal: "My one prayer today is that your day may be filled with all the joy the earth can hold," Haley wrote her (Haley to Emma Robinson, Thanksgiving 1937, Danny D. Smith Papers). When Hagedorn's biography came out, uncovering family secrets that distressed Emma and otherwise depicting Gardiner unfavorably, Haley sprang into action. He prepared a petition aimed at removing the book from the shelves of the Gardiner public library and the city's high school, and circulated it among local citizens for their signature. The petition spelled out the book's shortcomings.

> We, the undersigned, realizing that the Biography of Edwin Arlington Robinson written by Hermann Hagedorn does not give a true estimate of his character, and does not correctly portray the lives of members of his family, nor of many of our former citizens (containing as it does many items and incidents for which no proof can possibly be presented), feel that the book should not be officially sanctioned by the community.
>
> Out of respect for his memory, his family, his friends and our whole community, we ask that this book shall not have place in our Public Library, nor in the Library of our High School.

With the assistance of James L. M. Bates, another Gardiner resident and one of very few people capable of deciphering EAR's minuscule handwriting, Haley assembled twenty-one local signers for this document. It gave him "great satisfaction to do something for you all," Haley commented in sending the petition and list of signers to Emma Robinson (Haley to Emma Robinson, 31 October 1938, Danny D. Smith Papers). He duly presented these documents to the Gardiner public library as from a group designated as "the Committee on Morals and Manners."

All those signing were local citizens, with the names of Emma Robinson and Ruth Nivison leading the list and those of Bates and Haley bringing up the rear. Mayor Edwin P. Ladd, shoe magnate R. P. Hazzard, and a few others whose forebears Hagedorn had dealt with in cavalier fashion also signed. (Two who did sign later admitted they had not read Hagedorn's book and recanted.)

Notably missing were any signatories from the Richards family, or "the snob group," as Haley characterized them. In upholding "that vicious book," Haley told Emma Robinson, "the treacherously friendly" Richards clan revealed where it stood, not only with regard to the Robinsons but the entire community (Haley to Emma Robinson, 2 November 1938, Danny D. Smith Papers). Word that Haley and his committee had labeled Hagedorn's book as "vicious" reached Mrs. Richards, who responded with a letter dressing down Haley. The biography was *not* "vicious" in the sense of "immoral" or "spiteful," she maintained. On the contrary, she thought Hagedorn had "done a great work in placing in proper focus, the facts as he knew them." Besides, she noted with heavy sarcasm, the publicity "had been a most excellent piece of advertising, not only to help the sale of the book, but also to characterize the 'Committee on Morals and Manners' as a worthy lot of citizens of 'Tilburytown,'" the fictional name of the town inhabited by many of Robinson's characters (Richards to Haley, 11 November 1938, Harvard).

In arriving at its decision, the board invoked the library's proper function. As a democratic institution existing "for the benefit of all people in the community," it aimed to "have material on all sides of controversial subjects of interest to the people." Moreover, the library was building a collection of "material related to the life and writings of Edwin Arlington Robinson." On those impeccable grounds, it chose to retain the copy of Hagedorn's book already on its shelves. At the same time, however, the board of directors acknowledged the biography's "imperfections" and offered its hope that at some future date a completely revised edition might be issued, "omitting all items unnecessary to the book" (Anon., "Library Board Votes").

The economics of publishing did not allow for such a revised edition, and Hagedorn's book was to remain the principal life of Robinson for almost seventy years. Otherwise, however, the library board acted wisely in not banning the biography, or as the petition put it, in letting it "have place" on the shelves. In his campaign to honor all things Robinsonian, Eben Haley continued to rant against Hagedorn and, a few years later, invested 720 hours and 142 different shades of wool in creating a picture in needlepoint of EAR's Head Tide birthplace, "a real work of art along unusual lines" (Anon., "Depicts Home").

There were abundant reasons for Gardiner residents to be outraged by the biography. Hagedorn's superior attitude toward the community and its inhabitants contributed to almost all of these objections. He made unwarranted, undocumented, and even false observations sure to wound Robinson family pride: describing Edward Robinson as "a father who had not been a father" to his sons, mentioning an estrangement between EAR and his brother Herman, and maintaining that the poet's late financial success enabled him to support Emma and her nieces—all of this in addition to revealing the addictions that beset Dean and Herman (Hagedorn, 368, 222).

As for Gardiner itself, Ledoux had been right to worry that Hagedorn's privileged Germanic background and lack of a sense of humor might prevent him from understanding the culture of a small New England community. Hagedorn spent only two weeks there, yet clearly felt he had taken the measure of the place. "Charming, picturesque, redolent of old lavender," he wrote, "Gardiner's social life moved to the time-beat of Millard Fillmore." It "had nothing to say to a craftsman [such as EAR], struggling to shape a medium of expression . . . remote from the literary language which Gardiner recognized." Then Hagedorn went on to denigrate a number of the town's more "picturesque" citizens he'd heard about. Among them was "Southwest" Tarbox, the miser he equated with EAR's "Aaron Stark" as "[c]ursed and unkempt, shrewd, shriveled, and morose," and another Tarbox who (like EAR's "John Evereldown") never could "leave the women alone, lurking in doorways, disheveled and furtive-eyed. . . . There was Peg-leg Talbot, the disreputable 'tin knocker' who repaired stoves; Wash Benjamin, who had a mistress down the road and cursed the Episcopal Church every chance he had; Squire Whitmore who was so close he kept only one hen which, he said, could lay all the eggs he and his sister would want to eat" (Hagedorn, 52–53). In these capsule sketches, Hagedorn provided local color and suggested that he knew far more than he did. But or course there were people still living in Gardiner—descendants of those Hagedorn belittled—whose feeling were hurt. The son of Peg-leg Talbot, for instance, was one of the prime movers in circulating the petition against the book. He didn't want a copy on the high school library shelves where his children might read about their grandfather.

Even for readers without personal involvement, Hagedorn's disdain for Gardiner, its residents, and its values patently declared itself. His book could be read easily, and with some pleasure, as an entertainment. But the biographer included no notes to identify sources and was frustratingly vague about dates and locations. In addition, his volume was full of errors of fact and emphasis. David Nivison, for example, read it as a teenager and immediately perceived some things invented for effect. Hagedorn mentioned Gardiner's red clay, for instance, but Nivison knew from observation that there was not a speck of red earth in town, and later, studying at Harvard, read a book on geography that confirmed the fact. Hagedorn asserted that EAR "learned at home to be a gourmet," relishing snails and roast mussels, but Emma Robinson could not recall ever encountering either of those dishes in Gardiner. Such inventions did suggest, as David Nivison concluded, that Hagedorn "made a profession of colorful fakery" (Hagedorn, 200; David Nivison to SD, e-mail, 8 May 2009).

Worst of all, Ruth and Emma felt, was the basic proposition at the heart of Hagedorn's book: that Robinson was "plagued by the sense that the neighbors thought him a failure," and was "obsessed by what he imagined the people of Gardiner were saying about him." According to Hagedorn's account, EAR felt driven to achieve a measure of financial success as the only way to prove himself to his hometown while at the same time scorning its materialistic standards. Then, after finally having managed to make some money, in his late long poems EAR depicted the downfall of tycoons—Cavender, Nightingale, Matthias—who accumulated fortunes by ruining others, and so, in Hagedorn's construction, he repudiated the very men Gardiner "worshipped and called on its boys to emulate." This gave Hagedorn a theme, and Robinson a battle to wage and win, just as he fought off the demon of drink (Hagedorn, 87–89, 197, 360).

Tilbury Town, Robinson called the fictional town of his poems, and Hagedorn quite wrongly leaped to the conclusion that the place was "built around a cash-box, a till" (Hagedorn, 87), in so doing substituting a pun (EAR abhorred them) for the etymological meaning of the word "tilbury": a Scottish hill town. In order to make Hagedorn's narrative more dramatic, Gardiner in its guise as Tilbury Town became the villain of the piece. This offended almost everybody who lived there, and struck both Ruth and Emma as sheer nonsense.

In New York, James Barstow, a Gardiner native who with his brothers had known EAR since boyhood, became so upset about the brickbats hurled at his hometown that he produced a slim pamphlet, *My Tilbury Town*, in rejoinder. Barstow, who taught at Groton School and then became a private tutor, was a frequent drinking companion of the poet's during the years when EAR was struggling to establish himself in New York, and kept in touch with him throughout his life. After encouragement at the dinner Collamore hosted, Barstow decided to set down his objections to the biography. He was motivated to do so, at least in part, because he himself had supplied Hagedorn with data concerning the Gardiner of Robinson's earlier years. At the time, Barstow wrote, "[i]t did not occur to me that I was not speaking to a man of discretion, and I did not dream that this data would be used with the mention of names of people, some of whose relatives are still living." He objected even more to the revelation of "the tragedies that early befell the Robinson family." EAR, he knew, had not wanted those tragedies emphasized, and "it was a great pity" that Hagedorn had not "respected his wishes and used more restraint in dealing with the misfortunes of the family."

Hagedorn was a man of great energy, Barstow concluded, but not one overburdened by modesty. He "once said in my presence," Barstow observed, "that he could come to know New England and the New Englanders in a couple of weeks—a somewhat rash remark" (Barstow, 8–9, 11). In a letter to Barstow, Robert Frost suggested just how rash that claim was. "[Hagedorn's] utter misunderstanding of an American small town . . . arises from his being a city person, and even worse than that a European in mind and heart. I was surprised that he should have been called in or let in on the Robinson biography," Frost commented (Frost, *Selected*, 496).

By way of assisting Barstow in writing *My Tilbury Town*, Emma Robinson set down a one-page summary of what she found to be inaccurate in Hagedorn's book. This only scratched the surface of what she objected to,

Emma pointed out, for she objected "to a very great deal. As near as I can figure it seems to be mostly a eulogy to the Richards[es], certain N.Y. parties and to Peterboro[ugh], instead of a friendly, kindly interpretation of the man himself" (Emma Robinson to Barstow, Thompson EAR Notes, Gardiner). On 16 February 1939, when Emma and her daughter Ruth sat down to go through Hagedorn's biography in earnest, they noted first its dedication to "The Men and Women Whose Friendship Brightened the Road for 'EA' and Whose Recollections of Him Made this Book Possible." That, they believed, revealed what the book was really about.

Emma and Ruth made their annotations, with the assistance of Larry Thompson, as part of an endeavor to clear the path for a subsequent biography.

> Having done all in our power to persuade the Executors of E. A. R. that this was neither the time nor the man to undertake the writing of his biography and overruled on the ground that it must be done while there were people living who knew him personally, we feel on reading the book that it is based on the evidence of a selected group and not a true portrait of the man we knew. Earnestly desiring therefore to preserve those fine qualities in the man which seem to have eluded Mr. Hagedorn, and to correct errors of fact concerning his family and townspeople, for the possible use of later biographers we are making the following notes on the text. (Emma Robinson and Ruth Nivison, Thompson EAR Notes, Gardiner)

The notes ran to more than a dozen typewritten pages, and the exercise had a salutary effect on Ruth. "Glad to hear that Larry cheered your life," George Burnham wrote her on February 22. "Of course I shall be glad to get together with Larry and the rest of you to help get the record clear for the next book on the life of your uncle." Hagedorn's book "did not touch the real Robinson," he observed, "but time with our help will correct all that" (Burnham to Nivison, 22 February 1939, Colby). On the first of March, Emma and Ruth met again to annotate "the poems of E. A. R. in which we are able to recognize persons and experiences connected with his life at home and his family." These annotations, designed to "enable future readers to have a clearer understanding of the poetry," sometimes err by equating members of the family—particularly Herman and Emma—with characters Robinson invented or derived from other models, but on the whole they offer insights into family dynamics of substantial use to anyone embarked on a study of EAR (Annotations, Thompson EAR Notes, Gardiner). A few months later, at her summer home on nearby Squirrel Island, Emma and George Burnham went through Hagedorn's book yet again, making further comments and corrections.

Margaret Perry wrote Ruth several times early in 1939, commiserating about her distress over the biography and urging her and her mother to annotate it "very fully and carefully," even though the process might keep them "stirred up for some time longer, poor darlings." Perry herself found the book "amazingly dull," really not worth worrying about. "Just remember," she wrote Ruth Nivison, "an inept book can't hurt a man as big as your Uncle Win." She regarded both Hagedorn and Macmillan, his publishers, with scorn. "Didn't I hear that they paid H. H. $10,000 for the job?"—if true, a sizable payment in 1938 dollars (Perry to Nivison, 12 March 1939 and 23 May 1939, Colby).

Almost inevitably, the uproar in Gardiner led to a break between the Robinson and Richards families, who had taken opposing sides vis-à-vis Hagedorn's book. This rift caused Mrs. Richards considerable distress. "Ruth Nivison is one of the sweetest of women: has something of the characteristics of what is called genius," she wrote Olivia Torrence on 30 November 1938. The connection originally formed through EAR had solidified over the years. Rosalind Richards taught Ruth in a sort of kindergarten for girls she started in Gardiner, and later in a reading group. Then, during her married years, Ruth had generously given of her nursing skills to the Richards family. As Rosalind observed, "it would be impossible to say what her help meant to my Mother throughout long years of often-illness and of failing strength and [also] her freely given care to my beloved sister Alice . . . in the sudden illness that took her from us." Yet in the "bitterness and anguish" spawned by Hagedorn's book, Mrs. Richards lamented, "now [Ruth] has broken with us and believes all manner of evil of us" (Richards to Olivia Torrence, 30 November 1938, Gardiner).

The two families were also in disagreement about EAR's love life. As evidence accumulated over three generations has established, he first fell in love with Emma Shepherd when he was fresh out of high school. She was beautiful, bright, quick of movement and wit, something of a coquette, and she encouraged his youthful writing. But she was twenty-three to his nineteen, and chose to marry his handsome and personable older brother Herman, a promising young businessman. Young Win tried to argue her out of this decision, and could not bring himself to attend the wedding ceremony. Twenty years later, after Herman's death, he came back to Gardiner to court Emma once again—and once again she decided against marrying him, this time on the grounds that a wife and family would get in the way of his career.

To a degree remarkable even in New England, EAR and Emma kept their relationship secret. Not until after he died in 1935 did Emma say to her oldest daughter Ruth, "did it ever occur to you that he cared for me?" It was then that they set about annotating his poems—he had written her that "my poems will have to tell you all I cannot say" (SD, *Robinson*, 254–55)—as a private project. Hagedorn's biography, however, proposed another candidate as the love of EAR's life: unnamed in the book, to be sure, but in context manifestly Rosalind Richards.

As Hagedorn reconstructed it in ornamental prose, EAR early renounced "any relationship which might set drums beating in his veins," yet he was "hungry for a kind of fellowship that only a woman could give" (Hagedorn, 126). In 1897, a decade after he first courted Emma, he found that fellowship in the form of a young girl

> who could not have been fashioned more surely to stir a man so guarded and, at the same time, so romantic as Robinson. She was in her early twenties but she had lived away from the tides of life, and seemed scarcely more than a school-girl, some Tennysonian abstraction of feminine loveliness, moving among ideal conceptions and heroic forms, and wholly happy there. She had suffered much from illness, and he was first drawn to her by the compassion which he felt for any human being who seemed to need protection. She cared for his poetry, moreover, and saw a future for it; which shattered all his defenses. (Hagedorn, 127)

They tramped through the woods together, happily talking of books and their makers. And a year later, after his initial sojourn in New York, he came back to Maine to declare his love to this girl "of the woodland walks," and was rebuffed. Hagedorn rendered the scene elaborately:

> When at last he spoke, it seemed as though a fire, burning on the hearth, leapt up and suddenly were consuming the house.
> Shattering and uncomprehended, his declaration broke across her shimmering unrealities. His intuition allowed him no priceless moment of illusion. Her guileless joy of living had held no thought of him except as a companion, a friend.
> She was now as shaken as he.
> And it was he then who was giving comfort, trying to soften her dismay at having to give him pain. (Hagedorn, 123)

Reading this passage almost drove Emma Robinson to "spitting tacks!" She recognized Rosalind Richards from the description, and understood that the account must have come to Hagedorn from Rosalind or her mother. She wouldn't have been so upset if "the love affair they tell about was admitted to be mutual but to say in black and white that it was all on his side, that she did not return it," infuriated her. The feeling rankled even more because she could not express this indignation publicly, for doing so might have exposed her own not-yet-to-be-spoken-of love affair with EAR.

Emma and her daughter Ruth ventilated their resentment in conversations recorded by Larry Thompson: "The story of [EAR's] falling in love with Rosalind; of his proposal and her refusal; of Mrs. Richards refusing to let Rosalind marry a 'penniless' man is fabrication, according to RN and ELR, who are sure this grows out of Rosalind's own mind." According to later descendants of the Richards family, the issue was really one of social inequality: EAR, although upper middle class in status, lacked the required "pedigree" to qualify as a possible husband.

Emma and Ruth further maintained that Robinson's interest in Rosalind was merely friendly and that he wrote to her so rarely that the small packet of letters "addressed to her—each beginning 'Dear Person'—was so small as to indicate that the community of interest must have been short-lived" (Emma Robinson and Ruth Nivison, Thompson EAR Notes, Gardiner). For a long time Rosalind did not let anyone read those letters: not until 2005 were they opened for view at Harvard. They reveal no overt expressions of smoldering passion. Still, beneath EAR's extraordinary reticence, the letters make it clear that he went uncharacteristically far out of his way to encourage her ventures into authorship.

Emma Robinson died in the early summer of 1940, and some years later Ruth let a few close friends know of EAR's love for her mother. This did not particularly surprise John Richards, Rosalind's brother. Emma was "a very pretty woman," after all, he pointed out, "and [Robinson] saw her through some terrible times." But Richards insisted that EAR also confessed his love for Rosalind and "that the episode went deep." The emotion Hagedorn described "may not have lasted long (though I think it did)," he added, and there was "nothing strange" about EAR's having fallen in love with two different women at different periods in his life (John Richards to Peter Dechert, 26 November 1955, Danny D. Smith Papers).

Nor was it unexpected that each of those women should have believed she was EAR's real love. Young Bill Nivison remembered sitting in the music room at his family's home in Gardiner the morning of 13 May 1936, the date when Robinson's ashes were to be buried in Oak Grove Cemetery. He and his father were about to seal the urn when his grandmother Emma brought some rose petals to be placed inside. Then there was a knock at the door: a bunch of forget-me-nots sent by Rosalind Richards with a request that a sprig be put into the urn. Both women wanted something of themselves to go with EAR (SD, *Robinson*, 471).

Hagedorn relied on the reports and correspondence of those willing or eager to cooperate with him, and their names—Ledoux, Isaacs, Torrence—bulk large in his book. In her anger Ruth Nivison was inclined to believe that had the names of this group been omitted, their interest in Robinson would have ceased. At the opposite pole, Hagedorn earned the animosity of George Burnham by conspicuously avoiding mention of the importance to E. A. R. of his good friends Burnham and Ranck, quite possibly because Hagedorn had been unable to persuade Ranck to turn over the material he had collected toward a biography of his own.

The New York vs. New England issue also cropped up in Burnham's critique of Hagedorn's book. Had EAR lived longer, Burnham said, he planned to give up winters in New York in favor of an apartment in Boston that he and Burnham would share, while still going to the MacDowell Colony for the summer months. According to Margaret Perry, Robinson had been contemplating such a move for several years. He'd really rather stay in Boston, he'd told her mother, but did not want to offend James Earle and Laura Gardin Fraser, who had set aside an apartment for him in their New York home (Perry, Reminiscences, 21 May 1938, Colby).

The break between the Richardses and Ruth Nivison did not last long. By late March 1939, Rosalind Richards reported to Ledoux that the two families were friends again, a development that gave him "a glow of real happiness" (Ledoux to Rosalind Richards, 27 March 1939, Gardiner). The quarrel may have been over between them, but not their divergent opinions about the merits of Hagedorn's book.

For the most part, Robinson scholars and enthusiasts shared Emma and Ruth's judgment that the biography was "unsatisfactory" (Anon., "Library Notes," 205). Within months after its publication, Elizabeth Marsh—a close friend of EAR's at MacDowell—was being pestered by a young man from Oxford who, having heard of the "failure" of Hagedorn's work, was "frantic" to embark on a biography himself (March to Nancy Byrd, late 1938, Virginia). Nothing came of that initiative, and ten years passed before Emery Neff's *Edwin Arlington Robinson*, the Robinson volume in the American Men of Letters series, appeared. Neff concentrated on EAR's poetry, substantially avoiding any extensive exploration of his life. That approach pleased Margaret Perry, who after congratulating Neff on his "sound" and "sympathetic" book launched into a diatribe against Hagedorn. His book, she wrote Neff, was "much worse than nothing at all. . . . H. H. is only capable of writing to and of Boy Scouts, that is, Boy Scouts so full of Christian charity that they can endure his sickly sweet condescension" (Perry to Neff, 10 October 1948, Columbia).

In sharp contrast was Rosalind Richards's letter to Neff, who in the course of admiring his work insisted on "the value, beyond price, of Hermann Hagedorn's devoted book, written with what faithfulness." Rosalind knew, though, that the book had caused considerable agony to EAR's "beloved, lovely niece," and she drew a parallel "with the anguish, to Shelley's family, of any recording of his life" (Rosalind Richards to Neff, 2 May 1950, Columbia).

That rather far-fetched analogy—Robinson's circumspect life hardly compares with Shelley's adventurous, even scandalous one—moved Neff to reflect on a difficulty faced by biographers of living or recently dead authors. "The world feels it should know everything which shaped the writing of great poetry, and it is hard to draw the line between what is relevant to that end and what should be buried in oblivion as a family secret." Hagedorn may have rattled the family skeletons, but he probably knew "considerably more than he thought it proper to tell," Neff speculated. The important thing was to record the uncomfortable truths at once and privately, to be preserved for "the biographer of twenty or thirty years hence, who may not need to consider certain susceptibilities" (Neff to Rosalind Richards, 11 May 1950, Danny D. Smith Papers).

Five years later Peter Dechert, a dedicated Robinson scholar, had his say on the proper procedure for such preservation. He advised Ruth Nivison to write down her version of EAR's life, and counseled both Rosalind and John Richards to give up their defense of Hagedorn's biography, which he described as "inaccurate in many places," "superficial almost throughout," and "little more than an edited engagement book interspersed with appreciation." Nor was Neff's effort much better, he thought; both books depicted an emasculated figure who could not possibly have written the poems EAR left behind (Dechert to Rosalind Richards, 22 September 1955, Danny D. Smith Papers).

Dechert's attack spurred John Richards to the defense of his Harvard classmate Hagedorn. Many men he knew thought highly of Hagedorn's biography, Richards pointed out. Moreover, the author was hardly at fault if his book was not an entire success. It was written only three years after the poet's death "because [Robinson's] most intelligent and intimate friends [in New York, that is] knew of the threat of a biography that would have been cheap and inaccurate. Hagedorn was the third choice and undertook the work unwillingly [this seems false], doubting his powers, and laying aside important writing. The undertaking of E. A. R.'s Life was an act of friendship" (John Richards to Dechert, 14 November 1955, Danny D. Smith Papers). Hagedorn himself blamed the dispute on the "primordial jealousy" of the group, headed, he thought, by Collamore and Ranck, who were "madly hostile toward Isaacs, Ledoux, Torrence, and [himself]" (Hagedorn to C. P. Smith, 16 December 1961, Yale).

In 1965 Chard Smith brought out *Where the Light Falls: A Portrait of Edwin Arlington Robinson*. Using in part the annotations Emma and Ruth made, Smith traced his principal revelation—that EAR was in love with his brother's wife (not, as Smith originally thought, Olivia Dunbar Torrence)— directly from the poems to the life, riding his thesis hard. He also did some useful basic scholarship, discovering in legal documents, for example, that the Robinson family had purchased the stock of a drugstore in Gardiner, hence making it possible to supply Dean with the narcotics he required. Yet Smith "was plowing into the subject too soon," even thirty years after EAR's death, David Nivison observed (Nivison to Danny D. Smith, 17 July 2002, Danny D. Smith Papers). Lacking full disclosure, he arrived at incorrect and unjust interpretations of the triangular relations involving the poet and Herman and Emma Robinson.

That needed straightening out when, another forty years later, I had the good fortune to make another try at a thorough and accurate life of EAR, with the closet doors open and nothing withheld. By 2007 all of the antagonists fighting over Robinson had long ago faded from the scene. And for *Edwin Arlington Robinson: A Poet's Life*, I had thousands of letters to consult, as opposed to the paltry hundreds that the appeals from Macmillan had elicited for the rather bloodless *Selected Letters* of 1940. Does this mean that considerable time must pass before a sound life story can be created? Not necessarily, but there is much to be said, in the writing of biography, for coming along at the right time.

What was lucky for me was probably unfortunate for EAR and his posthumous reputation. The real loser in the sorry tale of Hermann Hagedorn's unsatisfactory biography and the two camps competing for control of Edwin Arlington Robinson beyond the grave may well have been the poet himself. Had a solid and sound book about him appeared a few years after his death, it could have helped to secure his standing as a great American poet and halted the unwarranted drift of his work into relative obscurity.

Summer of '24: Zelda's Affair

Scott and Zelda Fitzgerald came to France in May 1924 to get away from the frantic party life in the New York exurbs of Westport and Great Neck. Scott was deteriorating under a regimen of "drinking and raising hell generally,"

A preliminary version of this essay was presented at the 7th International Fitzgerald Conference in Vevey, Switzerland, 30 June 2004.

as he wrote Maxwell Perkins (FSF, *A Life in Letters*, 67). So he and Zelda and baby Scottie went to Europe for a fresh start, where he settled down to write a masterpiece. "[N]ever before," as he was to observe in looking back on that time, did he "keep his artistic conscience as pure as during the ten months" (FSF, *Gatsby* [Modern Library], viii) when he was working on *The Great Gatsby*.

He achieved that novel despite, or perhaps because of, a crisis in his marriage. After a few days in Paris, and a week or two trying this place and that on the Riviera, Zelda and Scott moved into the Villa Marie in Valescure, two and a half kilometers from Saint-Raphaël. It was a beautiful house, set high and cool above the beach with eucalyptus trees and parasol pines warding off the sun. While Scott immersed himself in the book, Zelda cast about for something to do. "What'll we do with ourselves this afternoon . . . and the day after that, and the next thirty years?" Daisy Buchanan inquires in *The Great Gatsby*. "What'll we *do* . . . with ourselves?" Alabama Knight echoes in Zelda's novel *Save Me the Waltz* (quoted in Levot, 172–73).

Scottie, not yet two, was under the meticulous care of an English nanny they'd hired in Paris. Servants looked after the house and prepared the meals. With time on her hands, Zelda swam in the Mediterranean, tanned herself to a biscuit brown, and began studying French. In the evenings she tackled the novels of Henry James, while Scott read lives of Byron and Shelley. Still, she was bored, while Scott was happily engrossed in the book he was writing. "We are idyllicly [*sic*] settled here," he wrote Perkins on June 13 (FSF, *A Life in Letters*, 76). The idyll would soon be interrupted.

Seeking companions during the long summer days, Zelda met three young French naval aviators on the beach. They were stationed at nearby Fréjus, and had rented quarters close to the Fitzgeralds'. The four of them played tennis together and took the sun. They chatted as well as they could, Zelda working from her French-English dictionary. After a time, she and one of the officers paired off; in the evenings they sometimes danced together. By midsummer she either did or did not have an affair with this young man, and this led to an emotional crisis.

The facts of the matter are beyond ascertaining. It was more than eighty years ago, and no one alive today was on the scene to observe or testify. What is clear is that whatever happened opened a rift in the Fitzgeralds' marriage that could not easily be mended. Neither Zelda nor Scott tried to hush up the affair. Both of them talked about it, wrote about it, worried it obsessively. It stands as a crucial and complicated chapter in their troubled life story.

The endeavor here is not so much to piece out the truth as to examine what biographers have made of Zelda's affair, or fling, or flirtation. The process may reveal as much about the craft of biography and its practitioners as about the Fitzgeralds themselves and what they did or said they did or imagined they did in the summer of 1924.

The French Aviator

It took more than thirty years to get the facts straight about the French naval officers who swam into Scott and Zelda's lives in the summer of 1924. Arthur Mizener in *The Far Side of Paradise* (1951), Fitzgerald's first biographer, devoted three and a half pages to the affair but did not do much digging. Relying on Scott's *Ledger* and *Notebooks* and Zelda's *Save Me the Waltz* (1932) as sources, Mizener assumed that Zelda and one of the Frenchman committed adultery. He was interested almost solely in the effect that this had on Fitzgerald. "Sexual matters were always deadly serious to him," Mizener commented, and "his capacity for being hurt by Zelda was always very great" (Mizener, 179).

In a long paragraph that he quoted from *Save Me the Waltz*, Mizener stressed the physical nature of Zelda's lover: a dark, romantic fellow with "broad bronze hands . . . convex shoulders . . . slim and strong and rigid" (Mizener, 178). His principal error was to get this man's name wrong. Mizener misidentifies him as René Silvé. One of the Frenchmen the Fitzgeralds came to know was indeed named René Silvy (not Silvé), but Silvy did not have an affair with Zelda Fitzgerald and may very well have been gay.

Eleven years later, in his *Scott Fitzgerald* (1962), Andrew Turnbull substituted another error for Mizener's. Like the previous biographer, Turnbull emphasized how shattered Scott was when he discovered what was going on. "He really believed in love, in what two people can build against the world's cheap skepticism." But Turnbull further speculated on Zelda's motives. "At twenty-three—almost twenty-four—she may have begun to fear that her looks were going, or she may have felt insufficient basking in her husband's glory. Perhaps she was trying to make him jealous, or perhaps she was bored and the seduction of the moment proved too strong."

As to the officer's identity, however, Turnbull remained as mistaken as Mizener. He quoted from "How to Live on Practically Nothing a Year," Scott's magazine article for the *Saturday Evening Post* of 20 September 1924. "[I]n half an hour, René and Bobbé, officers of aviation, are coming to dinner in their white ducks." Then in parenthesis, Turnbull equated "Bobbé" (not René) with Edouard Josanne, a name fetched from Fitzgerald's correspondence with Zelda's psychiatrists in the early 1930s (Turnbull, 145). This was wrong, in two ways. There was a Bobbé, all right, and he was probably René's partner, but Scott was not disguising Edouard Josanne as Bobbé. He simply left Josanne out of his lighthearted magazine piece, as a complication too painful (or valuable) to be addressed there.

At least Turnbull came close to getting the fellow's name right. "Edouard" was accurate, and "Josanne" was close. That was how Scott spelled his family name (he got Edouard wrong too, leaving out the "o"). For her part, Zelda spelled the name as "Josen." Not until Nancy Milford's *Zelda: A Biography* (1971) would someone spell the name correctly in print. Having located and corresponded with the man, Milford correctly identified him as Edouard Jozan, who went on from youthful indiscretions on the Riviera to a distinguished career in the French navy, winning medals for valor and retiring as an admiral. In a long letter to Milford, Jozan wrote that Zelda was indeed "a shining beauty," and he was attracted to her, but there was no affair. The supposed infidelity was a joint invention of the Fitzgeralds, he thought. "[T]hey both had a need of drama, they made it up and perhaps they were the victims of their own unsettled and a little unhealthy imagination."

Milford backed up this interpretation in an interview with Hadley Hemingway, Ernest's first wife. According to Hadley, Zelda liked to dramatize the supposed affair, going so far as to tell others that her lover killed himself when Scott broke off the relationship. "It was one of their acts together. I remember Zelda's face becoming very, very solemn, and she would say how he had loved her and how hopeless it had been and then how he had committed suicide. Scott would stand next to her looking very pale and distressed and sharing every minute of it" (Milford, 108, 112–14).

Ernest Hemingway, unlike Hadley, was inclined to believe that the affair was real. In *A Moveable Feast* (1964), Hemingway wrote that Scott told him several versions of the story about "something tragic that happened . . . at St.-Raphael. The first version that he told me of Zelda and a French aviator falling in love was truly a sad story and I believe it was a true story." Later versions were better told each time, "but they never hurt you the same way the first one did." Fitzgerald's storytelling was so persuasive, Hemingway wrote, that he could envision the lover's single-seater seaplane buzzing the diving raft "and Zelda's tan and Scott's tan and the dark blonde and the light blond of their hair and the darkly tanned face of the boy that was in love with Zelda" (Hemingway, *Feast*, 147–48).

Here two conflicting patterns begin to emerge in biographical treatment of the incident. A majority of the female biographers—with the exception of Kendall Taylor and Linda Wagner-Martin—tend to deny that the affair actually took place, and assume that the crisis it generated was more or less fabricated by the Fitzgeralds. Most of the male biographers, with the exception of James Mellow, follow the lead of Mizener and Turnbull in believing that Zelda and Jozan's relationship was indeed adulterous.

A year after Milford's biography for the first time concentrated on Zelda and not on her more famous husband, Sara Mayfield published *Exiles from Paradise* (1971). Mayfield, who had grown up with Zelda Sayre in

Montgomery, Alabama, adamantly maintained that nothing significant happened between Zelda and Jozan. "[T]heir 'affair' was nothing more than a summer flirtation, romantic, decorous, and slightly comic," she wrote, using *her* interview with Jozan—in which he talks of others' accounts of the summer of '24 as "raving mad" and full of "wild ideas"—to bolster her case (Mayfield, 96–97). In Mayfield's judgment, Scott practiced a double standard in overreacting to this flirtation. "If Zelda's eyes wandered, Scott's pride prompted him to attack her and the man to whom she was attracted; but if Zelda's *amour propre* was wounded by Scott's attentions to other women (including, she says, both "*poules de luxe* and stars of the screen and stage"), she wanted only to destroy herself" (Mayfield, 117). If anything, Mayfield demonstrated an even stronger bias against Scott than Milford had. In her account he emerged as something of a tyrant, unable or unwilling to understand and adapt to Zelda's Southern ways.

It remained for André LeVot to establish the background of the three Frenchmen stationed at Fréjus. In *F. Scott Fitzgerald: A Biography* (1983), LeVot fleshes them out as René Silvy, son of a Cannes notary public with literary ambitions; Bobbé (surname in some doubt, but possibly Croirier), a veteran of World War I who had fought at Verdun and shared a literary bent with René; and of course Edouard Jozan, son of a middle-class family in Nîmes who was about to embark on a fine career in the navy.

Curiously, various biographers presented conflicting accounts about Jozan's hair color. Mizener gave him "curly black hair" (Mizener, 178), and Milford described his hair as "dark and curling" (Milford, 108), but Mayfield—perhaps relying on Zelda's characterization in *Save Me the Waltz* of a golden-haired lover—cited his "curly blond hair," as did LeVot (Mayfield, 97; LeVot, 174). Then as late as 1993, Jeffrey Meyers's *Scott Fitzgerald* reverted to Mizener's account of the Frenchman as "a dark romantic man with curly black hair" (Meyers, *Fitzgerald*, 116).

Meyers also stood out among Fitzgerald biographers for having no reservations whatever about the relationship between Zelda and the naval aviator. Where others speculated about what might have happened, Meyers *knew* exactly what happened, and refused to pussyfoot around. He also adopted an air of superiority to the principals, exhibiting a bare tolerance for Scott and an alarming lack of sympathy for Zelda. He had no doubts, for example, about what motivated her summer infidelity. "After five years of marriage, [she] feared she had passed the peak of beauty and had to prove she was still attractive to men. She felt her life was empty, resented Scott's successful career, wanted to make him jealous." Hence it was easy for "Jozan, using his French charm . . . [to] invite Zelda to his apartment and seduce her." Then he abandoned her, leaving her suicidal. On the whole, Meyers concluded, this was a misfortune for Fitzgerald as a writer. "If Zelda had left him for Jozan in 1924, Scott would have had another lost love to inspire his work and been spared the horrors of her insanity in the 1930s" (Meyers, *Fitzgerald*, 116–17).

The Showdown

Arriving at the correct name and hair color of the French aviator who courted Zelda hardly ranks of importance as compared to what the Fitzgeralds *did* about the affair. Here, too, the reports of the various biographers vary widely.

Almost all of the chroniclers noted that Scott was used to men falling in love with Zelda and that generally it pleased him, though in this case matters got out of hand. Turnbull, however, was the first to assert that as a consequence Scott "forced a showdown and delivered an ultimatum which banished Josanne from their lives" (Turnbull, 146). This is vaguely worded— what sort of showdown? what was the ultimatum?—and given no documentation whatever.

Milford took up the issue in far greater detail, attributing her account to Scott's conversation with "a relative" years after the event. The relative was quite likely Scottie Fitzgerald, who after initially cooperating with Milford came to dislike her book as unfairly prejudiced against her father. According to this story, Zelda came to Scott in July, told him she loved Jozan, and asked for a divorce. Furious, Scott insisted upon a showdown among the three of them. Jozan would have to face him in Zelda's presence "and ask for her himself," he insisted. The confrontation Scott asked for never took place, although he invented such love-triangle scenes in both *The Great Gatsby* and *Tender Is the Night*.

Milford added that in a burst of anger, Scott locked Zelda in her rooms at the villa, and that she "apparently accepted [his] ultimatum passively and the subject of divorce was dropped" (Milford, 112). Milford further linked the end of the affair to Zelda's apparent suicide attempt in August. According to Calvin Tomkins, biographer of Gerald and Sara Murphy in *Living Well Is the Best Revenge* (1971), about three or four in the morning an ashen and trembling Scott Fitzgerald knocked on their door at the Hôtel du Cap in Antibes with the news that Zelda had taken an overdose of sleeping pills. Sara walked her up and down much of the night to keep her from slipping into the long sleep of oblivion (Tomkins, 209).

In her biography Mayfield dismissed the sleeping-pill episode as nonsense. Not only was Zelda's story (to Hadley Hemingway) that a young French flyer had committed suicide after their tragic romance "an absurd invention," but "almost equally incredible [was the Tomkins-Milford] story of Scott's going from St. Raphaël to . . . Antibes—a distance of fifty-two kilometers—at three or four o'clock in the morning, to get help from the Murphys, because Zelda had taken an overdose of sleeping pills" (Mayfield, 97). Here Mayfield was happily debunking the assertions of a previous biographer, and one whose book had more or less stolen her thunder. Still, she may well have been right: there is no mention of such a suicide attempt during August 1924 in Scott's *Ledger*.

Mayfield also expanded on the attractiveness of Admiral Jozan, emphasizing that she found him—during an interview no previous biographer had managed to arrange—"unusually charming and handsome." Mayfield described Jozan as "a born leader . . . healthy, athletic, and vigorous, assured": in fact, blessed with "all the qualities Scott would have liked to have." So when Scott became "violently and irrationally jealous" and threatened to "wring the aviator's neck" in a physical struggle (this development mentioned for the first time), Jozan, as the younger and stronger man, judiciously refused to beat him up. Further—another new twist in the story—Mayfield added that when Scott announced he would leave Zelda if she saw Jozan again, the Frenchman asked for and received a transfer to another station (Mayfield, 96, 98).

In the last of her three books about F. Scott Fitzgerald and their relationship in Hollywood, Sheilah Graham revealed a grandiose angle on the showdown relayed to her by Scott himself. According to Graham's *The Real F. Scott Fitzgerald* (1976), Fitzgerald told her that initially he liked "Jozanne" (yet another misspelling) and was glad he "was willing to pass the hours with Zelda," leaving him free to write. When the frolicking on the beach led to an affair, however, he was so furious that he bought a pistol and challenged Jozan to a duel, in which both men fired a shot without harming the other. "While he was telling me this," Graham remarked, she had the feeling that "the whole episode" had been invented to provide material for a book—as indeed it had, in the McKisco-Barban duel of *Tender Is the Night*. "Did the Fitzgeralds ever do anything just for the sake of doing it, and not to bolster the legend they had created about themselves or to provide Scott with [material] for his fiction?" she asked, with evident exasperation (Graham, 61–62).

A minor refinement of the tale emerged in Matthew J. Bruccoli's *Some Sort of Epic Grandeur* (1981). At more than six hundred pages (including apparatus), Bruccoli's was the longest of the Fitzgerald biographies, and contained the most factual material. However, inasmuch as he was primarily interested in Fitzgerald as a professional writer, and in his life only insofar as it had an impact on his career, Bruccoli devoted only a page and a half to Zelda and Jozan's summer romance. He accepted Hadley Hemingway's judgment that "the Fitzgeralds developed the Jozan affair into what was virtually a routine they performed, separately and jointly, for their friends." The new piece of information—and like all biographers, Bruccoli was inclined to attach undue significance to anything fresh he could add to the record— came from a letter Fitzgerald wrote to Dr. Robert S. Carroll, Zelda's doctor at Highland Hospital in Asheville: a document Bruccoli unearthed from a Sotheby Parke-Bernet catalogue. Therein Scott falsely claimed to have been a boxer in his youth, when, he says, he sparred with the champion professionals "Tommy and Mike Gibbons." He would have "annialated" [*sic*] Jozan in two minutes had the aviator been willing to fight him, he maintained (Bruccoli, *Grandeur*, 199–200, 408).

Sources and Interpretation

Reading through the biographies of Scott and Zelda Fitzgerald, one is struck by how much the story—and its interpretation—changes over time. As the evidence accumulates, with each biographer adding whatever he or she has discovered to the mix, the summer romance takes on greater resonance. In the end, examining a relationship that started and stopped in 1924 in books published from 1951 to 2004 makes it almost indisputable that whatever happened four score and some years ago in the south of France really *mattered* to the Fitzgeralds, their marriage, and their careers.

First let us consider who contributed what to the growing fund of information. Mizener quotes from Zelda's *Save Me the Waltz*, from Scott's *Ledger* and *Notebooks*, and from a letter of his to Max Perkins. From *Save Me the Waltz*, he derives not only the previously cited passage about Jozan's physicality but Zelda's (or her heroine Alabama's) semi-embittered, semi-resigned reaction to the end of the affair. Jozan went away, leaving her a long letter and a photograph of himself. The photo was "the most beautiful thing she'd ever owned," but she didn't see any point in keeping it. Whatever she'd wanted from him left when he did. "You took what you wanted from life, if you could get it, and you did without the rest." In a footnote Mizener calls Zelda's account of the romance "the most reliable," adding without further explanation that Scott "used his feelings about it" in depicting the relationship between Nicole Diver and Tommy Barban in *Tender Is the Night*, and in the story "Image on the Heart," published in the April 1936 *McCall's*.

Mizener's most important find in the *Notebooks* was Fitzgerald's retrospective comment: "That September 1924 I knew something had happened that could never be repaired." From the *Ledger*, presumably written contemporaneously with events like a journal or a diary, Mizener referred to only two entries, and compressed them to fit into the flow of his own prose. "A month after the crisis [Scott] noted that they were 'close together' again and in September that the 'trouble [was] clearing away.'" In the letter to his editor Maxwell Perkins, dated August 27, Fitzgerald suggests (without mentioning the affair) that he has matured as a result of the emotional crisis. "It's been a fair summer. I've been unhappy but my work hasn't suffered from it. I am grown at last" (Mizener, 178–80).

Turnbull added "How to Live on Practically Nothing a Year" to the source material, with its rhapsodic evocation of the setting: "the liquid dark" as night descends, "the heavy roses and the nightingales in the pines." From *Save Me the Waltz* he contributed the comment that Edouard somewhat resembled Scott. Jozan "was handsome—in feature not unlike Scott," but he was in Zelda's phrase "full of the sun" while Scott was "a moon person": like two sides of the same coin. From the same source Turnbull introduced the detail that the aviator zoomed his plane "perilously low over the Villa Marie" (Turnbull, 145).

Milford, the most extensive and conscientious researcher where anything pertaining to Zelda Fitzgerald was concerned, linked Jozan's stunting his airplane dangerously close to the villa's red-tiled roof to similar gestures of homage young American pilots had paid Zelda in Montgomery in 1918. Milford's single greatest coup, though, was locating Jozan and eliciting from him an extensive written account of his summer with the Fitzgeralds. They struck him as "brimming over with life" and so sophisticated that they "brought into our little provincial circle brilliance, imagination and familiarity with a Parisian and international world to which we had no access." Jozan thought of Scott as "intellectualist," while he described Zelda as eager to take from life every chance it offered (Milford, 108–9). The Frenchman acknowledged that he flirted with her and admired her, but matters went no further. This may or may not have been Gallic gallantry.

Judging from *Save Me the Waltz*, Zelda was extremely attracted to the handsome young French pilot. In this passage Zelda/Alabama vividly evokes the erotic power of Edouard Jozan. "He drew her body against him till she felt the blades of his bones carving her own," Alabama Knight recalls. "He was bronze and smelled of the sand and sun: she felt him naked underneath the starched linen. She didn't think of [her husband] David. She hoped he hadn't seen; she didn't care. She felt as if she would like to be kissing Jacques Chevre-Feuille on the top of the Arc de Triomphe" (quoted in Milford, 109–10). In his Goncourt Prize–winning 2007 novel *Alabama Song*, as yet untranslated into English, Gilles Simon portrays his fictional Zelda as carried away by Jozan's physical appeal.

Milford's citation of this "explicitly sensual" prose—as highly charged sexually as anything in Scott's work—is but one example of her intelligent use of sources. After consulting Scott's *Ledger,* for instance, she usefully provides the exact language of Scott's four monthly entries in 1924 about the affair. July: "The Big Crisis—13th of July"; August: "Zelda and I close together"; September: "Trouble clearing away"; October: "Last sight of Josanne" (Milford, 111–12).

These telescopic comments barely scratch the surface of what went on in Valescure. For further information, Milford interviewed not only Hadley Hemingway but also Sara and Gerald Murphy and Gilbert Seldes. The Murphys, who knew Scott and Zelda well and saw a good deal of them in the summer of 1924, apparently assumed that the affair—like so many among their Riviera friends—had become adulterous. "Jozan wasn't someone for her to talk to," Sara said. "I must say everyone knew about it but Scott." Yet Seldes recalled that when he and his new bride visited the Fitzgeralds early in August, a few weeks after the "Big Crisis," they detected "not a hint of discord" between Scott and Zelda (Milford, 110).

Given access to psychiatric records by Scottie Fitzgerald (records which have subsequently remained closed to biographers), Milford was able to quote extensively from an "autobiography" that Zelda wrote for Dr. Oscar Forel following her breakdown in 1930. In that document, Zelda cited two great emotional events of her life. First, "[m]y marriage, after which I was in another world, one for which I was not qualified or prepared, because of my inadequate education." Next, "[a] love affair with a French aviator in St. Raphael. I was locked in my villa for one month to prevent me from seeing him. This lasted for five years. When I knew my husband had another woman in California I was upset because the life over there appeared to me so superficial, but finally I was not hurt because I knew I had done the same thing when I was younger" (quoted in Milford, 174–75). As an avenue of escape, Zelda wrote, she immersed herself in the ballet.

The "locked in her villa" item may well have been a fabrication, like Zelda's elaborate sorrow over the tragic "suicide" of her lover. If she was so sequestered, no one else seems to have noticed. And this particular detail seems to trace back to Scott and Zelda's correspondence in 1919. At that time, even though they were engaged, she regularly wrote him provocative letters about her dates with other young men. These so disturbed Scott that he repeatedly proposed she ought to be locked up "like the princess in her tower."

Milford was also able to draw upon correspondence back and forth between the Fitzgeralds in 1932, after Zelda wrote *Save Me the Waltz* and sent it, without telling her husband, to Max Perkins, as well as Scott's letter to Dr. Mildred Squires at the Phipps Clinic in Baltimore, where Zelda was then confined. In that communication Fitzgerald stressed the lasting significance of his wife's summer romance. "Her affair with Eduard Josanne in 1925 and mine with [actress] Lois Moran in 1927 [in Hollywood], which was a sort of revenge shook something out of us, but we can't both go on paying and paying forever. And yet I feel that's the whole trouble back of all this."

By "all this" Scott presumably meant their then tortured marriage, the trouble compounded by Zelda's mental illness and his own excessive drinking. In a revealing remark, he traced a symbiotic connection between her psychological disturbance and his addiction to alcohol: "Liquor on my mouth is sweet to her; I cherish her most extravagant hallucinations" (Milford, 222). They were in it together, coveting each other's weaknesses.

Sara Mayfield, whose book closely followed Milford's, only slightly expanded on her predecessor's fund of information. From *Save Me the Waltz*, she noted that Jacques's fictional family name, Chevre-Feuille, meant "honeysuckle" in French. Interviewing Jozan face-to-face, she found him still charming at seventy years of age. Furthermore, Mayfield visited Scott and Zelda at Juan-les-Pins in the summer of 1926, and as an Alabama girl herself understood the ways of the southern coquette. In her confident assurance that Zelda's affair amounted to nothing more than an innocent summer entertainment, Mayfield stands at the opposite pole from Jeffrey Meyers, who took the liberty of following Zelda into Jozan's apartment to witness her infidelity.

It remained for André LeVot, in his 1983 biography, to make the most significant advance toward untangling the affair since the discoveries of Milford thirteen years earlier. Working from resources unavailable to or neglected by earlier writers, LeVot began to plumb the psychological depths. The first of these resources was Zelda Fitzgerald's unfinished novel "Caesar's Things," which she worked on during the last six years of her life. In that novel, she returned obsessively to the affair that had been central to *Save Me the Waltz*. The basic situation is much the same in both novels. The heroine is married to an artist who is committed to his work. She meets a young Frenchman who bears a certain similarity to her husband, but "whose work is not a rival to her and who is free to give her as much as she longs to receive." In "Caesar's Things," however, the given names are changed to emphasize the emotional interconnections between all points of the triangle. The woman is Janno, her husband Jacob, the lover Jacques.

The real reason Janno embarked on the affair, LeVot commented, was to "break out of the purgatory in which Jacob has confined her." Her husband invests all of his vitality in his painting, while she merely sits and waits, feeling dispossessed and withering away. Even when Jacob puts an end to the affair, he postpones dealing with the problem in order to complete his work in progress. "I'll get out of here as soon as I can," he says. "In the meantime you are not to leave these premises. You understand?" Janno understood, all right. She "told her husband that she loved the French officer and her husband locked her up in the villa": again the locked door, a detail in her autobiography for Dr. Forel (1930) that had gone unused in *Save Me the Waltz* (1932).

LeVot went back to Fitzgerald's *Notebooks* for still more important insights. In the same section of the notes that mention something having happened in the summer of 1924 "that never could be repaired," LeVot found two other comments that refer to the affair. In one of these Scott expresses compassion for Zelda's plight. "He was sorry, knowing how she would pay." The other suggests that Scott himself had been complicit in allowing or even arranging for his wife's dereliction. It reads, "Feeling of proxy in passion; strange encouragement." Something of what Scott apparently meant by "encouragement" was to emerge in "Caesar's Things." When Janno and Jacob first encounter Jacques, Janno is reluctant to approach him. Jacob insists that she do so.

Altogether LeVot establishes himself as a sensitive interpreter of the incident, with an apparent understanding of love affairs. When Zelda exercises her flirtatious charm, for example, LeVot observes that she "did it so outrageously . . . that the very exuberance she brought to it absolved her of any guilty intent." Flirting *that* openly, he suggests, could be an excellent way of warding off suspicion (LeVot, 174–77).

Relatively little new intelligence about the affair is advanced in my biography and those of James Mellow and Jeffrey Meyers. In *Fool for Love: F. Scott Fitzgerald* (1983), I discuss the way that Fitzgerald's story "Image on the Heart" (1936) parallels the events on the Riviera more than a decade earlier. In that story, the male protagonist, who has just married a younger woman, discovers that she had spent the day before their wedding with a French aviator. Although she maintains that nothing happened during that time, she offers her husband an annulment. He declines the offer, deciding to let her indiscretion pass. They ride away on their honeymoon, the husband silently thinking "that he would never know" the truth and worried that the question might "haunt their marriage like a ghost" (SD, *Fool*, 70–71).

As J. Gerald Kennedy points out in his essay on "Fitzgerald's Expatriate Years," both this story of 1935 and the account of the French mercenary Tommy Barban winning Nicole Diver away from her husband in *Tender Is the Night* the previous year strongly suggest that Zelda's luminous portrayal of Jacques Chevre-Feuille in *Save Me the Waltz* aroused Scott's "retrospective jealousy" (Kennedy, 139–40).

Zelda was acutely aware that this kind of uncertainty might trouble her husband. In her interview with Henry Dan Piper in 1947 that I introduced into the record, Zelda said she "regretted having flirted with so many men and never telling Scott how far she'd gone with them, letting him guess the worst" (quoted in SD, *Fool*, 71). Inasmuch as Zelda had become his lover in advance of their wedding, Scott was forever dubious about her virtue. As Hemingway mentions in *A Moveable Feast*, Fitzgerald asked him at their first meeting whether he had slept with Hadley before they were married.

Hemingway wasn't of much help. "I don't know," he said. "I can't remember" (EH, *Feast*, 127).

Like LeVot, Mellow emphasizes the psychological importance of Scott's "feeling proxy in passion" note. Mellow also wonders whether the fact that neither Scott nor Zelda ever spelled Jozan's name correctly might be construed as evidence of her marital fidelity, even though a letter she wrote Scott in 1930 (cited for the first time by Mellow) would seem to argue otherwise. "Then there was Josen," Zelda's letter admits, "and you were justifiably angry." In addition Mellow notes that René and Bobbé, as portrayed in *Save Me the Waltz*, were in all likelihood gay. The two of them, in Zelda's description, "protruded insistently from their white beach clothes and talked in undertones of Arthur Rimbaud" (Mellow, 210–14; Cline, 148).

It may well be that after Milford (especially) and LeVot, there was not much left for latter-day biographers to find out about the affair. But there was still room in which to venture new interpretations. In three twenty-first-century books, Kendall Taylor, Sally Cline, and Linda Wagner-Martin all attempt to understand what the affair of the summer of 1924 meant to the relationship between the Fitzgeralds—with particular emphasis on Zelda's subsequent position.

Taylor uncovered but one new scrap of evidence in *Sometimes Madness Is Wisdom* (2001): Zelda's card of entry to the Salon Privé of the Monte Carlo Casino dated June 10, 1924. For Taylor, this served as evidence that Zelda and Jozan visited the casino together on that date. Taylor also assumed that Zelda slept with the Frenchman. "When attracted," she wrote, "Zelda was sexually aggressive and Jozan had ample opportunities to respond."

In assessing the effects of the affair, Taylor invades Zelda's consciousness—a biographical leap based primarily on Zelda's observations in her 1930 autobiography for Dr. Forel. Whatever may have happened during the summer romance, Taylor observed, the incident "generated a deep distrust and left an indelible scar. When locked in the Villa Marie, Zelda realized she was also locked into her marriage and . . . determined to have no further romantic liaisons. Deeply troubled that she might never again be happy with Fitzgerald, yet aware of her inability to survive on her own, she recognized a power shift in their relationship and the reality struck her painfully" (Taylor, 138–40).

Cline's *Zelda Fitzgerald: Her Voice in Paradise* (2002) went further in postulating that the summer romance transformed the marriage, placing Scott firmly in control. Cline quoted more extensively from "Caesar's Things" than any previous commentator. In this unfinished work, her second fictional revisiting of the affair, Zelda described at least three occasions when her heroine, Janno, kissed Jacques long and with undue enthusiasm. In fact, Janno reflects, she should never have kissed him at all. "First she should never have kissed Jacques; then she shouldn't have kissed her husband; then after the kissing had become spiritual vivisection and half-masochistic there should not have been any more." Cline cited another section of "Caesar's Things" to provide a gloss on Janno's tortured feelings. "He that looketh on a woman to lust after hath committed adultery with her in his heart already," she quotes from the Bible, and then reflects that "adultery was adultery and it would have been impossible for her to love two men at once, to give herself to simultaneous intimacies."

Although "*no* concrete evidence" exists that Zelda slept with Jozan, Cline writes, "for the morbidly jealous Scott, who still had mixed-up Irish Catholic monogamous feelings for Zelda, the fact that she was entertaining a *desire* to commit adultery would be almost as much a sin as actually committing adultery." In the aftermath, Cline concluded, Scott appropriated the affair to establish his position as the controlling partner in the Fitzgeralds' marriage.

"The reason why Scott fictionalized and heightened the romance to include these fabrications [e.g., the confrontation, fight, or duel between himself and Jozan] was that he was then able to share it, thus once more taking over an important piece of Zelda's life. That she allowed him to do so illustrates her emotional dependency upon him." To back up these statements, Cline reverted once more to "Caesar's Things." Once the affair was ended, "Janno grew indomitably loyal and devoted to Jacob . . . Jacob was somehow the center of the whole business" (Cline, 150–54).

Linda Wagner-Martin's *Zelda Sayre Fitzgerald: An American Woman's Life* (2004) arrived at a psychological reading of the affair and its aftereffects that, like Cline's, placed Scott in a position of dominance. Feeling certain that Zelda did indeed attempt to kill herself in late August 1924, Wagner-Martin imagined how it must have been for Zelda once Jozan was banished from her life. Still "beautiful and vivacious" at twenty-four, but "with an increasing sense of her inferiority," Zelda suffered in two different ways: "from the loss of what she assumed to be the great love of her life" and also from her own sense of helplessness. "More than ever," Wagner-Martin observed, "she saw that she was in the control of her husband: Scott had the money, he had the power, he had the reputation. What would she do if she tried to leave him? How would she and Scottie live? And would she be emotionally strong enough to make a break?"

In Wagner-Martin's view, Zelda was so beset with these worries that she adopted a posture of submissiveness, ceding all authority to her husband. (That might explain why Gilbert Seldes and his wife, on their early August visit, observed only serenity between the Fitzgeralds.) Once the affair was over and Scott asserted his control, Zelda spent more time with Scottie and helped Scott with his revisions of *The Great Gatsby*. At least for a time, she submerged her yearnings for an identity of her own and became a virtual Stepford wife. Then, Wagner-Martin proposes, the Fitzgeralds' marriage descended into sadomasochism.

In support of this interpretation, she cited a November 1924 letter from Zelda to Scott, accusing him of "bestial behavior during love-making." Although this brought on a severe asthma attack, Zelda did not threaten to leave Scott. In effect Zelda accepted the sadomasochistic pattern of their marriage, assuming "the position of the masochist." But the longer they played these separate roles, Wagner-Martin suggested, the closer they came to "rational violence" and mental breakdown.

Wagner-Martin contributed an important fragment to the tale, drawn from the embittered confrontation between Zelda and Scott on the afternoon of 28 May 1933. With Dr. Thomas Rennie and a stenographer in attendance, the Fitzgeralds tried to talk out their problems on that day. In the 114-page account of this session, Scott repeatedly insisted that as the professional writer in the family, he should have sole access to whatever happened to either one of them for his fiction. According to his lights, Zelda had appropriated *his* material in *Save Me the Waltz*, and now she was threatening to take even more by writing about her illness. He went so far as to say, and say again, that Zelda had tried to destroy him by falling in love with Jozan while he was "doing the best work of [his] life" on *The Great Gatsby*. (Bruccoli, who printed a portion of the May 28 transcript in *Some Sort of Epic Grandeur*, did not include this detail.) "As far as destroying you is concerned," Zelda responded, "I have considered you first in everything I have tried to do in my life" (Wagner-Martin, 84–88, 168).

At bottom the conversation between the Fitzgeralds that May afternoon in 1933 boiled down to the issue of who was in charge of their relationship. Zelda wanted to be free of her husband's criticism and control, and to do her own writing. Scott wanted—and expected—her to be dutiful to him, as the breadwinner in the family. She criticized him for his persistent drinking and occasional cruelty. He disparaged her as an artist and a psychological cripple. It made for an ugly show of a marriage gone wrong—a marriage that may well have been beyond recovery after the summer of 1924, when something happened that could not be repaired, something they had to pay for during the rest of their lives.

Afterword

This study of Zelda Fitzgerald's affair with Edouard Jozan is based on fourteen biographical treatments of the subject written over more than half a century. Almost all of these contribute pieces of evidence into the record, and a few of them cite documents that are crucial to arriving at the facts of the matter. It is a cumulative process, with latter-day biographers standing on the shoulders of their predecessors as they survey the ground.

Obviously, you need the *facts* first, and then you proceed toward some version of the *truth*, in full awareness that the entire truth will, in all its complications, remain finally inaccessible. The process resembles the search for what Hemingway called the "true gen" in warfare, the phrase suggesting an analogy between the digging of the biographer and the work of G2, or military intelligence, in trying to make sense of reconnaissance photographs and prisoner interviews and intercepted communications. The biographer might also be compared to a forensic detective assigned to find whether a crime has been perpetrated, and if so, by whom and to whom, as well as when and where and—most difficult of all to ascertain—why. The elusive issue of people's motivations, motivations that those involved may well have been unable to understand themselves, forces the biographer into the role of an amateur psychologist. Manifestly, few humans are capable of doing all of these jobs thoroughly and well. It can safely be said that the single trait all biographers share is a certain arrogance as they undertake to understand how it must have been, say, for Zelda and Scott and Edouard a long time ago.

The literary biographer, at least, has the benefit of access to the writings of her or his subjects. In fact, the most persuasive testimony that the affair was adulterous and not an insignificant summer flirtation comes from Zelda and Scott themselves. Both of them made serious fictional capital out of the romance, and more than once. This strongly suggests that the affair meant far more to them than mere source material for a performance with which to entertain their friends

Still, the wide disparity between the judgments of the Fitzgeralds' various biographers testifies to the precarious nature of the craft. A few felt certain that Zelda was unfaithful to Scott with Jozan; others were sure that she was not. Some chroniclers thought the affair of little importance; others saw it as of great significance. From fourteen books you get fourteen different accounts—a scornful treatment, a bare recital of the facts, a modestly speculative approach, a fiercely authoritative one, several psychological readings, and so on. This illustrates what has often been remarked: that every biography conceals within itself the autobiography of its author. No matter how devoutly they embrace objectivity as their goal, biographers' personalities and opinions and biases emerge as they tell their separate stories.

Let my own case serve as an example. In writing *Fool for Love*, I emphasized an angle that others tended to ignore: the way in which *not knowing* what his wife had done exacerbated Fitzgerald's feelings of jealousy. It is true that taking this approach enabled me to introduce both "Image on the

Heart," Scott's 1935 story, and Henry Dan Piper's interview with Zelda into the record. Still, you might well conclude that at least as much as F. Scott Fitzgerald, I was somewhat troubled by epistemological uncertainties in these our lives, and shared his tendency to harbor and cultivate jealousy. You might even be right.

The Biographical Treatment

1. Arthur Mizener, *The Far Side of Paradise* (1951), 3.5 pages
2. Andrew Turnbull, *Scott Fitzgerald* (1962), 2 pages
3. Ernest Hemingway, *A Moveable Feast* (1964), 1.5 pages
4. Nancy Milford, *Zelda: A Biography* (1970), 7 pages
5. Sara Mayfield, *Exiles from Paradise* (1971), 5 pages
6. Sheilah Graham, *The Real Scott Fitzgerald* (1976), 1.5 pages
7. Matthew J. Bruccoli, *Some Sort of Epic Grandeur* (1981), 1.5 pages
8. André LeVot, *F. Scott Fitzgerald: A Biography* (1983), 5 pages
9. Scott Donaldson, *Fool for Love: F. Scott Fitzgerald* (1983), 1.5 pages
10. James Mellow, *Invented Lives* (1984), 10 pages
11. Jeffrey Meyers, *Scott Fitzgerald* (1993), 2 pages
12. Kendall Taylor, *Sometimes Madness is Wisdom* (2001), 4 pages
13. Sally Cline, *Zelda Fitzgerald: Her Voice in Paradise* (2002), 10 pages
14. Linda Wagner-Martin, *Zelda Sayre Fitzgerald: An American Woman's Life* (2004), 7 pages

Hemingway's Battle with Biographers, 1949–1954

Please never believe anything you read about Mr. Papa. It is all sheiss. I never aided it but may have abetted it by not comeing out everytime and formally denying crap. Your legend grows like the barnacles on the bottom of a ship and is about as useful. Less Usefull.
—HEMINGWAY TO LILLIAN ROSS, 28 JULY 1948, *SELECTED*, 648

Cowley, Ross, and Boal

By the midpoint of the twentieth century, Ernest Hemingway was well on his way to becoming the most famous writer alive and beginning to realize the costs of his celebrity. To a considerable degree, he had been complicit in establishing the public persona that generated his fame: that of the manly hard-drinking, hard-living warrior and outdoorsman who somehow managed to turn out books when not more vigorously occupied. Generally he had not shied away from publicity. Gossip columnists Leonard Lyons and Earl Wilson of the *New York Post* both visited the Hemingways at the Finca

Vigia in Cuba, for example. But brief items such as "Lunch at Papa Heming-way's" in the Lyons Den column seemed innocuous enough. Far more trou-bling were the long up-close-and-personal articles about him in the popular press, especially those by Malcolm Cowley in 1949 and Lillian Ross in 1950. These, he felt, compromised his privacy and threatened to handicap his future writing.

To begin with, Hemingway had few reservations about Cowley as a chronicler of his life and work. As early as the mid-1930s he identified Cow-ley and Edmund Wilson as the only worthwhile literary critics then practic-ing. He was pleased by Cowley's celebratory review of *For Whom the Bell Tolls* in 1940, and more pleased by the job Cowley did in editing and writing the introduction to the 1944 Viking Portable Hemingway. Then, working with Maxwell Perkins at Scribner's, Cowley came up with a plan to issue a three-volume edition of *A Farewell to Arms*, *The Sun Also Rises*, and *For Whom the Bell Tolls* with illustrations and an introduction showing the rela-tionship between the three novels—a proposal favored by Hemingway that foundered after Perkins's death in June 1947.

These good reasons helped Hemingway overcome his reluctance to cooperate when, early in 1948, Cowley approached him about an assign-ment he'd wangled from *Life* magazine for a long article about him. In doing research for the story, Cowley came across contradictory accounts about Hemingway's life, both in pulp magazines and mainstream publications, leaving him "in a state of profound confusion" about a number of matters, including Hemingway's World War I service. Was it true, he asked Heming-way, that he'd been wounded three times in Italy, once as a lieutenant with the crack Italian Arditi? Hemingway, who'd invented the Arditi connection, answered such queries, supplied Cowley with names and addresses of sources, and invited Cowley, his wife Muriel, and their son Rob to spend a week in Cuba in March 1948. During that visit and in correspondence afterwards, Hemingway habitually spun tales about himself in war and peace, and just as often warned Cowley against using this material. He trusted Cowley as a fellow professional, and went so far as to offer him a loan while the *Life* arti-cle was in process, Cowley felt "honestly and humbly grateful" but turned it down (MC to EH, 11 July 1948, Newberry). In a letter of 5 September 1948 he also granted Cowley permission to do a "book" on him.

Cowley's admiration for Hemingway pervades his "Portrait of Mister Papa," which occupied sixteen pages in the 10 January 1949 issue of *Life*. The lead photograph depicted the writer at his typewriter early in the morning, with three of the family cats as witnesses. Shoeless and shirtless, Heming-way looked fit in his fiftieth year, wearing shorts that showed his muscular calves and sporting a moustache (not yet a beard). "When he puts on his steel-rimmed Army-issued spectacles," Cowley commented, "he looks like a scholar poring over a Greek manuscript. When he grins he looks like a schoolboy masquerading in an iron-gray wig" ("Mister Papa," 90).

The article began with an extended account of Hemingway's war experiences, especially his World War II heroics—sub-hunting aboard the *Pilar*, attaching himself to the 22nd Infantry Regiment, forming his own freelance outfit that liberated the Ritz Hotel in Paris. Laudatory throughout, Cowley incorrectly predicted that *Across the River and Into the Trees*, Hemingway's novel in progress, would prove to be the best work of fiction to come out of that war.

The story moved from Hemingway's wars to his style of life: the fishing-hunting-boxing exploits, the multiple dinner guests, the staff in attendance, the fondness of Cubans for him and vice versa. A strong emphasis throughout was placed on Hemingway's dedication to his craft. Cowley quoted John Peale Bishop's recollection that during the early 1920s, when living on a pittance in Paris, Hemingway "could not be bought" ("Mister Papa," 98). The piece approvingly described his work regimen in Cuba—at the typewriter every morning from 8 A.M. to 12:30 P.M., keeping a daily count of words committed to paper, and stopping with a plan in mind for what would come next. Cowley quoted Hemingway on the difficulty and dignity of writing, and on his conviction that there was no such thing as a midwestern writer or an expatriate writer or any other kind of writer. He was a writer, period, Hemingway insisted, and that was difficult enough for anyone. At the end, Hemingway reflected on his attempt to achieve something lasting. A writer only had to "do it once to get remembered by some people," he said. "But if you can do it year after year after year quite a lot of people remember and they tell their children, and their children and their grandchildren remember, and if it's books they can read them. And if it's good enough it can last forever" ("Mister Papa," 101).

Cowley could hardly have finished with a more respectful passage. But his article was marred by a number of factually inaccurate reports about Hemingway. A few of these derived from Otto McFeely, a longtime Oak Park newsman Cowley hired to interview a number of Ernest's boyhood companions. "A Portrait of Mister Papa" had Ernest running away from home twice (false) and being kayoed by professional boxer Young A'Hearn (highly doubtful) when at fourteen he persuaded his father to let him take boxing lessons (true). Most of the misinformation, however, came from Hemingway's own yarns and his developing status as a celebrity. Among his friends, Cowley listed generals, priests, prizefighters, movie stars Gary Cooper, Marlene Dietrich, and Ingrid Bergman, Loyalist fighters in the Spanish Civil War, and convicts lately escaped from Devil's Island.

In the aftermath of the *Life* article, Cowley proposed writing a critical biography of Hemingway. He'd told Knopf that a full-length biography was out of the question, he wrote Hemingway on 3 May 1949 (MC to EH, New-berry). A shorter book was what he had in mind, and the time to do it was when *Across the River* was about to be published. Cowley abandoned the idea when Hemingway discouraged him. He did not like being character-ized—as Cowley had done in his *Life* article—as a literary boy instead of an athletic one. In so doing, he thought, Cowley was presenting his version of a great writer who resembled himself more than Hemingway. "[A]ll these guys have theories and try to fit you into the theory. Malcolm thot I was like him because my father was a Dr. and I went to Michigan when I was 2 weeks old where they had Hemlock trees" (EH to Harvey Breit, 23 July 1956, in *Selected*, 867).

Hemingway also felt a trace of resentment about Cowley making money out of his life. In correspondence, Cowley tried to minimize that resent-ment. "Did make some money out of writing about your life," he acknowl-edged in May 1951. "$2,000. Could have made more doing other things. Couldn't have had free trip to Cuba to see you and that's what tempted me. Tried hard to write the article in your interest." In December 1951 he returned to the same issue. "I hope I didn't say anything to imply that I wanted you to let me write the piece because I needed money." Cowley did need money, he admitted, and as a freelance man of letters would always need it, but chiefly he wrote the article because it gave him a chance to see Hemingway and because he "was sure that *somebody* was going to write it and was afraid that some snide bastard was going to get the assignment" (MC to EH, 16 May 1951, 25 December 1951, Newberry). Writing back the next month, Hemingway pointed out that when he'd initially expressed res-ervations about cooperating for the article in *Life*, Cowley assured him that the money would make it possible to send his son Rob to Exeter. Heming-way understood that wasn't the only reason Cowley took the assignment, he said, but it had a lot to do with his going along with it (EH to MC, 17 January 1952, JFK).

Cowley's story in *Life* fed the growing public appetite for inside infor-mation about Hemingway the man as opposed to Hemingway the writer. In the next year it was followed by Lillian Ross's controversial twenty-six-page *New Yorker* profile called "How Do You Like It Now, Gentlemen?" (13 May 1950) and by two articles from Sam Boal in the short-lived *Park East*. Ross had formed a friendship with Hemingway in advance of her piece, and Boal was an old friend of his wife Mary's. He'd gone along with their articles out of friendship just as he had with Cowley, but—he complained in December 1951—doing so meant that his writing was increasingly being "criticized from the standpoint of these friends' impressions . . . rather than from [that of] the work itself" (EH to Thomas Bledsoe, 9 December 1951, in *Selected*, 745).

Hemingway met Lillian Ross when she was doing research for her first *New Yorker* profile, on Sidney Franklin, the bullfighter from Brooklyn. Hemingway and Franklin had known each other since the late 1920s, and Franklin accompanied him to Spain when he was reporting on the Spanish Civil War in 1937. Either Ross arranged to interview Hemingway about Franklin by telephoning him, as she remembered it, or she arranged to do so after meeting his son Patrick in San Francisco, as Ernest remembered it.

Both agreed that she showed up unannounced at the door of the tourist cabin he was occupying in Ketchum, Idaho, at seven o'clock in the morning on 24 December 1947. According to Hemingway's lively account, he "was sitting on the can" when he heard Patrick talking to some woman outside. He didn't know who it could be, arriving on the day before Christmas (Patrick had failed to tell him about her visit), but she was invited to come inside and "had a good Christmas" with Ernest and Mary and his three sons and two of the Cubans who had been on the *Pilar* with him during the war (EH to Harvey Breit, 21 June 1952, in *Selected*, 767).

Hemingway and Ross hit it off at that initial meeting, and during the next few years frequently corresponded with each other. A total of eighty-one letters from Ross are archived in the John F. Kennedy Library's Hemingway collection, and he wrote her several letters as well. In those letters he played the role of the tutor holding forth for the tyro. As Ross put it, "Hemingway *told* me things" (Ross, "Told," 72). Told her how to play poker, how to ride a horse, how to get along in Hollywood, how to write. Instructed her about the difference between the porpoise and the whale, admitted that he'd actually had fun in the war, evaluated writers by comparing them to baseball pitchers. All of this was done in a casual, relaxed, humorous, dirty-talking style, as when he advised her that there was really no substitute in English "for the phrase 'Fuck off, Jack'" (EH to Ross, 28 July 1948, in *Selected*, 647). He also liked shocking her with descriptions of himself as a warrior—"killed 122, armed"—and as a lover—"in 1931–32–33 . . . I got so wor[n] out with the adultery that I practically gave up everything else" (EH to Ross, 8 May 1950, 11 May 1950, JFK). Ross was but twenty years old when she presented herself in Ketchum, and Hemingway, twenty-eight years her senior, took pleasure in playing Papa to her daughter. He let himself go in writing her, and often ended his letters by urging her to write again soon.

Ross's career at the *New Yorker* blossomed with her Sidney Franklin profile and another long account the following year on the making of John Huston's film of *The Red Badge of Courage*. When, late in 1949, she suggested writing a piece about his upcoming visit to New York, Hemingway said, fine, go ahead.

Her reportorial technique was to observe her subject closely and to write about what she saw without any authorial commentary: the "fly on the wall" approach. For the Hemingway profile, she placed herself in his company for nearly every waking hour of the three days he spent in New York, recording what he did and said during that time. The resulting account bore the stamp of authenticity, inspiring confidence in the reader that things happened pretty much the way Ross set them down. It also presented Hemingway in a highly unfavorable light.

Hemingway was on holiday at the time, and determined to enjoy himself in New York. He brought with him the nearly finished typescript of the novel he'd been working hard on, *Across the River and Into the Trees*. On the airplane from Cuba, he commandeered his seatmate into reading the script. At Idlewild (now Kennedy) Airport, he crooked his arm around this "wiry little man" and—speaking in what Ross called "Indian talk," bereft of articles—described the fellow's reaction. "Book too much for him. . . . Book start slow, then increase in pace till it becomes impossible to stand." The seatmate had only a single word to say before disentangling himself: "Whew!" (Ross, "Portrait," 195). In no hurry to leave the airport, Hemingway and his wife Mary repaired to the cocktail lounge for two double bourbons. At the bar he told Ross that he got along at least as well with animals as with humans. "In Montana, once, he lived with a bear, and the bear slept with him, got drunk with him, and was a close friend" (Ross, "Portrait," 197). So the profile began, establishing a picture of Hemingway as a buffoon given to improbable stories and a serious drinker who—later in the piece—would down champagne with breakfast and pull on his flask during a midday visit to the Metropolitan Museum of Art.

Ross's Hemingway also dispensed expert comments on sport, especially boxing. "Never lead against a hitter unless you can outhit him. Crowd a boxer. . . . Duck a swing. Block a hook. And counter a jab with everything you own" (Ross, "Portrait," 208). In the most damaging passage in the profile, he cast the contest for literary preeminence in prizefighting lingo. "I started out very quiet and I beat Mr. Turgenev. Then I trained hard and I beat Mr. De Maupassant. I've fought two draws with Mr. Stendhal, and I think I had an edge in the last one. But nobody's going to get me in any ring with Mr. Tolstoy unless I'm crazy or I keep getting better" (Ross, "Portrait," 202). At best this sounded immodest, at worst like braggadocio.

Here as elsewhere, Ross's stance as an observer who did not allow herself to comment on the proceedings worked against Hemingway. Many years later—without mentioning the passage above—she tried to take the curse off his extraordinary competitiveness. All writers wanted to be the best, she observed. Hemingway was simply more forthright about it than others, and in that respect "as touching as a child." Once he'd told her that he wanted to be Champion of the World. But Tolstoy was blocking him, and if he got by him he'd only run into Shakespeare. "What the hell do you do when they wrote it first?" (Ross, "Told," 73).

A few passages in the profile caught the flavor of Hemingway's humor. In conversation with Marlene Dietrich, he described a prominent motion-picture producer as "a sea heel." Dietrich wondered what a sea heel was. "The sea is bigger than the land," he explained (Ross, "Portrait," 204). Wishing he were elsewhere, Hemingway went to Abercrombie and Fitch to buy an overcoat. "I think I still have credit in this joint," he gruffly told the clerk (Ross, "Portrait," 212). Publisher Charles Scribner wondered whether Hemingway had the letters Scribner had recently written him. "I carry them everyplace I go, Charlie," he answered, "together with a copy of the poems of Robert Browning" (Ross, "Portrait," 220–21).

Generally, though, Hemingway emerged as basically ridiculous in Ross's article, and most readers regarded it as an attempt to belittle the author. In apologias of 1961 and 1999, she maintained that it was "a sympathetic piece" meant to capture Hemingway in high spirits, kidding around on a vacation, and that any careful reader could see that she wrote it out of "affection and admiration." Ross also insisted that the widespread public reaction against the portrait came as a complete surprise to her, to the *New Yorker*, and to Hemingway himself (Ross, "Portrait," 189–91).

Where Hemingway was concerned, this was not entirely accurate. Sent a copy of the profile early in April 1950—it ran in the April 14 issue—he wrote Ross that he "felt badly about being a character in the piece," but planned to "straighten up, now, and will fly right. Will speak a language that will put the late Henrietta James to shame and will confound all ticket holders with my erudition" (EH to Ross, 11 May 1950, JFK). On 23 May 1950 he told Dietrich that he hoped he didn't talk that way and didn't act "like such a conceited son of a bitch" (EH to Dietrich, JFK). Ross's piece would "make me plenty new good enemies" (EH to Scribner, 1 May 1950, Princeton). He himself and a good many others understood that the profile did him considerable harm. Cowley called it "the worst thing" ever written about Hemingway. "I think it was as bad as it could be—if it had been any worse it would have been better, because the malice of it would have been clearer" (MC to EH, 9 May 1951, Newberry)

At no time, though, did Hemingway condemn Ross herself, and their friendly correspondence continued without interruption. He liked her as well as he liked anybody, he wrote Robert Cantwell on 25 August 1950, "and anything she or anyone else writes about me, good or bad, is their own impression and I will not edit it nor correct it" (EH to Cantwell, JFK). Oddly, he felt it necessary to reassure Ross about the article. Some people called it "devastating," and believed that she had intended to "destroy" him, but she needn't worry about "the devastate people," Hemingway told her. And how could he be destroyed by a woman when she was a friend and they had never even been to bed and no money had changed hands? (EH to Ross, 16 June 1950, JFK).

In a letter Hemingway described the circumstances leading to publication of Sam Boal's two-part article of December 1950–January 1951. "[A] friend of my wife's from old London newspaper days named Sammy Boal crosses on a boat with us and I talk carelessly and cheerfully and without the necessary pomposity of the author and it turns out Sammy is or has been commissioned to write a profile on me. . . . Wonderful" (EH to Thomas Bledsoe, 9 December 1951, in *Selected*, 744). Boal's article showed little evidence that he had read Hemingway's fiction, but he described the man himself as "one of the greatest talkers of our time" (Boal, 18). He opened by listing the topics Hemingway discoursed upon during a ten-minute conversation: fighter planes vs. bombers, the origin of Thanksgiving, his new novel, the Crusades, Tintoretto, the football huddle, punchy prizefighters, cooking a grouse. On all such subjects, Boal maintained, Hemingway spoke with the authority of the expert. "He is right or wise about a thing or a place or a person simply because he *knows*," Boal observed. And he knows because with his "rat-trap memory" he remembers, his talk consisting almost entirely of recollections. Boal's Hemingway like Ross's dropped definite articles and sounded "relentlessly ungrammatical" in conversation. He was also given to improbable tales about himself. During a clandestine 1941 mission in China, Hemingway said, he'd built up his strength by "carrying horses across streams" (Boal, 18–19).

In this instance, and again like Ross, Boal failed to make it clear when or if Hemingway was fooling around. He was a serious but not a solemn writer, Hemingway objected after reading the two-parter, and he liked to joke when he wasn't writing. The best thing about the article was that it appeared in *Park East*, a magazine of limited circulation. The worst thing was that it came out in the wake of the disastrous reviews of *Across the River and Into the Trees*.

Hemingway had the highest of hopes for his novel. He'd put everything he could into it, he said after correcting the galleys, including "love and pride and a couple of other things you can't buy in every drug store." The book "killed" him emotionally every time he read it (EH to Ross, 8 May 1950, JFK). It aroused less charitable reactions from most reviewers. What was wrong with *Across the River and Into the Trees* paralleled what was wrong in the *New Yorker* profile. Hemingway's protagonist, Colonel Cantwell, is exactly his age, and shares the same habits. Ignoring a heart condition that will cause his death, Cantwell consumes heroic quantities of liquor and performs incredible feats of lovemaking with Renata, his nineteen-year-old mistress. But mostly he talks, discoursing for the benefit of the worshipful

Renata. The novel, as Richard Rovere noted in an early review, was "talky . . . almost garrulous." Hemingway's dialogue functioned "not as a tool of narrative but simply as a means for the author to unburden himself of opinions."

Among those who joined Rovere in dismissing the novel were some of the most distinguished literary critics then operating. Cyril Connolly: "*Across the River and Into the Trees* can be summed up in one word, lamentable." Alfred Kazin: "The book was obviously written under great tension . . . and can only distress anyone who admires Hemingway." Maxwell Geismar: "It is not only Hemingway's worst novel; it is a synthesis of everything that is bad in his previous work and it throws a doubtful light on the future." Several commentators looked forward to that future, however. Cowley called the novel "a tired book," although "beautifully finished as a piece of writing. . . . To see what the new Hemingway can do we still have to wait for his big novel" (Rovere, Connolly, Kazin, Geismar, Cowley reviews). Talk was then circulating about the three-part land, sea, and air novel that Hemingway had in prospect. Two years after *Across the River and Into the Trees*, he published a novella drawn from that prospective "big novel": the great popular and critical success *The Old Man and the Sea*. During those two years, between the fall of 1950 and the fall of 1952, Hemingway was often occupied in trying to impede the production of books about him and his work

Ernest Hemingway: The Man and His Work, a collection of a dozen previously printed articles, emerged at the same time as *Across the River and Into the Trees*. This volume began with two biographical portraits: artist John Groth's admiring account of Hemingway during World War II, when he was commanding his cadre of irregulars from a farmhouse on the Siegfried Line, and a reprint of Cowley's *Life* article. Most of the other essays were exercises in literary criticism, yet even in these, as editor John K. M. McCaffery pointed out in his introduction, "the personality of the subject has made a profound impact on the critic and has, in almost every case, affected the tone of the criticism" (McCaffery, 10). That was precisely the problem. Hemingway's public image bulked so large that it was almost impossible to avert one's eyes and consider his work on its own merits.

Mizener, Young, and Fenton

As a former journalist, Hemingway understood that professionals like Cowley and Ross and Boal had a right to turn out articles about him. But he did his best to ward off the potential biographers among them, not only Cowley but also Harvey Breit and Carlos Baker. He was corresponding regularly with Breit, of the *New York Times*, about baseball and boxing in particular. But he rejected the newsman's proposal for a biography. It was too early, Hemingway said in a letter of 1 September 1950. Too many people were still alive: his mother, for example, and other "womens," and above all himself. If he started thinking about himself, it might shut down his creative drive. In his own letters, he often talked about his adventures, feeling free to invent the facts as he went along (Baker, *Life*, 487). But he wanted to keep the actual details of his past off limits to prying scholars, especially after college professor Arthur Mizener brought out *The Far Side of Paradise*, his biography of F. Scott Fitzgerald, in the spring of 1951.

Mizener had contacted Hemingway while researching his book, and in response Hemingway unloaded several diatribes against his former friend. In his first letter to Mizener, he wrote that Fitzgerald "had a very steep trajectory and was almost like a guided missile with no one guiding him" (EH to Mizener, 6 July 1949, in *Selected*, 657). In his letter of 22 April 1950, Hemingway remarked that "[p]oor Scott . . . would have loved all this big thing about him now" and went on to provide two damning anecdotes. (1) One day when they were in New York, Scott said, "If only I could play football again with everything I know about it now," but backed down when Ernest suggested that they run through the traffic like halfbacks. (2) Zelda "ruined" Scott by telling him his sexual organ was too small to give her satisfaction. "Above all," Hemingway said, "[Fitzgerald] was completely undisciplined and he would quit at the drop of a hat and borrow someone's hat to drop. He was fragile Irish instead of tough Irish" (EH to Mizener, in *Selected*, 689–90). In other letters he inveighed against Fitzgerald's drinking and his childish behavior when drunk. If Scott were still alive, Hemingway added, he'd say these things to his face.

Some of these observations found their way into Mizener's *The Far Side of Paradise*, and those that didn't probably contributed to the deprecatory tone the biographer adopted toward his subject. As one perceptive reader put it, Mizener "doesn't approve of Fitzgerald; I don't think he likes him, and I'm damned sure he doesn't understand him" (Thomas Bledsoe to EH, 10 January 1952, JFK). This attitude troubled Hemingway, and he became incensed when the success of the book made Mizener a well-known and well-compensated author. Sections of the book were printed in advance of publication by the *Atlantic Monthly*. Afterwards, there was a feature in *Life*, and Mizener was widely heard and seen in the media. As Malcolm Cowley wrote Hemingway on 18 April 1951, "he's making a career out of Fitzgerald now in radio and television and he'd have the book in the movies too if Scottie [Fitzgerald's daughter] hadn't put a stop to that" (MC to EH, JFK).

What worried Hemingway most was the precedent. "Mizener made money and did some pretty atrocious things (to young Scotty and any offspring she might have) with his book on Scott and every young English professor sees gold in them dirty sheets now" (EH to Wallace Meyer, 21 February 1952, in *Selected*, 751). Letters started arriving in Cuba from would-be biographers saying they admired Mizener's book and would Hemingway mind sending them "all available details and any unpublished material" about his life, "this shit coming in the mail when [he was] trying to be a serious writer" (EH to MC, 1 June 1951, JFK). Hemingway considered Mizener a grave robber or, worse, a carrion crow feasting on his literary prey. Mizener, he maintained, had warned him that "we'll get you yet," but Hemingway was damned if he would be the next victim (EH to Fenton, 21 February 1952, JFK). Fitzgerald was dead and could not defend himself. But "through very much luck" he was alive, and anyone would do well to think twice before they got into a cold, hard fight with him (EH to MC, 13 May 1951, JFK)

Publicity, he was learning, was doing him actual damage as a writer. On a daily basis, Hemingway's increasing fame interfered with his work. Incoming letters asked him to explain his fiction, express an opinion, lend his name to a cause, approve of or cooperate in one sort of project or another. If he answered them all, he wouldn't have time to write anything else. Even saying no took time. Then there were phone calls, often late at night, from students trying to "get something to hang on [him] so they [could] get a Ph.D" (Young, "Foreword," 6) and from newspaper reporters who asked questions and twisted anything he said in response. He interviewed badly, Hemingway decided. If he talked straight, he sounded immodest. If he was cautious, he sounded as if he were pussyfooting around. Either way he made enemies (EH to Harvey Breit, 4 June 1952, JFK).

He wanted "more and truer stuff" written about his work, and fewer lies and distortions about his life, he told Charles Scribner. How could the "bumbling, Choctaw-speaking, punch-drunk wreck" of Ross's New Yorker profile be taken seriously as a writer? (Baker, Life, 497). The article preyed on his mind, as did the critical attacks on Across the River and Into the Trees and his dread of a hatchet job on himself similar to the one Mizener performed on Fitzgerald. Asked by the New York Herald Tribune Books to list his favorite books of the year, he invented a few titles he'd like to read if only they were available—among them He and Lillian: The Story of a Profile, by Mary Hemingway; The Critics: An Harpooner's Story, by Herman Melville; and Longevity Pays: The Life of Arthur Mizener, by F. Scott Fitzgerald (Reynolds, Final, 245).

Hemingway was especially wary of the academics on his trail, who sought—as he regarded it—to make their careers at his expense. In the middle of February 1951 Carlos Baker wrote him about the critical book he was planning on Hemingway's fiction. He wanted "to destroy the legend, puncture the windbags, clear the air a little, and show [Hemingway's] achievement in something like its true dimensions," Baker declared, and he promised not to invade private territory. Hemingway was not persuaded.

He wrote back that any extensive discussion of his life and work, whether public or private, threatened to infringe on material he might one day want to write. Nor did he want to read any outsider's account of his father's suicide, or how coitus interruptus ruined his marriage to Pauline. If a publisher had given Baker an advance, he offered to pay it back to stop the book (Baker to EH, 15 February 1951; EH to Baker, 17 February 1951, JFK).

As with Cowley, Hemingway was sending mixed signals to Baker. No, you can't write my biography, or a work of criticism with a biographical component. But by the way, here are a few of my most sensational secrets to entertain you. Eventually, Baker's assurances that he was not doing a biography won Hemingway over, and he began supplying him with detailed accounts on his work habits, the authors he'd learned from, and his early days in Oak Park. He also made corrections and comments on sample chapters from *Hemingway: The Writer as Artist* (1952), Baker's work in progress.

Still, Hemingway remained adamantly opposed to anyone telling the story of his life while he was still living it. In February 1951, the same month he heard from Baker, a letter came from Sam Boal proposing a straightforward biography. Hemingway said no, unambiguously (Reynolds, *Final*, 259). His decision on this matter was irrevocable, he told Cowley. "If they want to write about my books: o.k. Any mention of my life beyond what you published in *Life*: I stop the book. . . . Did it ever occur to any of these premature grave-robbers that when I was through writing books I might wish to write the story of my life myself if the people concerned were dead so they would be hurt no more than I would?" (EH to MC, 13 May 1951, JFK).

So Hemingway was very much on his guard when Cowley alerted him to Philip Young's book about him in an 18 April 1951 letter. In a passing reference, Cowley said he was "getting a pre-publication look" at the manuscript, which derived from Young's 1948 doctoral dissertation and which he was evaluating for Tom Bledsoe at Rinehart and Co. On the basis of the opening chapter on Nick Adams, Cowley reported that Young seemed to be "a close and careful reader with a great admiration" for Hemingway's work. Three weeks later, though, after reading the entire script, Cowley felt duty-bound to tell Hemingway about his reservations. He liked the beginning and the ending (a comparison of Nick Adams and Huckleberry Finn), but the "flabby" middle chapters, he reported to Hemingway, "show[ed] a deplorable tendency to confuse you as author with the various heroes of your novels and stories."

At the same time, Cowley advised Hemingway that not much could be done to prevent publication, since Young was working from printed sources and was "writing a sort of biographical criticism, not straight biography." He had sent a long report to Bledsoe suggesting "very extensive changes" and felt confident that Young would revise accordingly. "If he makes the changes," Cowley wrote, "it still won't be a book you like, but it will make sense and help your permanent reputation as a writer" (MC to EH, 18 April 1951, 9 May 1951, JFK).

Neither Cowley nor Hemingway, apparently, was aware of Young's November 1950 review of *Across the River and Into the Trees*, judging it "a pretty bad book" full of "outrageous and irrelevant attacks on recognizable living writers" and "wholly embarrassing conversations" (Young, review). Even without this information, Hemingway was alarmed enough by Cowley's report to express his determination to suppress Young's work. As he told Cowley, "[i]f Tom Bledsoe thinks he can publish a book on my life and works without my permission he is quite wrong because I have only to refuse permission from Scribner's for any extracts from my published works to be used and refuse permission for any of my letters to be used and then, if they continue, take the necessary legal action" (EH to MC, 13 May 1951, JFK).

It wasn't quite that simple, Cowley replied on 19 May 1951. Young didn't quote from any letters, confining himself to published sources. And where these were concerned, there was an unsettled point in copyright law as to how much could be quoted from any given work: from only a sentence to upwards of six hundred words. As a critic himself, Cowley said, he would hate to see the strict standard enforced by law. When he thought "of all the trouble and ill feeling and wasted time that would be caused by an effort to stop something like the Young book," he thought "the best policy by far would be to forget about it." Cowley said he would pass on Hemingway's letter to Bledsoe, and meanwhile he would try to make Young's book a better one if Hemingway would promise not to be sore at him for the result. Otherwise, Cowley was ready to "bow out of the picture." He didn't want such issues to "louse up" their relationship. On 8 June, following an incendiary response from Hemingway, Cowley said he'd planned to have another look at the book as revised, but that after that he'd "lay off it . . . keep away from it" (MC to EH, 19 May 1951, 8 June 1951, JFK).

This was easier said than done, for Hemingway relied on Cowley to serve as a intermediary between himself and Bledsoe, the Rinehart editor, who did not actually get in touch with Hemingway—though Cowley advised him to—for more than six months. He was keeping silence until Young's revised manuscript was completed, Bledsoe explained, but in the absence of any communication from the editor or author, Hemingway became increasingly apprehensive about dark doings at his expense. On 9 September 1951 he instructed Charles Scribner to forbid Young to quote from his works (Baker, *Life*, 654). At the same time, he permitted Baker— who had corresponded openly with Hemingway from the start—to quote as much as necessary.

His animus against Young derived in good part from the fact that Young had not contacted him directly. If Philip Young were an honest man, as he put it, "I would think he would have written me a letter outlining what he planned to do." This accusation was unfair to Young, Bledsoe maintained when he finally got around to writing Hemingway on 3 December 1951. Young hadn't written him because he knew Hemingway didn't want to be bothered and respected his desire to be left alone. And since Young was writing a book of criticism and not, as Hemingway feared, "a slanted biography disguised as criticism," he had no need to query Hemingway about details of his life. It was true that Young felt it necessary to include "some already well known facts" about Hemingway the man, Bledsoe acknowledged, but they were included "only to buttress the criticism" and were not personally intrusive. What he more or less desperately hoped, Bledsoe concluded, was that Hemingway would grant Young and Rinehart "permission to quote in the normal way for critical purposes." There wasn't much quotation—"only infrequent short passages"—but the quotes helped the book, "and it would look mighty funny if they weren't there" (Bledsoe to EH, 3 December 1951, JFK).

This attempt to dissuade Hemingway from forbidding quotation did not succeed. In a long letter, he explained to Bledsoe that there had been too damned much written about his private life and he was sick of it, citing the pieces by Cowley and Ross and Boal. After the *New Yorker* profile he'd decided to give no more interviews and discourage further publicity. When he heard from Cowley that Young was writing a book which "proves that I am all my heroes," that sounded awfully intrusive to him. His position remained the same as stated in his letter to Charlie Scribner: no quotations allowed (EH to Bledsoe, 9 December 1951, in *Selected*, 743–46).

Hemingway sent a copy of this letter to Cowley, who again advised him to let Young use the quotes—a total of only nine hundred words—but admitted that was Hemingway's business, not his. Eager to extricate himself from the affair, Cowley said he was sending back his $100 fee to Rinehart for vetting the manuscript and wouldn't look at it again under any circumstances and wished to God he'd never seen it "and let's not talk about it any more" (MC to EH, 25 December 1951, JFK).

But Cowley could not yet quit the field. Early in January 1952 Bledsoe wrote Hemingway again, hoping for a change of heart, and mentioning two things that further aroused Hemingway's suspicions. Bledsoe informed him (1) that Young had presented a paper on Hemingway at the Modern Language Association's annual meeting in Detroit, and (2) that Young was interested in "a standard pattern" in the Hemingway hero running through most of his work, a pattern closely resembling one in Hemingway's life, to which he appended a seemingly unrelated comment about Hemingway's "strong sense of the therapeutic value of writing" (Bledsoe to EH, 10 January 1952, JFK).

Reading between the lines, Hemingway arrived at the conjecture that Young's book was "some sort of psycho-analytic . . . treatment" of his writing in comparison with his life, and asked Cowley to clear up the mystery. Well, Cowley answered, Hemingway was right. "Part of [Young's] book, not the bigger part, [was] an attempt to psychoanalyze Mr. E. H. on the basis of his work." It was this part, making the error of confusing Hemingway with his heroes, that he'd counseled Young to revise. On the other hand, it was clear that Young valued Hemingway's fiction, "so that as regards your literary reputation the book is on the plus side." There seemed no way to stop publication, either, because Bledsoe—"a decent guy"—was willing to go ahead even without quotations (but with a prefatory note saying that Hemingway had forbidden them). Under the circumstances, Cowley once more advised Hemingway to allow quotations, and with that signed off on the whole sorry business. "This is my last will and testament on this subject signed malcolm cowley so help me god amen" (EH to MC, 17 January 1952; MC to EH, 28 January 1952, JFK).

This partial clarification stirred Hemingway's curiosity enough so that he wrote Bledsoe on January 31 asking for a letter from Young and a copy of the paper he read in Detroit. A week later, Young complied with this request, so that critic and author were at last in communication—albeit somewhat unpleasant communication, considering the contents of Young's paper. He'd presented it in a session on Hemingway at MLA, as a summary and response to papers by Frank Jones, Frederick Hoffman, and John Aldridge. Two of the other papers were psychoanalytic in approach, Aldridge's "Jungian" and Hoffman's "Freudian," and Young had come down on the side of Freud by describing Hemingway as the victim of a "traumatic neurosis." Hemingway saw only Young's comments, not those of the other panelists, and they made him angry (Young, "Foreword," 16).

Hemingway wrote Young that although he would not object to anyone quoting for the purposes of "legitimate literary criticism," he had definite objections to people writing about his life while he was alive and to the public psychoanalysis of living writers. Had Young and his fellow scholars at MLA secured medical degrees which authorized them to practice as psychiatrists? Did he see much difference between stating that a man had a traumatic neurosis and that he had syphilis? Did he not understand that either statement would be prejudicial and damaging, not to mention libelous? He was afraid that in his enthusiasm for his thesis Young had overlooked "some of the legal implications." These scarcely veiled threats aside, Hemingway was still in doubt about the precise nature of that thesis, about the mysterious something both Cowley and Bledsoe told him that he would not like in Young's book (Young to EH, February 1952, JFK).

The mystery, in fact, came from the second and most important half of Young's central thesis. Part one of the thesis argued that the "Hemingway hero" closely resembled Hemingway himself. Part two maintained, as Young put it, "that one fact about this recurrent protagonist, as about the man who created him, is necessary to any real understanding of either figure, and that is the fact of the 'wound,' a severe injury suffered in World War I which left permanent scars, visible and otherwise." To fight off the trauma of that wound, Young asserted, Hemingway and his heroes repeatedly felt compelled to test themselves in life-threatening activities—at war, in the bull ring, on safari, at sea (Young, "Foreword," 8). In that way they could demonstrate to themselves, and to others, that they had conquered their trauma, and by so doing achieve what the psychiatrist Otto Fenichel called "counter-phobic mastery."

This was not the first time a critic had advanced the idea that a wound underlay and animated Hemingway's work. Edmund Wilson, in *The Wound and the Bow* (1941), traced the origins of the creative impulse in seven writers—Hemingway among them—to one form of suffering or another, proposing that "genius and disease, like strength and mutilation, may be inextricably bound up together." This was damaging nonsense, Hemingway felt at the time, and he directed his editor, Maxwell Perkins, to threaten a libel suit against Wilson. A decade later, tempers having cooled, Hemingway wrote Wilson that he'd never been able to "understand the part about what my wound was. I tried to. But it wasn't any of the wounds I knew" (EH to Wilson, 10 September 1951, in *Selected*, 733).

Only a few months thereafter, the wound theory came back to haunt him in Young's somewhat reductive thesis. This time, Hemingway let loose both barrels in his correspondence. Young and the other professors at MLA wrote "unspeakably badly," thought "muddily," and obviously should not have been "allowed out unmuzzled without being on the leash of their analysts" (EH to Fenton, 21 February 1952, JFK). More specifically, he characterized "this Rinehart book by a Philip Young out of Thomas Bledsoe" as an attempt to psychoanalyze him "and prove that I am a coward and that as a compensation for my cowardice I write books, go to the available wars, etc." It was the old Max Eastman theory all over again, except that instead of letting off steam by wrestling Eastman in Maxwell Perkins's office, he had to decide what to do about it. He could forbid quotation, but then, as Bledsoe assured him, a prefatory note in the book to that effect would only draw further attention to himself. He could offer to read Young's book and then write a foreword attacking its contents. "Then the man can publish anything he damned well pleases, pay me for the foreword, pay for what he quotes, and hang and rattle." Or he could keep silent, and hence avoid "giving the book any publicity or importance by seeming to have held it up." In the end, he chose this last option, feeling confident that the book would be "dull enough to die of its own weight" (EH to Meyer, 21 February 1952, in *Selected*, 751; EH to Alfred Rice, 22 February 1952, JFK).

On 6 March 1952 Hemingway wrote that if Young would give his word "that the book [was] not biography disguised as criticism and that it [was] not a psychoanalytical study of a living writer" he could go ahead and quote from his works (EH to Young, in *Selected*, 760–61). After thinking it over, Young replied on March 19 that the book was definitely not a biography and neither was it a psychoanalytical study, but that it did "*contain* some material which may be called such—not much, a few hundred words out of 75,000." In those words he'd pointed out that "[h]ere is what psychologists (Freud and Fenichel) have said about wounds like the one Hemingway has written of so often. (*Only* about the wound, and nothing else . . .)" With that reservation, he could promise that his book was fundamentally a critical study of Hemingway's work, and he hoped to hear from him soon that it was all right to use quotations (Young to EH, JFK).

Disturbed by the notion that an injury he received when he was "a boy" should be used as a touchstone to understanding his life and his work, Hemingway did not soon answer. Sometime in April he cabled Rinehart: "sorriest delay been working hardest and thinking over mr. youngs letter as he did mine writing soon regards Hemingway" (EH to Rinehart, JFK). Young tried again on 23 May 1952, this time pleading poverty. It had been two months since he delivered his promise to Hemingway, Young wrote, and for over six weeks he had been "making three fruitless visits a day" to the post office. He was a teacher, and his "whole academic future" depended on publication of the book he'd devoted five years to.

He needed a job, Young went on, and it might be hard for Hemingway to understand why the book "should obtain [him] a job, and the means whereby [he and his wife could] continue to eat, but for young men in college teaching today that happens to be the way things are." He could rewrite and publish without the usual quotations, including a note saying Hemingway had refused permission. But he'd much prefer a go-ahead from Hemingway so that he "could get in touch with Scribner's regarding quotation arrangements." In closing, Young stated that he wished Hemingway absolutely the best, that he was "as staunch an admirer" of his work as anyone, that his book would make that clear, and that he "would deeply appreciate [his] formal cooperation" (Young to EH, JFK).

This request prompted Hemingway to four separate answers on March 26 and 27: two angry letters that were not sent, and a telegram and short typewritten note that were. The burden of the unsent letters was that Young's psychological interpretation of Hemingway and his work had "caused serious damage" to his work and his family. Disseminating such accusations to students, between stiff covers, was a sin beyond redemption. And yet, Hemingway said (in a favorite phrase of his), "I will be a sad son of a bitch if I will have anyone say that I am depriving him of his livelihood. Neither him nor his wife nor his kids nor his ox nor his ass." If Young's job and advancement depended on his book, okay: Hemingway granted him temporary liberty to attempt to destroy him as a writer. "So go ahead and publish. Then take a good look in the mirror sometime and . . . go outside and hang yourself. You've wasted too much of my time" (EH to Young, 26 and 27 May 1952, JFK).

The telegram itself was scarcely less nasty: "if it means your job if not published inform wallace meyer at Scribner's you have my formal permission to quote hope you're happy Hemingway." In the one-page typed note Hemingway added that he had written a six-page letter stating why he thought Young's book should not be published, but that inasmuch as he had granted the right to quote, reiterating these reasons would "only worry" Young. In addition, he was writing Scribner's to pay Young his permissions fee for quotation. "I am very sorry, kid, if you are up the creek financially," Hemingway ended, and offered to send him $200 (EH to Young, 27 May 1952, in *Selected*, 761–62).

Thereafter a few letters went back and forth between critic and author, mostly concerning specific material Young wanted to quote that was not controlled by Scribner's. The tone of this correspondence seemed pleasant enough. In one brief note, Hemingway told a joke at his own expense. He'd recently met a Texan whose wife "read everything" and was a great fan of his, Hemingway reported. The book of his she liked best was *Forever Amber* (EH to Young, 1 July 1952, JFK). But he continued to resent Young's thesis, and would have nothing more to do with his book. When Rinehart asked if it would be all right to use a photograph of him on the dust jacket, Hemingway wired that no pictures of him were to appear "inside or outside of Philip Young book" (EH to Rinehart, 2 August 1952, JFK). Young duly sent Hemingway the first advance copy of his *Ernest Hemingway* he could get hold of when it came out, and "was surprised by the speed with which [Hemingway] returned it—the wrapping reversed, [Young's] name and address carefully lettered in." That returned parcel was their last contact (Young, "Foreword," 26).

Hemingway expressed his feelings on the subject in a 4 June 1952 letter to Carlos Baker. What bothered him most, not having read Young's book, was the Detroit MLA paper alleging that he suffered from "a traumatic neurosis" and that everything he'd written stemmed from that. (He was also upset by

Young's accusation that he did not understand women and created fantasy women in his fiction.) He'd fought against this kind of invasive criticism, and perhaps he should have kept up the fight, but what was he supposed to do when "people say that by refusing the right to reprint you are depriving them of their livelihood?" Now, he supposed, he could expect further fouling of his work "by the two new schools of critics—the amateur detectives and the amateur psychiatrists" (EH to Baker, JFK). Young was the amateur psychiatrist he had in mind. The amateur detective was Charles Fenton.

By late August 1951, when he first heard from Fenton, Hemingway was on his guard against any and all intrusions on his private life. He had been made to look foolish and egotistical in magazine articles by Malcolm Cowley, Lillian Ross, and Sam Boal. He was upset by the hostile reviews of *Across the River and Into the Trees*, furious about Arthur Mizener's dismemberment of F. Scott Fitzgerald, and adamantly opposed to Philip Young's forthcoming book. The remarkable thing is that in spite of these reservations Hemingway gave Fenton an unusual amount of encouragement through the mails, at least at the beginning. Later, as the project appeared to veer away from Fenton's declared line of approach—a study of Hemingway's literary apprenticeship, how he shaped himself into a writer—into invasion of his privacy and appropriation of past incidents he himself wanted to write about, his anger boiled over.

The story emerges in interesting and at times combative correspondence between the principals: an ambitious young instructor at Yale and a world-famous author in Cuba. Over a period of fifteen months they wrote nearly fifty letters back and forth, including ten of Hemingway's most indignant ones, which he saved but did not send. Fenton initially earned the great man's trust by introducing himself as a fellow writer and fellow warrior. He'd won the 1945 Doubleday / Twentieth Century Fox prize for a first novel (never published), written a number of stories and articles for mainstream magazines, and worked as a reporter for metropolitan dailies. And he had enlisted in the Royal Canadian Air Force a year before Pearl Harbor and eventually flown as a tail gunner on bombing missions over the Ruhr. It also worked in Fenton's favor that, as he insisted in his first letter to Hemingway, "I couldn't care less about your private life, and I have no interest whatever in writing your biography" (Fenton to EH, 20 August 1951, JFK).

Believing as he did that writers were made and not born, Fenton set out in *The Apprenticeship of Ernest Hemingway* to trace the steps by which a talented midwestern youngster had transformed himself into one of the century's greatest authors. This necessitated a considerable amount of digging into Hemingway's past, from Oak Park schooldays and a stint as a cub reporter on the *Kansas City Star* to his wartime experiences, from feature writing and foreign correspondence for the *Toronto Star Weekly* to such

Paris mentors as Gertrude Stein and Ezra Pound. Fenton was a thorough and conscientious digger, getting in touch with just about everyone who could testify to his subject's progress along the way. His single best source, of course, was Hemingway himself, and for some time he fully cooperated with Fenton, supplying lots of valuable anecdotal material in letters of substantial length. But then he dug in his heels.

Three issues particularly troubled Hemingway. First, he regarded Fenton's research into his past as an invasion of privacy, and resented the Yale instructor for pursuing the companions of his youth like an FBI investigator. He reacted angrily, for example, when Fenton asked him about the stories he'd written in high school for the *Oak Park Tabula*. "What are you planning to do, boy? Publish all the crap I wrote as a kid trying to learn to write?" That would be like publishing the contents of his wastebasket. It reminded him of Arthur Mizener "looking for the stigmata of wet dreams on old pyjamas" in his biography of Fitzgerald. Then, in a pattern that ran through Hemingway's correspondence, he followed this outburst by volunteering unasked-for information, some of it accurate. False: his mother had held him out of school one year to study the cello, an instrument for which he had "absolutely no talent." True: in high school he'd had to try to be an athlete as well as to learn to write. "At Oak Park if you could play football you had to play it" (EH to Fenton, 13 September 1951, JFK).

Fenton assured Hemingway that he was no Mizener, and that he wasn't planning to reproduce his high school newspaper writings, only cite portions of them to illustrate his conviction that journalism "was a lot more important than the critics had realized, as a training not only in technique, but in the treatment of material" (Fenton to EH, 18 September 1951, JFK). Soon thereafter, though, he again managed to alienate Hemingway, this time by asking for a brief note authorizing the superintendent of Oak Park and River Forest High School to release a transcript of his high school grades. This request produced amusing commentary from Hemingway in two unmailed letters. First letter: Why did Fenton need a letter from him to get the grades? Didn't "they give them out without the permission of the accused?" Second letter: He was "touched by the school's solidarity in not sending grades without the permission of the graded or de-graded." Had Fenton got the grades anyway? "Did the principal break down or did [Fenton] have to filch them or was the matter just left in abeyance?" And if he did get the grades, just what did he plan to do with them? (EH to Fenton, 21 February 1952, 5 April 1952, JFK).

Among those Fenton contacted seeking information on Hemingway's high school career was Ernest's sister Ursula Jepson, then living in Hawaii. In querying her Fenton faithfully stuck to his apprenticeship theme. He inquired, for instance, whether the adolescent Hemingway demonstrated "a precocious sense of dedication about writing" and what he might have learned from Oak Park's English teachers. These inquiries seemed benign enough: "seems he must be trying to write a scholarly book on the Great Stein," Ursula wrote her brother. But Fenton also asked for names of others to get in touch with, and that might cause problems. "The insidious thing," she thought, might be "the trail of people he pick[ed] up," including those who wanted to get some of "their longstanding jealousy" of Ernest Hemingway out of their system (Jepson to EH, 4 August 1952, JFK). Ernest advised his sister not to answer Fenton's letter, and gave the same advice to Dorothy Connable, who was approached as a source for the Toronto period. Fenton was just as bad as Mizener, Hemingway insisted, and "the only way to stop these buzzards is to tell them *absolutely nothing*" (EH to Connable, 17 February 1953, JFK).

Working through his research chronologically, Fenton sent Hemingway drafts of his chapters on Kansas City and Toronto as they neared completion. These drafts confirmed Hemingway's conviction that Fenton, in sounding out the acquaintances of his newspaper days, was placing too much reliance on the testimony of unreliable sources. His "method of interrogation and cross-interrogation" produced at best only an approximation of the facts. Most people did not remember accurately, he told Fenton, and everything had changed in America over the past thirty years. You needed local knowledge to write with authority, needed "to have seen the hill before the bulldozer hit it." Besides, just as Ursula had suspected, a few of Fenton's sources—"professional survivors"—harbored grievances against Hemingway that they were only too glad to articulate.

Hemingway's second major objection was that cooperating with Fenton cost him valuable time and money. He wasted an entire working day trying to straighten out the Kansas City chapter, for instance, and he was further annoyed when Fenton sold that section to *New World Writing* for a pittance. He averaged between fifty cents and a dollar a word for his work, Hemingway pointed out. He wrote letters ranging between five hundred and fifteen hundred words that Fenton then incorporated into material that he sold for 2 1/2 cents a word. "Mr. Fenton, I hope you will agree this is economically unsound." Any man's autobiography was his own property, Hemingway went on, and he should certainly not feed it piecemeal into letters for another man to use. Under the circumstances, he thought Fenton ought to "drop the entire project." Either that, or organize it in such a way that both of them might profit (EH to Fenton, 29 July 1952, JFK).

At this stage in their correspondence, in early August 1952, Hemingway actually suggested that the two of them should collaborate. "You write the apprenticeship book," he proposed. "I will provide letters, as I have done so far giving you the true gen [intelligence] as I remember it." The resulting book would be published commercially, with royalties to be shared equally between them, and it would, he felt, make them both pots of money. In that way, when Hemingway wrote letters for Fenton to quote, he could consider that a legitimate part of the working day. There might even be sequels for 1925–35 and 1935–45 (the apprenticeship book covered the 1916–23 period). As a side benefit, Hemingway added, Fenton could help him deal with the Ph.D. candidates who were harassing him. One professor ought to "know how to tell another professor to fuck off: that he is working this side of the street" (EH to Fenton, 2 August 1952, JFK).

Hemingway was probably not serious in making this proposal, for it was made in a letter he wrote but did not send. When he next heard from Fenton, who sent him the Toronto chapter for comment, he replied with indignant exasperation. In the first pages of the chapter, Hemingway said in his letter of 9 October 1952, he found so many errors that he could spend the rest of the year correcting them and have no time left to write anything of his own. He was also upset about Fenton "collecting" the articles he'd written for the *Toronto Star Weekly*. Morally and perhaps legally, he had no right to publish such pieces. "I would no more do a thing like that to you than I would cheat a man at cards or rifle his desk or wastebasket or read his personal letters," Hemingway said. Then he moved on to even tougher talk. Fenton should examine his conscience before continuing with a project he'd "been warned to cease and desist on and which [would] lead him if not to jail at least into plenty of trouble" (EH to Fenton, JFK).

Back at Yale, where he was working to finish his dissertation/book, Fenton apparently decided not to answer this incendiary letter. Four months later, however, Hemingway followed up with a registered letter denying Fenton the right to quote from any of his work, just as he had with Philip Young. He claimed that he himself had in preparation a book on his apprenticeship as a young writer, and warned Fenton once again to "cease and desist" on a project that had "degenerated, or enlarged, into a full-scale invasion of privacy" and that had cost him irreplaceable working hours. He also maintained that he had copyrighted his bylined articles for the Toronto newspapers (EH to Fenton, 18 February 1953, JFK).

Again Fenton kept silence. Two months later, on 26–27 April 1953, Hemingway wrote his attorney, Alfred Rice, about a further plan to scare Fenton off. He instructed Rice to send Fenton a letter at his Yale address worded as follows: "My client, Mr. Ernest Hemingway has asked me to write you to ascertain why he has not received an answer to his registered letter to you of February 18th 1953. In the future, since Mr. Hemingway is traveling, will you address all communications to him through me?" This letter was to be registered also, and if Rice had no reply within a week, he was to send another registered letter to Yale's Department of English, enclosing the previous letter, to be sure that it was duly delivered.

In explaining his actions to Rice, Hemingway described Fenton as an unsuccessful writer who hated fiction and constantly confused it with fact and as an amateur FBI operative who by naming people in his book prevented Hemingway from writing about them and exposed him to libel suits. Fenton had interfered with his privacy "to an unbelievable extent." Furthermore, he had been forced to back away from a "wonderful story" about "some very bad and interesting trouble" he'd experienced up in Michigan—the time the law was pursuing him for shooting a heron out of season—because Fenton started identifying the people who were involved.

He didn't want to go to law, Hemingway added, but he wanted to keep Fenton "off balance" and he wanted his publisher—Farrar, Straus and Young—"too worried to touch the book." His objective was to drop a good roadblock ahead of and behind Fenton, and he understood that blocking his book boiled down to a question of who bluffed who. The thing to do now was to send the registered letter requesting an answer, for "[j]ust the sight of a legal letterhead spooks most people" (EH to Rice, 26–27 April 1953, JFK).

Rice's letter (if it was sent) drew no response from Fenton, who continued to plug away on the dissertation that would earn him his Ph.D, his academic "union card," in June. He was able to base the later chapters on close examination of the articles Hemingway turned out for the Toronto papers, on both sides of the ocean, thus avoiding in part the "trailing around" of sources that aroused Hemingway's anger and not troubling him with questions. In June Fenton mailed Hemingway a copy of his massive 630-page dissertation. In a reply Hemingway did not send, he once again brought up "the whole question of the reliability of something that happened 30 years or more ago" and singled out a few of Fenton's "unreliable witnesses." He admitted to feeling "pretty damned friendly" toward anyone who had done as much work as Fenton had on his beginnings as a writer. Yet at the same time he contended that the ground Fenton covered amounted to the "note book, oil resource, and basic material" for three novels he had yet to write (EH to Fenton, 26 June 1953, 2 August 1953, JFK). This accusation spelled out Hemingway's third point of contention: that Fenton was robbing him of subject matter for his fiction.

Over the summer and fall Fenton cut his "rock-like treatise" from 630 to 300 pages. The result, he wrote Hemingway on Thanksgiving Day, was "a good, sound, honest book" that invaded no privacy and left "completely undamaged all the material" Hemingway might want to use. He then appended a list of quotations he wanted permission to use from Hemingway's letters to him, to Sherwood Anderson, and to Gertrude Stein (Fenton to EH, 26 November 1953, JFK). Hemingway was on safari in Africa when he received this letter, and obviously in a good mood. Using the quotes was "perfectly ok," he wrote, and signed off with "Best always, your friend Ernest Hemingway" (EH to Fenton, 5 December 1953, Sotheby). Fenton, who had more or less been holding his breath for months, could finally exhale.

Fenton scrupulously kept his word by sticking to the apprenticeship process throughout, and his book has stood the test of time, remaining the best study of how Hemingway became Hemingway. As he put it in the final sentence, Ernest Hemingway had lived in several places during his seven-year apprenticeship—Kansas City, Chicago, Paris, and Toronto among them—"and he had been a newspaperman, but he had become a writer" (Fenton, *Apprenticeship*, 263).

The last few letters the two men exchanged were friendly communications, free of the rancor that Hemingway—and sometimes Fenton as well—was subject to. At the end, after the two terrible plane crashes Hemingway survived early in 1954 and the Nobel Prize later that year, his antagonist became "Dear Charlie." Hemingway even hoped that Fenton might make some money out of his book, adding that "[d]ough is the least part. Doing it well is first. Money is last" (EH to Fenton, 1954, 3 May 1954, Sotheby).

Despite the agreeable stance of these letters, Hemingway continued to disparage Fenton to others. In April 1955 he remarked that Fenton was "a disappointed creative writer and a disappointed FBI investigator" and that his book was "overdone." He did not judge Fenton as harshly as he had Philip Young, but he lumped them both together with Carlos Baker in a wholesale denigration of academic critics "Professor Carlos Back-up and Professor Charles Fender and Professor Philip Youngerdunger, wearing the serious silks of Princeton and Yale and N.Y.U." (Hotchner, 179).

Hemingway's last comment on Fenton came in a letter to Baker. By an unhappy coincidence, both Fenton and Hemingway committed suicide within a year's time. Fenton, forty-one, leaped from the twelfth floor of the Washington Duke Hotel in Durham, North Carolina, in July 1960. While undergoing shock treatment at the Mayo Clinic in Rochester, Minnesota, the following January, Hemingway wrote Baker about it.

> Had heard about Fenton jumping out of the hotel window. . . .
> Hope that won't set an example to my other biographers. Wonder what he thought about on the way down. Understand he had started to go down once and then decided to climb up and started all over again. He was supposed to have had some trouble when he was in the R.A.F. and that may have had something to do with it. Never met him but feel very sorry for him although

his school of biography and criticism was that type of F.B.I. treatment which I did not care for. I bought his book on Steven [*sic*]
St. Vincent Benet and it seemed a fair enough book to cause anyone inclined that way to window jump. Hope this levity is not
out of order. (Hemingway to Baker, 16 January 1961, JFK)

Six months later Hemingway, sixty-one, propped a shotgun against his head
and tripped both barrels.

THE CHEEVER MISADVENTURE

Writing the Cheever

On 30 June 1988, *John Cheever: A Biography* was published, six years to the month after Cheever's death and five and a half years after I first proposed the book to his widow, Mary. It was my fourth biography and by far the most difficult to bring into print. Midway through the process the Cheever family decided to fight the book. Their opposition, in the form of a possible lawsuit, combined with the judicial findings in the somewhat similar J. D. Salinger case to require considerable revision, held up publication for a year, and kept me and my publishers jumpy before and after the book came out.

In the beginning I was tremendously excited by the prospect of writing Cheever's biography. In the end I was primarily relieved that the ordeal was over. When I originally decided to write an article about that experience, in 1990, I was still angry and absolved myself of blame for what had gone wrong in my dealings with the family. Twenty years and more later, I can more judiciously see the mistakes I made along the way.

Research

Like many thousand others, I had been an avid reader of Cheever's fiction at least since the mid-1950s. I thought he captured the complications and uncertainties of contemporary existence, and showed us more about the way middle-class Americans lived in the middle of the twentieth century than any other writer. I read his stories and novels with pleasure and the occasional jolt of recognition. Cheever was the living American author I most admired, the one whose fiction most resonated with me. In the 1970s and 1980s, I wrote several essays about his work. As a matter of courtesy and in an attempt to establish communications, I mailed the first of these to Cheever at his home on Cedar Lane in Ossining, New York, and received a cordial response. On 17 October 1976, he thanked me for sending him this piece on Cheever and the suburbs ("The Machines in John Cheever's Garden"). He was pleased to see his work treated seriously and with understanding, he said. He did indeed mean to "be a Jeremiah," as I'd asserted: there were saints and angels and visions of hell abounding in his fiction. In closing, he remarked that it was good to know he had a friend in Virginia (I was teaching at the College of William and Mary) and he'd be delighted to meet me (JC to SD, 17 October 1976, Harvard).

Spurred on, I persuaded Leonard Unger, general editor of the *American Writers* series, that Cheever belonged in the eminent company of canonical American authors that series covered and that I was equipped to write his critical-biographical entry. For that project I read almost everything Cheever had published, along with everything I could find written about him, and went to see him—our sole meeting—on Nantucket in the summer of 1977. He told me then that "most people have fathers or mothers," but he was different: he had a brother instead (SD, *Cheever*, ix). This out-of-the-blue remark, delivered while he was driving me to catch the ferry to the mainland, lodged in my consciousness and helped inform both my fifteen-thousand-word *American Writers* essay (1979), the first thoroughgoing study of his work, and my biography, published a decade later. I sent him the long essay, along with a shorter article on his stories set in Italy, and he answered with characteristic wit. He could not himself gauge the importance of his contribution to literature but on the basis of reading my essays was "convinced that to make a contribution was [his] intent" (JC to SD, 24 August 1979, Harvard).

When word came of John Cheever's death in June 1982, I was keenly interested in doing a biography, but hesitant—so soon after his passing—to advance such a proposal. What moved me to action was a rumor going around the halls of the Modern Language Association convention in December 1982 that an authorized biography by a Jesuit priest was under way. A few weeks later I wrote Mary Cheever, his widow and executor, asking about that, expressing my interest in doing a biography about her husband, and sending along my curriculum vitae. No one was "entrenched and at work" on a biography, she replied, although her daughter Susan was in the process of writing a memoir. On the other hand, she cautioned that no biography could be undertaken until the family made a decision "about the disposition of John's journals," a massive quantity of notebooks and manuscripts on flimsy paper then reposing in a vault. "We survivors" had yet to decide whether to donate these journals or sell them or both, she said. My vita looked impressive—I had by that time written biographies of Hemingway, Fitzgerald, and the poet Winfield Townley Scott—but not having read any of my work, she could hardly make a judgment about my eligibility "for the job when the time [came] to do it" (Mary Cheever to SD, 16 February 1983, Harvard).

This was a long way from a yes, but not quite an outright no. Would-be biographers have to persist. On the strength of her last comment, I sent Mary Cheever the long essay on Cheever for the *American Writers* series and a copy of *Poet in America: Winfield Townley Scott*, my biography of a man whose work—as herself a practicing poet—she knew about. I also read her book, *The Need for Chocolate and Other Poems* (1980), with pleasure, discovering a number of truly excellent poems, and in May 1983 wrote her about the ones I'd especially liked. If it was all right, I proposed visiting her at the house on Cedar Lane in Ossining where the Cheevers had lived for more than twenty years. Were there scrapbooks? What about letters?

She'd started reading the biography of "W. T. S." (Winfield Townley Scott), Mary replied, and hoped to get him off to college before bedtime. But "alas, no doting granny nor dutiful child" ever kept a scrapbook about John. And he threw away letters, never kept copies," although some correspondents had given letters *from* him to repositories such as the New York Public Library and Chicago's Newberry Library. There would be "a lot of traveling, digging and interviewing to do for any life of him," as Susan had discovered in producing her memoir. Moreover, the consensus was "very much against authorizing any biography for some time." I might go ahead without authorization "and take a chance on our all liking it enough to cooperate later on," she supposed, but she couldn't be "very encouraging" (Mary Cheever to SD, 16 May 1983, Harvard).

Still, she would be happy to see me in June. I could see the house and "one very old dog" and look at a slew of old photos she'd never tried to organize. She picked me up at the Croton-Harmon station and drove us back to the handsome house on Cedar Lane. *Two* dogs greeted us there: Maisie, sixteen and failing, and Cocoa, one, a chocolate Labrador of great energy who bestowed his affection with abandon. There were also a couple of cats in residence, keeping their feline distance from the male intruder. Mary struck me as an attractive and intelligent woman, small in stature and with a high little-girl voice that did not seem to fit her assertive personality. She provided me with May wine and leftover doughnuts from the previous day's gathering of her fellow poets in Galway Kinnell's YMHA seminar. We spent a couple of hours sorting through the photographs, an extremely helpful procedure. Mary could identify all the people pictured—"That's Natalie

Robins and Chris Lehmann-Haupt"—and so alert me to people who knew Cheever well enough to be worth interviewing. She made no guarantees, but said it would be all right for me to go ahead and talk to them. I told her that I didn't want to write an "authorized" biography, for such books often distorted or twisted the truth to accommodate those doing the authorizing. Mary agreed that authorization was at best a minimal benefit. She would never want to censor any book, she said, but would be glad to correct errors of fact and emphasis when asked to do so. It was a good day in Westchester, and I left ready to plunge ahead and hope for the best.

Mistake: I hadn't read Mary's cautionary remarks carefully enough. She was her husband's literary executor, it was true, but—as she warned me—it was "we survivors" who would make the decisions. Any cooperation would depend on "our all" liking what I was doing. That meant, specifically, that I would need the approval not only of Mary Cheever but also of her children: Susan, who had already made her mark as a novelist; Benjamin (Ben), a former staffer at Reader's Digest *who would soon join Susan in producing a book about his father, as editor of a volume of his letters; and Federico, the youngest and least literary, who was then going to law school at* UCLA. *In my research on the biography, Mary Cheever was the sole member of the family I came to know at all well, and I relied on her recollections and reflections about the complicated family dynamics.*

Later that summer my wife Vivie and I spent a luminous day with Stella and Arthur Spear in Friendship, Maine. A down-east Yankee who lived most of the year only four miles from Cedar Lane in Briarcliff Manor and a longtime book editor and publisher, Spear was probably John Cheever's closest friend. He generously offered to rent us his house in Briarcliff Manor—only four miles from Cedar Lane—the following summer. There I could buckle down to work in the heart of Cheever country, while the Spears would once again be sojourning in Maine.

In the fall of 1983 I visited Mary Cheever again, this time accompanied by my intelligent and attractive wife. Vivie's presence—and wit—undoubtedly helped my cause. Mary recognized that I was not a "tourist" but a professional, and knew we'd be coming back the next summer for an extended term of research. She navigated us around old haunts in Scarborough and Ossining, and was forthcoming in the first of many interviews and conversations. I also talked to William Maxwell, Cheever's friend since the 1930s and his editor at the *New Yorker*, met Ben Cheever and his wife, Janet Maslin of the *New York Times*, and visited with Sara Spencer and Sally Swope.

At that time, too, I went into New York for a lunch conversation with Susan Cheever. She was late, so I waited on the stoop of her apartment building—and then inside while she downloaded her voice mail messages. Signals were being sent, but I steadfastly (or stupidly) chose to ignore them. Susan was almost finished with *Home Before Dark*, the memoir of her father published the next year. We agreed, or so I thought, that there was no necessary conflict between her memoir, which would treat her father's life from her intimate viewpoint as a daughter, and my biography, which would consider him from the more objective perspective afforded by hundreds of interviews, thousands of letters, and the interrelationships, such as they were, between the life and the fiction. Her principal concern was with John Cheever as her father, while mine was with him as one of the century's most brilliant writers. My goal was to provide an accurate and readable account of John Cheever's life, setting down as much of the truth as possible, and to help establish his position in the American literary canon. Nor were publication dates in conflict. Her memoir would come out well in advance of the biography. It seemed to me that the meeting had gone well. It did not seem that way to her.

Mistake: During our conversation I waxed expansive about all the things I was discovering about Susan's father and about hard-to-find early stories of his I'd located in obscure magazines. I also told her that I hoped to receive a grant to subsidize my research from the National Endowment of the Humanities and had applied for a highly competitive Guggenheim award for the same purpose. I was not in it for the money, I assured her. Having the opportunity to tell John Cheever's life story would be reward enough. It would have been useful to consult his journals, I acknowledged, but I knew there were many letters in various repositories and many people who would contribute their recollections. I also remarked that the best writing in any book about John Cheever would come from Cheever himself, in quotations or close paraphrase from his work and his correspondence. In retrospect I know I should have said less and listened more. The putative biographer should keep his mouth shut and, above all, should not make any show of superior knowledge. When I talked about Cheever stories that Susan had not read, it led to "bad chemistry." I'd offended her, she subsequently told a reporter, by acting as though I knew more about her father than she did and by "bragging" about research grants (quoted in Anita Miller, 326). So far as she was concerned, we were in competition, and it was a competition she did not mean to lose. Shortly after the lunch, she scotched my Guggenheim chances by herself applying for (and receiving) a Guggenheim to finance her memoir, never mind that the book was all but ready for the printer.

Still, by this time it was understood that I intended to work on a biography without official authorization. For the most part, Mary Cheever was most cooperative. She encouraged people to talk to me. She signed letters enabling me to copy Cheever correspondence in various archives and to obtain information from his doctors and psychiatrists. "Good luck. Work hard," she commented in a note accompanying that permissions letter (Mary Cheever to SD, 5 September 1983, Harvard). She suggested books and articles for me to read on the history of Quincy, Massachusetts, where John Cheever grew up, and on the history of Ossining, where he lived much of his life. We were getting along well, it seemed, except that you could never be sure—as Allan Gurganus put it—which Mary Cheever was going to open the door. Sometimes she was the soul of cordiality. Sometimes she was dismissive and sarcastic. One day at Cedar Lane, she backed her car the length of the driveway and banged into my parked car. "Oh well," she remarked, "it's just a rental," but it wasn't. Another signal, perhaps.

The semester grant from the National Endowment for the Humanities came through, enabling me to continue research. I spent most of the nine months between September 1983 and June 1984 poring over everything by or about Cheever that I hadn't yet read, using Dennis Coates's "John Cheever: A Checklist, 1930–1978" as a guide. Coates himself came through Williamsburg for a visit, revealing that during his contacts with Cheever the author had made intimate advances.

By far the most important research on the biography was done during the summer of 1984. The Spearses' house in Briarcliff provided an ideal location for soaking up the Westchester ambience and served as a jumping-off place to several points northeast. On trips to New York City I talked with Max Zimmer and Phil Schulz and Allan Gurganus, with Hope Lange and Raymond Carver and Hortense Calisher, with Ned Rorem and Shirley Hazzard, Robert Gottlieb and Candida Donadio. In Boston and environs I got acquainted with Quincy and the south-shore suburbs Cheever grew up in, looked around Thayer Academy under the guidance of Lucille Wentworth, and took the ferry to Martha's Vineyard to see John Hersey. On a trip to the Thousand Islands in the Saint Lawrence River, my wife and I stayed overnight on Whiskey Island with Mimi and Phil Boyer and visited with Fred Exley in Alexandria Bay. In Sherman, Connecticut, Muriel and Malcolm Cowley and Ebie and Peter Blume contributed fond recollections of John Cheever. Other rolling research trips in Connecticut took us to Old Lyme to meet Mary and John Derks, and to Cornwall Bridge for a conversation with Philip Roth.

One magic day we left Jim McConkey's Trumansburg, New York, farm before dawn to keep an 11 A.M. rendezvous with Saul Bellow in the health-food store on Route 9 in downtown Wilmington, Vermont, going on from there to an afternoon visit with Eleanor Clark and Robert Penn Warren in West Wardsboro. John Updike declined an interview but volunteered to answer questions in writing. He had often been quoted inaccurately, he explained. So I typed out three pages of single-spaced queries, and got back—miraculously, in the next mail—half a dozen single-spaced pages of unmistakably Updikean limpidity.

Heady as these experiences were to anyone of a literary bent, it was in northern Westchester County itself, in Ossining and Briarcliff and Scarborough and Croton, that I did most of that summer's exploration with Cheever's valued friends. Among the most helpful of this congenial group were Aline and Burton Benjamin, Clayre and Eugene Thaw, Jane and Barrett Clark, and Maureen and Roger Willson. Tom Glazer let me beat him at tennis and took me to a meeting of the Friday club. It was not easy to locate Donald Lang, a convicted felon Cheever had taught in a writing seminar at Sing Sing prison. He was out of jail, but had no phone or car and left no forwarding addresses. Finally I tracked him to a singularly unwelcoming structure in downtown Ossining. It would have been a perfect place to shoot a film about urban blight. Inside the stairwell was unlighted and forbidding. More or less terrified, I negotiated several floors in the dark and left a note with my phone number outside the room where Lang (or Donald Black, his alias) was supposed to be staying. Miraculously, he called back, and a few days later we talked about Cheever and what the criminals in Sing Sing thought about the small man with a Boston accent who had come to teach them how to write.

I had pleasant if less adventurous meetings across the Tappan Zee Bridge with Edward Newhouse and with the Ettlingers, Katrina and Don, who summoned up memories of their forty-year friendships with Cheever. Two of the psychiatrists he consulted spoke frankly about him, referring to their notes as they did so. From time to time I had a chance to go over my impressions and put a series of questions to Mary Cheever. Meanwhile I read through Cheever's letters to her, secured copies of his correspondence from a dozen libraries, examined the archive of his unpublished typescripts in the care of Glenn Horowitz in New York, and studied the two Cheever journals at Brandeis.

Like every biographer I was beset by gaps in the story, but gradually most of the blank spaces began to fill in. Rollin Bailey, a boyhood neighbor and friend of Cheever's, wrote at length about what it was like to grow up on Wollaston Hill in Quincy. Daniel and Sue Fuchs described Cheever at Yaddo in the mid-1930s, supplementing the recollections of others who had known him during those difficult years, including Lila Refrigier, Dorothy Farrell, Frances Lindley, and Elizabeth Logan. I made a visit to Yaddo, the Saratoga Springs artists' colony that functioned as a second home to Cheever, and chatted with his friend Anne Palamountain in the ornate splendor of the president's house at Skidmore College, In Chicago the writers Richard Stern and Eugene Kennedy provided their remarkable insights. In Iowa City I stayed in a room like the one Cheever occupied in the fall of 1973, and talked to John Leggett and John Gerber. Actually, his semester at the Iowa Writers' Workshop turned out to be the best documented of his life, because of the detailed reminiscences of his students and colleagues there, T. Coraghessan Boyle, Raymond Carver, Allan Gurganus, Lucy Miner, Ron Hansen, Sarah Irwin, and Gayatri Spivak among them. There was also a good deal of evidence about his disastrous eight months at Boston University the next year, furnished by Updike, Newhouse, Laurens R. Schwartz, Rick Siggelkow, George Starbuck, James Valhouli, and others. Writers, I had found, usually make excellent sources, for their remembrances emerged in the form of stories: concrete incidents and conversations, no vague generalizations. In London, Tanya Litvinova talked about her encounters with Cheever during his three journeys to Russia, and Will Wyatt showed me the film he made about the American author for BBC TV.

Cheever's interviews, both print and broadcast, offered a further avenue of information. Reticent about himself most of his life, he became far more open after winning his battle with liquor in 1975, and spoke of the most intimate matters with sometimes shocking candor. These interviews, particularly those with Dick Cavett, brought him a kind of public recognition he had never before enjoyed. The best of them are collected in *Conversations with John Cheever* (1987), a book I edited.

Letters and documents sent by friends and acquaintances of Cheever proved nearly as valuable as interviews. David Rothbart was among the few who replied to my appeal for reminiscences in the *New York Times Book Review*. A fellow enlisted man in Cheever's company at Camp Gordon, Georgia, in 1942, Rothbart sent along his World War II journal. Max Zimmer's 1981–82 journal and Laurens Schwartz's of the mid-1970s contributed essential background data. Samuel Coale and Dana Gioia shared their memories of meetings with Cheever. The Smithers Rehabilitation Clinic supplied its file on John Cheever during his life-altering stay there, battling alcoholism in the spring of 1975. Two years into the research I had fixed on an approach for the biography and was ready to write a proposal.

First, though, I wanted to read what Susan Cheever had to say in *Home Before Dark*, which came out in October 1984. So far as the biography was concerned, there were no surprises. Her powerfully affecting memoir disclosed her father's bisexuality and troubled marriage in print for the first time, and discussed his alcoholism and phobias as well. Better she should deliver the message, Susan believed, than someone who might present the material less sympathetically. By that time I had learned about these difficulties from the most immediate of sources: his lovers of both sexes, the psychiatrists who treated him, his friends and family, and, above all, his widow. Nonetheless *Home Before Dark* was valuable for its moving account of what it meant to be John Cheever's daughter. In fact it is substantially accurate, as Susan's brother Ben observed, that "there are only two people in that book." Susan rarely refers to her father's fiction in *Home Before Dark* except where it has something to do with herself. She recounts the time, for example, when the two of them were walking across the Queensboro Bridge in a high wind and her cap blew off into the East River. "After that," Susan observes, "my father was afraid of bridges" (Susan Cheever, 74). But the cap floated down no later than 1951, and it was to be half a dozen years before he developed his phobia about crossing bridges by automobile, and a decade before he wrote about it in "The Angel of the Bridge" (the angel in that story, by the way, bears a likeness to Susan). As in any memoir, the spotlight falls on the person doing the remembering.

Home Before Dark was enlivened by many verbatim passages drawn from John Cheever's journals and letters, more or less proving my contention about who would do the best writing in books concerning her father. The journals, except for the two at Brandeis and another published in a limited edition, were withheld from me on the grounds that they contained material that would be extremely painful for Mary Cheever to read or hear about. Cheever's journals do paint a distressingly dark portrait of his marriage, as he alternately excoriates his wife for her coldness and himself for the drinking that contributed to that coldness. A selection from the journals, edited by Robert Gottlieb with an introduction by Ben Cheever, was to appear in 1991.

Conflict

"John Cheever was a man divided against himself," I asserted in the proposal that went to my agent, Sterling Lord. Dark and light, drunk and sober, family man and aggressive seducer, heterosexual and homosexual: these bifurcations split Cheever down the middle. He was a man who tremendously enjoyed life, who reveled in the glory of mere existence, who could find rapture in blue sky and radiant light, wood smoke and sea breeze, the breasts of women and the laughter of children, Yet he was also oppressed by spells of deepest depression. His *cafard*, his blues, his Kafkaesque cockroach, he called these. Only in his last years did he become whole beyond confusion.

This was the basic idea shoring up *John Cheever: A Biography*, an idea prevalent in his work as in his life. He wrote time and again of the theme of two brothers opposite in temperament yet inseparably bound together. It's in all his novels, and in several stories, most notably "Goodbye, My Brother" (1951), the first story in the Pulitzer Prize–winning *Stories of John Cheever*

(1978). The setting is a summer house on Martha's Vineyard. Assembled for a reunion are the Pommeroy family, including the dour and much-disliked Lawrence, or Tifty. Tifty disapproves of everyone else in the family, of their drinking and infidelity, of their gambling at backgammon and foolish costume parties. His attitude becomes so intolerable that the narrator, one of his brothers, knocks him down and bloodies his head. Tifty then packs up and leaves, and the story ends in a kind of epiphany as the narrator's wife and sister emerge from the ocean, "naked and unshy," their uncovered heads "black and gold" in the water.

Clearly "Goodbye, My Brother" represents an attempt at exorcising the dark brother. But the curious thing about the story is that Tifty almost never articulates the distressing thoughts imputed to him by the narrator, and eventually one comes to understand that the amiable narrator and the depressing Tifty are two sides of the same person. In first draft, Cheever acknowledged, Tifty did not exist—only the narrator. The brother lies within as well as without, just as Cheever had a brother he simultaneously loved and hated and was himself inhabited both by the demon of depression and the angel of joy.

Pervasive though this pattern is in Cheever's fiction, I tried not to apply it programmatically to his life. As every graduate student knows, once you have a thesis the world lies at your feet, and the danger is that one will reshape all available evidence to conform to that thesis. Still, throughout the writing of the book, I assumed that there were lines of interconnection between Cheever's life and his fiction, while recognizing that these lines were rarely straight. "Art is never real life," Wallace Stevens warns, and manifestly Cheever's greatest gift was his capacity to bewitch quotidian existence into something magical. His father, a man he repeatedly tried to come to terms with in his fiction, studied the tricks of the magician's trade in his youth, but it was his second and neglected son, John, who became a literary magician. On the surface he depicts recognizable people and mundane places, often burnished upper-middle-class suburbs seemingly impervious to any hint of disorder (in one such fictional town, it is illegal to die in Zone B). Yet a madwoman may walk in the door any minute, and a man's life may whiz by in the space of an afternoon's swimming. In his late fiction Cheever even embraced the miraculous. It is only by a miracle that Ezekiel Farragut escapes from Falconer Prison and into the company of free men.

Early in 1985 my proposal circulated among interested publishers, and Random House contracted to publish the book after a lively auction. The contract called for delivery of a typescript in September 1986, with publication sometime in 1987. It remained only to complete the research over the spring and summer, teach full time in the fall, and then, not least, actually write the book during the ten months thereafter.

At this point my relations with the Cheever family rapidly worsened. Apparently they felt that they should have had a right to approve of the proposal, though Mary had made it clear that she did not expect or want to exercise any power over what I wrote.

Mistake: It did not help that I managed to offend both of Cheever's sons. On a trip to Los Angeles in February 1985, I met Federico (Americanized to Fred) and his wife, Mary McNeil Cheever. During our advance correspondence, I'd asked Fred if I could see the long letter of reminiscence—containing domestic anecdotes and a short account of the trip to Russia he'd made with his father—that he'd sent Susan for use in her book. Yes, he said, I had his "unreserved permission," but he'd made no copy of his letter and I'd have to ask his sister for it. "If she gives you any trouble let me know," he added. Overtly there was no trouble, but neither did she forward the letter. "I'm looking! I'm looking!" was the last word from her about it (Fred Cheever to SD, 7 January 1985, and Susan Cheever to SD, late January 1985, Harvard).

This minor disappointment had nothing to do with alienating Fred Cheever. I accomplished that during the trip to Los Angeles. In addition to talking with Fred, I had conferences with several others who lived there and knew Cheever well. One of them was a former student of Cheever's at the Iowa Writers' Workshop who was establishing himself as a prominent American novelist. He told me about witnessing a confrontation between John Cheever and his son Fred ten years before, in the summer of 1974. John and Fred were keeping house together, Mary having gone to visit her father and other family members in New Hampshire. In her absence, Cheever proposed to invite a female student from Iowa to stay in the Cedar Lane home. Fred rebelled against this plan, and a heated argument ensued. According to my informant, who was visiting at the time, blows were struck.

On the one hand, this tale seemed unlikely. Cheever was particularly fond of his youngest child, and it was out of character for him to lash out physically against anyone in his family—even when drinking was involved, as it had been in this case. Yet there was no good reason for the witness to have invented the story. And Mary had told me that sometimes Fred struck his father in anger and frustration at his drunkenness. On one of my first visits to the Cheever house, she pointed to one of the living room chairs. "That chair was broken twice," she told me, "when Fred hit his father in it." Rightly or wrongly, I decided I had to ask Fred himself about it. That turned out to be one question too many. Not only had his father never struck him, Fred replied, but he would have been incapable of doing so—and I should have realized that.

In a subsequent letter, Fred, who was then serving as president of the law review at UCLA, expanded on the point. His father, he pointed out, was one of the least violent persons he had ever known, someone who spent most of his time in the company of his family, his dogs, and a few friends. Quite sensibly, he advised me "to have a long honest conversation with at least one member of the Cheever family." Why was it, he asked, that the three extremely different Cheever children were all so fond of their father—a man who he was afraid I would portray as "something of a monster" (Fred Cheever to SD, 1 April 1985, Harvard). *In a telephone conversation, I tried to reassure Fred on this issue. In fact, I told him, I tremendously admired John Cheever not only for his work but for taking control of his difficult and troubled life, shaking off his dependence on alcohol and coming to terms with his sexuality: an admiration that pervaded the biography I eventually published.*

Mistake: *Yet another complication came to light when it developed that Ben was going to edit a volume of his father's letters. Actually this did not strike me, at first, as a problem. The only conflict, it seemed to me, would come if the biography and the collection of letters came out in the same season (in the end that very nearly happened:* John Cheever: A Biography *was published in June 1988 and* The Letters of John Cheever *in November 1988), but Ben assured me that the letters project would take some years to bring to fruition. I offered to send him copies of the nearly two thousand letters I had accumulated, or to help in establishing chronology and identifying references. This offer was not welcomed. We discussed the matter after dinner at Ben and Janet Maslin's home in Westchester. As I was leaving, Ben saw me out and said that he was not inclined to grant me permission to quote from his father's letters, on the grounds that such quotations in a biography might diminish the appeal of the letter collection he was editing. It was hard to believe that he would insist on so restrictive a prohibition, one that contradicted his father's practice of allowing scholars and critics to quote at will from their correspondence with him. Rather cavalierly I remarked, "Well, there's fair use," meaning that copyright law would permit limited quotation or short paraphrase from the letters with or without permission. That comment would have been better left unsaid. The next time Ben and I talked on the phone, in a long and desperate conversation, I argued that brief quotation from his father's entertaining letters would serve to whet reader appetite for his volume, and suggested that after all we shared the common goal of encouraging appreciation of his father's work. Ben thought otherwise, vehemently, and started yelling. Subsequently, I offered a percentage of my royalties in exchange for minimal use of quotation, to no avail.*

Looking back on the experience, it becomes clear that I remained too much the Pollyanna throughout, refusing to accept the accumulating evidence that the Cheever children—and especially Susan and Ben—would do whatever they could to undermine my biography, a practice they followed up to and beyond its actual publication more than three years later. After all, when I'd telephoned Mary to tell her of the news that Random House had contracted to publish the book, she called back to ask who the editor would be. Soon after that, Robert Loomis, the editor in question, had a call from Susan Cheever asking if he knew I did not have access to the journals. Yes, he did know, since it had been made clear in the proposal. In our personal contacts, Susan had always been cordial, but it was difficult to construe that call as other than malicious in intent. Some years later, she told a reporter that she "might" have made that phone call to Loomis. "I wasn't out to get [Donaldson]," she insisted, "but we were competing. I wished he hadn't been writing [his biography]."

Just how fierce a competition came to light in June 1985. On our way to New Haven for a college reunion, Vivie and I called on Mary Cheever in Ossining, and she behaved toward us both with unconcealed animosity. After that terrible afternoon, I seriously considered abandoning the book, despite the years already invested in it. Then at the reunion itself my Yale classmate Robert K. Massie, author of *Nicholas and Alexandra* among other excellent books, told me that he had heard Susan announce that my biography would never be published if she could help it. So she'd made that phone call to Loomis, and so—as I was discovering—she'd been advising people I'd contacted for interviews not to be forthcoming, in effect closing doors that her mother had been opening. A few weeks later Mary wrote me that I would not be granted permission to quote from the letters. Though she was officially the executor, she made it clear that this drastic decision was not hers alone. It had been arrived at out of "family loyalty and unity." She was not, as I would surely understand, willing to make decisions "directly contrary to the wishes of his other heirs, our children" (Mary Cheever to SD, 26 June 1985 and 12 July 1985, Harvard).

Mistake: *In that same letter Mary Cheever pointed out that I should have obtained permission from the estate to make use of letters and journals before stating in my proposal that I intended to do so. Up to that point, considering Mary's cooperation in making copies of the letters available, it had not occurred to me that such a step would be required. But of course she was absolutely right. Eighteen months later, I asked for—and somewhat surprisingly received—permission to quote from poems she'd written directly based on her marriage. I also sent her sections of the book dealing directly with herself, making changes for accuracy that she proposed in response.*

Consequences

"Shoot the widow," according to distinguished literary biographer Justin Kaplan, stands as the first axiom of the genre. The major problem in my case, however, lay with Cheever's children and not his widow. Which brings to mind another dictum propounded by Edgar Johnson, the great biographer of Dickens. "Never write a biography of someone whose children are still alive," he counseled. For a biographer of twentieth-century American writers like myself, this was advice that could not be taken.

In previous biographies of Winfield Townley Scott, Ernest Hemingway, and F. Scott Fitzgerald, I had not encountered trouble with either widows or children. Nor did difficulties arise in those I later published about Archibald MacLeish and Edwin Arlington Robinson. In the course of writing those books I was lucky enough to become a friend of Scott's widow Eleanor, of Fitzgerald's daughter Scottie, of MacLeish's son Bill (whom I'd known at Yale), and of Robinson's grandnephew David Nivison. In the case of Hemingway, my book did not delve into intimate family matters. Besides, Mary Hemingway, Ernest's fourth and final wife, was a professional writer herself and had already published her memoir *How It Was* (1976) a year before my *By Force of Will: The Life and Art of Ernest Hemingway* emerged.

In a 1990 article I blithely claimed to have done nothing to warrant the opposition of the Cheever children. Not so, I realized later. Among other things I could have said less and listened harder. But they had no reason to be worried about what I would write. *John Cheever: A Biography* presents a sympathetic portrait of their father and a laudatory assessment of his writing, without undue or sensational emphasis on his struggles with alcohol and sex—struggles that Susan's memoir had already made public. In addition, it seemed to me that there could be no real competition among those of us—Susan, Ben, myself, others interested in exploring the writings and the life of John Cheever—who were aimed toward the common goal of advancing a greater public understanding of his importance as a major American author.

Mistake: *I should have realized from the beginning that my real affront was intruding on the children's turf. John Cheever was their father. How could any outsider, no matter how well-intentioned (I leave aside the question of competence), presume to write about him at all? "What the family wanted was "what everyone wants in life," as Louis Menand put it: "to control the narrative" (Menand, 24)—and to manage John Cheever's literary estate to the family's profit, as well they should have done. I looked on my biography as an endeavor complementary with theirs, but they saw me as an unwelcome competitor. I was in competition with a cottage industry that has produced Susan's memoir, Ben's edition of the letters, another book by Susan about her mother's family, a novel by Ben with distinct parallels to his own experience with his father, a selection from Cheever's journals with an introduction by Ben.*

The Cheevers' position on quotation imposed a barrier to my biography, but hardly an insurmountable one. Many biographies are written without use of any letters at all, and through other sources I had accumulated enough material to write several books. Moreover, under existing copyright laws, I could indeed make fair use of the information in the letters I had located and read and annotated. I might even quote from them, if that were done sparingly. On that understanding I started writing hard in September 1985.

The Salinger Case

When I was writing in earnest, news broke about the Salinger-Hamilton legal dispute, a case that had a chilling effect on the writing of history and biography in the United States. Ian Hamilton, a well-known British biographer, had written a book about J. D. Salinger's life that Random House contracted to publish. The typescript Hamilton delivered in September 1985 relied in large part on quotation from about seventy letters Salinger had written in his youth, letters Hamilton found in various university libraries. When bound galleys came out in May 1986, Salinger got hold of a copy, moved immediately to copyright his letters, and through his attorneys demanded that Random House delete the unpublished material. What troubled the famously reclusive Salinger was the *invasion of privacy* that Hamilton's biography represented. Unable to find legal relief on this ground, he turned to *copyright infringement* laws to impede or inhibit publication.

In response, Hamilton set about amending his book, converting most of his direct quotations into rather artful paraphrases. In September 1986 he resubmitted his biography, and once again it went into the publisher's production cycle. Salinger did not find the changes acceptable, however, and sued for a preliminary injunction to restrain distribution of the book. Meanwhile Mary Cheever's lawyers wrote me and Random House in May 1986 reiterating that I did not have permission to quote from the letters and journals—or anything else Cheever had written, they added, whether published or unpublished. In effect this letter placed us on warning of a potential lawsuit, but I went ahead and finished the first draft of the biography. This arrived at Random House while the Salinger case was being considered by Judge Pierre N. Leval of the United States District Court for the Southern District of New York. Random House placed the Cheever biography on hold while awaiting the decision in the Salinger case.

Leval's decision came down on November 5, and was everything we could have wished for. He found against Salinger's request for a preliminary injunction in an opinion that reflected his First Amendment sensitivities. Hamilton's revised biography, he ruled, made minimal use of Salinger's copyrighted material. Only in about thirty instances had he quoted or closely paraphrased "a word or a phrase or an image." Therefore the book did not "exploit or appropriate" the literary value of the letters, diminish their commercial value, or "impair Salinger's control over first publication."

Enjoining publication of a book was too serious a matter, he concluded, to be undertaken when the degree of infringement was "trifling and inconsequential." Salinger's desire for privacy deserved respect, but did not warrant protection under the copyright law. Hamilton had stayed within the acceptable boundaries of fair use.

As to fair use itself, Leval observed that this doctrine should be sparingly applied to quotation from unpublished work, for the creator of the work, or his heirs and executors, must be able to control the circumstances of first publication before the work became part of the public domain. On the other hand, when the proposed use did not adversely affect the financial rights of the copyright holder, no good reason could "justify so extreme a rule as would absolutely bar the fair use of unpublished matter." Besides, copyright did not encompass "facts and ideas," whose free public dissemination was of great importance to historians. Instead copyright protected the art or craftsmanship involved, "the author's particular manner of expression." Hence a biographer could report his subject's thoughts and feelings as expressed in a letter, so long as he did not "overstep permissible limits by taking the author's craftsmanship." These limits would vary from case to case, but "extensive verbatim copying or paraphrasing" was prohibited.

Working from this decision, I went back through the Cheever typescript and made a few minor changes. The auspices looked hopeful for publication in the fall of 1987, a year later than the original publication date. My biography would have come out then but for Salinger's appeal of Leval's ruling. Random House, paying heavily for litigation on the Salinger biography, was not eager to invite another lawsuit. So once again we folded our hands and awaited a judicial finding. On the basis of Judge Leval's ruling I felt a certain optimism. "Salinger's position," he concluded, "demonstrated no likelihood of success." Unfortunately, he was wrong about that.

On 29 January 1987, the United States Court of Appeals for the Second Circuit reversed Leval and ruled that a preliminary injunction should be issued against Hamilton's biography. The decision, written by Circuit Judge Jon O. Newman, held that Leval had erred in two ways. First, he had not differentiated sharply enough between copyright of unpublished as opposed to published material. Citing the U.S. Supreme Court's finding in *Harper & Row v. Nation Enterprises* (1985) that "the scope of fair use is narrower with respect to unpublished works," Judge Newman speculated that the court had meant to prohibit *any* use of "protected expression" in unpublished writing.

But what constituted "protected expression"? The appeals court ruled that Judge Leval had not given enough weight to Hamilton's "close paraphrasing" from Salinger's letters. Such paraphrasing, the judges held, was to be regarded on the same basis as direct quotation. In appealing Leval's decision, Salinger identified fifty-nine instances in which Hamilton quoted from or closely paraphrased forty-four of Salinger's unpublished letters. When close paraphrase was combined with direct quotation, the court found, Hamilton had appropriated the expressive content of many of those letters. If these did not make up the "heart of the book," to a large extent they made the book worth reading. Both quantitatively and qualitatively Hamilton had exceeded the limits of fair use. On those grounds the appeals court barred publication of the biography "in its present form."

In the footnotes to its decision the appeals court noted particular paraphrasings that in its judgment were impermissible. These thus became a matter of public record, and in due course were printed in the *New York Times* and elsewhere, an occurrence that the privacy-seeking Salinger must have regarded with some irony. For example, the court's opinion compared a passage from a Salinger letter written in 1943 to Whit Burnett with Hamilton's paraphrased account. Distressed that Oona O'Neill, whom he had been dating, had married the much older Charlie Chaplin, Salinger imagined this satirical scene: "I can see them at home evenings. Chaplin squatting grey and nude, atop his chiffonier, swinging his thyroid around his head by his bamboo cane, like a dead rat. Oona in an aquamarine gown, applauding madly from the bathroom. Agnes [her mother] in a Jantzen bathing suit, passing between them with cocktails. I'm facetious, but I'm sorry. Sorry for anyone with a profile as young and lovely as Oona's."

Hamilton might justifiably have reported that Salinger was upset about the Chaplin-O'Neill marriage or that he could imagine how disastrous their life together might be, the court recommended. Instead he ventured upon this paraphrase: "At one point in a letter to Whit Burnett, [Salinger] provided a pen portrait of the Happy Hour Chez Chaplin: the comedian, ancient and unclothed, is brandishing his walking stick—attached to the stick, and horribly resembling a lifeless rodent, is one of Chaplin's vital organs. Oona claps her hands in appreciation and Agnes, togged out in a bathing suit, pours drinks. Salinger goes on to say he's sorry—sorry not for what he has just written but for Oona, too youthful and exquisite for such a dreadful fate." Any reader, it seems to me, will detect the difference between Salinger's vivid and angry passage and Hamilton's yeomanlike but comparatively pallid attempt to paraphrase the unparaphrasable. In other words, the paraphrase did *not* capture the expressive content of the author. Still, according to the court's opinion, "[e]ven the briefest similes [were] closely paraphrased," and I suppose that is true. (Doing the best he could, Hamilton went back to his desk and some months later produced *In Search of J. D. Salinger*, a book making almost no use of the letters and chronicling his frustrations about the biographical process. *How I Didn't Get That Story*, it might have been entitled.)

In the Chaplin passage as in others, the court ruled that Hamilton was illegally appropriating Salinger's distinctive manner of expression. But the decision went further, placing limits on the use of *information* from unpublished work. The biographer (or historian or scholar) who took only facts ran no risk of an injunction, it acknowledged, but the biographer who copied the correspondent's "expression of facts" did face that risk. "[Unpublished] works normally enjoy complete protection against copying any protected expression."

This radically restrictive provision led to almost comic consequences in my revision of the Cheever biography. Let's assume that in an unpublished letter Cheever wrote that he and his family "sailed for Naples on the *Conte Biancamano*, traveling first class because of Mary's pregnancy." In point of historical fact that's what happened in the fall of 1956, and yet, according to the appeals court, I could not repeat it in that way or in the same order. Tracking the original too closely, even if the original conveyed only facts expressed in everyday language, might infringe copyright.

Alarmed by this ruling, Random House began a series of appeals. First it petitioned for rehearing on the basis of Judge Leval's color-coded chart of the allegedly infringing passages in Hamilton's biography. Leval marked the passages in five colors to designate "an infringing quotation, an infringing paraphrase, a non-infringing quotation, a non-infringing report of historical facts, or a non-infringing report of ideas." On 5 May 1987, the court entered Leval's meticulous exhibit into the record, but refused a rehearing. Leval's document, the court observed, only reinforced its conviction that he had misapplied the governing standards. Later that summer an *en banc* appeal for rehearing by the full complement of judges in the Second Circuit was also rejected. In September Random House appealed to the U.S. Supreme Court to overturn the decision, and to consider three questions: whether the fair use doctrine of the Copyright Act barred quotation from unpublished letters, what was meant by the term "expression" in the 1985 *Harper & Row v. Nation Enterprises* decision, and whether prior restraint of a publication violated the First Amendment. The Association of American Publishers joined the appeal. So did several distinguished authors represented by the attorney Irwin Karp, including Kenneth S. Davis, John Hersey, A. E. Hotchner, Justin Kaplan, J. Anthony Lukas, and Ralph G. Martin, all of whom feared that the denial of fair use privileges to unpublished letters would "unduly hamper reasonable use of such works for normal biographical, historical and scholarly purposes." The Supreme Court decided not to reconsider the matter.

James Atlas, who was soon to embark on his biography of Saul Bellow, sounded the alarm in a November 1987 article for *Vanity Fair* subtitled "Will J. D. Salinger's Successful Suit Against Random House Bowdlerize the

Biography Boom?" Atlas called particular attention to the delays it had caused in publication of my Cheever biography, and quoted editor Robert Loomis's warning that the Salinger case offered "a remedy for which there was no disease" and was "going to have a more detrimental effect than anyone realizes" (Atlas, "Biografiends," 46).

For decades scholars assumed that they could safely quote or paraphrase unpublished documents, within the imprecise boundaries of fair use. The Salinger decision threatened that practice, imposed far tighter restrictions on the use of facts and ideas from such documents, and promised to inhibit free expression in other unanticipated ways. In effect it invited public figures (and their heirs/executors) to use copyright law not to ensure the right of first publication but to control what others might say about them. By withholding permission to quote from correspondence, they could discourage or in some cases prevent the writing and publishing of history, biography, and other scholarship. Alternatively, they could use the right to quote as a means to bargain for approval over whatever was written.

In a 1989 case involving a biography of L. Ron Hubbard, founder of the Church of Scientology, the Second Circuit Court of Appeals upheld and strengthened its ruling in the Salinger case that all but minimal quotation and paraphrase of unpublished material constituted infringement of copyright, once again reversing a finding by Leval that the quotations were justified by fair use. This inspired an article in *Newsweek*'s Christmas issue for 1989 speculating about "The End of History," for historians customarily relied for information on memoranda, notes, diaries, journals, and correspondence—all unpublished documents. In February 1990, the Supreme Court declined an appeal to review this decision from the publisher Henry Holt, joined by the American Association of Publishers, PEN American Center, and the Authors Guild.

These two decisions had a drastic effect on the writing of biography and history. Manuscripts accepted for publication were shelved or placed on hold. The entire publishing industry—publishers, editors, copyright lawyers, scholars, historians—was unnerved. Finding no remedy in the courts, they banded together and took their protests to the Congress. Their appeal was fortified by Judge Leval's March 1990 essay "Toward a Fair Use Standard" in the *Harvard Law Review*. His analysis considered each of the four factors affecting fair use, with particular attention to the first factor, "The Purpose and Character of the Secondary Use." Leval argued that quotation from unpublished documents was justified if the challenged use was "transformative"—if the book or article was "productive" (advancing knowledge and progress of the arts) and if it employed "the quoted matter in a different manner or for a different purpose from the original." You could not "merely repackage, free riding on another's creation." You could not take unpublished material that was created for and on its way toward publication. Otherwise, it was important to recognize the value of accurate quotation as a necessary tool of the historian and journalist. Fair use balanced "the social benefits of a transformative secondary use against injury to the incentives of authorship" (Leval).

The basic principle allowing "transformative use" of unpublished material was duly written into law after an unprecedented joint meeting of the House and Senate committees charged with responsibility for copyright. In October 1992 the Congress amended the Fair Use part of the Copyright Act (Section 107) to provide the following standard: "The fact that a work is unpublished shall not itself bar a finding of fair use if such finding is made upon consideration of all the [fair use] factors," in particular the "transformative use" doctrine. The Supreme Court's unanimous decision in *Campbell v. Acuff-Rose* (March 1994) reiterated that criterion. There Justice David Souter cited Section 107 in ruling that fair use depended on whether a new work merely superseded the original or whether and to what extent it was "transformative." The congressional amendment nullified the threat to literary biographical and historical works posed by the Salinger and Hubbard findings, and such works went back into the publishing pipeline. These corrective actions stemming from Leval's work, important though they were, came too late to alleviate the problems confronting my Cheever biography.

Revising and Publishing

By the spring of 1987, Random House editor Bob Loomis had gone over the script for my Cheever biography with his acute sensitivity for whatever did not look or sound right on the page, and I had made alterations accordingly. Copyediting, relatively light, was also completed. There seemed little point in holding up the book on the outside chance that a legal appeal might succeed. A week after the circuit court denied rehearing on the Salinger biography in May, we began to revise the biography to conform to its ruling. Difficult and painstaking though it proved to be, Random House attorney Gerald E. Hollingsworth believed it imperative to consider every use of an unpublished document. There were hundreds of such cases, and we tackled each one individually. To begin with, I went back through the manuscript, highlighting passages where an unpublished letter or journal fragment shed light on Cheever's life or work. Then I assembled all the corresponding notes—copies of letters, most often—indicating in red pencil where the information came from.

Next we had to determine whether the use I made of this material was permissible under the law. For many years publishers had guessed that five hundred words constituted the maximum allowable amount a secondary user could quote from a *published* work. But in the case of *unpublished* work, with the Salinger decision reverberating around the halls, Random House arrived at a much more restrictive standard. The publishers decided, arbitrarily, that I could quote (or closely paraphrase) approximately ten words or 10 percent of a given letter, whichever was less. Since letters ordinarily ran much longer than one hundred words, in effect the limit was ten words per letter. We also kept in mind that even facts and ideas, if presented in the same order and showing the same thought processes, were not usable beyond the ten-word barrier. These restrictions, as Loomis pointed out, made it almost impossible to paraphrase something. Nonetheless we tried. Lord, how we tried.

On the morning of May 14, Loomis and Hollingsworth spent two and a half hours on the Scarborough chapter and slogged through only one page. It was a terribly frustrating process, as a single example will serve to illustrate. Just after Labor Day in the late 1940s, the Cheevers came back to New York City from the New Hampshire countryside. In the course of a long letter to Don and Katrina Ettlinger, Cheever complained about how oppressive the city seemed.

"Susie seems to be having less trouble adjusting to the city than Mary and me," he began (this letter is published in Ben's selection, albeit with some unacknowledged deletions). "I walked up Sutton Place yesterday, a sultry day, and saw half a dozen people I knew. They all looked sickly and one of them asked us to a cocktail party. Today is one of those overcast mornings when everything smells of drains and the air is like a piece of dirty grey felt. Morrie Werner came up last night and said that Dewey will be the next president, the cost of living is up nearly thirty percent since June." Later in the same letter Cheever expanded on this melancholy mood. "It's a gloomy picture but from where I sit I can see, as I could see all last winter, the interminable funeral processions moving across the Queensboro Bridge to the enormous graveyards in Long Island" (JC, *Letters*, 120–21).

In this chapter, dealing with his move to Westchester, I wanted to convey something of Cheever's ambivalence about living in New York. This letter provided valuable evidence, most of it in the form of facts—the people he saw, the funeral corteges on the Queensboro—and his thoughts about them. Initially, before the appeals court decisions, I had written that the Cheevers found it difficult to come back to the city from summer vacations, then added: "On one such return . . . Cheever walked up Sutton Place and saw half a dozen people he knew, all looking unwell. Everything smelled of drains and the air was 'like a piece of dirty grey felt.' It looked as if Dewey would be the next president and the cost of living had gone up thirty per cent since June. The rumble of traffic on the Queensboro bridge seemed ominous: one funeral procession after another crossed the bridge to the vast graveyards of Queens." Before the Salinger decision this would probably have qualified as legitimate paraphrase, for it is basically a report of facts and ideas, with the only distinctive expressive content in the "dirty grey felt" simile. By the circuit court standard, though, it was far too long and tracked the original too closely. Loomis and Hollingsworth, in their morning's struggle, proposed this revision: "Cheever seemed particularly depressed by what he found on one such trip . . . foul smells, sickly friends, and air 'like a piece of dirty grey felt.' And the sight of funerals on their way to Queens didn't help his mood. Besides, it looked as if Dewey might win." That slightly rearranged the order Cheever had used, and introduced some language ("didn't help his mood") I was reluctant to adopt.

In the end I combined Cheever's observations in the letter to the Ettlingers with those he made in a separate letter to Josephine Herbst about working in New York during the stifling heat: "Sometimes Cheever left Treetops (New Hampshire) in midsummer in order to work alone in the city. These trips were rarely successful. On one such visit the air smelled 'like a piece of dirty grey felt.' On another the inhabitants looked 'like the citizens of hell,' and he soon fled northward." This version sacrificed absolute fidelity to the facts—it was not on a *midsummer* trip to the city that he found the air so odious— in the interests of economy and vigor. On balance I preferred that revision, which reduced two paragraphs of medium length to two short sentences. In this instance, as in many others, staying within the court's guidelines improved the book. That was to be expected, for the effect of the legal restrictions was to mandate cuts, and as I was forever telling myself and my writing students, you can make almost any piece of writing better by cutting it.

Yet if the biography gained by virtue of tighter writing, it certainly lost some of the engaging tone of Cheever's voice. This was a considerable loss, so it was a painful process that Loomis and Hollingsworth and I embarked upon in the summer of 1987. For one long week we labored over the manuscript, stripping Cheever's prose and my paraphrasing of all unpublished documents to the requisite ten words or less. We began early each day, ahead of the rest of Random House's employees, for there were bound to be extensive interruptions later on, especially as Hollingsworth was called away to confer about the firm's acquisitions in every corner of the globe.

It boggles the mind, the spectacle of these three men—the chief legal officer of one of the world's leading publishers, an executive editor and vice president of the same company (and one whose authors were to win both National Book Awards for 1988), and a writer-professor of at least considerable mileage—sitting around a conference table counting to ten and debating (the most frequent point of disagreement) whether repetition of concrete fact could possibly be construed as impermissible borrowing. What

Bob Loomis and Gerry Hollingsworth and I were engaged in was decidedly picayune. Yet the broader issues posed by the Salinger decision were of great significance for the writing of history and biography.

The job was about half done by the end of the week, but the guidelines had been firmed up, so I did the rest of the revision alone, slapping myself on the wrist when ten words stretched to thirteen, eliminating names of people and places because they too were considered part of the word count, and otherwise satisfying the unreasonable restrictions deriving from the Salinger case. I kept thinking, in frustration, of the cliché "If it ain't broke, don't fix it."

One saving grace was that despite limited access to letters the biography retained many of Cheever's words from other sources. These included his interviews for newspapers, magazines, and radio and television programs, for example. I could also quote from his stories and novels, so long as I kept within the more liberal confines of fair use for *published* work.

I relied on Cheever's fiction to furnish not the facts but the emotional truth about otherwise undocumented areas of his life. As with any gifted author, it was often hard to tell what was invented and what was real. Cheever rarely spoke or wrote letters about his father, for instance, yet in a series of stories—most of them uncollected—he sketched out portraits of him. Did his father actually invite an abortionist to dinner when he learned that his wife was pregnant with John? Very likely not, but Cheever depicted that incident several times in his fiction (in which the characters are of course not designated as John Cheever, Frederick William Cheever, and Mary Liley Cheever). He also converted the story to autobiography in more than one interview, adding that he knew about the abortionist because his mother told him—if she did. Whatever the hard facts, it surely signifies that Cheever believed his father wanted him aborted. And that conviction fits into the pattern of his emotionally troubled youth as a late-begotten child neglected, as he saw it, by both parents but most of all by his father. In addition, Cheever's fiction usually functioned as an accurate barometer of his psychological weather. *The Wapshot Scandal* and *Bullet Park* are dark books, and while writing them he felt nearly suicidal. *The Wapshot Chronicle* is full of sunshine, and the sensual joy of the book reflects Cheever's own sense of happiness at the time.

John Cheever: A Biography was advertised in the Random House catalog for spring 1987, so as the months dragged on people occasionally asked what the problem was. "It's in legal review," I'd say, letting it go at that. By October 1987 I had finished revising to avoid copyright infringement, Random House had approved the result, and the book was only a few hurdles away from production. First it had to pass the customary legal tests for libel, invasion of privacy, and related legal concerns. Random House's external lawyers posed a number of queries along these lines, seeking reassurance, for example, that Eugene O'Neill's father was dead. Next I sent off copies of relevant pages to interviewees who had asked to see what I would write as a result of our conversation. This led to some useful alterations: among others, William Maxwell and Shirley Hazzard were helpful in clearing away confusion and suggesting more accurate and felicitous language. Then I went to work on the photo section—a handsome one, as it turned out, though assembled without the assistance of the Cheevers.

Each of these chores took time, and the book was postponed until summer 1988. I anticipated publication with eagerness and with a measure of trepidation. Despite the care we had taken to conform to the Salinger decision, we were by no means certain that a lawsuit might not crash around our ears. When bound galleys went out to reviewers and book clubs and paperback houses weeks in advance of the June 30 publication date, we held our collective breaths and listened hard. Never has silence sounded sweeter.

John Cheever: A Biography came out as scheduled in June, and was widely reviewed. There were front-page reviews in the Sunday book sections of the *New York Times, Chicago Tribune,* and *Los Angeles Times.* Most of the reviews were good, some were excellent, and the three really bad ones (out of dozens) seemed to emanate—or so I persuaded myself—from New York literary circles inhabited by Susan and Ben Cheever. Writers (as opposed to professional book reviewers) generally liked the book, especially those with a particular affinity for Cheever's work. The novelist Tom Boyle, who had been Cheever's student at Iowa, remarked that my biography was for him "as readable and 'unputdownable' as any thriller" (quoted in Libman).

The best review—the one that meant the most to me—came from James Salter in the *Los Angeles Times Book Review.* He found too many inconsequential details in the book, a crime to which I must plead guilty. When you know something about your subject—something you've found out in the course of your research, something no one else has noted—you are strongly inclined to put it in, even if doing so does not much advance the reader's understanding. Too often in the Cheever biography, I succumbed to that temptation. But otherwise Salter praised the book. "There are many sections of great poignancy, many funny things, many of electric intimacy and candor. . . . There is spellbinding power, never more so than in describing Cheever's death, pages that are both terrible and deeply moving; one is losing an old, beloved friend" (Salter, review). That's the kind of review you do your work hoping for.

Still, it doesn't do to make too much of reviews, for if you won't believe the bad ones, how can you credit the good? In practice, most reviews of nonfiction books do little more than summarize those segments the reviewer found to be particularly interesting. Some of them add a few words about the way the story is told, and it's those brief comments that biographers—who are writers, after all—look for. Most reviews of the Cheever biography had laudatory things to say about my writing. I wrote "lucidly," several observed. The biography was "entirely readable," "written with clarity and compassion." What set the book apart was its "graceful narrative style," the "ease and variety" of the prose. Yet a few dissenters criticized my "hackneyed . . . pedestrian" manner, my susceptibility to "stale expressions." Were these people reading the same book?

A number of reviews compared the biography to Susan's memoir, making two points. (1) I covered a considerable expanse of territory she'd neglected. (2) My book lacked the passion and poignancy of hers. Fair enough. But she need not have worried that I would treat her father's personal problems with insensitivity. My "sympathy for Cheever" gave the book "an almost elegiac tone," one reviewer remarked. I had "a feel and reverence for my subject," said another. The book was "done with compassion and not a trace of viciousness."

What mattered was that the biography was at long last published, that it had a good though hardly a best-selling run, including a paperback edition, and that lots of people read it and went back to read more of Cheever's fiction: exactly what literary biographies should accomplish. My admiration for Cheever's writing is as strong now as it was when I first wrote Mary Cheever early in 1983. She'd asked me then about what approach I planned to take. "To tell John Cheever's story as well as I can, and to make a case for him as a major American writer," I told her. That's what I tried to do, and during the months and years when I was reading his words and talking to his friends, I came to see his life as a triumph over the demons of drink and depression that haunted him. There's a tenderness near the end of the book that Salter and other readers felt, for all of us who loved his work felt diminished by his death. And I remain tremendously grateful to have had the chance to tell his story.

Would I do it all over again? I've been asked a few times since the biography appeared. Yes, I would, for writing the Cheever was the most stimulating and fascinating work of my life. But I'd go about it differently, for it was also the most frustrating and frightening project I'd ever undertaken. What would I do differently? Well, in the fall of 1988 I contracted with Houghton Mifflin for a biography of the poet and patriot Archibald MacLeish, shooting for a May 1992 publication date to mark the centenary of MacLeish's birth. Once again I was entering upon my usual three- to five-year gestation period for producing a biography, with a complicated and interesting story to tell. I did not begin before obtaining in writing the executor's authorization to quote from MacLeish's work, both published and unpublished. A decade later, I followed the same procedure when beginning work on the life of the poet Edwin Arlington Robinson.

The Lawsuit

Family of John Cheever vs. Academy Chicago Publishers

It may well be that Academy Chicago, a small midwestern publisher, saved my biography from litigation. During the months immediately preceding publication of *John Cheever: A Biography*, the Cheevers became involved in an exchange of lawsuits with Academy Chicago that took more than three years and a million dollars in legal fees to resolve. David Streitfeld of the *Washington Post* then called it "the most expensive, protracted and vicious court battle to take place in recent years over a book" (quoted in Anita Miller, ix). Martin Garbus, the eminent First Amendment lawyer who represented the Cheevers, devoted a chapter to the case in his memoir *Tough Talk*. Anita Miller, who with her husband Jordan founded Academy Chicago, wrote an entire book about it, called *Uncollecting Cheever*, both books appearing in 1998. In a minor yet significant way, I was drawn—or dragged, really—into the contest.

Here's the background. Early in 1987 Franklin H. Dennis, a publicist representing Academy Chicago (among other publishers), proposed the idea of assembling the previously uncollected stories of John Cheever in a book. Dennis, who came from Westchester County, admired Cheever's work and knew there were a number of stories he had published in magazines but never collected in book form. Initially he didn't realize how many there were, and probably the Cheever family didn't either. But he did sense the commercial possibilities of publishing them. After all, *The Stories of John Cheever* (1978), containing sixty-one stories, had become a best seller and won both the Pulitzer Prize and the National Book Critics Circle award. He took his idea to the Millers at Academy Chicago, who told him to follow up, and so in June Dennis wrote Ben Cheever asking for his advice on how to proceed with a volume of stories not in the 1978 edition. Might Ben be interested in editing such a book? Ben was not, but he said the collection sounded feasible and told Dennis to write his mother. Dennis did so, he and Ben discussed the matter over lunch, and in due course Academy Chicago sent a contract to Mary Cheever.

This contract offered only a minuscule advance—a mere $1500—and provided that royalties should be split half-and-half between the Cheever estate and Franklin Dennis, who was to serve as editor. These terms seemed strikingly out of line for a book by a major American author. Nonetheless ICM, Cheever's agents, signed off on the deal, and so did Mary Cheever herself. The contract did not make it entirely clear how many stories the book would include, or how they would be chosen. This lack of specification led to the legal disagreement between the parties. Academy Chicago planned to include all of the uncollected stories, whether in copyright or not, and began vigorously promoting the book. The Cheevers, who had originally believed that the contract was for a small edition aimed at an academic market, maintained that they had the right to determine how many and which stories to include, and even whether the book should be published at all. In fact, they contended that their copyright had been violated and that the contract should be invalidated. As in most lawsuits, partisans on each side felt absolutely positive that they were in the right. Eventually, the Cheevers' position prevailed.

Once the contract was agreed to, Academy Chicago set itself the task of unearthing stories Cheever wrote and published as long as half a century earlier, some of them in obscure magazines. With the help of Dennis Coates's bibliography they located almost all of these uncollected stories— sixty-six of them—and planned to issue them in the fall of 1988, a few months after my biography came out. In January 1988 Jordan Miller sent me a table of contents for the volume and asked if I knew of any stories they'd missed. No, I answered, I thought they'd caught them all. I also pointed out that in researching for the biography, I'd read all of the stories and made copies of most of them. I sent along a copy of one story they knew about but had been unable to find.

A few weeks later Jordan Miller telephoned me, wondering if I would like to write an introduction to the book. (I did not know that the firm had previously asked John le Carré and Raymond Carver to perform this task.) Yes, indeed, I said. I knew the stories well and had some things to say about them that had not fallen within the compass of the biography. I thought that the stories deserved publication, not only on their merit but as evidence of the apprenticeship of a major writer. And the early stories, particularly, dealt with locales and subject matter very different from the East Side apartment houses and suburban enclaves that the upper-middle-class readers of Cheever's *New Yorker* stories were familiar with. In those early stories, Cheever was manifestly depicting his own family-in-decline as well as invented characters struggling to scratch out a living during the depression years.

To write such an introduction struck me as the kind of professional work for hire I was uniquely qualified to do. Moreover, I had the time, with the biography finished and awaiting publication—it was early March 1988—to do the job immediately. It did not seem to me that my differences with the Cheever family would in any way inhibit or compromise the task, and the rumor was that the lawsuit between Academy and the family was about to be settled. Jordan Miller promised an honorarium of $1000, to be paid on submission. I delivered the forty-five-hundred-word manuscript on March 30, two weeks ahead of deadline. Academy Chicago was "absolutely delighted" with it, Jordan Miller wrote me. My focus, my insights, my writing were all first-rate. A check would go out to me "within the next couple of weeks" (Jordan Miller to SD, 3 March 1988). It did not.

Before long, the lawsuit sprang back to life, and my introduction became a bone of contention between the parties. I learned of this problem in an odd and somewhat terrifying way. One morning in May, I was staying at the Yale Club in New York when Herbert Mitgang of the *New York Times* called. "What did you think of Mary Cheever's letter?" he wanted to know. My heart skipped a beat, for the bound galleys of my biography had recently gone into circulation. "What letter?" I asked, my mind racing toward the worst possible explanation. I hadn't seen it, for Mary had sent the letter to me at the College of William and Mary, and I was on the road. Still, how could a letter to me from Mary Cheever wind up in the hands of the *New York Times*? Mitgang explained that her *attorneys* had sent him a copy of the letter, and at that point I was sure that the jig was up and we were going to court over my biography. Not only was I hearing from her through her lawyers, but on a subject newsworthy enough to interest the *Times*. Then Mitgang read the letter, which contained Mary Cheever's extensive critique of my introduction to the uncollected stories. This was unpleasant news, but considering the alternative I was awfully glad to hear it. In any case, as I wrote Mary, it was a hell of a way to conduct correspondence.

Inasmuch as Cheever's *Uncollected Stories* was never published, neither was my introduction, save in the form of bound galleys prepared by Academy Chicago. This is what I wrote, slightly revised.

Introduction to The Uncollected Stories of John Cheever

To begin with, these are uncollected stories of John Cheever, not unpublished stories. He wrote them, sold them to magazines, and saw them into print. They are part of his corpus, not drafts or false starts he thought better of and decided to abandon. The distinction is a crucial one in a time when the discarded dross of some authors is dug up, drastically reshaped, and tricked out for presentation as, say, the legitimate work of Ernest Hemingway. No such editorial liberties are involved here. These are John Cheever's stories, and hence worth reading.

On the other hand, these are also stories that Cheever (and his editors) chose not to print in book form. Some of them are short sketches, some are written to a predictable boy-gets-girl pattern, some read like minidocumentaries. Yet even the slightest radiate an occasional glow—a rhetorical sparkle, a brilliant scrap of dialogue, an incisive detail of characterization— that marks them as uniquely Cheever's, the work of a master in the making. Those who admire his writing will find much to delight them here. And of course it is a good thing to have so much of his work rescued from dusty periodical shelves and presented in one volume. John Updike, paging through old copies of the *New Yorker* after the death of his friend and fellow artist, found gem after gem among the uncollected stories, and encouraged their publication.

Issues of merit aside, these stories throw considerable light on Cheever's art and life. He was a writer who in effect repudiated his apprenticeship and his formative years. *The Stories of John Cheever*, the 1978 collection that won the Pulitzer Prize and made it clear to everyone breathing that he commanded the form, contained nothing written before "The Enormous Radio" (*New Yorker*, 17 May 1947). Yet in fact he wrote and published eighty-one stories before that date, the work of a lifetime for many an artist. Fifty of those eighty-one are among the sixty-six stories reproduced here.

The *New Yorker* printed about half of Cheever's early stories. Others appeared in such periodicals as the *New Republic, Collier's,* and *Mademoiselle* (among the better known) and the *Left, Pagany,* and *Hound and Horn* (among the little magazines). In his early years Cheever published where he could, seeking to establish himself. Like a gambler who will forever be hooked, he rolled high dice on his very first try. Kicked out of Thayer Academy in the spring of 1930, the eighteen-year-old youth produced an eloquent fictionalized account of that experience and sent it off to the *New Republic,* where Malcolm Cowley plucked it out of the slush pile and published it as "Expelled" on 1 October 1930. Five years later, after Cheever moved to New York City, Cowley again was instrumental in advancing his career. He looked at the stories Cheever had been writing (and not selling) and advised him to try shorter pieces. In response, Cheever turned out four short sketches in four days. The *New Yorker* took two—"Brooklyn Rooming House" and "Buffalo," published on 25 May 1935 and 22 June 1935—and so began an association that was to link author and magazine together in the public mind throughout his lifetime. The *New Republic* took the third, a piece about a burlesque performer called "The Princess." The fourth, "Bayonne," went to *Parade,* not the Sunday supplement but an ephemeral periodical that printed one issue in the spring of 1936 and quietly expired.

By disavowing the first fifteen years of his professional career, Cheever helped contribute to a public image of himself that the fiction of his early work might have undermined. To most people the name "John Cheever" summons up a picture of an upper-middle-class suburbanite, well-to-do, well educated, and more gifted and wittier than his neighbors. The facts are that he never went to college, that until the success of the last half decade he rarely had much money, and that he was often uneasy in the Westchester environs he inhabited from 1951 until his death. Despite having his picture taken mounted on a horse for *People* magazine, he did not ride to hounds;

he rarely rode at all, except on bicycles. His stories of the 1930s and 1940s portray a very different world from that of the prosperous suburbs. For one thing, they take place in urban settings—in New York City, mostly. And, especially in the earlier stories, they depict characters who must struggle to make a living and keep their dignity intact. An anthropologist from another culture, given only these Cheever stories as artifacts of the time, would have no difficulty in ascertaining that the people in his fiction were suffering through the depths of a depression.

The second story he published reads like a doctrinaire proletarian document. "Fall River" appeared in Autumn 1931, when the author was still a teenager. (He signed himself "Jon" Cheever in those days.) It ran in the second issue of *The Left: A Quarterly Review of Radical and Experimental Art*; the initial issue called on the intellectual and artist to rise "from his blind bourgeois psychology, his pathological introspection, his defeatism and futile liberalism" in order to proclaim "the disintegration and bankruptcy of the capitalist system." That is precisely what Cheever's story attempts to do. Hard times have fallen on Fall River, Massachusetts, a mill town where the mills have closed down, people have "very little money and no food," and the complaints of the workers echo "like thunder beneath the hills." The church tries to silence the thunder, but "there were few," as the narrator observes, "who could forget the sound of the Internationale." Like most proletarian fiction, "Fall River" is long on polemics and short on plot and character development. Yet it portrays the distressing economic conditions that—rather less programmatically—Cheever was often to explore in the decade ahead.

In three of these stories, the principal character is a middle-aged woman who is reduced to keeping a boardinghouse to make ends meet. (Cheever's own paternal grandmother may well have kept a boardinghouse in Boston; his own mother operated a gift shop in Quincy, Massachusetts, after his father lost his position in the shoe business.) Perhaps the most poignant case is that of Mrs. Moreno, who tries to keep a "respectable house" in "Brooklyn Rooming House" and clings pathetically to the pretense that all her roomers, even the drunken louts, are really gentlemen guests. The out-of-work musician in "Play a March" plays the blues on his accordion while his wife maunders on about the house in White Plains they can't afford; they keep the apartment dark to save on the electric bill and share a can of spaghetti for dinner. The unemployed Swedish sailor in "A Picture for the Home" wants his photograph taken with his meager possessions—even his alarm clock—to prove to his mother that he is not a failure. "Things were better once" is the refrain running through these stories, "things were much better once." Sad though that lament may be, it also implies a hope that in the future things might take a turn for the better, once again.

This capitalist capacity for hope undermines the recruiting tactics of the Communist organizer Girsdansky in "In Passing" (*Atlantic Monthly*, March 1936), Cheever's most overt confrontation of the two economic systems. Girsdansky's message is simple and straightforward. "Anyone who has been poor and helpless and hungry, day after day after day, with no prospect of ever being anything but poor and helpless and hungry, must eventually" join the revolution. A man without vices, Girsdansky speaks earnestly to the down-and-out on street corners and in church basements, but they resist the lesson he delivers in his voice that is "a little flat, like the voice projected by the phonograph." They are unwilling to give up their dream that tomorrow, or some day, their ship will come in—and so long as they cling to that dream, they will not join the Communist cause. At the end, the narrator walks away from Boston Common, where Girsdansky, oblivious to the cold, continues his harangue.

"In Passing" not only represents Cheever's rejection of Communist ideals, it also contains a highly autobiographical component. He himself was cold and hungry and broke in the mid-thirties, yet never without hope for the future, never without the drive to succeed where his father had failed. That failure is vividly captured in the scenes that focus on the loss of the family home. The narrator's mother is devastated. "We haven't a place to rest in, a place to die in," she cries. "We may die in a hotel. On the street." His father, however, manages to shut out his present distress by reliving the glory of the past. "We drank every quart of champagne they had on that train," he gaily recalls. "We had plenty of money then," he says, and "we'll have it again—don't you worry." Cheever's parents were in fact dispossessed of their home on Wollaston Hill in Quincy, the home he grew up in. "In Passing" is notable for its incisive portrait of Girsdansky, and for its evocation of the mother dispossessed of her home, yet Cheever did not include it in any of his six story collections or in the 1978 *Stories*, perhaps because it dealt so closely and painfully with his immediate family and forebears. Other stories uncollected until now fall into a similar pattern.

The most poignant of these attempt to come to grips with the ghost of Aaron Waters Cheever, his grandfather, who died of alcohol and opium abuse in 1882, and with his own father, Frederick Lincoln Cheever, another man who drank and whose career ended in failure. Growing up in Quincy, the young writer could find no male ancestors to identify with, and yet in writing about them he tended to glamorize and rationalize their fate.

His paternal grandfather, Aaron, was to remain a shadowy figure throughout Cheever's life. No one would talk to him about Aaron Waters Cheever, least of all his father. He could only glean the information that his grandfather had abandoned his wife and two sons in Boston, and gone to the devil. Left to the resources of his imagination, he imagined the details of that decline and fall in "Homage to Shakespeare" (*Story* magazine, November 1937). In the story, the narrator implicates William Shakespeare in the collapse of the protagonist, who is given no name but called "my grandfather." As a youth, he ships out to India and falls under the spell of Shakespeare's plays during the long months at sea. When he returns to Newburyport, it is with the words of the bard ringing in his ears—particularly the words of the great tragic figures as they damn lesser mortals for their lack of faith and understanding. The grandfather takes on the airs, and even adopts the rhetoric, of those characters. (Aaron Waters Cheever had two sons. The younger was Cheever's father, Frederick. The older he called Hamlet.) In his overweening pride, he does not deign to work, leaves his family, and devotes himself to wenching, drinking, and railing against fate. In his grandson's fictional formulation, he becomes the victim of his own sensitivity to the magic of Shakespeare.

His father is also fashioned as a victim in "The Autobiography of a Drummer" (*New Republic*, 23 October 1935). The drummer (or traveling salesman) of the title is clearly modeled on Frederick Lincoln Cheever, and the sketch traces his downfall in much the same terms Arthur Miller was to adopt for *Death of a Salesman*. At one time, the shoe salesman (nameless in the story) had enjoyed tremendous success. He sold carloads of "expensive and beautiful" shoes to buyers who valued the workmanship that went into them. At his peak, he had "ten suits of clothing and twenty pairs of shoes and two sailboats." He traveled all over the United States, living in the best hotels. But a new set of business practices destroyed his career. Cheap shoes mass-produced in factories replaced the handmade shoes of the past. Individual buyers gave way to chain-store representatives, less interested in quality than price. In the end the salesman lost his customers, defeated not through any fault of his own but because of the tawdry commercialism of the times.

In "The Autobiography of a Drummer" Cheever was apparently trying to justify his father's financial collapse. He was less inclined to excuse what he regarded as Frederick Lincoln Cheever's unwillingness to love him. Cheever was the second and last child of his parents' marriage, born in his father's forty-ninth year, and he thought of himself as an unwanted child. His mother told him, he maintained, that his father wanted him aborted—a conversation that crops up several times in his fiction. Certainly his father had little time for him when John was growing up. He had established a strong alliance with John's brother, seven years older, and did not trouble to form another with his late-begotten son. So, at least, Cheever envisioned the family situation, and time and again, he tried to deal with it in his stories and novels.

In *The Wapshot Chronicle* (1957), for instance, he fashioned a loving portrait of his father. Leander Wapshot is depicted as an engaging and eccentric character, rather unfairly dominated by the women in his life. It is true that he is alienated from and intolerant of his younger son Coverly (a character modeled on Cheever himself), but Leander is for the most part a likable figure, and the one who speaks for the author at the end of the novel.

A far less flattering image emerges in "The National Pastime" (*New Yorker*, 26 September 1953). Here the father (nameless, like the other protagonists in these family stories) neglects to introduce his son into the mysteries of baseball, and so places the lad in a position analogous to that of a Polynesian boy who has not learned to swim. The father in this case is almost sixty years old when his son is born, and soon thereafter suffers a business failure that leaves him focused on the end of things. "How can you ask me to play baseball when I will be dead in another month?" he demands of his son, but this is not true: the father in the story will live many more months and years, and what keeps him from teaching his son to play baseball—and from participating in other rites of passage involving father and son—is an overwhelming egotism that will not allow him to think of anyone but himself. In an unlikely ending, the now-adult son makes a barehanded catch of a foul line drive at Yankee Stadium, and the pain is succeeded by "a sense of perfect joy" as the unhappy memory of "the old man and the old house" fades at last from his dreams.

Like the ending, the other details of this story rendering a harsh judgment on a father who does not and will not love his son may well have been invented by John Cheever. He was from his youth blessed with the story-making capacity. But the stories did not come from the ether. He wrote *out of* his experience, if not directly *about* it. As James Salter has pointed out, "[w]e know that most great novels and stories come not from things that are entirely invented, but from perfect knowledge and close observation." Cheever's gift for invention and his transformative imagination saw to it that there was almost never a one-to-one correspondence between fiction and fact. Fiction, he frequently insisted, was "not crypto-autobiography." Yet the creation of stories, he proclaimed nearly as often, provided him with a way to make sense of his life.

"Homage to Shakespeare," "The Autobiography of a Drummer," and "The National Pastime" are deeply felt, emotionally powerful stories that cut close to the bone. Two other stories in this collection—one early, one late—apparently deal not with family but with events in Cheever's life. In the first of these, "In the Beginning" (*New Yorker*, 6 November 1937), the author does not disguise himself through anonymity or a fictional name. He is simply "John Cheever," reliving the afternoons and evenings of his dancing school in Quincy. The instructor, a dignified and somewhat terrifying woman named Miss Barlow, tries to instill in her young charges the rudiments of proper social behavior on the dance floor. In the second, "The

President of the Argentine" (*Atlantic Monthly*, April 1976), Cheever applies a fictional veneer to that desperate period in his life—1974 and 1975—when he was badly depressed, sexually conflicted, and sliding into the abyss of alcoholism. The story adopts various concealments, but the narrator walks down Commonwealth Avenue from Kenmore Square to the Ritz, just as Cheever used to do during his months living alone in Boston. The avenue is punctuated by statuary, and en route the narrator is overcome by the desire to place his hat atop the massive statue of the President of the Argentine. A young man, apparently on the make, strikes up a conversation with him, and a policeman shouts at them to break it up. "You boys . . . spoil everything," he says. Next the narrator charms a young girl who has flunked out of the embalming school in Kenmore Square (real enough) and in the final sentence raises the scrim to reveal his own rather foolish and lonely self: "The man who wanted to put his hat on the statue of the President is I." Not one of Cheever's best, the story offers a glimpse into the mind of the writer looking back on his most degraded period.

Many other stories demonstrate how Cheever was able to transform his experience. Reading through them chronologically, one can learn a good deal about him. This is even true, in a muted way, of the formula fiction he wrote for *Collier's* and *Mademoiselle* in the late 1930s and early 1940s. Three of the *Collier's* stories are conventionally plotted racetrack yarns in which true love is confronted by obstacles that the characters manage to hurdle in the final scenes. Each story is centered around the Saratoga Racetrack near Yaddo, the artists' and writers' colony where Cheever spent many months during his poverty-ridden years. The novelist and screenwriter Daniel Fuchs, who was at Yaddo with Cheever in the late 1930s, recalls that one day there was a frantic phone call from the editor of *Collier's*. The magazine planned to run one of Cheever's racetrack stories in the next issue, but the typescript had vanished. Could Cheever rush a carbon to New York? He could not, since he had made no carbon. Instead he sat down, rewrote the story from memory in a day, and shipped it to New York to beat the deadline.

"A Present for Louisa," in *Mademoiselle*'s Christmas 1940 issue, resonates with personal overtones. A young couple, Roger and Louisa, are trying to decide whether to get married on a shaky financial footing. Marriage "isn't a lark," Roger warns, and they shouldn't embark on it until absolutely sure they can support themselves. In the end he relents and the couple happily take their vows. Much the same difficulty faced the author in the fall of 1940, when—despite his not having a steady job or a reliable source of income—he and Mary Winternitz decided to be married.

"Family Dinner," a *Collier's* story of 25 July 1942, departs from the standard conventions of the popular magazines. The marriage of Frank and

Frances has gone bad, and they are about to separate. To keep up appearances, they go through the ritual of a dinner with her family—carving the roast beef, Chopin afterwards, the glass of brandy Frank drinks with her father—before riding back to the city in different cars on the same train. Told in an understated style reminiscent of Hemingway (there are many Hemingway echoes in Cheever's early stories), "Family Dinner" nicely exemplifies Cheever's feeling for ceremony, and anticipates later stories of marital conflict.

Ten of the stories in this volume have to do with life in the United States Army during World War II, and derive from Cheever's own service as an enlisted man, particularly during his infantry training in Camp Croft, South Carolina, and Camp Gordon, Georgia. (Cheever did not see combat: he spent most of his army career writing propaganda films for the Signal Corps.) There is a sturdy sense of comradeship in these tales, an awareness that the thirty-year-old writer from New York City was working in concert with the longshoreman and the bartender, the chicken farmer and the five-goal polo player. Together these men go through bayonet drill and on bivouac; together they are herded into and out of the mess hall for a turkey dinner on Thanksgiving; together they chip in to make up the loss when a fellow soldier's money is stolen. Whatever their differences in mental and physical ability or social and psychological orientation—and these are vast—these men are unified by a common purpose. They are even bound together, in the most interesting of the stories, by a shared hatred of their basic training sergeant.

The title character of "Sergeant Limeburner" (*New Yorker*, 13 March 1943) is a sadistic noncom who abuses the men in his company unmercifully. As Cheever's letters home testify, this character was modeled on his platoon sergeant during basic training. Cheever began by loathing this sergeant, but eventually came to realize that his tormentor was driven by compulsions over which he had no control, and that he was terribly lonely. In bringing this man to life on the page, Cheever not only showed him at his worst—driving the men until they drop in the sun, calling them out for nighttime drill, allowing them no respite from ill treatment—he also produced a measure of justification for Limeburner at the end. Badly beaten by one of his recruits, the sergeant is relieved of his post and led away in humiliation. But the men who watch him as he goes, feeling no pity at all, pleased to be rid of him at last, were in fact, the narrator concludes, "soldiers he had destroyed himself to make."

Another group of six stories almost constitute a short book of its own within this collection. These are the "Town House" tales, published between April 1945 and May 1946 in the *New Yorker* and based on an experiment in communal living that the Cheevers and two other young families undertook just after the war. Pooling their incomes, the three couples (each with one child) rented a large townhouse on 92nd Street. The place had five floors, eight bathrooms, and plenty of bedrooms to go around. This apparently felicitous arrangement soon degenerated into bickering. One couple loves to party, while another prefers Great Books and classical music. One of the wives is a beauty who flirts outrageously, another a mousy type whose husband is bewitched by the beauty. The couple modeled on the Cheevers tries to keep the peace amid the general disorder and hysteria. Cheever saw the comic potential in the situation and exploited it in his six "funny, funny pieces" (as he called them).

The "Town House" stories, widely read and talked about at the time, were soon bought as a vehicle for the stage. On 2 September 1948, a dramatization of *Town House* by playwright Gertrude Tonkonogy opened in Boston to good reviews. A few weeks later, after George S. Kaufman had shined it up by adding more gags, the play opened—and promptly closed—on Broadway. Cheever, hoping for a financial windfall, made $54. Producer Max Gordon lost a hundred thousand. Whatever their fate on the stage, however, the stories still read well. And Cheever turned the Broadway disappointment to literary profit in such tales of the theatrical world as "The Opportunity" (*Cosmopolitan*, December 1947).

Noteworthy among the later work in this volume are two sketches for the *Reporter*, whose editor, Max Ascoli, was the Cheevers' neighbor in Westchester. "The Journal of a Writer with a Hole in One Sock" (29 December 1955) offers a glimpse into the situation of a middle-aged writer who—very much like the author at that time—was able to make ends meet through the patronage of those who let him rent his home at reduced rates. "How Dr. Wareham Kept His Servants" (5 April 1956) seems to be founded on Cheever's father-in-law and the Eastern European immigrants he employed at his summertime retreat in New Hampshire. The story's sympathy goes to the immigrants, who are blackmailed into serving Dr. Wareham because of their Communist beliefs. Cheever was in fact friendly with one such employee, who used to lecture him about his bourgeois failings as they toiled in the vegetable garden.

In "The Leaves, the Lion-Fish and the Bear" (*Esquire*, November 1974), Cheever presents a rationale for the sort of manly homosexuality he endeavored to practice late in life. A traveler picks up a hitchhiker on a trip to the Rockies, and when they are snowed in for the night, the two men make joyful love. The next morning, the weather clears and they part, without guilt or sorrow or any ill consequences. One man can love another without compromising his marriage, the story argues, for the encounter has done nothing to diminish the traveler's fondness for his wife. It was a theme Cheever developed and extended in *Falconer* (1976), where a homosexual affair in prison serves to liberate the protagonist's capacity to love all of his fellow human beings.

"The Island" (*New Yorker,* 27 April 1981) was the last story Cheever wrote, and despite its brevity a highly significant one. Published the year before he died, it describes a sort of Shangri-La in the Caribbean, where the great musicians and actors and athletes of the past—and even the great prostitutes and trapeze artists—are "leading happy and simple lives." They have not had to pay for their success by fading into shadows of their former selves. Instead they keep busy "digging and trapping shellfish, weaving baskets, and reading the classics." Though only on the island for a few hours, the narrator cannot stop thinking about this magic place. Perhaps, as the story does not explicitly say, the island represented a version of heaven Cheever conjured up. Perhaps that was where he was headed.

In the letter Mitgang telephoned me about, Mary Cheever objected to two assumptions I'd made in this introduction. First, she said, I'd incorrectly assumed that John Cheever had chosen which stories to include in his prize-winning 1978 collection, leading me to speculate that in omitting everything written before 1947 he might have been "insisting on a public image" of himself that those early stories "served to undermine." It was not that way at all, Mary wrote me. Cheever granted Robert Gottlieb, his editor at Knopf, a somewhat grudging permission to bring out *The Stories of John Cheever,* and contributed a preface to the volume. Otherwise, he'd had nothing to do with the book. "The selection of stories was Gottlieb's alone," she maintained. Yet at the same time, she went on to state in contradiction that *her husband's* "only standard (and Gottlieb's)" in making selections "was the excellence of the stories" and that "early stories were dropped because 'they were embarrassingly immature,' as Gottlieb and Cheever agreed" and as Cheever himself commented in his preface to the collection.

A second false assumption of mine—one, she supposed, that biographers were "particularly prone to"—was that "a story, however immature and imitative, is interesting for what it reveals about the writer's life, the more private the more interesting." To this charge I could only plead guilty. Yes, I was interested in tracing connections between a writer's life and his work. The life illuminated the work, and vice versa. But I did not consider this approach in any way sensational, as Mary apparently did. "Maybe you think your preface will cause a lot of people to rush to buy the book the way shoppers do at supermarkets, as if John were a movie queen or rock star?" she wrote me (Mary Cheever to SD, 3 May 1988, Harvard).

The Cheever family was upset by the aggressive steps Academy Chicago was taking to promote the book. The firm rapidly put together "a Cheever sampler" for distribution at the American Booksellers Association over

Memorial Day weekend, containing three stories and the first few pages of my introduction, issued a flyer hailing *The Uncollected Stories of John Cheever, 1930–1981* as a "Major Fall Production" with a first printing of fifty thousand copies, and ran off bound galleys of the book to stimulate the sale of book club, paperback, and foreign rights.

Upon reading Mary's letter, I made some modifications in the introduction. In part I did this to avoid further straining relations with the family. But I also saw her point that I'd been guilty of leaping to conclusions about Cheever's motives for ignoring his early work. This, she pointed out, represented an example of the *post hoc ergo propter hoc* fallacy. It was true that John Cheever, in later periods of his life, presented himself as a gentleman to the manor born—an affectation that Mary herself, who had no patience with any display of what New Englanders call "side," had called my attention to—while in fact he'd come from a family suffering through the hardships of poverty.

Susan Cheever, in *Home Before Dark*, wrote that her paternal grandfather, Frederick Lincoln Cheever, had once been co-owner of a shoe-manufacturing firm: her father had told her as much. A search of the records uncovered no such company, and almost certainly her grandfather worked as a shoe salesman: the profession assigned to him in "Autobiography of a Drummer." Yet in her book also, Susan described her father's assumption of an aristocratic New England background as "show" and characterized the handsome house on Cedar Lane as representing "some place of his own that might confirm his credentials as a gentleman and soothe his insecurities" (quoted in Castronovo, 208–9). In calling attention to these pretensions, I was hardly invading family privacy. It was also true that Cheever chose not to reprint in book form the stories that dealt with those troubled years. But I may well have been wrong to assume that he had done so in order to maintain his public persona. After all, as Mary also reminded me, Cheever had frequently spoken in interviews about the hard times of the 1930s.

So I made brief alterations to eliminate any statement of his intentions, for example cutting the phrase about his "insisting" on an image of himself as the reason behind rejecting his early work. He might have done so (we have nothing on the record) because he didn't think anything he'd written before 1947 was good enough to deserve collecting in hard cover. If so, though, I thought he had judged those early stories too harshly. I balanced the deletions on this issue by adding a few sentences arguing that fiction was not diminished by parallels to reality, and that those parallels were worth exploring. I told Jordan Miller about making changes, and he wrote in response that doing so would constitute "a grave mistake" (Jordan Miller to SD, 13 May 1988).

By this time, the attitudes between the legal adversaries were hardening. Mary Cheever made accusations against Academy Chicago in her letter to me, and Jordan Miller responded in kind. Each party served papers on the other. Lawsuits were filed both in New York (Cheever country) and Illinois (Academy Chicago territory). Newspapers and magazines ran stories in which the parties lobbed verbal grenades back and forth. I was situated in a no-man's-land between them.

On May 22 Mary Cheever wrote, saying she was relieved about my proposed changes, but asking me to go one step further. In this letter Mary spelled out what was to become the family's most potent legal argument. Cheever would never have approved the volume of uncollected stories, for they were simply not good enough. As caretakers of his estate, they were compelled to defend his reputation from the harm that would ensue from its publication. As Mary expressed it, "John would have been horrified by this collection, as I am and have been since I came to understand that it is being promoted in a big edition as if it were the Knopf collection in literary merit all over again with, as well, an Introduction and Editor's Note suggesting that these stories contain some previously suppressed information about the author."

"You have always respected my opinions whether or not they differ from your own, as I must respect yours," Mary went on. "But this book will have my name on the copyright page and will be seen as a work approved by me as John's executor and widow. As my duty as executor and out of loyalty to his memory, I must ask you to withdraw this Introduction" (Mary Cheever to SD, 22 May 1988, Harvard). That I was unwilling to do.

Three weeks later, the parties to the lawsuit met in New York in an attempt to work out their differences. The first item on the agenda at that June 15 meeting was my introduction, which whether altered or not continued to infuriate the Cheever family. The Millers, seeking a reconciliation so that the book could appear as announced, were willing to make further changes to satisfy the Cheevers. What specifically did they object to? Just about everything, it turned out, including the first and second paragraphs. At that stage, Mary Cheever "suddenly became agitated," as Anita Miller reconstructed the scene in *Uncollecting Cheever*. With her face contorted, her voice breaking, her arms trembling, she declared that "it was not true that John Cheever had repudiated his formative years." "Did you know I hated Scott Donaldson when you commissioned this?" Ben then "asked pleasantly." Couldn't the introduction be scrapped? he suggested, and the Millers—who must have anticipated the demand—agreed (Anita Miller, 91–93).

Perhaps, Anita Miller immediately proposed, Susan and/or Ben could write an introduction, hence keeping outsiders out of the loop. Or, better yet, they could use Cheever's own "Why I Write Short Stories," composed for *Newsweek* when Susan was a staffer there, preceded by a few words from Susan/Ben. Both parties agreed to that solution, and the meeting went on to discuss the financial terms of the contract. On this point as well, Academy Chicago retreated, offering to raise Mary Cheever's share of royalties from 50 to 80 percent and to reduce Franklin Dennis's share accordingly. The disputants then departed, the Millers hoping that the issues between them had been resolved and going forward with plans for the book.

The paperback auction scotched any chance of a settlement. The timing could not have been worse for Academy Chicago. On the night after the meeting in New York, the Cheevers learned from Ben's agent, Andrew Wylie, that Academy Chicago—working through its agent, Scott Meredith—had received a floor bid of $100,000 from Dell for paperback rights, with an auction scheduled for June 29. The offer was based on bound galleys of the entire book, including my introduction as then unrevised, and the Millers had said nothing about this, or about other bound galleys going out to reviewers, during the meeting in New York. As a consequence, the Cheevers' lawyer, Martin Garbus, accused Academy of negotiating "in bad faith," hence disavowing any apparent agreements reached at the meeting, and sought an injunction against the paperback auction (not granted) and a restraining order against further distribution of the bound galleys (granted). The auction took place as scheduled on the twenty-ninth, Dell winning with a bid of $225,000. That same day, Judge Gerard Goettel, the federal judge in White Plains, New York, issued a preliminary injunction against publication of *Uncollected Stories*. The disputants were going to trial.

I learned of these matters only years later, in Anita Miller's *Uncollecting Cheever*, a detailed, readable, and bitterly indignant account of the legal proceedings in the case that encompasses depositions, evidentiary hearings, and trials both in New York and Illinois. I was not summoned to testify at any of these venues, and glad of it. Yet going into and during the first trial in New York, the Cheevers repeatedly presented my introduction— never mind that Academy Chicago had agreed to abandon it—as a major cause for complaint. As Mary Cheever told the *Chicago Tribune*, what really bothered her was my implication that her husband wanted to suppress the early stories because they "revealed something about John that he didn't want known." This amounted to an airing of "dirty laundry . . . gossip," she said (quoted in Anita Miller, 106). Readers are invited to scan the introduction to detect any hint of what might be called "dirty laundry."

Both sides to the dispute thought ill of their adversaries. The Cheevers felt they'd been hoodwinked into a contract under false pretenses. When Mary Cheever signed the contract for a tiny advance and inequitable royalty terms, she assumed that Academy Chicago had in mind a small book with a small press run. She and her children were outraged, subsequently, when the publisher decided to reprint all the previously uncollected stories in a book that promised to make them a great deal of money. The Millers, they contended, had discovered a "literary gold mine" and were taking advantage of it. This was intolerable, and when they sued to stop publication—both on copyright and contract grounds—they took the position that they were defending John Cheever's literary reputation against exploitation and the damage that would result from issuing his least meritorious work.

Academy, on the other hand, thought that they'd negotiated the contract in good faith. They had not realized, at first, how many uncollected stories there were. As they located and read them, they began to understand just how valuable a literary property they constituted, and determined to bring out a book containing all of them. The Cheevers' objections, they felt certain, were motivated by money alone. "It is true," Anita Miller wrote me in 1999, "that your introduction appeared to play a significant part in the lawsuit, but I don't think you need to worry about its having triggered Cheever animosity against the collection. The Cheevers were motivated by greed, pure and simple." In writing her about *Uncollecting Cheever*, I asked for payment of the still outstanding $1,000 fee for the introduction. "We have long since written off all obligations connected with what you aptly call 'the lawsuit from hell,'" she replied (Anita Miller to SD, 4 March 1999).

The Cheevers prevailed in the courts, barring Academy Chicago from issuing its collection of all the uncollected stories. In an attempt to salvage something from their failed lawsuit, the publishers brought out a slim volume of *Thirteen Uncollected Stories by John Cheever* in 1994. All of these were stories that had gone out of copyright and reverted to the public domain—any publisher could have reprinted them—and ranged in date of origin from 1930 to 1949. With freedom from copyright the sole principle of selection, the book lacked coherence. As John Updike pointed out in his review, the thirteen stories "begin with some formless, vaguely anti-capitalist effusions by a teenager and progress to some pat, hokey confections by a young man trying to survive the Depression by selling to the slick magazines." Despite these reservations, however, Updike found it "fascinating to see a splendid natural talent grow its wings" and singled out a few of the stories, including "In Passing" and "Family Dinner," as particularly interesting.

At the end of his commentary, Updike proposed that "in order to placate those who find something to love in all [Cheever's] work, his estate might eventually arrange an edition of his uncollected stories more generous and orderly than this baker's dozen born of bitter litigation." Such a book, he suggested, might include everything in *The Way Some People Live* (1943), Cheever's first book of stories, as well as the forty uncollected stories in the *New Yorker's* files. The resulting volume might serve as a companion to Cheever's 1978 collection, satisfy his readers, and dispel "the tainted air that lingers in the wake of the Academy Chicago squabble" (Updike, "Posthumous Output," 448, 450, 452–53). That hasn't happened yet, but it's still a good idea.

The Next Biography

I first heard from Blake Bailey in April 2004. He e-mailed me with word that he'd contracted with Knopf for a new biography of John Cheever, inasmuch as the journals were "now available in toto" and nearly twenty years had elapsed since my "admirable" book had come out. A lot of people I'd interviewed or corresponded with had died during those two decades. Bailey wondered if I still had the tapes/transcripts/notes from my Cheever book, and if I'd be willing to share them with him.

It is always somewhat daunting to find out that one's work is going to be superseded, especially when the aftercomer will be granted access to materials you were denied. But with the passage of time, such things will happen. So I replied that he certainly could see my work, and directed Bailey to Swem Library at William and Mary, where the papers for the Cheever and other biographies are located (Bailey and SD, e-mails 26 April 2004).

I knew of Bailey's well-received book on Richard Yates, another discontented soul who like Cheever located much of his fiction in the suburbs. Bailey and I were both practicing the same craft, I figured, and he was welcome to use any of my research findings. It was no more than any early biographer should do for a later one, as I'd learned through the generosity of Carlos Baker, who let me examine the Hemingway papers in his office at Princeton, and of Arthur Mizener and Henry Dan Piper, who allowed me to pore over their Fitzgerald documents at Cornell and Southern Illinois, respectively. Besides, I'd gone on to other subjects, and in the spring of 2004 was two hundred pages along on the biography of Edwin Arlington Robinson that came out in 2007.

For a few months thereafter, Blake Bailey and I communicated regularly through e-mail. He'd read the "Writing the Cheever" essay in the *Sewanee Review*, which documented my struggles with the family, and particularly with Susan and Ben Cheever. "Butter Susan," I advised him in an e-mail, but there was no need of that (SD to Bailey, 17 May 2004). Susan immediately liked Bailey, thinking how wonderful it would be for her mother, Mary, then ninety, to have this handsome, charming fellow coming to call and hanging on her every word.

It was Ben Cheever and not Susan, however, who chose Bailey as his father's biographer. Ben's wife, Janet Maslin, wrote a rave review of Bailey's Yates biography in the *New York Times* and urged Ben to read the book.

Subsequently, Ben invited Blake to participate in a literary talk show he hosted in Westchester County. At dinner afterwards, they got along so well that Ben proposed that Blake undertake a new account of his father's life, with total permission to read and quote from his journals and letters and without any requirement of family approval of the result. Blake was initially reluctant—he wanted to be the first to tell the story. But it was too good an offer to refuse. This story was to be repeated many times over during the next five years in almost every comment on and review of Bailey's book.

Blake didn't make the trip to William and Mary until September 2004 (his first child was born during the summer months, and I'd warned him against the summer heat in Williamsburg). On his first visit he spent six hours a day for four days looking through my Cheever papers and "scarcely put a dent in Box III." He came back again, twice, in the spring of 2005 to finish the job, spending three weeks in all. "I hope you don't mind my squatting on your shoulders like this," he remarked (Bailey to SD, e-mail, 21 September 2004).

In his initial research, Blake often wondered if I had an address or could put him in touch with some of my interviewees. Where was Max Zimmer, the young writer who'd become Cheever's late-in-life protégé? What about Donald Lang, the ex-convict Cheever taught at Sing Sing? And Lucy Miner, his student at the Iowa Writers' Workshop? Usually, I could only aim Bailey in the general direction of these contacts. But he proved to be a determined digger, who obviously enjoyed it: "he won't escape me, oh no," he said of one chap. He was caught up in the biographical process, the excitement of unearthing a piece of the puzzle almost every day and seeing how it fit with the others. In the end, after spending half a decade on the job, he located just about everyone I'd interviewed who was still alive. He also contacted a number of other people I might have talked to but didn't.

By a curious coincidence, Francis J. Bosha's extensive summaries of the Cheever journals at Harvard's Houghton Library arrived in the mail on 17 May 2004, three weeks after I first heard from Blake Bailey. A selection from these journals—a valuable literary property whose publication rights sold for $1.2 million—had been published by Knopf more than a decade earlier as *The Journals of John Cheever*, edited by Robert Gottlieb. But that book contained only 5 percent of the three to five million words (the estimates vary) Cheever actually set down between the late 1940s and his death in 1982. A dedicated bibliographical scholar with a strong interest in Cheever, Bosha went up to the Houghton, read through all twenty-eight looseleaf notebooks, and provided useful summaries of what they contained.

I'd done a review of the journals as excerpted by Gottlieb for the *Chicago Tribune*. The story they had to tell, in exquisitely written prose, was almost unrelievedly one of woe, an attitude standing in contrast to the blue-sky endings of many of his stories. His characters are usually in distress of one kind or another, but often Cheever let them find renewal or regeneration through immersion in the natural world. Hawthorne had done the same thing in his stories, a century earlier. This happens much less often in the journals, which are full of self-excoriation, self-pity, and downright despair. I quoted one entry from 1962 to illustrate the point:

> The span between living and dying is brief and anguished, and the soul of man is reflected not in snug farmhouses and great monuments but in fourth-string hotel rooms, malodorous and obscure. That is all there is. There is nothing. Tired but sleepless, lewd but alone, hopeless, drunk, sitting at the window on the air-shaft in some other country: this is the image of man. All the rest of it—the cheering lights of morning, sweet music, the towers and the sailboats—are fantastic inventions, evasions, lies, vulgarities, and politenesses poorly invented to conceal the truth.

The troubled life Cheever described in these journals derived largely from "two astonishing contests, one with alcohol and one with my wife." Aware that he "could very easily destroy himself" with liquor, he repeatedly commented on his daily "booze fight"—the struggle to hold off taking his first "scoop" until noon, or eleven, or ten, or after breakfast. Among modern American writers, his addiction was not at all unusual. Yet he was one of the very few—John O'Hara, he noted, was another—who at long last "kicked the shit" and continued to work.

The marital battle, on the other hand, seems to have persisted to the end. The portrait of Mary Cheever in her husband's journals is devastating. She is cold, mean, sarcastic, unwilling to applaud his accomplishments or satisfy his persistent sexual desires. These maldispositions were related to his drinking, Cheever realized, but they continued even after he became sober in 1976. The fault, he speculated, lay in her unhappy childhood, but it might as easily have been traced to his own. It is easy to see why I was forbidden access to the journals on the grounds of their depiction of the marriage, and why Mary persistently refused to read them.

In his final years, Cheever turned increasingly to other men as sexual partners (earlier, there had been affairs with both men and women). These were discussed in the published journals, along with childhood anecdotes tracing homosexual inclinations to his formative years. Even within the family, he felt the strongest ties to male relatives. "My own true love was my brother" Fred, he comments. The child who could deliver him from darkness was his late-begotten son Federico.

In brief, then, Gottlieb's abbreviated version of the journals introduced the basic themes running through all of them. It is probably true, as Gottlieb observed, that *any* extensive selection from the journals would reveal "the same life and the same talent: in fact, the same man" (SD, review). From a biographical standpoint, the Cheever who emerges in the 5 percent version of his journals in 1991 is not notably different from the one Blake Bailey describes in his 2009 biography. Yet as I discovered after reading through Bosha's detailed 170-page summary of all twenty-eight looseleaf folders, many entries in those journals invited further examination by scholars. From Bosha you could pinpoint precisely where to find Cheever's reflections on other writers, including Bellow, Updike, Mailer, and Capote. You could also discover the location of his early approaches—drafts, some of them—to different books-in-the-making: the foreground of *Bullet Park* and of *Falconer*, for example.

I alerted Bailey to Bosha's work, and sent him an e-mail about a few of its more striking revelations—material that I wished I could have known about when writing my biography. Childhood incident of older brother Fred "punching an Irishman" who said John looked like a girl, when they were skating one winter day at Braintree Dam. News that Cheever applied for OCS (he wasn't admitted) during World War II. Self-reproach (in 1960) for the "monotony of my central characters who are never anything but myself," followed by a list of exceptions. Excoriation for practicing "gross indecencies" in Hollywood with Calvin Kentfield. Examination of his slightly built self in a mirror, 1968 or so, and seeing an "aging boy—a runt—in a blue sweater." These were revelations to me but not to Bailey, who had his own forty-three-hundred-page copy of the journals to wade through and assess (SD to Bailey, e-mail, 25 May 2004).

Before Bailey and I wished each other good luck and drifted out of touch, he sent me a copy of the 9 April 2004 *Westchester Journal News* article announcing a "New Cheever Biography Planned." That piece, based on interviews with Bailey and Ben Cheever, established the basic rationale for a new biography of Cheever. The "crux of the matter" was that Bailey would have access to and permission to quote from the journals, fresh material and 95 percent unpublished: an advantage that "Cheever's first biographer, Scott Donaldson, did not have." True enough, and entirely unobjectionable. But Ben Cheever went on to take several sidelong swipes at my book. In others' writing about his father, he observed, he'd always felt that "the pathology [took] up all the room." And, more specifically, "my father used to say that to have a bad biographer was to be stuck with a bad roommate for eternity. I like the idea of him getting a good roommate at last" (Canfield).

When Blake Bailey's biography was nearing publication five years later, the family comments dismissing my previous book adopted an apologetic tone. Ben in the *Washington Post*: "Now, *in Donaldson's defense*, he didn't have the rights to quote from my father's letters or journals the way Blake did. . . . Still, we felt that Donaldson didn't understand our father. He talked about him in a way that was both simplistic and crude" (Haygood): two damning adjectives that had gone unused in any previous discussion of my work. Susan in the *New York Times*: "We wouldn't give him permission" to quote. "It's not a very good book, but *I can't say we made it easy on him*" (McGrath, "First"). And Bailey himself, postpublication, in the *Wall Street Journal*: "I think *to be fair* to Scott Donaldson, he pounced before the corpse was even cold and at that time Susan was writing her own memoir, Ben was editing a book of the letters and they had this more proprietary feeling toward their father. Enough time has passed that they wanted the definitive treatment" (Speakeasy). On the whole, I'd just as soon do without such defenders.

The unkindest cut of all came with the arrival, compliments of the author, of Bailey's *Cheever: A Life*. I immediately tackled the book, all 770 pages, and found much of it fascinating. The book is singularly well-written, and I was impressed by the extent of Bailey's research discoveries, not only in the journals but from his dedicated exploration of all possible sources of information. Bailey unearthed fresh revelations about Cheever's parents and brother. He did an admirable job of folding remarks drawn from journals and letters into his own highly readable prose. He included relevant information from the notes I'd deposited at William and Mary, duly crediting them in his fifty pages of endnotes. But nowhere in his biography—not in front matter, not in the notes, not in an epilogue—did he acknowledge by name the existence of my *John Cheever: A Biography*. That stung, so in otherwise congratulating Bailey for doing an excellent job, I remonstrated with him for not so much as mentioning the title of my biography (SD to Bailey, e-mail 31 March 2009). He replied with reasons for the omission, but it was a point on which we agreed to disagree (Bailey to SD, e-mail 1 April 2009).

Bailey's biography achieved a notable critical success, winning the National Book Critics Circle award and becoming a finalist for the Pulitzer Prize. Most of the reviewers followed his lead by ignoring the biography I'd published twenty years before. Most of them had not read it. This was not true of Geoffrey Wolff and Jonathan Yardley, who wrote the kickoff reviews for the Sunday *New York Times* and *Washington Post*. Wolff had reviewed my biography unfavorably, in particular, and in my paranoid moments it occurred to me that he may have been chosen by the *Times* to review Bailey's biography *because* of his dismissal of mine. In expressing admiration for the new work, Wolff praised Bailey for his wit and "attention to shifts in tone" in interpreting Cheever's fiction, for his "sound moral judgment" and "critical sensibility," for his sketches of people in Cheever's life that were "short stories in themselves," for his "wise and serious" approach. His sole objection was to the "explosively candid cries of despair, resentment and lust" in Cheever's journals, representing "the bent perceptions and attenuated judgment of an alcoholic": "Cheever, having started drinking as a youngster, finally stopped in 1975, on Page 518. Watching the years unroll via page headings throughout Bailey's 'Cheever,' this reader reached Page 79, the year 1935, and realized with panic that I was to be pent up with a depressive drunk for 40 more years. Boo-hoo for me: think of Cheever's wife, sons and daughter! He bullied them all, with his younger son Federico receiving the least calumny but the most onerous caretaking responsibilities" (Wolff).

Yardley overtly compared the two biographies. "Two decades ago, reviewing Scott Donaldson's 'John Cheever: A Biography,' I commented that, at 416 pages of text and apparatus, the book told us far more than we needed to know about Cheever's life. What, then, is to be said of Blake Bailey's "Cheever"? It weighs in at a stupefying 679 pages of text plus 89 pages of acknowledgments, notes and index, 770 pages in all, making for a vast inert pudding of a book that leaves the reader with a severe case of indigestion."

Yardley went on to deplore the "all-too-intimate disclosures" about Cheever. "There was plenty of that in Donaldson's biography, but in Bailey's it overwhelms everything else, the writing included. This is the chronicle of a man who was obsessed with sex and who drank 'murderously,' and it positively drips with detail about both." No doubt, he concluded, it was important to know that Cheever the man was sexually promiscuous and a fall-down drunk—and perhaps that told us "a bit about Cheever the writer as well"—but it was one thing for a biographer to arrive at an understanding of these shortcomings and "quite another simply to record, over and over and over again, their quotidian details."

From the journals, as from his own exhaustive research involving hundreds of hours of interviews and unearthing of previously unlocated letters, Bailey was able to show "how exasperating Cheever was as a drunk, and how pompous/manipulative he could be even at the best of times" (Yardley). As Bailey told interviewers, he was not shocked by these failings. He reported them objectively with a kind of humorous detachment. But he fell into the trap—as I had also done in my Cheever biography—of putting in too much of what he had found out. The reader is weighed down by repetitive mentions of Cheever's obsessive drinking, sexual yearnings, marital complaints, cruel parenting, and terrible loneliness. John Updike, reviewing for the *New Yorker*, could locate little sight of the often witty and amusing Cheever he'd come to know. It made for "a dispiriting read," he thought

(Updike, "Basically"). Alternatively it resulted in what a British reviewer characterized as "a great, tough read" (Homberger).

Several reviewers wondered how Cheever's children could possibly have welcomed Bailey's biography. Did they actually want their father's faults "exposed to the full glare of daylight?" The answer apparently is yes, they did, for they preferred honesty above all else. Bailey might have provided too many details, but by and large he caught the way it was around the "shark tank" of the family dinner table. Both Ben and Susan Cheever gave the biography their enthusiastic endorsement, and Fred agreed, with perhaps some reservations. "Blake Bailey did a very, very careful and thorough job," he commented. "He found sources no one else had found, he interviewed people no one knew existed, he solved all sorts of family mysteries. Is it entirely the story someone else would tell? Of course not. It's his."

Only after turning off the switch on my ego have I finally been able to accept Bailey's darker version of Cheever's life as closer to the truth than my kinder, gentler account. I presented Cheever as "a man divided against himself," the division in his spirit taking "its toll on the man even as it invigorated his work." That still seems to me a viable approach. But it may well be that I took too sunny a view of his final years, when I portrayed him as finding renewal through his escape from alcohol. "Rejoice, rejoice," Ezekiel Farragut counsels after his improbable escape from prison in *Falconer*. That, I thought, was the message Cheever wanted to leave behind. Yet in Bailey's book it becomes clear that conquering the demon of drink one day at a time did not substantially change Cheever's personality or improve the acrid atmosphere at the house on Cedar Lane.

Probably I should have known better, if only through my interviews with two of the psychiatrists Cheever consulted. One of them, who had seen not only the author but his wife and children, concluded that most of the family's troubles derived from Cheever himself. The other declared him a victim of pathological narcissism, a phrase that I decided not to use as too cruel and fixating. Lost in admiration for his fiction, I *wanted* him to be a better man, I *wanted* him to achieve a final victory.

Forty years ago, Malcolm Cowley warned me against the tendency to become judgmental he detected in a first draft of *By Force of Will: The Mind and Art of Ernest* Hemingway. At first I objected that I hadn't sat in judgment on that great writer. Certainly I hadn't meant to, but when I went back to the script, there it was: evidence of clear disapproval that I thereupon set about to eliminate. My job as a literary biographer was to try to understand the authors whose lives and works I was examining, and to convey that understanding without prejudice. I had no permission, no right, to serve as judge and jury about their behavior.

Most writers lead difficult lives. Sometimes they are cruel to others. In telling their stories, the biographer has to find a balance between, say, admiration for Hemingway's "The Snows of Kilimanjaro" and abhorrence for his practice of casting off friends and wives. Over time—thinking of one's own mistakes—I have become less judgmental about the writers who were my subjects. God knows they were hard enough on themselves. Six of them were alcoholics. Two of them killed themselves, and two others made attempts at suicide. Perhaps no life ends happily, but I depicted Cheever—as I had Fitzgerald, a man he resembled in many ways—as heroic for overcoming addiction and soldiering on. In doing so, I may well have traveled from unjustified faultfinding to unwarranted praise. Or, perhaps, I did not.

BIBLIOGRAPHY

Anesko, Michael. *Monopolizing the Master: Henry James and the Politics of Modern Literary Scholarship.* Stanford: Stanford University Press, 2012.

Anon. "Depicts Home of E. A. Robinson in Needlepoint." *Kennebec (Maine) Journal,* 8 May 1943.

———. "Library Board Votes to Retain Poet's Life Story." *Kennebec (Maine) Journal,* 8 November 1938.

———. "Library Notes for E.A.R.'s Birthday." *Colby Mercury* 6 (November 1938): 205–14.

Atlas, James. "Biografiends and the Law." *Vanity Fair,* November 1987, 46–50.

———. "My Subject, Myself." *New York Times Book Review,* 9 October 2005, 24–25.

Authors Guild Symposium. "Almost Like Falling in Love." *Authors Guild Bulletin* (Winter 2003): 17–32.

———. "The Art of Interviewing." *Authors Guild Bulletin* (June–July 1982): 13–25.

———. "Whose Life Is It, Anyway?" *Authors Guild Bulletin* (Winter 1999): 13–26.

Backscheider, Paula R. *Reflections on Biography.* New York: Oxford University Press, 1999.

Baker, Carlos. *Ernest Hemingway: A Life Story.* New York: Scribner's, 1969.

———. *Ernest Hemingway: The Writer as Artist.* Princeton: Princeton University Press, 1952.

Barnes, Julian. Review of *The Family Idiot,* by Jean-Paul Sartre. *London Review of Books,* 3 June 1982, 22–24.

———. *Flaubert's Parrot.* New York: Vintage, 1990.

Barstow, James. *My Tilbury Town.* Gardiner (Maine) Public Library, 1939.

Benson, Jackson J. "Ernest Hemingway: The Life as Fiction and the Fiction as Life." In Scafella, *Hemingway,* 155–68.

Bentley, Toni. Review of *A Book of Secrets,* by Michael Holroyd. *New York Times Book Review,* 7 August 2011, 1, 10–11.

Berg, A. Scott. *Max Perkins: Editor of Genius.* New York: Dutton, 1978.

Berlinerblau, Jacques. "Philip Roth's Next Book and Biography: What's Going On?" *Chronicle of Higher Education* (4 June 2012).

Boal, Sam. "I Tell You True." *Park East* 10 (December 1950): 18–19, 46–47, and 11 (January 1951): 36, 48–49.

Bosha, Francis J. "The John Cheever Journals at Harvard University's Houghton Library." *Resources for American Literary Study* 31 (2006): 199–311.

Bowen, Catherine Drinker. *Biography: The Craft and the Calling.* Boston: Little Brown, 1969.

Bradbury, Malcolm. "The Telling Life: Some Thoughts on Literary Biography." In Homberger and Charmley, *Troubled Face of Biography,* 131–40.

Bram, Christopher. *Eminent Outlaws: The Gay Writers Who Changed America*. New York: Twelve, 2012.

Brenner, Gerry. *Concealments in Hemingway's Work*. Columbus: Ohio State University Press, 1983.

Brooks, Peter. "Obsessed with the Hermit of Croisset." Review of *Flaubert's Parrot*, by Julian Barnes. *New York Times Book Review*, 10 March 1985.

Bruccoli, Matthew J. *Some Sort of Epic Grandeur: The Life of F. Scott Fitzgerald*. New York: Harcourt Brace Jovanovich, 1981.

Bush, Harold K., Jr. "Cradling Lives in Our Hands: Towards a Theory of Cultural Biography." *Christianity and Literature* 57 (Autumn 2007): 111–29.

Canfield, Kevin. "New Cheever Biography Planned." *Westchester (N.Y.) Journal News*, 9 April 2004.

Cassuto, Leonard. "The Silhouette and the Secret Self: Theorizing Biography in Our Times." *American Quarterly* 58 (December 2006): 1249–61.

Castronovo, David. *The American Gentleman*. New York: Continuum, 1991.

Cheever, John. *Bullet Park*. New York: Knopf, 1969.

———. *The Letters of John Cheever*. Edited by Benjamin Cheever. New York: Simon and Schuster, 1988.

———. *Thirteen Uncollected Stories*. Edited by Franklin H. Dennis. Chicago: Academy Chicago, 1994.

———. *The Uncollected Stories of John Cheever, 1930–1981*. Bound galleys. Chicago: Academy Chicago, 1988.

Cheever, Susan. *Home Before Dark*. Boston: Houghton Mifflin, 1984.

Cheney, Alexandra. "Blake Bailey on His Award-Winning John Cheever Biography." *Speakeasy* (blog), *Wall Street Journal*, 12 March 2010.

Cline, Sally. *Zelda Fitzgerald: Her Voice in Paradise*. New York: Arcade, 2002.

Clark, Roy Peter. "The Line Between Fact and Fiction." In Kramer and Call, *Telling True Stories*, 164–69.

Coates, Dennis. "John Cheever: A Checklist, 1930–1978." *Bulletin of Bibliography* (January–March 1979): 1–13, 49.

Cox, James M. Remarks at Robert Frost session. Modern Language Association Convention, Washington, D.C., December 1984.

Connolly, Cyril. Review of *Across the River and Into the Trees*, by Ernest Hemingway. *London Sunday Times*, 3 September 1950, 3.

Cowley, Malcolm. *The Literary Situation*. New York: Viking, 1954.

———. "A Portrait of Mister Papa." *Life* 25 (10 January 1949): 86–101.

———. Review of *Across the River and Into the Trees*, by Ernest Hemingway. *New York Herald Tribune Book Review*, 10 September 1950, 1, 16.

Crowley, John W. "John Cheever and the Runty Little Man: Some Reflections on Biography." *Syracuse Scholar* 11 (Spring 1991): 64–71.

Davison, Peter. "To Edit a Life." *Atlantic* (October 1992): 92–100.

Day, Douglas. Remarks at seminar on biography. Modern Language Association Convention, Chicago, December 1971.

Donadio, Rachel. "Bio Engineering." *New York Times Book Review*, 4 November 2007, 39.

Donaldson, Scott. *Archibald MacLeish: An American Life*. Boston: Houghton Mifflin, 1992.

———. *By Force of Will: The Life and Art of Ernest Hemingway*. New York: Viking, 1977.

————, ed. *Conversations with John Cheever*. Jackson: University Press of Mississippi, 1987.

————. *Death of a Rebel: The Charlie Fenton Story*. Madison: Fairleigh Dickinson University Press, 2012.

————. *Edwin Arlington Robinson: A Poet's Life*. New York: Columbia University Press, 2007.

————. *Fitzgerald and Hemingway: Works and Days*. New York: Columbia University Press, 2009.

————. *Fool for Love: F. Scott Fitzgerald*. New York: Congdon and Weed, 1983.

————. "Hemingway Encounters: A Biographer Reminisces." *Hemingway Review* 31 (Fall 2011): 96–106.

————. "John Cheever." In *American Writers: A Collection of Literary Biographies*, supp. 1, pt. 1. New York: Scribner's, 1979.

————. *John Cheever: A Biography*. New York: Random House, 1988.

————. *Poet in America: Winfield Townley Scott*. Austin: University of Texas Press, 1972.

————. "Recovering Robinson." *New Letters* 73 (2006): 146–59.

————. Review of *The Journals of John Cheever*, edited by Robert Gottlieb. *Chicago Tribune Books* (22 September 1991).

————. "Toward a Definitive Biography." In Scafella, *Hemingway*, 93–103.

Edel, Leon. "The Figure Under the Carpet." In Pachter, *Telling Lives*, 16–34.

————. *Literary Biography*. Toronto: University of Toronto Press, 1957.

————. *Writing Lives: Principia Biographica*. New York: W. W. Norton, 1984.

Ellmann, Richard. *Golden Codgers: Biographical Speculations*. New York: Oxford University Press, 1973.

————. "Freud and Literary Biography." In *a long the riverrun: Selected Essays*, 256–70. New York: Knopf, 1989.

Epstein, Joseph. *In a Cardboard Belt: Essays Personal, Literary, and Savage*. Boston: Houghton Mifflin, 2007.

Fenton, Charles A. *The Apprenticeship of Ernest Hemingway*. New York: Viking, 1954.

Fitzgerald, F. Scott. *The Great Gatsby*. 1925. New York: Modern Library, 1934.

————. *A Life in Letters: F. Scott Fitzgerald*. Edited by Matthew J. Bruccoli. New York: Simon and Schuster, 1994.

Fitzgerald, F. Scott, and Zelda Fitzgerald. *Dear Scott, Dearest Zelda: The Love Letters of F. Scott and Zelda Fitzgerald*. Edited by Jackson R. Bryer and Cathy W. Barks. New York: St. Martin's, 2002.

Fitzgerald, Zelda. *Save Me the Waltz*. 1932. Carbondale: Southern Illinois University Press, 1967.

Frost, Robert. *The Poetry of Robert Frost*. Edited by Edward Connery Lathem. New York: Holt, Rinehart and Winston, 1979.

————. *Selected Letters of Robert Frost*. Edited by Lawrance Thompson. New York: Holt, Rinehart and Winston, 1964.

Fruman, Norman. "The Biases of Biography." Lecture at Eötvös Loránd University, Budapest, 13 May 2000.

Garraty, John. *The Nature of Biography*. New York: Knopf, 1957.

Geeslin, Campbell. "Along Publishers Row." *Authors Guild Bulletin* (Fall 2003): 2.

Geismar, Maxwell. Review of *Across the River and Into the Trees*, by Ernest Hemingway. *Saturday Review of Literature*, 9 September 1950, 18–19.

Gellhorn, Martha. "Martha Gellhorn: On *Apocryphism*." *Paris Review* 79 (1981): 280–307.

Glendinning, Victoria. "Lies and Silences." In Homberger and Charmley, *Troubled Face of Biography*, 49–62.

Graham, Sheilah. *The Real F. Scott Fitzgerald Thirty-Five Years Later*. New York: Grosset and Dunlap, 1976.

Gregory, Horace. Review of *Edwin Arlington Robinson*, by Hermann Hagedorn. *New York Herald Tribune*, 30 October 1938, 7.

Hagedorn, Hermann. *Edwin Arlington Robinson: A Biography*. New York: Macmillan, 1938.

Hall, Brian. *Fall of Frost*. New York: Penguin, 2008.

Halperin, John. "The Biographer's Revenge." In Salwak, *Literary Biography*, 149–66.

Hamilton, Ian. *Keepers of the Flame: Literary Estates and the Rise of Biography*. London: Hutchinson, 1992.

Harrington, Walt. "Toward an Ethical Code for Narrative Journalists." In Kramer and Call, *Telling True Stories*, 170–72.

Hart, Henry. *James Dickey: The World as a Lie*. New York: Picador, 2000.

———. "Natural Enemies: Reflections on Writing the Biography of James Dickey." *Salmagundi* 174–75 (Spring–Summer 2012): 97–121.

Haywood, Wil. "John Cheever Biographer Blake Bailey Peels Back the Layers of a Life." *Washington Post*, 20 March 2009.

Hemingway, Ernest. *Death in the Afternoon*. New York: Scribner's, 1932.

———. *Ernest Hemingway: Selected Letters, 1917–1961*. Edited by Carlos Baker. New York: Scribner's, 1981.

———. *A Moveable Feast: The Restored Edition*. Edited by Seán Hemingway. New York: Scribner's, 2009. Originally published 1964.

———. *The Nick Adams Stories*. New York: Scribner's, 1972.

———. "Prologue." In Scafella, *Hemingway*, 3–5.

Hendrickson, Paul. *Hemingway's Boat: Everything He Loved in Life, and Lost, 1934–1961*. New York: Knopf, 2011.

Hillyer, Robert. Review of *Across the River and Into the Trees*, by Ernest Hemingway. *Atlantic* (December 1938).

Holmes, Richard. *Footsteps: Adventures of a Romantic Biographer*. London: Hodder and Stoughton, 1985.

Holroyd, Michael. *A Book of Secrets*. New York: Farrar, Straus and Giroux, 2010.

———. "How I Fell into Biography." In Homberger and Charmley, *Troubled Face of Biography*, 94–103.

Homberger, Eric. Review of *Cheever: A Life*, by Blake Bailey. *Independent*, 18 December 2009.

Homberger, Eric, and John Charmley, eds. *The Troubled Face of Biography*. New York: St. Martin's, 1988.

Honan, Park. *Authors' Lives: On Literary Biography and the Arts of Language*. New York: St. Martin's, 1990.

Hotchner, A. E. *Papa Hemingway*. New York: Random House, 1966.

Hutchison, Percy. Review of *Edwin Arlington Robinson*, by Hermann Hagedorn. *New York Times*, 16 October 1938, 5.

Johnson, Edgar. Remarks at session on biography. Modern Language Association Convention, Chicago, December 1967.

Johnson, Samuel. *Letters to and from the Late Samuel Johnson*. Edited by Hester Lynch Piozzi. London: Printed for A. Strahan and T. Cadell, 1788.

Jones, Howard Mumford. Review of *Edwin Arlington Robinson*, by Hermann Hagedorn. *Boston Transcript*, 8 October 1938, 1.

Junkins, Donald. "Shadowboxing in the Hemingway Biographies." In Scafella, *Hemingway*, 142–53.

Kakutani, Michiko. "From Chaplin to Groucho to T. S. Eliot." Review of *Hello Goodbye Hello: A Circle of 101 Remarkable Meetings*, by Craig Brown. *New York Times*, 6 August 2012, C1, C4.

Kaplan, Justin. "A Culture of Biography." In Salwak, *Literary Biography*, 1–11.

———. "The Naked Self and Other Problems." In Pachter, *Telling Lives*, 36–55.

———. "In Pursuit of the Ultimate Fiction." *New York Times Book Review*, 19 April 1987, 1, 24–25.

———. "What Biographies Can't Do." *Boston Review*, June 1986, 9–10.

Kazin, Alfred. Review of *Across the River and Into the Trees*, by Ernest Hemingway. *New Yorker*, 9 September 1950, 101–3.

Kellman, Steven G. "Biographer: Get a Life!" *American Scholar* 67 (Summer 1998): 140–42.

Kendall, Paul Murray. *The Art of Biography*. New York: W. W. Norton, 1965.

Kennedy, J. Gerald. "Fitzgerald's Expatriate Years." In *Cambridge Companion to F. Scott Fitzgerald*, edited by Ruth Prigozy, 118–42. New York: Cambridge University Press, 2002.

Kidder, Tracy. "Securing Consent." In Kramer and Call, *Telling True Stories*, 176–77.

Kimbrel, William W., Jr. "Carlos Baker and the 'True Gen.'" *Hemingway Review* 16 (Fall 1996): 83–96.

Kramer, Mark, and Wendy Call, eds. *Telling True Stories*. New York: Plume, 2007

Krug, Julie. "Raising the Dead." *The Writer* (April 2013): 36–39.

Kundera, Milan. *The Art of the Novel*. New York: Grove, 1988.

Laing, Olivia. *The Trip to Echo Spring: On Writers and Drinking*. New York: Picador, 2014.

Lang, Cecil Y. Talk on Byron and biography at College of William and Mary, 29 November 1984.

Lee, Hermione. *Philip Roth*. 1982. London: Routledge, 2010.

———. *Virginia Woolf's Nose: Essays on Biography*. Princeton: Princeton University Press, 2005.

Leval, Pierre N. "Toward a Fair Use Standard." *Harvard Law Review* 103 (March 1990): 1105–36.

LeVot, André. *F. Scott Fitzgerald: A Biography*. Translated by William Byron. Garden City, N.Y.: Doubleday, 1983.

Libman, Gary. "Who's Reading Whom." *Los Angeles Times Book Review*, 4 July 1988, V-5.

Lord, Alice Frost. "Hagedorn's Biography of Poet Robinson Is Ready." *Kennebec (Maine) Journal* (8 October 1938).

MacLeish, Archibald. *Collected Poems, 1917–1982*. Boston: Houghton Mifflin, 1985.

Maddox, Brenda. "Biography: A Love Affair or a Job?" *New York Times Book Review* (9 May 1999).

Malcolm, Janet. *Psychoanalysis, The Impossible Profession*. New York: Knopf, 1981.

———. "The Silent Woman." *New Yorker*, 23 August 1993, 84–159.

———. *Two Lives: Gertrude and Alice*. New Haven: Yale University Press, 2007.

Mariani, Paul. "William Carlos Williams." In *The Craft of Literary Biography*, edited by Jeffrey Meyers, 133–53. London: Macmillan, 1985.

Martin, Jay. "Historical Truth and Narrative Reliability: Three Biographical Stories." In *Biography and Source Studies*, vol. 1, edited by Frederick Karl, 25–72. New York: AMS Press, 1994.

———. "William Faulkner: Construction and Reconstruction in Biography and Psychoanalysis." *Psychoanalytic Inquiry* 3 (1983): 320–37.

Mayfield, Sara. *Exiles from Paradise: Zelda and Scott Fitzgerald*. New York: Delacorte, 1971.

McCaffery, John K. M., ed. *Ernest Hemingway: The Man and His Work*. Cleveland: World, 1950.

McCullough, David. "The Unexpected Harry Truman." In *Extraordinary Lives: The Art and Craft of American Biography*, edited by William Zinsser, 23–61. Boston: Houghton Mifflin, 1986.

McGrath, Charles. "The First Suburbanite." *New York Times Magazine*, 1 March 2009.

———. "Philip Roth to Cooperate with New Biographer." *NYTimes.com*, 5 September 2012.

McGrath, Charles, et al. "The Real Story: Literary Fact and Fiction." *PEN* America 1 (Winter 2000–2001): 115–29.

McPhee, John. "Progression." *New Yorker*, 14 November 2011, 36–42.

Meade, Marion. "Budd Schulberg, the Blacklist, and the Interviews That Got Away." *The Biographer's Craft* 7 (July 2012): 3–4.

———. *Dorothy Parker: What Fresh Hell Is This?* New York: Penguin, 1989.

Meanor, Patrick. *John Cheever Revisited*. New York: Twayne, 1994.

Mellow, James R. *Invented Lives: F. Scott and Zelda Fitzgerald*. Boston: Houghton Mifflin, 1984.

Menand, Louis. "Lives of Others." *New Yorker*, 6 August 2007, 64–66.

Meyers, Jeffrey, ed. *The Biographer's Art: New Essays*. New York: Amsterdam, 1989.

———. *Scott Fitzgerald: A Biography*. New York: HarperCollins, 1993.

Middlebrook, Diane Wood. "Spinning Straw into Gold: A Biographer's Story." *Stanford Magazine*, June 1991, 47–50.

———. "Telling Secrets: The Ethics of Disclosure in Writing Biography." Remarks at session on biography at Modern Language Association Convention, San Francisco, December 1991.

Mihm, Stephen. "The Biographer's New Best Friend." *New York Times Book Review*, 11 September 2011, 9.

Milford, Nancy. *Zelda: A Biography*. New York: Harper and Row, 1970.

Miller, Anita. *Uncollecting Cheever: The Family of John Cheever vs. Academy Chicago Publishers*. Lanham, Md.: Rowman and Littlefield, 1998.

Millgate, Michael. *Testamentary Acts: Browning, Tennyson, James, Hardy*. New York: Oxford University Press, 1992.

Mizener, Arthur. *The Far Side of Paradise: A Biography of F. Scott Fitzgerald*. Boston: Houghton Mifflin, 1951.

Munker, Dona. "Dealing with Black Holes in Your Narrative." *The Biographer's Craft* (June 2013).

Nadel, Ira Bruce. *Biography: Fiction, Fact, and Form*. London: Macmillan, 1984.

Nettels, Elsa. "Henry James and the Art of Biography." *South Atlantic Bulletin* 43 (1978): 107–24.

Niven, Penelope. "'Biographizing': Thornton Wilder on How to Write Biography." Talk at First International Wilder Conference, College of New Jersey, October 2008.

Oates, Joyce Carol. *Wild Nights! Stories About the Last Days of Poe, Dickinson, Twain, James, and Hemingway*. New York: HarperCollins, 2008.

Oates, Stephen, ed. *Biography as a High Adventure: Life-Writers Speak on Their Art.* Amherst: University of Massachusetts Press, 1986.

Ozick, Cynthia. "Who Am I?" *Authors Guild Bulletin* (Winter 2001): 33.

Pachter, Marc, ed. *Telling Lives: The Biographer's Art.* Washington, D.C.: New Republic Books, 1979.

Pearce, Joseph. *The Unmasking of Oscar Wilde.* New York: HarperCollins, 2000.

Perry, Thomas Sergeant. *Selections from the Letters of Thomas Sergeant Perry.* Edited by Edwin Arlington Robinson. New York: Macmillan, 1929.

Price, Reynolds. *Clear Pictures: First Loves, First Guides.* New York: Atheneum, 1989.

Reynolds, Michael. *Hemingway's First War: The Making of "A Farewell to Arms."* Princeton: Princeton University Press, 1976.

———. *Hemingway: The Final Years.* New York: W. W. Norton, 1999.

———. "Up Against the Crannied Wall: The Limits of Biography." In Scafella, *Hemingway,* 170–78.

Richardson, Robert D. Remarks at American Literature Association Conference on Biography, Puerto Vallarta, Mexico, December 2001.

Robbins, J. Albert, ed. *American Literary Manuscripts.* Athens: University of Georgia Press, 1977.

Robinson, Edwin Arlington. *Collected Poems.* New York: Macmillan, 1937.

———. *Selected Letters of Edwin Arlington Robinson.* New York: Macmillan, 1940.

Roiphe, Katie. "Portrait of Marriage." Review of *Two Lives: Gertrude and Alice,* by Janet Malcolm. *New York Times Book Review,* 23 September 2007, 7.

Rose, Phyllis. "Confessions of a Burned-Out Biographer." *Civilization* (January–February 1993): 72–74.

———. "The Impulse to Explode." Review of *Ralph Ellison: A Biography,* by Arnold Rampersad. *American Scholar* 76 (Spring 2007): 21–26.

Ross, Lillian. "Hemingway Told Me Things." *New Yorker,* 24 May 1999, 70–73.

———. "Portrait of Hemingway." In *Reporting,* 187–222. New York: Simon and Schuster, 1964.

Rovere, Richard H. Review of *Across the River and Into the Trees,* by Ernest Hemingway. *Harper's,* September 1950, 104–6.

Rovit, Earl. "Literary Lives." *Sewanee Review* 119 (Spring 2011): 225–36.

Runyan, William McKinley. *Life Histories and Psychobiography: Explorations in Theory and Method.* New York: Oxford University Press, 1984.

Salter, James. Review of *John Cheever: A Biography,* by Scott Donaldson. *Los Angeles Times Book Review,* 17 July 1988.

———. *Selected Letters of James Salter and Robert Phelps.* Edited by John McIntyre. Berkeley, Cal.: Counterpoint, 2010.

Salwak, Dale, ed. *The Literary Biography: Problems and Solutions.* Houndsmill, Basingstoke, Hampshire: Macmillan, 1996.

Scafella, Frank, ed. *Hemingway: Essays of Reassessment.* New York: Oxford University Press, 1991.

Schlesinger, Arthur M., Jr. "The Perils of Pathography." Review of *Power, Privilege and "The Post": The Katharine Graham Story,* by Carol Felsenthal. *New Republic,* 3 May 1993, 36–38.

Schorer, Mark. "The Burdens of Biography." In *The World We Imagine,* 221–39. New York: Farrar, Straus and Giroux, 1968:.

Secrest, Meryle. *Shoot the Widow.* New York: Knopf, 2007.

Shipman, Pat. "Missing Links: A Scientist Reconstructs Biography." *American Scholar* 70 (Winter 2001): 81–86.

Sisk, John P. "Biography Without End." *Antioch Review* (Winter 1990): 449–59.

Skidelsky, Robert. "Only Connect: Biography and Truth." In Homberger and Charmley, *Troubled Face of Biography,* 1–15.

Smith, Amanda. "Victoria Glendinning." *Publishers Weekly,* 15 December 1989), 49–50.

Smith, Chard Powers. *Where the Light Falls: A Portrait of Edwin Arlington Robinson.* New York: Macmillan, 1965.

Smith, Paul. *A Reader's Guide to the Short Stories of Ernest Hemingway.* Boston: G. K. Hall, 1989.

Smith, Wendy. "Edmund Morris: Writer Behind the Throne." *Publishers Weekly,* 11 October 1999, 49–50.

Solomon, Deborah. "The Queen." *New York Times Magazine,* 17 October 2010, 20.

Spacks, Patricia Meyer. "Biography: Moral and Physical Truth." In *Gossip,* 92–118. New York: Knopf, 1985.

Storr, Anthony. "Psychiatry and Literary Biography." In *The Art of Literary Biography,* edited by John Batchelor, 73–86. New York: Oxford University Press, 1995.

Taylor, Kendall. *Sometimes Madness Is Wisdom: Zelda and Scott Fitzgerald; A Marriage.* New York: Ballantine, 2001.

Taylor, Welford Dunaway, ed. *Sherwood Anderson Remembered.* Tuscaloosa: University of Alabama Press, 2009.

Theroux, Paul. "Memory and Invention." *New York Times Book Review,* 1 November 1998, 39.

Tomkins, Calvin. *Living Well Is the Best Revenge.* New York: Viking, 1971.

Trogdon, Robert. Review of *Dear Papa, Dear Hotch: The Correspondence of Ernest Hemingway and A. E. Hotchner,* edited by Albert J. DeFazio. *Hemingway Review* 25 (Spring 2006): 140–42.

Turnbull, Andrew. *Scott Fitzgerald.* New York: Scribner's, 1962.

Underwood, Thomas A. "Mr. Tate and His Biographers: The New Criticism and the Problem of Literary Biography." *Princeton University Library Chronicle* 50 (Spring 1989): 206–19.

Untermeyer, Louis. "Unfinished Portrait." Review of *Edwin Arlington Robinson,* by Hermann Hagedorn. *Saturday Review of Literature,* 15 October 1938, 34.

Updike, John. "Basically Decent." Review of *Cheever: A Life,* by Blake Bailey. *New Yorker,* 9 March 2009.

———. *On Literary Biography.* Columbia: University of South Carolina Press, 1999.

———. "Posthumous Output." In *More Matter,* 442–53. New York: Knopf, 1999.

Vaill, Amanda. *Hotel Florida: Truth, Love, and Death in the Spanish Civil War.* Bound galleys. New York: Farrar, Straus and Giroux, 2014.

Wagner-Martin, Linda. *Zelda Sayre Fitzgerald: An American Woman's Life.* New York: Palgrave Macmillan, 2004.

Weinberg, Steve. "Biography, the Bastard Child of Academe." *Chronicle Review,* 9 May 2008, B15–B17.

Weintraub, Stanley. "Reviewing Literary Biography: Apprehending the *Daimon.*" In *Literary Reviewing,* edited by James O. Hoge, 29–43. Charlottesville: University of Virginia Press, 1987.

West, James L. W., III. "An Accidental Boswell: Writing the Life of William Styron." *Sewanee Review* 119 (Summer 2011): 445–50.

———. *Making the Archives Talk: New and Selected Essays in Bibliography, Editing, and Book History.* University Park: Pennsylvania State University Press, 2011.

———. *The Perfect Hour: The Romance of F. Scott Fitzgerald and Ginevra King, His First Love.* New York: Random House, 2005.

Whitman, Walt. *Leaves of Grass.* Comprehensive reader's edition. Edited by Harold W. Blodgett and Sculley Bradley. New York: New York University Press, 1965.

Wilder, Thornton. *The Bridge of San Luis Rey.* New York: Boni, 1927.

———. *Selected Letters of Thornton Wilder.* Edited by Robin G. Wilder and Jackson R. Bryer. New York: HarperCollins, 2008.

Wilkinson, Alec. "Remembering William Maxwell." *American Scholar* 73 (Winter 2004): 39–46.

Wilson, Edmund. "Hemingway: Gauge of Morale." In *The Wound and The Bow: Seven Studies in Literature*, 214–42 Boston: Houghton Mifflin, 1941.

Winchester, Simon. Remarks at the Third Annual Leon Levy Center for Biography, New York, 10 March 2011.

Wolff, Gregory. "Suburban Suffering." *New York Times Book Review*, 12 March 2009.

Woolf, Virginia. *Collected Essays.* Vol 4. London: Hogarth Press, 1967.

———. *Moments of Being: Unpublished Autobiographical Writings.* Edited by Jeanne Schulkind. New York: Harcourt Brace Jovanovich, 1976.

Yalom, Irvin D., and Marilyn. "Ernest Hemingway: A Psychiatric View." *Archives of General Psychiatry* 24 (June 1971): 485–94.

Yardley, Jonathan. "Good Writer, Bad Man." *Washington Post Book World*, 15 March 2009).

Young, Philip. *Ernest Hemingway.* New York: Rinehart, 1952.

———. "Foreword: Author and Critic: A Rather Long Story." In *Ernest Hemingway: A Reconsideration*, 1–28. University Park: Pennsylvania State University Press, 1966:.

———. Review of *Across the River and Into the Trees*, by Ernest Hemingway. *Tomorrow* 10 (November 1950): 55–56.

INDEX

Previously published titles in the Penn State Series in the History of the Book

Peter Burke, *The Fortunes of the "Courtier": The European Reception of Castiglione's "Cortegiano"* (1996)

Roger Burlingame, *Of Making Many Books: A Hundred Years of Reading, Writing, and Publishing* (1996)

James M. Hutchisson, *The Rise of Sinclair Lewis, 1920–1930* (1996)

Julie Bates Dock, ed., *Charlotte Perkins Gilman's "The Yellow Wall-paper" and the History of Its Publication and Reception: A Critical Edition and Documentary Casebook* (1998)

John Williams, ed., *Imaging the Early Medieval Bible* (1998)

Ezra Greenspan, *George Palmer Putnam: Representative American Publisher* (2000)

James G. Nelson, *Publisher to the Decadents: Leonard Smithers in the Careers of Beardsley, Wilde, Dowson* (2000)

Pamela E. Selwyn, *Everyday Life in the German Book Trade: Friedrich Nicolai as Bookseller and Publisher in the Age of Enlightenment* (2000)

David R. Johnson, *Conrad Richter: A Writer's Life* (2001)

David Finkelstein, *The House of Blackwood: Author-Publisher Relations in the Victorian Era* (2002)

Rodger L. Tarr, ed., *As Ever Yours: The Letters of Max Perkins and Elizabeth Lemmon* (2003)

Randy Robertson, *Censorship and Conflict in Seventeenth-Century England: The Subtle Art of Division* (2009)

Catherine M. Parisian, ed., *The First White House Library: A History and Annotated Catalogue* (2010)

Jane McLeod, *Licensing Loyalty: Printers, Patrons, and the State in Early Modern France* (2011)

Charles Walton, ed., *Into Print: Limits and Legacies of the Enlightenment, Essays in Honor of Robert Darnton* (2011)

James L. W. West III, *Making the Archives Talk: New and Selected Essays in Bibliography, Editing, and Book History* (2012)

John Hruschka, *How Books Came to America: The Rise of the American Book Trade* (2012)

A. Franklin Parks, *William Parks: The Colonial Printer in the Transatlantic World of the Eighteenth Century* (2012)

Roger E. Stoddard, comp., and David R. Whitesell, ed., *A Bibliographic Description of Books and Pamphlets of American Verse Printed from 1610 Through 1820* (2012)

Nancy Cervetti, *S. Weir Mitchell: Philadelphia's Literary Physician* (2012)

Karen Nipps, *Lydia Bailey: A Checklist of Her Imprints* (2013)

Paul Eggert, *Biography of a Book: Henry Lawson's "While the Billy Boils"* (2013)

Allan F. Westphall, *Books and Religious Devotion: The Redemptive Reading of an Irishman in Nineteenth-Century New England* (2014)